Growing Pains

Environmental Management in Developing Countries

Edited by Walter Wehrmeyer and Yacob Mulugetta

Growing Pains

ENVIRONMENTAL MANAGEMENT IN DEVELOPING COUNTRIES

EDITED BY
WALTER WEHRMEYER AND YACOB MULUGETTA

Greenleaf
PUBLISHING
1999

To Aida
and to Sue and Alma

Published by Greenleaf Publishing Limited
Aizlewood Business Centre
Aizlewood's Mill
Nursery Street
Sheffield S3 8GG
UK

Typeset by Greenleaf Publishing Limited and printed on environmentally friendly, acid-free paper from managed forests by Bookcraft, Midsomer Norton, UK.

British Library Cataloguing in Publication Data:
Growing pains : environmental management in developing countries
1. Environmental management - Developing countries
2, Environmental policy - Developing countries
I. Wehrmeyer, Walter II. Mulugetta, Yacob
333.7'091724

ISBN 1874719136 Hbk
ISBN 1874719233 Pbk

Contents

Foreword

Carlos Magariños
Director-General,
United Nations Industrial Development Organisation

THE JOB OF GOVERNMENTS can be defined as maximising public 'goods' and minimising the 'bads'. In that sense, I wish that, as the minister responsible for mining and industry in Argentina in the early 1990s, I and my cabinet colleagues could have had access to the advice inherent in the following pages. Admittedly, global concerns were elsewhere at the time. Most developing countries were more preoccupied with recovering from the lost decade that went before than with preserving the environment, whether national or global.

In the meantime, we have moved on. Structural adjustment and macroeconomic stabilisation have proved their worth—and their limitations. From an environmental perspective, market reforms have so far *not* fulfilled expectations that privatisation would foreshadow investment in new (and therefore cleaner) technologies, that marketisation would reallocate out of unproductive (i.e. environmentally wasteful) sectors, and that the state's divestment of production functions would enable it to take on supervisory and regulatory ones.

Governments today are concerned to link macroeconomic stabilisation to microeconomic performance. To spread the benefits of both to as many voters as possible, their reform programmes increasingly recognise the natural environment as a national public good. Trading standards, investment strategies or international agreements such as the Montreal Protocol on Ozone-Depleting Substances and the Kyoto Protocol to the United Nations Framework Convention on Climate Change, should ensure the natural environment's international dimensions.

That is the current expectation. But, even when the political will is there, we still need to understand a lot more about linking environmental best practice with theory, and whether the relevant global and national institutions and mechanisms are the right ones for all situations. This book contributes to such understanding.

As a public good, the natural environment is unique among such 'goods' in that it exists, and for all practical purposes is sustainable, independently of the human species. Clean air and water, biodiversity and a protective ozone layer are present naturally. It is their use or abuse by humankind that diminishes or destroys them. This is why they are best understood in relation to their counterparts, 'public bads'—air and water pollution, biodiversity depletion, monoculture and desertification, and holes in the protective ozone layer. It is also why regulations, standards and (as this collection of essays emphasises) the behaviour of multinational corporations as global citizens all play an important role in containing and minimising them.

Growing Pains is a monitor of how well we are doing in protecting environmental goods in developing countries. Key actors—theoreticians (development economists in particular), government ministers and policy planners, chief executive officers in the private sector and their advisers, and heads of institutions (national and multilateral)—will surely identify with specific issues explored in this book. Heads of national and multilateral institutions like my own and each of our member states will pay attention to three essays in particular: Neil Harrison's 'Joint Implementation of Climate Change?', Frank Vorhies's 'Biodiversity and Globalisation' and Ans Kolk's 'Environmental Management and Organisational Change' (at the World Bank).

The prevailing climate is a quintessential *international* public good. Its 'bads', global warming and climate change, are to be prevented through international co-operation in the form of *joint implementation* (JI) of the Kyoto Protocol. But, as Neil Harrison notes here, JI has to compete with other economic and political goals of nation-states. If the national interests of investor countries dominate project selection, global efficiency of climate mitigation will not be optimised and the development plans of developing countries inhibited. Harrison concludes that, while, on available evidence, national-interest bias in project selection is not inevitable, project efficiency could be improved and investment could enhance rather than inhibit development.

The international public good, *biodiversity*, is commonly held to be about access to, control over and economic uses of the planet's biological sources. Vorhies rightly adds that it is also about social equity in the distribution of their benefits and costs, and conserving the ecological systems of the planet. There are roles for both public and private institutions in the management of biodiversity—roles that, Vorhies argues, are being changed radically by globalisation. Whether the strategy of *stakeholder participation,* described by Murray Jones, for Peru's development of world-class hydrocarbon reserves in one of the world's foremost areas of natural biodiversity proves a satisfactory model, only time will tell.

Ans Kolk's review of the impact of the World Bank on environmental management and climate change has two messages: great multilateral institutions can be wrong (and the combined opinion of NGOs and some industrialised-country governments can be correspondingly right); and they *can* be turned around. Kolk shows why the Bank underwent what amounts to a revolutionary change from 'frontier economics' to 'environmental management'. Member states and heads of other multilateral institutions facing similar problems of cultural and institutional change will identify with the conclusion that the feasibility of reforms depends on the extent to which an organisation succeeds in reconciling diverging demands.

I leave Matthew Cole's contribution on the environmental impact until last because it is a story only just begun—the clash between two international public goods: free international trade and a sound environment. It is also the field for another major clash between increasingly well-co-ordinated NGOs and a major multilateral institution, the World Trade Organisation. At this point, Cole offers a methodology for estimating the impact of the Uruguay Round in terms of three effects: scale, technique and composition. If the Uruguay Round achieves its own objective of increasing the scale of economic activity, some negative impact on the environment must be accommodated—as with other economic growth mechanisms. If it allows greater access or enforces use of cleaner production techniques, the Round will be beneficial. If it changes the composition of what countries produce, the impact will depend on which sectors expand and contract. Bearing in mind NGOs' and the European Union's concern that environmental standards have already been deemed unfair trade restrictions, I look forward to reading in a future book such as this how well the proposed Millennium Round in Seattle was able to make the compromises.

Introduction

Walter Wehrmeyer and Yacob Mulugetta

IN THE LAST FEW YEARS, environmental management as a concern for corporations in Western Europe, North America, Australia and Japan has come a long way: evolving quickly from being a matter of mere legislative control on a few and specific concerns—such as noise, effluent, air emissions and waste disposal—to being seen currently as a set of complex issues that permeate all business activities up and down the value chain. Moreover, the role of environmental management has shifted from being a 'hygiene factor' (issues that need to be addressed but which by themselves do not contribute to organisational success) to being a 'motivator' (issues that add value to the company, improve the economic and social standing of the organisation, help motivate and retain employees, and improve the corporate image, all of which are necessary elements of competitive firms).

The situation in developing countries is somewhat different. The vast majority of companies in the developing world have so far not found an adequate response towards environmental management and its larger cousin, sustainable development. Yet both worlds, the North and South, with substantially different environmental and social agendas, are nominally and practically promoting efforts towards sustainable development. Just how different both worlds are and how concentrated economic and political power is in the North is briefly illustrated in the statistics given below, all taken from the *World Development Report* (World Bank 1997c) and the *Human Development Report* (UNDP 1999).

- Annual GNP per capita in the ten poorest countries was $159; in the ten richest countries, it was 188 times as much—$29,922 (at 1995 prices).
- The national GNP of the ten richest countries was 750 times more than that of the ten poorest countries.

- 42% of people (993 million) in the 46 countries classified as 'low-income' lived on less than $1 per day. In total, 1,159 million people are said to live on less than $1 per day—about 22% of the global population.
- The assets of the top three billionaires are more than the combined GNP of all least developed countries and their 600 million people.
- Per capita CO_2 emissions in the 46 low-income countries was 771 kg (1992 data); that of the 26 high-income countries was 10,512 kg—13.6 times as much. A similar ratio could be found for per capita waste production.
- The 1996 per capita commercial energy consumption in industrialised countries was 5,388 kg oil equivalent, compared to 300 kg oil equivalent in the least developed countries.

These figures paint a sombre picture of the significant inequality that is prevalent in income distribution, in consumption patterns, in access to resources, and in opportunities to alleviate poverty at the national and global level. In view of these differences in the levels and intensity of consumption patterns, it is only a matter of straightforward extrapolation that the 20% living in the industrialised North (OECD) are bound to have a substantially higher per capita environmental impact. Indeed, the gap in the per capita environmental burden between the residents in the North and their counterparts in the South is widening. However, the past decade has seen a continued growth in public awareness in the North concerning environmental issues and the policy interventions required to ensure that further degradation is, at the very least, kept to a minimum. This has contributed to local pressures on industry to improve their environmental record, either voluntarily or by enforcing stringent environmental legislation, as well as the proliferation of a consumer market that is willing to pay an environmental premium for environmentally friendlier goods. The implications of these developments are that people in the North may lead environmentally unsustainable lifestyles, but that lifestyle is perceived as desirable because of the breadth of choice that it entails.

In contrast, there are more people living in the South, with significantly smaller per capita resource use. The very fact that consumption levels have been too low to meet basic needs for more than a billion people is seen as one of the main causes of economic stagnation, particularly in the least developed countries. Poor countries need to accelerate their consumption growth if they are to ensure that the capabilities of their people are enhanced and their lives enriched, and effective poverty alleviation strategies are embarked upon. Requirements for increased access to resources, however, need to be ushered by proactive and real measures to minimise the attendant environmental impacts and to advance human development. Quite simply, the path taken by the rich and high-growth economies over the past century cannot be repeated if the desired objective is to create a future that is truly sustainable.

Regrettably, badly written or ill-enforced environmental legislation have littered the landscape of environmental interventions in the developing world, which makes proper control and accountability of resource use difficult at best, impossible at worst. For instance, Peru has more than 6,500 individual items of environmental legislation, with different laws (and standards) for different economic sectors, regions, products and manufacturing techniques, and it is estimated that about a third of these are redundant, with another third probably outdated, obsolete or contradictory to other laws. Yet there are no enforced pollution control standards on cars in Lima—a city of more than seven million people with weather conditions that support smog for significant periods, leading to poor air quality, respiratory ailments and the like.

It is also worth noting that societies in the poor South are typified by an enormous chasm between the urban rich, who epitomise the (environmentally unsustainable) practice of Northern lifestyles, and the (often rural) poor, frequently subsisting on marginal agricultural land and vulnerable to the effects of environmental damage. The fact is that the 'well off', wherever they are, benefit from the cornucopia of consumer choices at their disposal. But the poor bear many of its social and environmental costs, which continue to diminish their capacity and access to basic living resources. It is important to stress that poor people depend on natural resources for their livelihoods, and therefore natural resource degradation often becomes an immediate and livelihood-threatening crisis—a question of survival (Broad 1994). Thus, poverty and environment are closely linked in a nexus of mutually reinforcing causality chains where past resource degradation deepens today's poverty, while today's poverty creates impediments to the care and rehabilitation of the resource base in future years. The challenge should therefore be how to mobilise the same actors who 'contributed' to local environmental degradation to become the custodians of the environment and its regeneration.

In this effort, the first area that calls for attention is enhancing the level of awareness regarding the environment and outlining the opportunities and advantages gained from its preservation. Through such processes, the hope is for consumers to have a genuine stake in safeguarding the environment, and to place their demands on producers to adhere to higher environmental standards and quality control. While this may well be the case in the industrialised countries, environmental awareness and consumer power in the developing world are at levels that are far from satisfactory. Here, there is rarely an environmental awareness that goes beyond pride over the national riches of one's country, let alone consumer demand for 'greener' products.

Inasmuch as there are enormous differences in consumption patterns and access to resources between people in the North and South, there are inevitably going to be differences in the strategies adopted. This is most evident in the way industrialised and developing nations approach the concept of sustainable development, and what its relevance is to their respective societies, and most importantly how the concept itself finds meaning within the confines of different states at different stages of development. In general terms, while policy-makers in the North struggle with a maintenance and eventual reduction in per capita resource use at given levels of lifestyles, the main social, political and economic concern in the South is poverty alleviation. From this perspective, the North is in a better position to improve matters environmentally as it has some political backing and, more importantly, the technological competence and the resources. However, all is not rosy here, either. For example, the CO_2 reduction targets set at the Kyoto Climate Change Conference in

1997 for the North are still unlikely to be met, as public and corporate pressures to maintain economic growth in a traditional manner are too strong for a significant reduction in emissions. It seems that we all want to go to paradise, but nobody wants to leave their cars at home.

There is now a general agreement that environmental problems are best addressed at their source, through appropriate environmental and economic policies. Ideally, these policies should include three fundamental principles: the **precautionary principle**, the **polluter pays principle** and the **user pays principle**. The precautionary principle dictates that government undertake more extensive risk assessments before authorising activity and that the acceptable margin of risk be narrowed (UNCTAD 1991). The other two principles mainly refer to the incorporation of environmental concerns into public decisions whereby the costs of environmental measures are internalised and reflected in the prices paid by producers for inputs, and by consumers for final goods and services. The purpose is to more accurately reflect the full costs in the production and consumption spheres. Through these mechanisms, the North can play a greater role in reducing environmental impacts on human behaviour than the South, since environmental standards now constitute an important arm of economic policy in the former. Developing countries, on the other hand, are less likely to consider the environmental soundness of the products that they consume, and indeed may not have the necessary technology or the financial resources to afford the luxury of rendering their products sufficiently environmentally friendly to meet Northern standards. This 'fault line' remains at the heart of problems concerning the harmonisation of environmental standards, the formulation of which would go some way to reducing the potential for conflict over the use of environmental trade measures and decreasing the competitive advantages attained through environmentally unsound practices.

The notion of internalising external environmental and social costs for traded goods, however, may not always be appropriate as a policy tool, particularly in cases where the environmental losses in question are irreplaceable and therefore difficult to price. This realisation is of immense importance to developing countries in view of the fact that considerable shares of global biodiversity and raw material wealth are located within their boundaries. At the risk of contradicting the argument about the 'pricelessness' of certain environmental resources, biodiversity resources have been valued at multiples of countries' GNPs: the value of biodiversity for pharmaceutical research alone has been estimated at over $200 billion p.a. (Simpson *et al.* 1996). The message is, therefore, that other policy instruments are required to grapple with issues such as damage to the regenerative capacity of ecosystems, extinction of species and loss of biodiversity, and threats to protected sites of internationally recognised ecological, cultural or historical significance. Already, there is a plethora of United Nations agreements and protocols on issues such as climate change, endangered species and biodiversity.

Undoubtedly, the South is in a difficult position to respond to its impending environmental problems. The realistic scenario is that, given the low levels of consumption discussed earlier and the likelihood of growth in economic activity and consumption patterns, growth in environmental impacts are also expected that are higher than those triggered by the same growth rates in the North. In addition, the growing populations are likely to put additional pressures on countries to promote growth. Yet the poorest—those who would benefit most from sustainable development—have traditionally very short payback periods[1] and, for most, the environment remains the source of their livelihood. In this, environmental disasters demonstrate a 'ratchet effect', where insurance is an alien concept and each flood or drought causes loss of income or assets from which they are unlikely to recover economically.

In addition, a dichotomy exists in the industrial composition of countries in the South. In many such countries, one finds two distinct sectors: those that are export-oriented and those that are domestic market-oriented. The former is frequently geared towards resource extraction and is foreign-owned, which allows better access to capital markets, a subsequently higher capitalisation, and more modern technologies with greater innovative potential and, accordingly, also has better access to more recent management ideas, such as Total Quality Management (TQM). It is this sector that knows about, and is concerned with, environmental management, if there is such corporate environmental awareness to start with and if the foreign owners are prepared to operate to standards similar to the ones they have in the North. Normally, the main areas of concern are health and safety, ISO 14001 and other eco-labels. The principal focus of such businesses is predominantly servicing the environmental agenda in the North or 'keeping a foot in the door', i.e. to secure access to international markets or resources.

The second sector, which is typical of a Southern economy, is directed toward the domestic markets, and has a much thinner capital base, which results in the downwards business spiral of poor training and poor technology leading to poor profit margins. This, in turn, leads to weak R&D efforts and capital re-investment, with a low likelihood of product quality being improved; which also implies that competition is driven more towards the price rather than the product. It comes as little surprise that this sector is also frequently the more polluting and the less resource-efficient. As competition between these two industrial sectors intensifies over time, the export-oriented sector is likely to use, with some justification, environmental arguments to add pressure to the domestic-market sector.

The frequently heard argument that the industrialised North is exporting its pollution activities into the South remains unproven. While it is more likely that poorly managed plants are being maintained at inadequate levels of investment and management, and therefore are more prone to accidents—for example, the Bhopal case—the evidence that industry is relocating into developing countries to avoid stringent legislation is not persuasive. It appears that other factors, such as levels of technology, access to markets or resources (qualified labour force, raw materials and infrastructure) as well as quantity and quality of government support (or government taxation) are more important (Leonard and Duerksen 1980; Leonard 1982; Wilson 1994).

1 The World Bank (1992a) cites a study showing that the poorest are only willing to sacrifice part of their income in anticipation of future improvements if payback periods are typically below 18 months or with rates of return in excess of 15%.

Herein, lax environmental regulation or poor enforcement of regulatory standards seem to be coincidental arguments for the location of industry. Given the low cost of environmental control,[2] and the global nature of pressure groups and the increasing phenomenon that companies' environmental and social performance in one country is seen as indicative for the company as a whole (see Shell's performance in Nigeria, for example), the export of pollution is unlikely to be a significant factor. The exception to this is hazardous waste disposal where some countries in the developing world, such as French Guyana, have developed a strange fondness for accepting it (Singh and Lakham 1989).

This short and somewhat stylised outline of the pattern of environmental management in the South suggests that it may be a dangerous fallacy to assume that, since environmental problems are global, each country in the South can adopt the environmental management approaches of the North. The socioeconomic, organisational regulatory or political circumstances and the environmental demands may be too different from the North. For instance, the usefulness of ISO 14001 must be questioned in countries that have no clear legislative control and very little tradition and experience of formalised management systems—or with formalised and working bureaucracies for that matter.

In the quest for sustainable development, the North and South have different options, which are evidently dependent on the positions either are in. The North faces the difficult challenge of having not only to reduce pro-rata environmental effects, but also to reduce the environmental impacts of accepted lifestyles. This is politically and economically very difficult, as product choice and product use also offer opportunities for social diversification, status maintenance and personal freedom. For example, the status gained from driving a new sports car cannot be offered by public transport, regardless of how much environmental sense the latter makes over the former. In fact, much product differentiation depends on consumers' desires to establish their identities, or to satisfy social and psychological needs that are frequently not met by environmentally superior alternative products. As such, the challenge of the North lies in reduced resource consumption to achieve a given living standard. In this, 'sustainability' rather than sustainable development is the key phrase. Here, the title of this book, *Growing Pains*, can serve to symbolise the increasing pain and consumptive sacrifice that are required to amend unsustainable lifestyles in the North.

The challenge of the South clearly lies in development, rather than the maintenance of the status quo. The identification and promotion of strategies towards the socioeconomic growth of their societies must lie at the heart of the sustainable development agenda. It is questionable whether the development strategies that are originating in the North are the optimum ones: they are most certainly the best available at short notice and, by means of the bilateral and international aid agencies, the best supported. Here, *Growing Pains* suggests the often painful trade-

2 MacNeill *et al.* (1991) suggest an approximation of about 2% of turnover, with large variations between industry sectors. Also, Luken (see Chapter 5) suggests a figure of about 2% of production costs.

offs that have to be made in the process of economic and social growth in the countries concerned. It also indicates the increasing 'pain' the Western lifestyle causes the ecosystems globally. On a more principled point, the efforts to implement Northern-style environmental management in the socioeconomic context of the South may appear unjustified: *should* the South learn from the polluting North how not to pollute when (a) the North's own development path has not been a model of cleaner production; and (b) the overall environmental impact of the North is still growing as pro-rata environmental improvements of some firms and consumers are nullified by increases in the levels of consumption overall?

Sadly, what the North and the South have in common is that both are low on alternative development models. The former has few alternatives as it sees market-based solutions and the increasingly dominant role of corporations as the only politically and economically acceptable form of commodity exchange, thus limiting itself unnecessarily towards a narrow range of economic options.[3] This explains the propensity of tradable permits and other market-based mechanisms towards environmental pollution reduction, as well as the increasing use of voluntary approaches. They are unlikely to deliver the environmental improvements scientists tell us we need.

The South is in the unenviable position of having to improve living standards rapidly while maintaining environmental quality *and* to do this without the necessary capital (financial or human), without proven sustainable development models, and without much time before environmental and social problems become more acute. Curiously, countries in the South rarely look towards each other to develop or disseminate ideas.

This book addresses some of the issues that arise from corporate environmental management in developing countries. It is designed to stimulate the discussion about the role corporations have in sustainable development, and to highlight (mostly poor but also good) practice in this field. We do not offer panaceas, as each country has its own opportunities and its own problems; and, after almost 50 years of failed panacea-oriented economic development policy transfer from the North to the South, we think that it is time to abandon the hope for a universal solution to country-specific problems, and to begin to develop individual approaches that work, and to disseminate knowledge and understanding of these within the South.

An overview

The book is loosely structured around five themes, namely: globalisation; the role of business; a focus on national strategies; as well as issues surrounding international trade and its effect on the environment at large. The final section on environmental management and sustainable development aims to highlight the organisational and structural challenges that this concept entails as well as providing an outlook for the challenge ahead.

3 In fact, the apparent success over the Eastern Bloc has arguably blinded the West towards its own structural deficiencies (Galbraith 1992) and may have produced an aura of superiority that makes it difficult to accept change or to learn form other models, however rare these may be.

There are three facets to globalisation that are of interest here. First, at the supranational level, we can witness a loss of control from national governments, which can be seen in the increased network of political groupings and their increased sphere of influence. This can also be seen economically, where the economic muscle of some individuals or of corporations far exceeds that of some countries, as shown earlier. The tools that facilitate the loss of economic control include transfer pricing between subsidiaries of the same global corporation which allows the geographical allocation of profits and losses to minimise tax burdens or regulatory control. Other examples where the economic grip of a government on 'its' economy is being eroded include: offshore tax havens, cheap shipping flags and on-line gambling, among others.

Second is the rise of corporate power, where globally operating businesses shape markets and product demand to an unprecedented degree. Coincidental to this, we can also witness increasing international transparency on environmental or ethical issues where a mismatch between espoused and actual behaviour is being communicated at Internet speed. For example, Nike's use of child labour in developing countries and Shell's plans to sink the Brent Spar were both brought to the attention of consumers quickly and effectively. Globalisation here means greater transparency and much greater competitive pressures.

Third, globalisation means a rapid loss of local specificity, such as a loss in product diversity and a loss in local uniqueness. This can be found in the startling similarity in the tourism experiences on offer, whether tourists venture to Kenya or to Brazil, the globalised range of duty-free goods in airports, or the similarity in services being offered in international hotels, down to the ubiquitous CNN. The question that arises is what constitutes local identity in a globalised world?

From an environmental perspective, we are *de facto* managing very different ecosystems with a quite small toolbox of environmental management practices. In fact, the ISO 14000 series was specifically designed that way, to ensure no environment-based trade barriers can be set up, which is in turn the biggest deficiency of this standard (Gleckman and Krut 1996). Such an approach has inevitably little regard for local specificity and, given the above point about the increasing transparency of corporations, the headquarters may have greater influence in the design of the environmental management programme than the local people that the programme (or its absence) ultimately affects. There may be situations where national circumstances prevent this from being a suitable approach, as Mike Di (Chapter 7), Alexey Voinov *et al.* (Chapters 8 and 10), Peter Koffel (Chapter 22) and Barbara and Eric Ribbens (Chapter 20) show in this book.

In the **Globalisation** section, Gib Hedstrom and colleagues at Arthur D. Little (Chapter 1) competently lay out in practical terms what globalisation means for firms. This is followed by a perspective from Frank Vorhies of the IUCN (Chapter 2) on the need to find and to promote suitable international mechanisms to protect biodiversity in an increasingly globalised policy world. Neil Harrison (Chapter 3) then provides a necessary overview of the current practice in linking climate change objectives with economic development aid: joint implementation. David Barkin (Chapter 4) rounds off this section by outlining how globalisation and the increasing mobility of finance have affected sustainable development in Mexico.

The **Focus on Business**—the second theme—begins with a review by Skip Luken (Chapter 5) of the efficacy of environmental regulation on developing countries, which concludes that, at the industrial level, environmental regulation in developing countries will have a similar effect as it had in the developed world between 1970 and 1990. Dennis Rondinelli and Gyula Vastag (Chapter 6) present a strong case of environmental excellence as a cogent counter-point to the common prejudice of the polluting and poorly run subsidiary in a developing country.

The difficulties of using global standards in a nationally divergent context is presented by Mike Di (Chapter 7), who outlines the inadequacy of ISO 14001 implementation in China. He also argues that there are structural advantages for global businesses in the implementation of the environmental management system standard, which puts national businesses at a disadvantage. The section is concluded by Alexey Voinov *et al.* (Chapter 8), who outline the difficulties caused by corruption and poor regulatory standards when combined with a weak economic system. Using Russia as an intriguing and rapidly evolving case, they argue that market-based mechanisms may not necessarily be the best solution and that corruption and weak national policies are frequent contributors to environmental damage.

The third theme—**National Focus**—presents case-based contributions that highlight the complexities of environmental management in a small number of countries. Percy Garcia and his colleagues (Chapter 9) produce an interesting and challenging overview of the implementation problems of effective environmental management in the Andean region. Their sobering catalogue of barriers and driving forces may be a model for many, if not most, developing countries. Voinov and colleagues (Chapter 10), again using Russia as a case in point, argue that the implementation of economic or business-oriented 'solutions' from one economic system may not be appropriate in another system. Jeannie Sowers (Chapter 11) then scrutinises the intriguing situation of the need to develop environmental management in a social climate that is clearly unaffected by the Judaeo-Christian notions of environmental protection that pervade and underline postmodern environmental management. She asks, 'what happens in countries that do not share the environmental ethics of the West' and arrives at the answer that corporate environmental protection still occurs, but only to the extent to which it is politically expedient. Mandar Parasnis (Chapter 12) provides a sound country-based overview for Thailand, as does Emilio Latorre for Colombia (Chapter 13). Both argue that environmental management is being taken seriously by business, despite significant obstacles and much less economic, social and regulatory pressure to do so than in the North.

The fourth theme discussed in this book, **Trade and Environment**, highlights the linkages between trade and environment. Integrating trade, environment and development policies in the framework of sustainable development objectives is one of the most important challenges for developing countries (UNDP 1998). An impassioned debate has been going on for sometime now on whether unrestricted international trade, as embodied in proposals for GATT and WTO, will harm or help the environment.

Those arguing in favour of trade liberalisation maintain that freeing trade from inefficient restriction may well be the best way of achieving environmental protection while also safeguarding economic growth. This group also argues that trade has the potential to contribute significantly to alleviating poverty in the South if each country recognises its 'comparative advantage', i.e. produces goods in which it is relatively more efficient, and trades for products in which it is relatively less efficient. Invariably, this would lead to an enhanced investment climate, improvements in the rate of technological development, and the creation of a fertile ground for a healthy and competitive economic activity. Thus, trade liberalisation can benefit the environment by increasing economic growth and providing resources to resolve environmental problems, and by creating new trading opportunities in 'environmentally friendly' consumer products. If pursued on a manageable scale, trade and environmental protection would therefore be compatible goals and the aversion to free trade and GATT/WTO that most environmentalists display may be unfounded.

The groups arguing against trade liberalisation insist that free trade unleashed would harm both the environment and human welfare. They take the view that the notion of 'comparative advantage', which is the central tenet of the free trade argument, may have worked in the economies of the 19th century when David Ricardo first formulated the concept, but, in today's world, where money can be transferred between nations at the speed of light, it is fallacious to consider that comparative advantage still exists. In other words, if firms are free to relocate their capital internationally to wherever their production costs would be lowest, then the favoured countries have not merely a *comparative* advantage but an *absolute* advantage (Daly 1993). The struggle for capital investment, in turn, may lead to the lowering of environmental quality and standards.

Moreover, countries that are heavily dependent on the production and export of non-energy commodities have yet to benefit from the world marketing system currently in place. Sub-Saharan countries are especially vulnerable, as their economic survival depends largely on single commodity exports such as cotton, coffee and cocoa, comprising over 50% of their total exports in many cases. Unfortunately, the export prices for these commodities have been liable to large fluctuations, and in 1992 were at their lowest levels in 30 years (Cheru 1992). In the short term, such lower commodity prices and capital deficits are offset by producing ever-greater quantities, which in the long term places a heavy strain on the natural resource base.

All in all, it is important to remember that the links between trade and environment are complex and depend on a wide range of factors. Although more needs to be done in understanding the relationship between international trade and environmental protection, the experience thus far has been mixed, with both positive and negative interactions identified. This may indicate that trade and environment issues differ across countries depending on the specific environmental and developmental conditions. In view of the differences from country to country, it is difficult to draw generalised conclusions on how to achieve compatibility between trade and environment. As more information becomes available, a clearer understanding will, no doubt, emerge.

The chapters presented in this section are selected to help the reader understand the range of issues associated with international trade and their effect on the environment. Chapter 14, by Matthew Cole, presents an elegant review of the Uruguay

Round and its implications for the welfare of the environment. He argues that, while modest gains are expected from the Uruguay Round in terms of economic growth and income levels, the associated local air pollution and health issues in developing countries require attention. Efficient use of resources and the use of clean technologies, supported by appropriate environmental legislation, could provide some of the answers for the anticipated industrial expansion. Of course, success in integrating trade opportunities with environmental stewardship is dependent on the kind of partnership established between Northern consumers and Southern producers of services and goods. Nick Robins and Sarah Roberts from the IIED (Chapter 15) provide an informative piece on the lessons to be learned from the small number of pioneering companies in the South that have already taken advantage of the new trade opportunities created in the aftermath of the Earth Summit in 1992. The main reason for their success is to do with their long-term commitment in combining sustainable production and profitability, and building the necessary capacity to adapt to new business opportunities. Meeting the demands of consumers and other stakeholders is also receiving much attention from multinational corporations (MNCs) in their pursuit of sustainable development. Titus Moser and Damian Miller (Chapter 16) succinctly argue that, although sustainable business practice among MNCs in the South tends to vary case by case, there are some common themes that transcend individual cases. They identify four themes to highlight the sustainable development debate involving MNCs and their activities in developing countries. Consolidating the above two chapters, David Sonnenfeld (Chapter 17) presents a useful case example of the pulp-manufacturing industry in South-East Asia to highlight the need for analysis at multiple levels (national, international, political, economic and technological) when applying the principles of industrial ecology, i.e. dematerialisation and decarbonisation.

The fifth and final theme covered in this book explores the links between the ever-elusive concept of **Sustainable Development** and its other important constituent, **Environmental Management**. Of course, the connection between the two concepts was always significant owing to the fact that the very idea of sustainable development arose essentially from the concerns relating to the depletion of natural resources and damage to the environment. The need to rehabilitate and manage the environment was seen as an important policy consideration, particularly following the Rio Earth Summit in 1992, some five years after 'sustainable development' entered the vernacular of the academic domain worldwide. The commitments made at this Summit, encapsulated in *Agenda 21*, apportioned equal weight to economic (and social) development, and environmental protection, recognising the intrinsic relationship between them and the need to use an integrated approach to global and local problems. Moreover, the principal political agreement at the Rio Summit was the recognition that global ecological problems had to be solved in an equitable way, through North–South partnership. In essence, this takes on board the notion of 'common but differentiated responsibility' of each nation, with a view that the North would change its production and consumption patterns and assist the South with financial aid and technology transfer, while the South for its part would give high priority to good governance, prudent economic management, improved pollution standards and policies directed to poverty alleviation.

Some eight years after Rio, there are very mixed opinions on whether the 'spirit of Rio' has been translated into practical action. On the positive side, there has been some progress at the institutional level with the establishment of over a hundred national councils or co-ordinating bodies in sustainable development. Further, the post-Rio period has been marked by a dramatic rise in public awareness, contributing to enormous activities in Local Agenda 21 worldwide, in both the North and South. Modest improvements in the area of energy efficiency are observed in the North, in addition to reductions in air, water and soil pollution.

Regrettably, the post-Rio record in much of the developing world has not produced the intended results in terms of environmental protection and poverty reduction. Many countries remain enmeshed in problems of external debt and low commodity prices, forcing producers to intensify production with fewer resources available to confront the environmental consequences of intensification. Those Southern countries that are industrialising rapidly are also facing the pressures of urbanisation and high growth in their industrial sector, putting additional pressure on the environment, concerns for which remain secondary to the imperatives of growth. Another factor that has also impeded the progress towards sustainable development is that the industrialised countries have not lived up to their commitments to help the South. Contrary to the commitments made in Rio to increase financial assistance and technology transfer from North to South, official development assistance (ODA) dropped from 0.34% of OECD countries' GNP in 1992 to 0.22% in 1997, far distant from the 0.7% fixed by the UN in 1969, following the recommendation made by the Pearson Commission (UNDP 1999). Little progress has also been made in technology transfer of environmentally sound technologies.

Collectively, the chapters in this section attempt to contribute to the ongoing discussion and debate in the post-Rio era, and underpin the complexities involved when addressing sustainable development. Each chapter is unique in its own right, and new case examples or new ways of approaching and treating sustainable development are presented. This can only be constructive, since sustainable development depends on new experiences and new findings about the interaction of different systems in order to maintain its permanence and relevance, and not just be another development fad.

This process of 'permanent flux' is no less real in influencing organisational change. Chapter 18, by Ans Kolk, describes the evolution of the World Bank over the past two decades, and how external pressures and internal contradictions led to the review of its policy on environmental practice. This is expected to impact on future development (and environmental) projects in developing countries in the light of the Bank's latest concern in poverty alleviation and environmental protection issues. However, the extent to which the World Bank has shed its 'technical fix' approach to environmental problems and poverty alleviation remains to be seen. Govindan Parayil (Chapter 19) eloquently warns against such an approach, using the development experience in the Indian state of Kerala, which has achieved remarkably high levels of social development with minimal environmental costs and low throughput. The reason for Kerala's success has much to do with radical nature of its early (post-independence) development path, which prioritised economic equity and distributive justice over economic growth. In stark contrast to the case of Kerala, Barbara and Eric Ribbens (Chapter 20) provide an insight into the dismal scenario of environmental degradation and social and economic underdevelopment of the Marshall Islands. They attribute the current unsustainable condition to specific local physical realities and weak institutional and human capacity. The value of social capital in enabling local communities to manage their activities effectively is well presented in Chapter 21 by Murray Jones. Using the case of the Camisea gas and condensate development project (Peru), he points to the great advantages of extending the participation of stakeholders to embrace the full spread of people who would have been affected by the (now abandoned) project in some way. This process is seen as a useful exercise if the aim is to maximise input and transparency and, by so doing, ensure that all views are represented in all decisions. The lack of accountability and transparency in decision-making is at the heart of the ecological crisis that Indonesia currently faces, according to Peter Koffel in Chapter 22. This process, in turn, has contributed to the practice of 'business as usual', which urgently needs to be reversed so that common-sense thresholds can be put in place. Finally, Patrick Bond and Robyn Stein present in Chapter 23 a similarly alarming scenario in post-apartheid South Africa, where companies still expect society to shoulder the burden of externalised environmental costs. Yet the distribution of South Africa's environmental resources, such as water, is alarmingly unequal when measured according to class, race and gender. In essence, part of the problem is that technical and market-oriented solutions dominate with no consideration for ecological values, public health, and the equalisation of quality of service. The authors propose popular mobilisation and coalition building of those affected by poor public services and environmental management problems.

A short outlook

The world has made a start in addressing the issues that have long troubled the development agenda. There is now a clearer view of the political economic nature of the environment and development debate and the need for co-ordinated action at international level. Already, it is evident that globalisation is integrating consumer markets around the world at breakneck speed, and that action at the global level can produce results faster than ever before. However, it is possible that global opportunities may not be shared equitably among nations and people. In fact, the alarming outcome of globalisation is that inequalities within countries and between countries have been rising apace as the relentless competition for investment and access to markets in the face of disappearing borders creates winners and losers in the global market. One important step would be to take advantage of this growing interdependence of people's lives to enhance global action to develop technologies for human development and poverty reduction, take stronger global action to tackle global threats, and bring people together to share knowledge and information. Globalisation can improve prospects for environmental management—through the spread of environmentally friendly technologies, standards and pressures by consumers and activists (UNDP 1999).

All in all, the management of environmental resources and sustainable development should address the long-term implications of all policies and actions on development, and consideration ought to be given to the needs of future generations equal to that given to the wellbeing of present generations. Thus, it would be reneging on the principles of sustainable development if there was emphasis only on *intergenerational* equity without taking on board *intragenerational* equity. Not only would it be morally unacceptable but also practically unworkable to treat the present and the future separately, as they constitute part of one continuum where the paths embarked on today will have bearings on tomorrow in making the relations of human and natural resources more compatible.

I

GLOBALISATION

1
The Environmental Challenge of Going Global*

Gilbert S. Hedstrom, Ronald A.N. McLean and Bernhard H. Metzger

CONVENTIONAL WISDOM holds that, as transnational companies expand into new sites and markets, they leave behind North America's and Northern Europe's stringent environmental, health and safety performance requirements. The reality is quite different. Leading transnational companies have known for some time that sound EHS performance is vital to success wherever they operate. Host countries expect the best from firms with global resources. The financial community is very sensitive to the risks and liabilities of mediocre environmental performance. Advocacy groups don't hesitate to hold companies accountable for lapses in EHS practices wherever they occur. And consumers—especially in Europe—can be motivated to punish companies at the cash register when they perceive them as environmentally irresponsible.

When transnational companies first took the measure of the global EHS challenge, many took steps to review and revise their worldwide corporate policies (*Prism* 1994). Now, as companies become more familiar with the ongoing reality of managing EHS performance globally, they are applying these standards in the light of newly won insights and best practices.

The challenges to industry

Our experience suggests that major transnational corporations in a range of industries face similar challenges in managing EHS globally. These challenges include

* This chapter is reprinted with permission from *Prism*, 2nd quarter, 1997, Arthur D. Little's journal for senior management.

split-level expectations, public scrutiny and demand for consistent performance and business effectiveness.

Split-level expectations

Many of the countries into which transnationals are expanding have extensive EHS regulations on the books. Often—in the former Soviet Union, for example—these regulations may include stricter standards on matters such as site contamination and emissions than those in Germany, the Netherlands or the US. In other cases, as in some Latin American countries, the standards may he borrowed from existing US or European regulatory codes. Transnationals have found, however, that, under these regulatory schemes, compliance expectations are often very different for themselves than for domestic firms. While much is expected of the transnationals, who are seen as technically and financially equipped to achieve high environmental performance, much is overlooked among domestic firms.

Public scrutiny

Just as officials in developing countries are increasingly aware of the EHS requirements and expectations transnational companies meet in Europe and North America, consumers and advocacy groups are increasingly paying attention to how these companies operate worldwide. In a number of instances, non-governmental organisations are working with local communities and officials in developing regions to help them use political processes to ensure that environmental performance requirements are part of business deals with transnational firms. These organisations are deeply sceptical about transnational companies' global EHS commitment and performance. Any company that takes pride in its EHS record or promotes it at home should be certain that its operations anywhere in the world can stand up to public scrutiny.

Demands for consistent performance

Worldwide EHS standards and policies have become common among transnational corporations. The challenge now is to strike a balance among competing priorities—especially in energy chemicals, pharmaceuticals and other industries that have undergone corporate downsizing, restructuring and decentralisation. Boards of directors and senior management need to be certain that, in newly decentralised structures, their companies' EHS performance continues to provide long-term worldwide protection from liability. At the same time, heads of the businesses and regional managers want flexibility to adapt quickly to competitive shifts in local and global markets, and they need assurance that corporate policies support business and financial targets while minimising risk.

Demands for business effectiveness

Corporate approaches to environmental, health and safety issues must make business sense as well as EHS sense. Internally, EHS managers are being challenged to link EHS performance issues to the business matters that take priority with most line managers. Externally, companies should be prepared to negotiate with officials and other stakeholders in terms of risk-based approaches that provide cost-effective solutions to EHS problems.

Best practices

To address these challenges, leading companies have developed a number of best practices. Some examples follow.

Know what your values are.

Companies with strong internal cultures find it much easier to sustain environmental, health and safety controls worldwide. Robust corporate values provide a consistent basis for negotiating with local regulators, maintaining a consistent approach across diverse local standards and building trust with stakeholders at home and abroad. Environmental values are well established among leading multinationals. Conoco, for example, believes that considerations of sustainability must drive future development and operations, especially in fragile or sensitive environments such as rainforests and tundra. At Alcoa, six core values—including a commitment to environmental, health and safety excellence—help shape the company's decision-making.

Applying strong corporate values to specific real-world industrial situations is not always simple. Alcoa's company policy (see Chapter 6) mandates that its facilities everywhere meet or exceed the requirements of local law and of internal company standards, which, in many cases, are stricter than regulatory standards. In some instances, this approach has compelled the company to weigh the environmental benefits against other social benefits of a specific investment. What should a company do when a facility provides otherwise scarce jobs and income to local residents but cannot rapidly be improved environmentally without capital costs that would make it non-competitive? Environmentally, the ideal decision may be to shut the plant down. Economically and socially, the benefits may be greater if the plant keeps operating. One solution is to spread the environmental investment over a period of years, so that production costs remain competitive, jobs are retained and clear progress is being made toward a higher standard of environmental performance.

At Novartis, the life sciences company created by the merger of Ciba and Sandoz, worldwide EHS standards are based on Swiss, European Union and US models, according to Dr Kaspar Eigenmann, Head of Corporate Health, Safety and Environment. Novartis finds that adhering to these standards seldom requires the company to back out of a venture. Instead, when problems have been identified at one of its partner facilities, Novartis focuses on improving environmental performance. To make this approach work, Novartis looks for partners that share its view of environmental issues and are prepared to apply Novartis's standards.

Integrate EHS into your global growth strategy.

One EHS activity that has long been a part of transnational business procedure is environmental due-diligence assessment of acquisition targets. Dr Max Kogelnig, Technical Director, Environment and Safety at Solvay, the Belgian multinational chemical and pharmaceutical company, indicates that Solvay requires at least a Phase I due-diligence assessment for all acquisitions of industrial property. For many acquisitions where significant contamination is suspected, Phase II sampling for soil and groundwater is conducted. These assessments are also used as a basis for establishing environmental improvement action plans.

These activities cover now-familiar aspects of the total potential risk and liability picture for a project. A next step for some companies is to integrate risk-based approaches to environmental health and safety issues into business risk analysis and decision-making. One initial effort in this area has been made by Scotford, a US importer and distributor of petrochemicals and a subsidiary of Shell Canada Chemicals Company. Scotford decided to expand its distribution and sale of monomer styrene throughout the US. The company used a study of the EHS risks of various transport options in its present operations to obtain a baseline understanding of potential risks in future, expanded operations. Scotford then integrated semi-quantitative comparisons of these EHS risks in various transport alternatives with business-related factors. The company used the results of the integrated analysis to incorporate EHS risk thinking in major long-range strategic planning.

Overall, however, companies could be doing more to include EHS issues fully in their planning for expansion. Most of the time, technical and financial staff members review new projects first, and EHS staff contribute their review only later, after many parameters with EHS implications have already been set. To include EHS thinking earlier, companies will need to change mind-sets about EHS matters among business and technical staff, a shift that EHS staff must help to drive. Conoco is approaching this challenge by decentralising many of its EHS functions and establishing a five-member worldwide project group whose mission is, in part, 'to get safety, health and environment staff in on the ground floor with new projects', in the words of Dennis Parker, the company's Vice-President for Safety Health and Environment. Conoco's operational managers give the new approach favourable reviews.

Put performance first.

Many in industry believe and hope that performance-oriented environmental regulation and management will increasingly displace the command-and-control approach to environmental protection. Choosing their own route toward regulatory standards, companies are often able to use cost-effective technologies and approaches, freeing up resources that can be applied to other EHS priorities.

In terms of global expansion, a focus on performance gives companies an opportunity. In many countries, environmental, health and safety regulation and enforcement are still evolving. When transnational companies negotiate performance-based approaches with regulators and then excel at meeting agreed-upon standards, they build credibility not only for themselves but for the performance-based approach.

A performance-based focus also means accepting—within reason—host-country expectations that ventures backed by transnationals will set an EHS example and perform at a higher level than domestic firms. Benefits of this 'high-road' strategy include access to important natural resources, the opportunity to set the standard and influence external and domestic firms to come up to the same level, a more secure franchise to continue operations long term and a better image worldwide.

Several years ago, Conoco needed to weigh risks and benefits to the company's image while deciding to go forward with the Polar Lights project in northern Russia. To go forward, Conoco would need to build a pipeline system to connect Polar Lights with Russia's export pipeline system. Frequent and sizeable spills in Russian pipelines in the Arctic and west Siberia have given these systems a bad reputation. Conoco decided that the opportunity to establish a system that would be a model of environmental performance was greater than the risk of being associated with poorly performing Russian pipeline systems. Polar Lights is now up and running successfully.

A major international foods company identified a problem with waste-water at a dairy plant in Brazil. The company faced a choice between installing treatment options to meet European waste-water standards or then-current Brazilian standards. Despite the considerably higher cost of meeting European standards, the company chose that route for the dairy plant. Three years later, the wisdom of this decision was confirmed when Brazil adopted European standards for waste-water. The company not only adhered to its own values and standards, but got the jump on competing dairy facilities in terms of meeting the new requirements.

Chevron Overseas Petroleum Incorporated (COPI) 'feels a responsibility to help raise the environmental performance of the industry in its host countries,' says Jim Koerber, Manager, HSE, COPI. Chevron is convinced that host governments bring in Western companies in part to pressurise local companies to improve their performance. In Kazakhstan, as part of its involvement in the giant Tengiz project, Chevron has worked hard to get permission to use international environmental, health and safety standards that are more appropriate for the company's technology than standards based on outdated Russian technology. In return, the company is committed to operating at a high level of environmental protection and accepts that local firms are on a slower track toward meeting the same level of performance.

☐ *Build partnerships.*

Any expert on expanding your business globally will tell you that local partnerships are vital to success. What, specifically, does that mean in the environmental, health and safety arena?

On one level, building partnerships can mean taking a leadership role in changing the way EHS needs are met. At the Eco 1997 Conference in Paris in February of that year, David Buzzelli, Vice-President, The Dow Chemical Company, reported that a group of transnational chemical companies that operate in Thailand are working with the Thai government and chemical industry to introduce the Responsible Care programme of the Chemical Manufacturers' Association to the chemical industry there.

In energy ventures in the former Soviet Union, working together also extends beyond business relationships to other stakeholders. Ed Caldwell, Co-ordinator of Environment, Safety and Regulatory Affairs, Exxon Ventures (CIS), comments that local scientists and institutes are key stakeholders in the environmental permitting process. The public respects them, and they are the ones who developed existing Russian environmental and technical standards. Companies that try to go it alone and disregard the contributions of experts in host countries may well be seen as arrogant and may encounter greater obstacles in negotiations.

◻ *Challenge your assumptions.*

Much of the current focus on environmental, health and safety performance is on the process. Some transnational companies that think broadly about the environmental impact of their activities have concluded that, in the long run, their products affect the environment more than their processes. Terry Thiele, Associate General Counsel for AB Electrolux's North American subsidiary, White Consolidated Industries, notes that up to 90% of the environmental impact of the company's products occurs while they are being used. Electrolux believes that the greatest long-term opportunity for environmental protection will come from reducing the environmental impact of its products. For a worldwide company such as Electrolux, which ranks first or second in many of the markets in which it competes, that means understanding what consumers in widely disparate markets want, in environmental terms, from products, and giving it to them without losing any competitive ground.

Similarly, Mercedes has recognised that a clean product is more important from an environmental standpoint than a clean site. Mercedes believes that producing cars is now a relatively clean process—especially when compared to the environmental burden imposed by cars over their life. Seeking to develop an emissions-free vehicle, Mercedes is focusing on fuel-cell technology that generates electricity from hydrogen. If a car of this sort becomes commercially successful, the worldwide positive impact on air quality could be substantial in the long term. Meanwhile, the company continues to scrutinise every stage in the making of its products to further minimise environmental impact.

The hallmark of environmental thinking at Mercedes (and its parent company Daimler-Benz) and at Electrolux is a willingness to break through the conventional time-frame for environmental planning and strategy and take steps toward goals that may not be realised for a decade or more. In the global marketplace, where investments in new regions can take years to bear fruit, a long-term outlook is critical

Anticipate trends: integrate EHS thinking now.

If the current trend toward the lowering of trade barriers and the globalisation of markets and industrial activities continues, companies that manage environmental, health and safety performance at a consistently high level worldwide can expect to see their efforts pay off. In this atmosphere, companies are likely to see a continuing harmonisation and convergence of EHS protection and performance standards. This will occur in part as regulations such as the European Union's Eco-Management and Audit Scheme and standards such as ISO 14001 spread through supplier networks, and in part to ensure that environmental issues don't become trade barriers.

To keep ahead of these global forces—and keep their environmental, health and safety costs lower than the competition—companies will need to give much more attention to integrating EHS thinking across the product and process value chain. It will become increasingly expensive to tack on good EHS performance once basic planning and implementation is complete. The integration process is likely to work best for those firms that have learned how to work closely with line management worldwide and team with them on solutions to EHS challenges that make sense locally. Bringing the corporate vision down to ground level is challenging even for companies operating primarily in one country. It gets much harder on a global scale. The closer the business and EHS visions are to begin with, the less difficult aligning them will be.

2

An Essay on Biodiversity and Globalisation

Frank Vorbies

The political economy of biodiversity

'BIODIVERSITY' IS NOW WIDELY ACCEPTED as a scientific concept encompassing the diversity of life on Earth. This diversity is generally described at three levels: diversity of ecosystems, diversity of species, and diversity of genes. As a scientific concept, biodiversity is a more precise description of what most people call 'nature'.

Biodiversity, however, is more than a scientific concept. It is also a political concept embracing a trinity of globally agreed objectives:

- Conservation of biodiversity
- Sustainable use of biological resources
- Equitable sharing of the benefits arising from this use

The political concept of biodiversity is particularly relevant to globalisation as it deals with the interface between global ecological, economic and social processes. Biodiversity is about control over and access to our planet's biological resources. It is about the economic uses of these resources. It is about social equity with respect to the distribution of associated benefits and costs. And it is about conserving the ecological systems of our planet.

Biodiversity is also an economic concept, in that biological resources provide a complex array of goods and services for the benefit of humankind. Some of these goods and services are critical to the survival of the human race, such as management of the climate system and the provision of fresh-water. Others respond to core demands for nutrition, shelter and clothing. Still others respond to demands for scientific inquiry, natural beauty or outdoor recreation.

Some of the goods and services provided by biodiversity are public in that society at large benefits from their provision, such as watershed services and carbon sequestration. Other examples are more private such as food products and nature-based tourism. This implies that there are roles for both public and private institutions in the management of biodiversity. However, as discussed in more detail below, biodiversity has generally been managed by public institutions. As globalisation changes the roles of these institutions, it is directly impacting the way in which these institutions can or should manage biodiversity.

The meaning of globalisation

Ruud Lubbers, the former Primer Minister of the Netherlands, is one of the world's best-known experts on globalisation. He has run a well-known seminar on the subject at Harvard University's John F. Kennedy School of Government. The course description offers a good introduction to the concept of globalisation. It is quoted here from the website at some length:

> The emergence of a global economy compels national governments to reappraise their assumptions of economic governance and, in doing so, to adopt a more systematic approach to the implementation of socio-economic policies. At the same time, *the new global economy also demands a reconsideration of the role of international institutions* (the GATT, WTO , IMF, OECD, NATO, WEU, UN) as fashioners and sustainers of the ground rules for numerous international transactions in the domains of security, human rights and sustainable development.
>
> We define globalisation as a process that widens the extent and form of cross-border transactions among peoples, assets, goods and services and that deepens the economic interdependence between and among globalising entities, which may be private or public institutions or governments. This process is driven by economical (adoption of the system of free-market economy and economic liberalisation, both within and between countries) technological (advances in information and communications technology) and political (the demise of communism and a movement towards democracy in former communist countries . . .) developments.
>
> Globalisation differs from other forms of intensified interdependence between national economies: true economic globalisation involves a qualitative shift toward a system based on a consolidated global market place for production, distribution and consumption rather than on autonomous national economies. Equally important, globalisation involves more than economics or economic interconnectedness. It increases risks and opportunities for individuals and communities seeking to transform local traditions and modes of behaviour in reaction to processes of globalisation that emphasise mobility, simultaneity, pluralism and alternate routes to the satisfaction of needs and services.
>
> Finally, *globalisation may create a need for supranational global governance regimes to maximise welfare globally*. Such institutions and regimes may be needed to address cross-border market failures that national governments are unable to surmount or fully compensate for. The fields of satellite communications, seabed exploration, nuclear proliferation and protection of the ozone layer, for

> example, may demand the attention of global institutions to reduce the coordination and transaction costs of such activities or to capture the external benefits of intergovernmental networking. *These international public and social goods will increasingly require pluralist governance structures* if they are to produce truly global public value [emphasis added].[1]

As the italicised sections show, Lubbers clearly sees a need for new or restructured global institutions to manage globalisation and its impacts. With respect to biodiversity management, this chapter supports Lubbers's call for new institutional structures.

Biodiversity and the global economy

Globalisation is fundamentally an economic phenomenon. Yes, as indicated above, there are technological aspects of globalisation, such as the rapidly developing global information and transportation networks, as well as energy aspects, such as readily affordable and abundant petroleum supplies. These aspects lower the costs of globalisation by lowering the costs of supplying goods and services on a global scale. The forces behind such supply-side aspects are, however, fundamentally economic and have been made possible by a particular economic development path: the market economy. The essence of globalisation is the ascendancy of the global market economy.

Though the market economy has had and always will have its shortcomings, socialist alternatives are no longer credible options. Even communist China is no longer communist in an economic sense. Virtually all political parties, from the new Labour Party of the UK to the African National Congress of South Africa, fully accept the market as the basis of their economies. Additionally, the market economy is now widely recognised and accepted as a global reality.

Modern economic policy debates now centre not on socialism versus capitalism but rather on the role of markets to address government failures and the role of governments to address market failures. In this context, however, support for *politically administered* or *mercantilist* economic policies remains strong. This is particularly the case in developing countries and in government divisions responsible for the management of biodiversity. But globalisation is now undermining these traditional mercantilist approaches to managing biodiversity.

To explain further, *mercantilism* was the economic system of the European colonial powers. The Portuguese, Spanish, British and French exported this system of politically managed economies to their colonies in the Americas, Africa and Asia. Up to today, strong mercantilist elements remain in many of the national structures of these former colonies. The Peruvian economist, Hernando de Soto, defined mercantilism as follows:

> Mercantilism was a politically administered economy in which economic agents were subject to specific, detailed regulation. The mercantilist state did not let consumers decide what should be produced; it reserved to itself the right to single

1 *http://www.globalize.org*, 1999.

> out and promote whichever economic activities it considered desirable and to prohibit those which it considered inappropriate . . . To achieve its objectives, the mercantilist state granted privileges to favoured producers and consumers by means of regulations, subsidies, taxes and licenses (de Soto 1989).

While globalisation has emerged from the ascendancy of the market economy, mercantilist approaches remain strong in terms of internationally agreed rules for international trade. They also remain strong at the national level, as evidenced by the attempts of governments to maintain controls over their economies through central banks, national transport systems, national communication systems, national energy systems, and even national systems of protected areas.

Biodiversity conservation and the management of biodiversity-based sectors, such as agriculture, forestry and fisheries, have traditionally been the responsibility of government agencies. Government conservation agencies almost universally prefer to rely on administrative procedures and regulatory instruments to manage biodiversity rather than market processes and economic incentives. They remain true to the mercantilist tradition and are thus increasingly 'out of sync' with the process of globalisation.

The preference for politically administered management systems for biodiversity is probably rooted in the development of the modern nation-state. In earlier days, monarchs and emperors strove to monopolise access to natural resources. With the emergence of the nation-state, national governments maintained the tradition of state monopolies over natural resources. Even a bastion of capitalism such as the United States maintains widespread state monopolies over forests, mountains, river systems, lakes, coastal zones and wildlife.

Thus, today, in the face of globalisation and the *marketisation* of most sectors of the economy, the management of biodiversity continues to be dominated by outdated mercantilist systems. Yet, with the ascendancy of the global market economy, there is also now increasing pressure on governments, especially in developing countries, to *privatise* nature by turning over the management of biodiversity to market forces. At the global level, this pressure is evidenced in the potential conflicts between the rules of international trade and the objectives of the global biodiversity agreements. At the national level, this pressure is reflected both in the belief that protected areas must 'pay for themselves' and in the trends towards commercialisation of access to and management of biological resources.

The biodiversity community, with its long history of reliance on and use of the mercantilist structures, is currently ill-equipped to deal with the pressures globalisation and increasing demands to commercialise or privatise biodiversity. This situation is especially serious because many proposed market-based approaches to managing biodiversity have not been tested and indeed may not work. Thus, there is a critical need to strengthen the commercial acumen of the biodiversity managers and at the same time there is a critical need to develop precautionary approaches to the marketisation of nature. As suggested by Lubbers,[2] there is a need for new or strengthened global institutions to deal with these challenges.

---

2 See footnote 1.

Global biodiversity agreements

The global biodiversity agreements provide the political framework for strengthening existing approaches and developing new approaches to managing biodiversity, especially in the context of globalisation. With the reach of the global economy, it is becoming increasingly necessary to develop global agreements on the interactions between economic activities and our planet's ecological systems. Without such global agreements, the processes of globalisation will remain ungoverned and their potentially negative impacts on the biodiversity unchecked. This section briefly introduces a few of the key global biodiversity agreements and then proposes that the linkages between them need to be strengthened.

The Convention on International Trade in Endangered Species

One of the oldest biodiversity agreements (early 1970s) interestingly enough focuses on a key feature of globalisation: international trade. CITES—or the Convention on International Trade in Endangered Species of Wild Flora and Fauna—regulates trade in endangered or threatened wildlife. Through a listing system, it bans trade in critically endangered species and limits trade in threatened species to exports that are shown to be non-detrimental to the species.

Given the mercantilist nature of biodiversity management, it is perhaps not surprising that there has been a much stronger emphasis on using CITES to stop trade or to limit trade rather than to develop trade measures and practices that promote sustainable use. The many anti-trade decisions under CITES are, of course, in apparent conflict with international free trade policies. In this context, the critical role of CITES needs to be reconsidered.

The World Heritage Convention

Another early biodiversity agreement, the World Heritage Convention, focused on identifying key natural (and cultural) sites that should be protected. In so doing, it recognises that there are specific sites of global significance that should be formally recognised as such. Thus this agreement supports the understanding of biodiversity as a global resource generating global intangible benefits.

The Ramsar Convention on Wetlands

A third early agreement focuses on the conservation and wise use of wetlands. The Ramsar Convention on Wetlands (named after the Iranian town in which it was launched) focuses on a component of biodiversity that does not easily fit into traditional government structures. While most governments have ministries or divisions to manage forests, coastal zones and protected areas, few have had explicit divisions to manage wetlands. Furthermore, the legal status of a wetland is often a mixture of public and private ownership and many important wetlands stretch over national boundaries. Thus an agreement to recognise wetlands of international significance as well as to develop common principles and practices for their management was an early recognition of global responsibilities for biodiversity at the ecosystem level.

The Framework Convention on Climate Change

In the early 1990s, the world's governments met in Rio to agree on a joint programme in support of sustainable development. Known as Agenda 21, this agreement included the creation of three new conventions to address the topics of climate change, biodiversity and desertification. It also created an intergovernmental process to address forests. One of these agreements, the Framework Convention on Climate Change, boldly addresses one of our planet's major public goods: the climate system.

Under this agreement, governments are also attempting to develop economic instruments compatible with the globalised market economy to manage the climate system. These instruments include a central role for biological resources in the sequestration of carbon. Development of new global markets for carbon sequestration, however, poses a serious challenge to the institutions managing biodiversity. As discussed above, these institutions are universally ill-equipped to operate within such market processes.

The Convention on Biological Diversity

The most visionary and holistic biodiversity agreement is the Convention on Biological Diversity. Now ratified by almost all the countries in the world—with the notable exception of the United States—this Convention is attempting to develop a global framework for the management of biodiversity. It is striving to meet the trinity of biodiversity objectives—conservation, sustainable use and equitable benefit sharing—through globally agreed policies and procedures for managing biodiversity. These policies and procedures are also intended to support the overall goal of sustainable development and the corollary objective of poverty alleviation. But, given the tradition of biodiversity management, the Convention is understandably yet to address the pressures of globalisation head-on. There is, however, an increasing recognition that the private sector must be an active player in managing biodiversity, but this recognition has yet to be articulated into clear roles and responsibilities for the private sector and global market processes.

Merging the biodiversity agreements?

Because of its all-encompassing vision, the Convention on Biological Diversity, or the CBD, provides the best global framework agreement for managing the ecological systems and biological resources of our planet. In this sense, all other agreements, including those mentioned above and others such as the Convention on Migratory Species and the Convention to Combat Desertification, ought to be merged under the CBD to form a coherent and effective body of biodiversity laws and policies.

Today, however, the various global biodiversity agreements operate virtually independently from one other. Their secretariats are scattered around the globe; their meetings take place at different times and in different places; and their decisions are not harmonised. Though there is now some collaboration between the agreements, most successfully between the CBD and Ramsar, this collaboration is far from adequate. In the face of globalisation, this balkanisation of global biodiversity policy seriously threatens our ability to manage biodiversity.

As a matter of urgency, serious consideration should be given to bring the global biodiversity agreements together.

Biodiversity agreements and trade agreements

Unlike global biodiversity agreements, global trade agreements are harmonised under the management of the World Trade Organisation (WTO). This new institution is dedicated to expanding and strengthening international free trade. In this sense, it stands at the front line of globalisation.

Global trade agreements are evolving in a highly coherent and effective way while global biodiversity agreements flounder in a myriad of disconnected meetings and resolutions. This state of affairs not only makes the management of biodiversity less effective in its own right, but also in the context of addressing the globalisation of trade.

International trade has significant direct and indirect impacts on biodiversity. As noted above, the direct impacts were recognised some time ago by the biodiversity community with the creation of CITES. The CBD is also concerned with international access to genetic resources and the transfer of bio-technology. And increasingly there is a realisation that the promotion of free trade in developing countries that lack good governments and effective civil society structures is likely to encourage the over-exploitation of biological resources. Thus well-organised trade policies in the face of balkanised biodiversity policies are likely to expand the global economy in ways that seriously undermine biodiversity.

If biodiversity agreements are to become an effective counterweight to trade agreements, they must 'get their act together' and become more focused with respect to biodiversity measures for managing international trade.

Global biodiversity organisations

In addition to bringing the global biodiversity agreements together, we need to look at opportunities to strengthen the position global biodiversity organisations. This section covers some of the key institutions and then considers whether mergers among them might be appropriate.

IUCN: The World Conservation Union

The world's major biodiversity organisation is IUCN. Founded in the 1940s, its 900-plus members include states, government agencies and NGOs. IUCN also has large commissions of experts on species, protected areas, ecosystems and environmental law. And the IUCN Secretariat is an institution in its own right with a global programme and offices in 40 countries.

The mission of IUCN is to conserve the integrity and diversity of nature and to ensure that any use of natural resources is equitable and ecologically sustainable. That this mission is fully compatible with the trinity of biodiversity objectives is not surprising, as IUCN was instrumental in creating most of the global biodiversity agreements. Also, IUCN has key responsibilities for the implementation of CITES, Ramsar and the World Heritage Convention and is increasingly being asked to play key roles with respect to the CBD.

Ironically, however, just as globalisation was becoming a real force, IUCN decided to decentralise and to regionalise focusing locally more than globally. Also, as a union of governments and non-government organisations, IUCN has yet to build a strategic partnership with the private sector. Nevertheless, IUCN remains the major global multi-stakeholder biodiversity institution and could be positioned to address the impacts of globalisation on biodiversity.

World Wide Fund for Nature

The World Wide Fund For Nature, or WWF, is the world's largest independent conservation organisation, with around five million supporters and a global network of 27 national organisations, five associates and 21 programme offices. WWF was established in the 1960s as a funding mechanism in support of the work of IUCN. Until the mid-1990s, the two institutions were headquartered in the same building in Gland, Switzerland. They are now in separate buildings, about 500 metres apart.

The missions and programmes of IUCN and WWF are essentially the same. Like IUCN, WWF is a global institution with a strong focus on the ground and with undeveloped links to the private sector. Unlike IUCN, however, WWF's members are individuals and not organisations.

In addition to WWF, there are other international biodiversity NGOs such as the Flora and Fauna International, Birdlife International and The Nature Conservancy. None of these, however, has the global reach of IUCN and WWF. Also, all of these are members of IUCN and so in a sense form part of its global biodiversity union.

United Nations Environment Programme

Founded in the 1970s, the UN Environment Programme, or UNEP, was the first significant intergovernmental agency to address the environmental agenda. In comparison, IUCN is a non-intergovernmental organisation with its mixture of government and non-government members. When UNEP was set up, IUCN was already 25 years old and, in its early years, the green side of the intergovernmental environmental agenda was in many respects simply contracted out from UNEP to IUCN.

Today, however, UNEP plays a key role with respect to biodiversity including hosting many of the biodiversity conventions including the CBD and CITES.

With respect to globalisation, UNEP faces many of the same problems as the other UN agencies. Being essentially a club of governments, it is not able to easily accommodate either the NGO community or the private sector. Hence, UNEP is not well positioned to bring together various stakeholders to address the impacts of globalisation on biodiversity.

UNEP's role of hosting the biodiversity conventions, however, does offer an important opportunity to bring these together as discussed above. An obvious first step would be to bring all the convention secretariats together under one roof.

The World Bank Group

Most people would not think of the World Bank Group as a global biodiversity organisation, but increasingly the Bank sees itself as one. During the 1990s, the Bank greatly increased its environmental programme and now has one of the largest environmental staffs and budgets or any organisation. In its proposal for a comprehensive development framework, the Bank integrates the environment as a core component. It is also taking a very active interest in funding projects related to climate change and biodiversity.

With its focus on economic development and its private-sector capacity, particularly in the International Finance Corporation, the Bank is technically well placed to address the pressures of globalisation. Its now strong environmental capacity also makes it well placed to address the impacts of globalisation on biodiversity. However, its constituency—like UNEP and unlike IUCN and WWF—is government-based and thus far too narrow.

Global Environment Facility

In the early 1990s, the world's governments also established a new funding mechanism for the environment. Known as the Global Environment Facility, or the GEF, its mission is to provide incremental funding for global environmental benefits. This mission fits well with the process of globalisation as it focuses on global impacts rather than national or local impacts. A large part of GEF funding is either directly or indirectly supporting projects on biodiversity.

Though the GEF is a global financial mechanism for biodiversity, it is not really structured as an independent institution. It operates through windows in UNEP, the World Bank and the UN Development Programme. Thus it is not well positioned to act on its own with respect to globalisation. In close association with other institutions, however, it could play a key role.

Towards the World Biodiversity Organisation?

Just as global biodiversity policy is balkanised under the various biodiversity conventions, global programmes of work on biodiversity are also balkanised under a host of global biodiversity organisations. This is presents a particular problem with respect to the interface between international trade and biodiversity. Today we have no clear biodiversity counterpart to the World Trade Organisation.

It is also a problem with respect to the multinational corporations. One of the key features of globalisation is the globalisation of corporations. We are witnessing an ongoing series of mergers and acquisitions creating huge global corporations in all sectors of the economy, including banking, petroleum, autos, airlines, telecommunications, information technology and even fresh-water. Without a strong 'World Biodiversity Organisation', there will be no credible biodiversity counterpart to these global corporations.

The timing may be right for strategic mergers and acquisitions within the biodiversity sector. Already the World Bank has collaborative agreements with IUCN and WWF. IUCN also has an agreement with UNEP. The intergovernmental agencies, however, are unlikely to be able to find a meaningful place for the civil sector and the private sector within their structures. Hence global 'non-intergovernmental' and non-governmental organisations may provide the best opportunity.

At the moment, it appears as if a strategic merger between IUCN and WWF would be our best chance of creating a World Biodiversity Organisation that is strong enough to seriously take on the challenges of globalisation, including providing a counterbalance to the WTO and a counterpart to the global corporations.

Biodiversity and the global corporations

As already alluded to, a major biodiversity challenge of globalisation is the emergence of huge global corporations. These companies have the ability to exploit biological resources and to impact the status of biodiversity throughout our planet. In an increasingly globalised world, their global economic power means that *de facto* they play a major role in managing our planet.

If we want to manage global biodiversity effectively, we must engage the global corporations. Global biodiversity policy cannot be developed by and for a club of national governments. Policies must be developed by and for global corporations as well. For example, just as we expect national governments to develop biodiversity strategies and action plans, we should also expect global corporations to develop their own biodiversity strategies and actions plans. This is especially true for the biodiversity-impacting industries such as mining and transport as well as for the biodiversity-based industries such as agriculture and tourism. And, once again, there is a need for a credible World Biodiversity Organisation to engage substantively with these global corporations.

Interestingly, engaging the global corporations in the biodiversity agenda may actually have more far-reaching results than our current focus on improving the performance of national governments. It is precisely these corporations that operate across the face of our planet. Getting them to act positively with respect to managing biodiversity will produce globally significant results on a global scale.

Biodiversity and global information

As Lubbers explains,[3] globalisation has many dimensions in addition to the economic ones. A key dimension is information. If we are to conserve biodiversity and to ensure that the uses of biological resources are sustainable and equitable, we need to gather and synthesise much more information than we have currently about biodiversity management. We need not only more complete and detailed biological information, we also need a better understanding of the roles of economic instruments, legal structures, social practices and cultural traditions in managing biodiversity. The global information and communications revolution allows us for the first time to begin to understand how our planet functions on a global scale and which human actions support or undermine the integrity and diversity of our planet's ecological systems and biological resources.

Concluding remarks

In May 1998 at the WTO/GATT 50th anniversary celebrations, US President Bill Clinton remarked: 'Globalisation is not a policy choice—it is a fact.' Globalisation is a fact that the biodiversity community cannot ignore. If properly harnessed, aspects of globalisation can help us to better manage biodiversity. If not properly managed, aspects of globalisation will seriously threaten the diversity and indeed the integrity of our living planet.

Global biodiversity policy must come together into a coherent and influential body of laws and practices. It must be able to address key components of globalisation such as international trade and global corporations.

Global biodiversity organisations must take a serious look at their internal operations and external partnerships. Strategic mergers and alliances should be considered to ensure that biodiversity conservation is promoted and managed on a global scale alongside the many global processes promoting and managing international trade, finance and commerce.

Failure to address the reality of globalisation on the part of the biodiversity community will open the door to an accelerated decline of the quality and quantity of life on our planet.

3 See footnote 1.

3

Joint Implementation of Climate Change?

Distortions in Practice and Effects on Developing Countries

Neil E. Harrison

THE PURPOSE of international environmental policy is to organise the international co-operation necessary to mitigate environmental problems that extend beyond political borders. International environmental policy must co-exist with other economic and political preferences of developed and developing countries. This chapter assesses the influence of competing economic and political goals on the application by states of the rules for 'joint implementation' (JI) of the United Nations Framework Convention on Climate Change (the Convention)[1]—a 'positive' measure designed to minimise the global cost of mitigating climate change. If the national economic and political interests of investor countries dominate project selection, the global efficiency of climate mitigation may not be optimised and development plans of developing countries may be inhibited.

The first section explains the practical requirements of JI and analyses the principles for JI projects set out in the Convention and its Protocol. The second section develops measures to discriminate national political and economic goals from participation in the pursuit of global efficiency as criteria for project selection.

The third section analyses the available data—much of which is incomplete or not comparable—on JI projects. The data shows that national interests often do influence project selection but that this is not inevitable. Finally, I draw tentative conclusions on the motivations for JI projects, their effects on global mitigation efficiency and development in poorer countries. I then offer suggestions: (i) for ensuring

---

1 All official documents of the Convention and the Conference of the Parties that it establishes (and its subsidiary bodies) and the JI national reports may be found at *http://www.unfccc.de/fccc/*.

that JI projects efficiently mitigate greenhouse gas (GHG) emissions without distorting development; and (ii) for private JI investments that could enhance rather than inhibit development.

Joint implementation

In the Convention signed in 1992, the developed countries accepted that they should 'take the lead' without explicitly accepting that they were responsible for climate change. They insisted that mitigation of climate change must occur within an 'open international economic system' and free trade and that obligations under the treaty should not inhibit 'economic development [that] is essential for adopting measures to address climate change' nor prevent 'sustainable growth'. Principally in response to pressure from the United States, the Convention permits efforts to address climate change to be 'carried out co-operatively by interested Parties'. In anticipation of an emissions trading system, JI allows a party to the Convention to satisfy its emissions mitigation obligations under the Convention wherever the least-cost emissions reductions may be achieved (Articles 3.3 and 4.2[a]). It makes possible a form of emissions trading in which one party (the host country) does not have an emissions cap or reduction target.

The First Conference of the Parties to the Convention (COP 1) agreed to a pilot programme—'Activities Implemented Jointly' (AIJ)—through 1999 to assess the feasibility of joint implementation without assigning credits for emission reductions (Decision 5/CP.1). At COP 3 in Kyoto the JI process and reporting was modified—now targeting 'sustainable development'—and became the 'Clean Development Mechanism' (CDM) (United Nations 1997: Article 12). After 1999, states may earn certified emissions reductions (CERs) from investments in GHG mitigation projects in other countries. CERs may be credited against emissions targets, which developed countries must meet by between 2008 and 2012. The Kyoto Protocol also laid the groundwork for a tradable emissions permit.

In establishing the AIJ pilot project COP 1 decided that projects 'should be compatible with and supportive of national environmental and development priorities and strategies, contribute to cost-effectiveness in achieving global benefits' and should comprehensively address all relevant sources and sinks of GHGs (Decision 5/CP.1). JI projects must result in GHG reductions additional to any projected in the host country and the investment must be additional to any official development assistance (ODA) flows. All projects must be accepted by all states involved ensuring some political oversight of private-sector JI investment.

The benefits to investor countries of AIJ projects include opening up new markets and opportunities for exports, receiving future tradable emissions credits, and the opportunity to participate in JI international decision-making on changes to the programme. Private-sector investment from investor countries may reduce the need for domestic regulation and both private investors and investor countries earn 'green' bragging rights. Summarising experience through early 1997, the World Bank (World

Bank Group 1997) concluded that there had been a 'virtual pilot phase failure' from uncompetitive investment returns from environmental projects, little direct private-sector participation, and an absence of serious environmental policy concern in investor-country governments. Further national reports in 1998 on JI activities showed increasing private-sector participation. The availability of credits after 1999 may encourage more governments to provide the incentives necessary to entice substantial private-sector JI investment.

Host countries expect to receive additional development aid and investment, transfers of technology, and local 'spin-off' in environmental benefits in reduced local pollutants, such as reduced sulphur emissions (*Financial Times* 1995). However, developing countries have opposed JI on three counts. First, it may distract the developed countries from making domestic changes to reduce their emissions. This may be part of the developed countries' reasons for pursuing JI in the first place. Second, it potentially challenges developing-country sovereignty and their development autonomy. Large quantities of JI investments directed by the developed countries may not easily integrate with host-country objectives. Finally, developing countries are concerned that financing for JI might reduce bilateral ODA and reallocate private foreign direct investment from more productive investments. It was hoped that JI would encourage transfer of energy-efficient technologies, practices and processes to developing countries as they industrialised. However, there is no mechanism established by the Convention for transfer of technology at less than market rates as had been demanded by the developing countries. Thus, JI may create technological dependence of second and third world countries on the developed countries, permit the developed countries to 'export' social dislocation from meeting the goals of the Convention, and subordinate mitigation of climate change to rent-seeking by transnational corporations.

National interests and global efficiency

JI projects to date are summarised in Table 1. No projects have been attempted in the industrial processes, solvents, waste disposal or bunker fuels: projects more appropriate in developed countries. Experience has been gained in the types of JI project that take advantage of the natural conditions and technological capabilities in developing countries and countries with economies in transition.

Investor countries preferred different types of projects, different costs per ton, and different hosts. Norway and the Netherlands have been quite eclectic in their interests and have had an effect on the GHG impacts of JI disproportionate to their economic or political importance. The US, with its much greater resources, has favoured large projects in forest preservation, fugitive gas capture and renewable energy, in Latin America and Russia. Sweden, with a large number of small projects, has invested only in energy efficiency and renewable energy projects and shows a clear preference for projects in three neighbouring Baltic states. These patterns indicate the effect of national political and economic interests—beyond global efficiency—in project selection.

Project type	Number	GHG impact	Average impact	Range of project impacts
Afforestation	1	292,728	292,728	
Agriculture	2	3,065,770	1,532,885	437 to 3,065,333
Energy efficiency	36	7,787,789	216,327	800 to 1,575,040
Forest preservation	6	74,750,089	12,458,348	134,379 to 9,834,120
Forest reforestation	5	9,572,482	1,914,496	57,640 to 7,216,000
Fuel switching	3	3,023,416	1,007,805	7,400 to 2,408,866
Fugitive gas capture	2	30,007,966	15,003,983	7,300 to 30,000,666
Renewable energy	40	33,148,162	828,704	13 to 19,765,628
Totals	95	161,648,392	1,701,562	

Table 1: SIZE AND TYPE OF JOINT IMPLEMENTATION PROJECTS

If efficiency were the sole criterion for investor project choice, investor states would seek the least-cost option and only the host states and JI projects with the lowest mitigation costs would attract investment. Differences in project type and location would only reflect investor financial capabilities and host conditions and capabilities. However, if JI is used to pursue the national political and economic goals of investor states, global efficiency would not be optimised and the economic and political dominance of poor by rich states would continue. Are investor states selecting those projects that will optimise mitigation efficiency or are they pursuing through JI their individual political and economic agendas?

Usually only in-depth case studies can fully explain the many influences on foreign policy. However, such case studies do not exist and the data is not available to make an accurate assessment of decision-making for each project. Analysis of the available data for the 95 official AIJ projects and of national JI reports shows that criteria other than efficiency entered into the project selection of some states. As some developed countries (for example, the US) have greater resources than others (Norway or Sweden), project size would be important only if investment was grossly non-proportionate to the investor's influence in the global economy.

Three characteristics of developed countries' investments in JI projects would indicate an apparent divergence from an objective standard of efficiency. First, an apparent preference for certain types of JI project. In pursuit of efficiency alone, all countries should choose a similar distribution of project types. Second, a willingness to accept a higher than average cost per ton of carbon dioxide equivalent mitigated. Efficiency demands that all projects should have comparable mitigation costs per ton for each project type. Investor acceptance of substantially larger than average costs would indicate the intrusion of other interests. Finally, an investor preference for selected host countries would demonstrate the effect of other decision criteria. Because of differences in host-country conditions (e.g. tropical forests) and capabilities (e.g. technological and institutional), certain types of project might be more effective (and

	Australia	Belgium	France	Germany	Netherlands	Norway	Sweden	USA	Total
Afforestation								0.18	0.18
Agriculture								1.90	1.90
Energy efficiency	0.01	0.03	0.10	0.14	0.86	2.15	0.55	0.97	4.81
Forest preservation					6.08			40.15	46.23
Forest reforestation						0.14		5.78	5.92
Fuel switching					0.01	1.49		0.38	1.88
Fugitive gas capture					0.00			18.56	18.56
Renewable energy	0.00			0.01	0.02	0.01	1.46	19.02	20.52
Totals	0.01	0.03	0.10	0.15	6.97	3.79	2.01	86.94	100.00

Table 2: INVESTOR COUNTRY PROJECT PATTERNS BY PERCENTAGE OF TOTAL GHG IMPACT

efficient) in some host countries than others. Forest preservation projects are likely to be least costly in poor, large developing countries with tropical forests. Projects with a substantial technological component (e.g. energy efficiency or renewable energy) are likely to require some technical capability in the host country. Differences between the hosts selected by investors for any project type, or an apparent preference for a few hosts for a range of project types by a single investor, would suggest that other investor economic and political interests influenced project selection. The next section uses these three characteristics to assess four countries' patterns of JI investments.

Investor countries' uses for JI

It is reasonable to assume that investor countries have comparable technical capabilities and that they all have comparable knowledge of the availability of least-cost mitigation projects. Only four countries have invested in more than two projects. These four countries—the US, Netherlands, Norway and Sweden—accounted for almost 93% of the projects and nearly 98% of the estimated mitigation (Table 2).

Sweden

Sweden has used JI projects to enhance its economic and political influence in three host countries. Because of its high domestic mitigation costs, Sweden established a programme for JI projects in 1993, before the AIJ rules were defined (Government of Sweden 1998). Sweden's policy is comparable to AIJ rules with three additional requirements: that the projects can be implemented quickly, that they are affordable,

Investor	Number	GHG impact	Project types (1 per type, or as noted)
Australia	2	13,863	Energy efficiency; renewable energy
Belgium	1	50,250	Energy efficiency
France	1	168,000	Energy efficiency
Germany	2	237,579	Energy efficiency; renewable energy
Netherlands	7	11,256,820	Energy efficiency (4); forest preservation; fuel switching; fugitive gas capture; renewable energy
Norway	6	6,134,308	Energy efficiency (3); forest reforestation; fuel switching; renewable energy
Sweden	50	3,257,449	Renewable energy (26); energy efficiency (24)
USA	25	141,530,123	Renewable energy (10); forest preservation (5); forest reforestation (4); agriculture (2); afforestation; energy efficiency; fuel switching; fugitive gas capture
Totals	95	161,648,392	

Table 3: INVESTOR COUNTRY PREFERENCE FOR PROJECT TYPES

and that they use reliable technology. It also intended to invest exclusively in its Baltic neighbours and Eastern Europe.

The range of Sweden's projects is small, being restricted to either energy efficiency or renewable energy (see Table 3). Most use similar well-tested technology. Within each project category its projects are remarkably similar in type and cost per ton mitigated and all projects are in only three host countries: Estonia, Lithuania and Latvia (see Table 4). Two of these countries have historical ties with Sweden and all three are natural (and historical) trading partners in which Sweden is heavily investing. Most projects are fully financed by Swedish government entities through grants for feasibility work or loans for project implementation. Projects with host-country financing generally are expected to have negative long-term costs. The high

Investor country	Number of projects in host countries (1 project in host unless otherwise indicated)
Australia	Solomon Islands; Fiji
Belgium	Croatia
France	Czech Republic
Germany	Russia; Latvia
Netherlands	Hungary (2); Russia (2); Latvia; Romania; Czech Republic; Bhutan
Norway	Burkina Faso; Mexico; India; Costa Rica; Poland; Slovakia
Sweden	Latvia (22); Estonia (19); Lithuania (9)
USA	Costa Rica (7); Russia (4); Mexico (4); Honduras (3); Ecuador; Indonesia; Belize; Panama; Czech Republic; Nicaragua; Sri Lanka

Table 4: INVESTOR PREFERENCE FOR HOST COUNTRIES

proportion of projects fully funded by the Swedish government further suggests that Sweden has used JI to enhance its political and economic influence in these three countries. With its entry into the European Union (EU), Sweden has committed to participate in joint EU climate policy, including JI in other countries (Government of Sweden 1998: 2), largely separating JI from its national interests.

United States

The US's 25 projects account for more than 86% of the total projected GHG impact of JI. Its projects are usually larger than the average for any project category and more costly per ton. Only the US has projects of each of the types listed and US projects also exhibit wider geographical distribution.

Most US JI projects are also qualitatively different. The design of many US projects reflects commercial interests and the desire of profit-motivated firms to expand their markets and test their technologies simultaneously. They involve a range of private-sector entities, including consulting firms and universities, utilities, equipment suppliers and host entities. Few US projects receive any direct US government financing and much of that comes from agencies designed to finance the export of goods and services. US projects also include a number of large projects with substantial capital investment requirements such as wind farm equipment or land purchases for a forest plantation. Although it plans to use bank financing for capital expenditures, this increases the cost per ton.

The design of the US Initiative on Joint Implementation (USIJI) explains this distorted pattern of JI investment. The US was a strong proponent of JI in the Convention and afterwards and began its JI programme in October 1993. Participants were promised input into development of international criteria for JI, public recognition, technical assistance including facilitating acceptance of the projects by the host government, and access to new market opportunities (US Initiative on Joint Implementation 1995). Private for-profit and not-for-profit organisations were encouraged to propose projects. These were assessed by technical experts and a USIJI panel comprising (in 1995) members from the Environmental Protection Agency (EPA), the Departments of Energy, State, Agriculture, Interior and Commerce and the US Agency for International Development (in the State Department). The stated objective was 'to increase the availability of renewable energy or to change the way that land is used' in order to 'expand the scope of potentially interested parties beyond those that are normally involved in international development' (US Initiative on Joint Implementation 1995).

Because of the emphasis on private-sector initiatives ($40 million in the first round and $200 million in the second round in 1996), the USIJI Secretariat acts as 'marriage broker' between domestic entities and host-country governments and private entities, supervises the appropriateness of the project under the AIJ guidelines, and assesses coincidence with national goals (Joint Implementation Network 1996). Both national goals and private-sector interests can best be met by investing in stable Latin American countries, especially after agreement on the North American Free Trade Area. Private-sector organisations often have the greatest overseas experience in these countries and, since the Monroe Doctrine, the US has pursued political and economic influence in its 'backyard'. Although second-round proposals were received from Latin America, Asia and the former Soviet Union, the final selection of projects included only projects from Latin America and one in Russia. The choice of projects was aided by the bilateral agreements to facilitate JI co-operation signed with several Latin American countries in 1994 and 1995 (Joint Implementation Network 1996). The only significant exception to the general US preference for Latin America is Russia where the US has attempted to support the economy to reduce political instability. It hosts four projects, including the some of the largest.

Within Latin America the most business-friendly and stable should be expected to receive the bulk of the investment. Costa Rica, a stable Central American country with strong commercial and political ties to the US seeking inward investment and a national ecological plan, is host to seven projects, including the largest single US project, predicted to reduce GHGs by over 57 million metric tons over 25 years.

Netherlands

Dutch project selection reflects a preference for investing in Eastern European countries, especially those that are actively seeking membership in the European Union (Joint Implementation Network 1995). The Netherlands has projects in six countries, five in Europe and a small micro-hydroelectricity project in Bhutan. The European projects are much larger projects and make use of the technical capabilities in the ex-Soviet or ex-Soviet satellite host countries. The Netherlands set aside funding in addition to regular ODA grants of approximately $6 million for co-financing pilot projects in developing countries between 1996 and 1999 and the same amount for projects in Central and Eastern Europe between 1997 and 1999.

Perhaps because, since August 1996, the Netherlands JI programme has been administered by the Dutch Joint Implementation Registration Centre on behalf of the Ministry of Environment, the Dutch objective of a range of project types has been met (Joint Implementation Network 1996). JI projects must also meet the requirements of decision 5/CP.1, have no negative environmental side-effect, and include a training component for local authorities and partners (Joint Implementation Network 1997). Costs per ton are usually comparable to averages for project types. Only the forest preservation project—to establish a national park in the Czech Republic—is of unusual size or cost.

Norway

The structure of Norway's project selection process, its co-operation with the World Bank, its stated policy and the range of JI projects attempted point to a seemingly genuine Norwegian effort to seek benefits both for itself and for host countries. Although only Norway operates its JI activities through its Foreign Ministry, it shows less preference than the other three countries for using JI to enhance relationships with developing countries to advance its national interests. Its six projects are spread across four project types and six host countries on four continents. Norway has also invested in the only JI project in Africa. All of Norway's costs per ton are at or below average cost for their project type.

Since 1995, Norway has given priority to JI projects as 'an important supplement to measures implemented domestically' (Government of Norway 1997: 2). It hopes to 'catalyze opportunities for broad participation among interested Parties and relevant actors with the view to maximizing learning value' and sees JI as one of many possible 'cost effective mechanisms for the mutual benefit of all Parties'. Norway's policy is to build institutional capacity in host countries and to encourage private-sector participation, though neither of the last two criteria would disqualify a proposed project if not met.

There are three competing explanations for the apparent preference of some investor countries for certain host countries. First, an investor desire to implement a specific project type may lead them to work with certain host countries. Second, historical economic and political relations should make it easier to design and implement projects in certain host countries. Finally, host country efforts may enhance these connections. The next section argues that effective JI institutions in developing countries can attract JI investments and ensure that projects comply with the host country's development priorities.

JI in developing countries

Both domestic factors (such as a 'weak' state) and systemic factors (e.g. terms of trade) limit developing countries' abilities to choose their development path. Although the Convention was careful to protect state sovereignty, it states that international climate mitigation policy should not take precedence over international free trade or preservation of intellectual property rights. Thus, systemic constraints on development remain. In an effort to make JI investment complement and conform to host-country development plans, AIJ rules require that the host-country government specifically accepts the project and all its terms and conditions. However, as in other cases of inward investment, their need for scarce capital may encourage developing countries to turn a blind eye to possible negative local social, ecological or economic impacts, and institutional incapacities may prevent developing countries from assessing negative impacts before approving projects.

Unfortunately, the local impacts of JI projects completed or in progress through 1998 cannot be identified. The Convention Secretariat has commented that the reporting format and the quality of reporting within that format are inadequate for judging the local impacts of JI projects because 'environmental, social/cultural and economic benefits and negative impacts are generally not described in a detailed manner' (United Nations 1998). The impacts of JI projects can only be assessed from investor-country national reports. Among host countries only Costa Rica and Poland have submitted national reports to the Secretariat and no independent research on local impacts has been published. Four other developing countries are known to be developing national institutions for assessing and accepting JI investments.

Some national reports from investor countries claim substantial local benefits and no negative local externalities. However, it appears that these assertions reflect hopes from project proposals rather than appropriate *post facto* research. The beneficial effects of JI projects on local ecosystems can sometimes be more readily predicted than the social disruption of new technologies and changed resource use and employment patterns. For example, assessments of the conversion of power-generating equipment from coal to gas may extol the local ecological benefits (reduced acid rain and other harmful pollution) but ignore the social dislocations (unemployment and reduced local resources for education and health) of reduced coal mining. Technological innovation often affects social relations and development always implies some social change. If JI is to become a major part of an international climate mitigation effort, assessment of the impacts of environmentally friendly investments cannot ignore calculation of the social and institutional disruption such projects may cause.

Institutional capacities in developing countries are indicated by the efforts they have made to assess JI projects for their complementarity with national development plans and their potential for negative local impacts. For example, in 1994 Costa Rica institutionalised a process for assessing proposed JI projects prior to acceptance. That year it also established the Costa Rican Office on Joint Implementation (OCIC), a co-operative effort between the government, represented by the Ministry of Environment and Energy, and private-sector organisations (Government of Costa Rica 1998). OCIC's mandate is to provide 'international marketing to attract additional investment to finance the country's long term sustainable development priorities' (Government of Costa Rica 1998: 2), which are enumerated in detail and centre around its tropical rainforests, quality of life and local capacity building. Costa Rica has also established funding for its share of AIJ projects and a means to allocate credits for GHG reductions to JI investors. Not only does this institutionalisation of AIJ indicate that Costa Rica has controlled JI investment but it has also attracted substantial JI investment. Costa Rica is the host for projects that will mitigate nearly 42% of the total of all JI projects. In addition, Costa Rica is an attractive investment partner because of its privatisation programme and its liberal policy on inward investment (AMCHAM 1998).

Other potential host countries, including the Russian Federation and Poland (Government of Poland 1997), have established AIJ programmes. From the sketchy data available, it appears that projects in countries with economies in transition are appropriate for the host's technological capacity. No national report defines how the national JI institution(s) assess negative local impacts before project acceptance and during and after project implementation. Thus, there is not enough evidence to judge whether host institutional capacity is sufficient to prevent negative local impacts.

Increasing the (very small) financial assistance and mitigation effect of JI will require large increases in private-sector investment. However, AIJ rules on financial and environmental additionality tend to inhibit private-sector participation: 'strictly interpreted, [financial and environmental] additionality sets companies off to look for anything but profitable investment opportunities' (World Bank Group 1997: 12). If JI is to become a significant channel for additional development funds, developing countries must offer firms profitable investment opportunities that complement local development goals and avoid negative local social or ecological impacts. Thus, JI differs from other foreign direct investment or ODA only with respect to its ecological objective. Because Costa Rica's 'national environment and development priorities and strategies' (Government of Costa Rica 1998) are largely expressed in terms of ecological goals (e.g. biodiversity, forest conservation, clean water, etc.), JI projects in that country co-ordinate especially well with its development plans.

For private firms considering CDM or JI projects, four lessons are clear. First, JI should be seen as a laboratory in which to design the technology, techniques, administrative methods and political connections for future large-scale and profitable environmentally benign projects that assist poorer countries to develop. Good relations with host countries may lead to special access and favoured treatment (such as market access) as developing-country production and markets grow rapidly in the next few decades. JI projects that benefit host development and environment can build these relations. Second, because of the supervisory interest of intergovernmental organisations and national and international reporting requirements, firms should be clear about their commercial goals. Firms will need to maintain elaborate records, including extensive engineering data. As JI is not a quick profit opportunity, profit-seeking organisations must have clear objectives, not all of which need to be financial.

Third, private-sector organisations would benefit by focusing their efforts on those potential host countries with well-developed JI institutions (as in Costa Rica and Poland). Doing so will reduce the complexities of working with government bureaucracies. Finally, private-sector organisations need to recognise that, in addition to learning and constructing a working relationship with developing-country states, there is a value to the 'green' imagery of JI projects. Customers in developed countries are increasingly concerned about the negative environmental effects of growth. As some multinationals have already understood, JI appropriately pursued is an opportunity to assist development while conserving the environment (Percy 1997) but may not itself be highly profitable. Profit-seeking firms would find participation in JI and CDM projects easiest in those developed countries that have appropriate and effective institutions for governing inward JI investment.

Conclusion

JI projects before and during the AIJ pilot period are a foretaste of the effects of the global emissions trading that came two steps closer with the CDM and decisions made at COP 4 in Buenos Aires in November 1998. This chapter has shown that many investor countries have used JI to pursue national political or economic goals, which should reduce global mitigative efficiency. Such practices carried through to global emissions trading may reduce its efficiency and cement the economic and political dominance of the developed countries.

Developing countries may optimise their benefits from JI and similar activities (and protect themselves from negative local impacts and environmental neo-imperialism) by constructing appropriate host-country institutions. Costa Rica's relative success may not be directly replicable across the globe but it is indicative of the benefits of reducing transaction costs and institutional barriers to appropriate inward investment while maintaining a state right of veto. Host-country institutions should have the capacity to assess negative local impacts before project acceptance and during and after project implementation. Clarification of national environmental and development criteria would help to guide appropriate investment and simplify private-sector investment.

More research is required on the local impacts of JI projects. Little is known about the social and economic externalities of JI, making developing countries appropriately nervous about participating. Many technical and methodological problems also remain to be solved (which are beyond the scope of this chapter) before developing countries can be assured that JI and CDM will aid their development and have few negative local impacts (Heller 1997; World Bank Group 1997).

As a precursor of emissions trading, JI shows that the economists' favourite solution to environmental problems is no panacea in the current international system. With the lessons learned from AIJ, JI and CDM may enhance climate change mitigation and development in the poorest countries. Then again, business-as-usual in investor countries may only continue the dominance of the poor countries by the rich.

4

Financial Globalisation and Sustainable Development in Mexico*

David Barkin

AS THE FIRST LATIN AMERICAN NATION to join in the United States' project to forge a 'Free Trade Area of the Americas', the Mexican authorities wholeheartedly assumed a new role for themselves as ideological and political marshals, shaping a new policy environment in which institutional changes might occur. This process, which began with the North American Free Trade Agreement (NAFTA), is an example of the heightened sensitivity of its leadership to the demands for greater 'environmental responsibility' as part of the process of international integration. The environmental side agreement, negotiated as part of NAFTA, with its new oversight and consultative institutions, was the price that the governments were 'forced' to pay in exchange for the approval of the expanded free trade agreement.[1]

This chapter offers a discussion of some of the environmental impacts resulting from globalisation. Mexico's remarkable reversal from its historic position of inward-oriented development to the wholehearted embrace of international integration was never subjected to domestic debate. From this analysis, it is clear that, in spite of Mexico's heightened awareness of and sensitivity to environmental problems, the increased volume of international financial flows is having a significant deleterious impact on the environment.

---

* This chapter summarises a lengthy report prepared for the World Resources Institute project: *International Financial Flows and the Environment*. For information on that project and the original version, please consult the web page: *http://www.wri.org/iffe*.

1 The decision not to pursue the GATT finding that the US tuna fish embargo constituted a violation of international agreements is evidence that the Mexican government was more fearful of angering the environmental community than protecting the interests of the Mexican fishing community (Barkin 1994).

The new importance of international financial flows in Mexico

There have been significant increases in financial flows since 1990. The principal characteristics of these flows and some significant developments in the domestic economy can be summarised as follows:

1. The tremendous increase in the volume of financial inflows. With the recuperation of the Mexican stock market (BMV) from the 'Black Monday' in October 1987, portfolio investments have increased sharply. These inflows are the result of important changes in international financial markets and the new importance of mutual funds and pension funds that diversified into emerging markets as part of their search for higher investment returns. In Mexico, policy-makers were shaping the macro-economic environment to attract this foreign capital as part of a campaign to reinforce the image of international responsibility.

2. These capital inflows were principally in the form of short-term funds channelled into equity markets but then increasingly into high-interest paper of the Mexican government. These inflows were used to finance the growing foreign trade deficits, provoking dollarisation of the domestic public debt (transforming of peso-denominated debt instruments into foreign currency obligations), which was the proximate cause of the devaluation and loss of confidence in December 1994. Internally, the high priority placed on servicing the foreign obligations has led to a systematic reduction in other areas of public expenditure.

3. Foreign direct investment (FDI) flows were being encouraged principally in a narrow group of export-oriented industries: *maquiladora*,[2] automobiles and computers. Total flows increased from about $5 billion in 1990 to more than double that in 1994, falling somewhat after the crisis of December 1994.

4. There was an important increase in the volume and value of international trade along with an apparent diversification towards the export of non-traditional manufactured and agroindustrial products. Natural resource-based production still continues to weigh heavily in exports.

5. Private domestic productive investment remains at a standstill because of high internal interest rates and the decline in purchasing power in local markets. Most of the reported increase in domestic production can be attributed to improved use of existing capacity rather than the addition of new facilities.

---

2 *Maquiladora* is the Latin American term for 'export platforms'. These are plants that use a large proportion of parts in the assembly process imported under temporary licences free from duties, which are re-exported in the form of finished consumer goods, paying duty only on the value added in the assembly process (or none at all if the Mexican products are sent to the USA, under the rules of the free trade area).

6. There were important changes in the financial services industry in Mexico and in the behaviour of individual families who were owners of domestic enterprises. New stock issues allowed the scions of industry to increase capitalisation of their firms while reducing personal holdings, without sacrificing effective control over the enterprises. Similarly, the re-privatised banking system became vehicles for private enrichment as they issued credits to their own associates, through questionable arrangements that would lead to massive defaults, the burden of which is being transferred to the public sphere in 1998.

The changing policy context of globalisation

The combined effect of the far-reaching institutional and policy changes implemented in the post-1985 period was to substantially increase the freedom of action of a small group of investors who were afforded privileged access to a very profitable segment of the Mexican economy. These reforms set the stage for a new period of 'free-market' activity that has further polarised Mexican society and re-organised the geographic distribution of activity, placing increasing pressures on fragile ecosystems throughout the country and unsustainable demands on available land and water resources elsewhere. To facilitate the globalisation, institutional arrangements were changed dramatically.

Institutional changes for globalisation

The accelerated integration of Mexico into the global economy began with accession to the GATT in 1986. Subsequently, negotiations began to join the NAFTA; to create the free-trade agreement with Colombia and Venezuela, and later with Chile, Mercosur (Argentina, Brazil, Paraguay and Uruguay), and most recently with the European Union. These negotiations were accompanied by a dramatic unilateral opening of the economy beginning in 1986; the removal of trade barriers accelerated in 1988, as a tool of domestic inflation control, through the mechanism of unfettered consumer goods imports that resulted in a severe contraction of employment and output.

In 1989, the law to regulate foreign investment was substantially modified to facilitate direct ventures by foreign corporations without the need for domestic partners. With notable exceptions such as telecommunications, banking, some petrochemicals and air transport, foreign investors encountered a new permissiveness that allowed them much greater latitude in their Mexican operations. Agricultural protection was also reduced. Irrigation districts were placed under the direct management and self-financing of users' associations, excluding most peasants and indigenous groups. Price supports and extension services were virtually eliminated along with bank credit for all but the most profitable of crops; only corn and bean support programmes remained, and even these were used to systematically restructure production, encouraging production by the country's most modern farmers and discouraging continued cultivation by the nation's four or five million peasant families.

The highly disputed modification of the land reform legislation removed individual protection in order to facilitate transfer of land rights and their sale to third parties. The modification of the National Forestry Law confirmed a tendency towards encouraging private management of natural resources, historically under the control of the social (*ejido*) sector; this reform encourages a plantation approach to commercial farming, with tax incentives for private enterprises willing to engage in these activities. Similar changes opened the country's coasts to private investment in aquaculture.

The Mexican government implemented a very strong wage-containment policy that substantially reduced the real purchasing power of minimum wages, beginning in 1987. Even though some industrial wages (for a shrinking number of workers) were allowed to increase at a higher rate, incomes declined markedly, forcing a rise in labour-force participation rates (especially for women), increasing the importance of the service sectors and international migration. Employment in the *maquiladora* sector has increased to more than one million since the activation of the NAFTA, with most new establishments remaining in the border region, in spite of efforts to promote decentralisation.

Public-sector enterprises were sold or auctioned off, creating a new group of very wealthy people which was so exceptional as to provoke a caustic commentary from *Forbes* magazine (July 1994). The privatisation of the telephone company and a new competitive regime in long-distance service led to joint ventures with foreign partners that accelerated the introduction of new technologies. The re-privatisation of the banking system was followed by the deregulation of the rest of the financial services sector, permitting an important expansion of non-banking services, such as insurance, factoring and stock trading, along with the introduction of new financial derivatives, such as options, futures and leasing. Of particular note was the fragility of the new groups, which became evident in the aftermath of the 1994 crisis.

Private concessions for the construction and management of infrastructure are having an important impact on the productive system and on the environment. The process raised serious questions about the way decisions are made, since no public debate was allowed on these crucial issues.

More than 6000 km of private toll-roads were built during the first half of the 1990s, but mismanagement forced a government bail-out. This shifted support from improving the rail system, which might have reduced emissions. Poor route design and low construction standards led to important damage in adjacent regions, particularly affecting poor peasant and indigenous groups as a result of modifying the course of rivers and the topography to ensure a smooth high-speed ride for those who can afford the high tolls.

In other areas, infrastructure projects have a chequered history. The port system is being modernised; the improvement and expansion of container ship facilities in Mazatlan is leading to a redeployment of cargo throughout the country. In contrast, an ambitious but controversial multi-modal transport and energy corridor on the Isthmus of Tehuantepec in southern Mexico, with complementary manufacturing and processing facilities, is moving ahead slowly as opposition from peasant communities, the environmental community and academic analysts affects its financing. Similarly, a proposed inter-coastal canal from the Texas border to Tampico has stalled because of opposition from environmental groups on both sides of the border and inadequate financial support from US interests.

The privatisation of energy generation and natural gas distribution has proceeded apace. While the national energy company (CFE) remains responsible for electricity distribution, several contracts have been let for new thermo-electric generation capacity. Local markets have been assigned to some companies to promote the expansion of natural gas use, as a mechanism for reducing urban contamination. One particularly troublesome development is the recent award of a contract for a megaproject to produce nitrogen to maintain and increase gas production by injecting it into a large oil field in the Gulf of Mexico. The environmental problems posed by this questionable project add to the concerns raised by the enormous volumes of associated natural gas that are currently being flared in the region.[3]

The relationship between financial flows and macroeconomic policy decisions

Although the Mexican economy was already in crisis, the 1982 liquidity crisis and debt moratorium and the ensuing macroeconomic changes were clearly the most immediate antecedents of the implantation of neoliberal economic policies. During the first half of President de la Madrid's term (1983–85), public expenditures were reduced, provoking a recession that led to several stand-by agreements with the International Monetary Fund. The country was placed under international scrutiny, a process that was contained in a secret (at the time) letter of intent about the process and objectives of economic management.

'Preparing' for Mexico's accession to the GATT was an underlying theme for policy-makers from about 1985. Profound changes in domestic policy were required to move from protected markets and a highly articulated system of social balance; a new group of economists set out to remake national institutions in the light of the new international orthodoxy, creating an economic structure guided by market signals that determined favoured sectors and regions. Public policy would facilitate private decisions, attracting resources and encouraging more investment by creating a favourable investment climate. Inflation was considered to be 'public enemy number one' and all public-sector management tools were brought to bear in the struggle.

The regressive tax system was made even more 'competitive' in comparison with alternative destinations for private investment; rates for corporate taxes were adjusted and exemptions well defined to attract international capital. Even with an exemption on capital gains from stock market transactions, tax evasion continues to be a major problem. The administration of a major revenue source, the value added

3 The debate surrounding the nitrogen project uncovered an especially alarming feature of decision-making: technological choice is based on its profitability for the international consortium in which important domestic firms would participate as junior partners as well as for the public-sector officials. Alternative technologies would have afforded substantial savings and reduce the environmental damage, but would strengthen the position of the petroleum workers, their union and local 'low-tech' engineering firms.

tax, remains a problem as the government estimates evasion at as much as 47% of potential revenue.

There is no willingness to develop a coherent or progressive tax policy designed to promote new (re)investment and the adoption of new technologies that would be in accord with the needs of the community. An ideological commitment to decentralisation became a tool to reduce the size of the central government budget and bureaucracy, especially in education and medical care, but insufficient resources, both financial and of trained people, cripples the process.

Monetary policy focused on the domestic money supply and interest rates, although the Bank of Mexico also plays a major role in the administration of the foreign exchange reserves and their markets. Since the principal focus was on attracting foreign capital, little concern was shown for the high rates of interest for Mexican borrowers. Traditional instruments are proving increasingly inadequate to achieve their goals, and currency fluctuations now reflect international uncertainty. Although never openly discussed, after more than a decade, it is clear that the lack of experience, combined with sheer greed and corruption, led to many unfortunate decisions, requiring massive government intervention to rescue myriad firms and financial organisations that had made bad choices or whose founding members had artfully decapitalised. This corporate welfare package now amounts to more than 13% of GNP, seriously affecting resources that might otherwise be available for social welfare programmes and environmental management.

The major focus of domestic policy, however, was the level of real wages. Although lip service was paid to promoting productivity, the state did not adopt an effective technology policy. The burden of industrial policy was placed on heavy wage controls as a means for reducing costs and offering attractive profits to investors. The decline in purchasing power of the minimum wage began just after the first round of adjustments to the crisis of 1976, but accelerated sharply with the formal establishment in 1987 of a system of a formally negotiated tripartite incomes policy, known locally as 'Pactos'.[4]

As with many other aspects of Mexican political life, the macroeconomic policy framework is in the process of change as a result of the 1997 elections. Although the government is still controlled by a strong executive, the increasing participation of the various opposition parties in the political arena is opening new areas of policy to debate. Similarly, opposition control of government in Mexico City is raising expectations of important changes in the way in which public participation may affect local management. While it would be premature to venture a judgement about these changes, it seems clear that the movement in the direction of democratisation will contribute to a broader discussion of many issues of public concern. This is likely to be particularly important in the area of environmental quality and policy, because conditions are deteriorating rapidly and because well-organised local NGOs exist and are searching for ways to become more effective. As we shall see below, however, the

4 Until 1994, wages for the organised industrial labour force actually rose in contrast to those for most other workers, but since then even these workers have begun to experience important declines in real incomes.

prevailing complacency in official circles that economic growth itself is the best remedy for environmental problems is not only unwarranted but probably wrong, at least in the short run in Mexico.

Structural adjustment, international financial flows and the environment

Structural adjustment policies (SAPs) have had profound impacts on the environment (Reed 1992; Hansen-Kuhn 1993). Perhaps the most significant impacts relate to the deterioration in the material conditions of workers and peasants throughout Mexico. Similar declines were observed in the real purchasing power of other sectors of society. The middle classes were sharply affected by the macroeconomic mismanagement that climaxed with the devaluation of more than 100% in December 1994: because they had accepted the declarations of the return to long-term growth, the middle classes had begun to borrow from the recently privatised banking system. With this crisis and the banks' decision to raise interest rates sharply on peso loans, to impose penalty charges and rates on late payments, and then to capitalise all overdue payments, millions of people suffered an immediate decline in their incomes while many were threatened with foreclosure on their homes, cars, businesses and other assets. Peasant producers were also heavily affected by the changes in policy motivated by the rules of the international economy: production subsidies were eliminated and direct producer payments offered were lower than before.

In these circumstances, people, businesses and government were obliged to engage in many marginal activities. Frequently these had negative impacts on the environment for want of human, material and financial resources; environmental management tasks were postponed, as were maintenance and investment throughout the society. As conditions deteriorated further, more people were forced into more marginal activities and the migratory stream, further reducing the quality of life. This relationship was recently examined in some detail by the National Heritage Institute (1997), which concluded that the 'intuitive link between land degradation and migration is borne out' in Mexico. In the countryside, dry-land cultivation continued, but with less intensity, as migrants and those remaining in the countryside paid contract labour to cultivate and harvest basic crops; production increased, but with lower yields, and more erosion. In this sector, as in others, worker remittances (from economic refugees, both local and international) continue to play an important role in permitting families to survive and continue their traditional activities (be it dry-land farming, artisan activities or small-scale manufacturing and commercial activities). Despite the fact that they are not 'profitable' by market standards at prevailing market prices, they continue in these jobs for want of other alternatives in a society that has no collective safety net.

Because of the centrality of wage-repression policies to the SAP mechanism used to encourage large-scale imports of capital, their evaluation is crucial. An econometric analysis of this matter in the case of deforestation in Bolivia concludes:

> The Bolivian case raises important questions regarding the capacity of developing country governments to implement macro-economic and environmental policies. In theory, the most appropriate way to address undesirable environmental effects of SAPs might be through environmental policies, rather than adjusting the economic policies themselves. In practice, however, developing countries typically lack the institutional capacity to implement such environmental policies, so the undesirable effects may continue (Kaimowitz *et al.* 1999).

Similarly, a more recent article that examines the environmental effects of agricultural trade liberalisation (May and Segura Bonilla 1997) poses many of the same questions, and comes to similar conclusions:

> further pressure on degraded resources and marginal farmers, and a reinforcement of sectoral policies that benefit commercial export crop growers as opposed to food producers may make increased trade more of a bane than a blessing for developing countries. In the context of emerging regional trading blocks, removal of trade barriers between participating nations has led to dislocation of production whose localised impacts, it is hoped, would be resolved through 'reconversion' of agriculture in affected subregions. It may be, however, that internalisation of socio-environmental costs of such dislocation would indicate that production, despite competitive disadvantages, would best have been left where it was (May and Segura Bonilla 1997: 5).

They conclude—citing an important study by the IICA—that 'the problem [of generating sustainable behaviour] does not lie in the market mechanism per se, but in how the players are organized and how effective are the rules established to promote environmentally sound behavior' (Otero *et al.* 1992).

In spite of the sophisticated discourse about protecting the environment in Mexico, there are still many institutional barriers that prevent implementation of the existing regulatory package. The administration itself complicates the task because of its deep-seated opposition to grass-roots organisations and intermediate NGOs' efforts to organise themselves and their constituencies into effective groups in order to forge alternative productive projects and community political structures that would be socially and environmentally responsible. The new political environment generated by the victories of several minority parties throughout the country is beginning to open up space for dissension on many issues, including the environment.

There is widespread agreement that the Mexican government's environmental regulatory and enforcement process is particularly weak. In spite of the fact that a new ministry was created to oversee these efforts, with a high concentration of the country's most informed people in the areas of natural resource management and environmental regulation, the conflict between competing goals of economic growth and environmental quality has almost always been resolved in favour of the former. Inevitably, the first reaction of high-level officials to any accusation is to deny the existence of a problem, or to minimise its importance and then to resist third-party attempts for investigation.[5] The notable cases of the dock on the island of

---

5 The Ministry of Industrial Development tries to block all efforts to examine the environmental

Cozumel and the massive death of migratory birds in Guanajuato are just two examples brought to the NAFTA Commission on Environmental Co-operation.[6]

Environmental sustainability: case studies in Mexican development

To examine the environmental impact of Mexico's global integration we turn to the *maquiladora* industry and rural development policy. Following these brief discussions, we turn to two other related issues that are pertinent for this analysis: the private sector's role in improving voluntary compliance and self-regulation as part of a broader worldwide move towards creating a code of ethics for corporate accountability; and the attempts by the 'social sector' to circumvent the process of government and corporate control by undertaking its own efforts to promote greater local autonomy to promote self-development, including the cultivation of export markets.

Maquiladoras *in the border region*

The *maquiladora* industry has grown dramatically during the past 15 years. Today it is the largest such export-oriented assembly operation in the world, dramatically outpacing the number of establishments and employees in the Asian tigers; only the manufacturing operations in the People's Republic of China dwarf the Mexican industry (and these are not generally considered to be *maquilas*). In spite of its size, the industry employs less than 3% of the national labour force. The industry has gradually diversified its output, and slowly begun to decentralise away from the border region. In view of the substantial diseconomies associated with the environmental and socioeconomic problems of the border region, it seems surprising that the move towards the centre and to the Yucatan Peninsula has not accelerated; this is no doubt due, in large measure, to the substantial problems with road transport, insecurity and official corruption that significantly increase transaction costs in other parts of the country for these enterprises.

The principal environmental issues related to the *maquiladoras* in the border region are: infrastructure; water availability and quality; sewage treatment and disposal; air quality; toxic wastes; and housing. These issues are occasioning important social and political conflicts. With the implementation of the NAFTA, a new Border Economic

---

and social impacts of integration and discredit Mexican researchers undertaking the work; it is ironic that they have been ineffective in this effort, sending lower-level personnel whose heavy-handed interventions provoke more hostility than sympathy. On the other hand, when the former head of the [official] National Ecology Institute became overly protective of industry interests in the environmental arena, he was quickly replaced; he now heads a private-sector think-tank conducting research and training on problems of 'sustainable development'.

6 The serious forest fires of early 1998 offer another tragically poignant example: the government insisted that 'only' half a million hectares were affected, while the local organisation engaged in combating the conflagrations placed the figure at more than twice that amount (Barkin and Garcia 1999).

Co-operation Commission (BECC), and its affiliated North American Development (NAD) Bank, were created to handle the planning and co-ordination of environmental management and remediation. While they generated opportunities for community groups to air their grievances, the resources available to confront the problems are minuscule in comparison with the tasks at hand; the NAD Bank has been the target of widespread criticism for the lethargy with which it has geared up its operations (e.g. USGAO 1995). One notable benefit of the integration process, with its avalanche of new private investment, is the burgeoning of information about the tremendous human and environmental costs of this style of industrialisation, a cost that has been imposed on society for a long time but which is now becoming broadly known and documented (Gumbleton and Bhargava 1995; USGAO 1995; Public Citizen and RMALC 1996).

Perhaps the most serious problem with the current trend towards accelerated industrial development is that it probably already exceeds the border region's physical carrying capacity. The allocation of water rights has long been a contentious issue that has never been resolved adequately; the International Boundary and Water Commission, created in 1889 to administer agreements in this area, has never forthrightly addressed the overriding constraint that available water supplies should place on regional development. This issue must be combined with an evaluation of the implications of present technological choices for waste disposal and treatment systems, which are also intensive in water use.[7] Overall, there is a clear need for implementing a growth management programme for each of the border's sub-regions; but this task is still not on the agenda for the region's principal actors.

Some analysts suggest that the increasing flows of foreign direct investment into the region will help confront these problems. They argue (most articulately on the Internet conference BeccNet) that the newcomers are particularly sensitive to the criticisms being raised against foreign companies as 'environmental runaways', searching for ways to escape from the tougher regulatory framework prevailing in the USA. In contrast, others note than an important segment of the *maquila* industry is composed of small plants or leased local facilities contracted to Mexicans; generally these operators are not sensitive to social problems and have not distinguished themselves for their adherence to environmental regulations. Thus, the *maquiladora* complex is rather heterogeneous and cannot be simply characterised as being more environmentally responsible or mature than other segments of Mexican industry. Inadequate human and financial resources leave local governments on both sides of the border unprepared to face the challenges of accelerating growth.

In sum, even if the firms in the region were dealing responsibly with their obligations to the environment, it seems clear that the burden of regional growth is not being squarely faced. The increased trade flows resulting from liberalisation, greater production, and a larger urban population are increasing pressures on local

7 The lack of adequate drinking water and sewage systems for most of the population in the border region is perhaps the most egregious violation of basic guarantees of health and safety for the region. The technological choice for waste-water treatment reflects a fundamental disdain for people's need for reprocessed water in their communities for local productive projects.

infrastructure and other resources and on the woefully inadequate waste treatment and disposal system. Air quality, too, is deteriorating without any objective basis for believing that the trend can be reversed in the near future. Although desperately needed, an effective growth management strategy is not yet on the agenda. As a result, growth financed by foreign investment will continue to bear negatively on the environment.

The changing shape of primary production

Changes in public policy in rural Mexico were promulgated in anticipation of the process of international integration and the need for foreign capital. In the new model, production would be reoriented towards higher-valued products, abandoning the rhetorical commitment to peasant-based food self-sufficiency. A new land reform is titling small-scale beneficiaries of agrarian reform and stimulating a land market; promoting organisational and technological changes to raise productivity and output; and using the most modern technology in irrigation, biotechnology and agrochemicals. This new focus opens a discussion of fundamental questions about Mexican society. We might list some of the most salient as:

- The viability of Mexico's indigenous population as unique social groups
- The desirability of protecting the peasantry and the communities of rural Mexico
- The role of the rural economy in food security
- The importance of rural employment opportunities
- The responsibility of society to provide viable alternatives for people who cannot be absorbed into the globalised sectors
- The resource-intensity of Mexico's foreign trade
- The contribution of the rural population to environmental management and water supplies

In Mexico, internationalisation has disadvantaged the vast majority of rural producers. To defend their communities, many peasant and indigenous groups have begun to form intermediate organisations with support from local and international NGOs to prosecute their demands.[8] Encompassing one-third of the population, these groups have undertaken a remarkable programme of self-conscious resistance and survival; remittances from family members in non-rural Mexico and in the United States now account for an injection of more than 40% of the value of rural production. Although they lack support to develop new technologies for dry-land

8 The Zapatista uprising of January 1994 is the culmination of years of frustrated efforts to assert these rights, and its transformation into a non-violent effort to achieve their goals has expanded into a broad attempt by 'civil society' to obtain some measure of autonomy for these groups (Collier 1994).

agriculture or to use inherited knowledge of ecosystem management and germplasm, they are experimenting with alternative approaches and new activities that recognise their legitimate rights and the need to create opportunities for their survival as communities.

The communities are seeking to increase the productivity of their traditional cropping systems by using resources earned by selling 'profitable' services from other sectors. Such alternatives include traditional activities such as artisan production, but this is also being extended to new activities such as eco-tourism, wildlife preserves and farms, fishing and marine life expeditions, as well as the protection of endangered species, all of which have proven markets, if organised correctly. One particularly interesting approach proposes to compensate communities for providing environmental services that would benefit the country as a whole, while reducing inequalities and dependency.[9] These efforts are designed to contribute to the consolidation of the communities' long-term agenda of social and economic development (cf. Schroyer 1997).

Without a change in national policy, however, these constructive local approaches are actually inimical to sustainable development. Although these alternative models generally offer possibilities for a better quality of life for their participants, it is remarkable that they engender aggressive and often hostile reactions from the government, which attempts to block them; it would seem that productive activities undertaken by grass-roots organisations are less worthy of protection and promotion than those conducted by large corporations. Today, this resistance to local initiatives contributes to the further polarisation of rural society, creating barriers to international financial flows and transforming local demands into violent social movements.

Private-sector activities for environmental improvement

The private sector in Mexico has begun to define an important role to pre-empt public pressures for greater regulation of its environmental impact. It has created a number of important institutions in the corporate structure to offer a strong defence of their activities. These activities are being supported by the National Ecology Institute (INE), a semi-autonomous entity responsible to the Secretary of the Environment, Natural Resources and Fisheries (SEMARNAP).

There is a growing awareness among the larger corporations of the need to take vigorous action to forestall direct government intervention. Among their actions, the industry cites 'costly' measures to replace phosphates in detergents by biodegradable ingredients (20 years after such changes were implemented elsewhere), advances in the control of air- and water-borne contaminants, and the growing number of firms working for ISO 14000 qualification.

Other initiatives are emerging on a sporadic basis throughout society and the economy. In response to the dramatic deaths of more than 40,000 migratory birds, the Commission on Environmental Co-operation (CEC) of the NAFTA helped the

9 One such project involves rebuilding an aquifer on the Pacific Coast of Oaxaca to supply water to a languishing resort community (Barkin and Pailles 1998).

tanning industry of Guanajuato to implement some of the necessary technical changes through a fund that has been set up for such initiatives. The UNIDO, in collaboration with the National Polytechnical Institute, established a Center for Clean Production, which chose the galvanoplasty industry as its first showcase example in collaboration with the University of Massachusetts at Lowell. Similarly, a private university, the Technical Institute of Monterrey, has created a Clearinghouse for Eco-efficiency in Business, as part of the Mexican chapter of the World Business Council on Sustainable Development (WBCSD), to undertake research on technical programmes for promoting eco-efficiency in industry. The élite Center for Studies on Sustainable Development produces its own environmental discourse, as well as serving as a conduit for private-sector concerns about excessive regulation in national and international forums.

While this set of activities represents a significant advance over what had been occurring previously, it is seriously flawed. Only a small part of industry is directly involved in making changes in the production process that will reduce the negative impact of industrial activity: it is difficult to obtain credits for modernisation; there is no culture of worker–management collaboration to implement changes, and this is compounded by a well-grounded fear that better-trained workers will be 'stolen' by competitors in a labour market characterised by a paucity of 'good' workers. Finally, many observers note that the changes being implemented by the 'school' of 'eco-efficiency' are fundamentally oriented towards 'end-of-the-pipe' efforts by reducing discharges and recycling waste products, rather than redesigning production processes to create fewer wastes.

Social sector strategies in the era of globalisation

The increasing pressures created by the deepening economic crisis have motivated numerous groups to seek out alternative solutions for strengthening their local economies. One common thread in these approaches has been the search for some greater measure of autonomy in their dealings with the international economy.[10] Among the most notable of these are the many examples of peasant communities that are searching for new markets for traditional exports. The most successful of these efforts are those that recognise the need to ensure that these non-traditional products remain complementary to the panoply of activities that have been important; without going into greater detail, it is important to note that there is an ongoing discussion within grass-roots communities about the importance of defending and strengthening these inherited traits in their social and economic structure.

These developments are particularly important in the light of the changes in international financial flows. Although foreign direct investment (FDI) has been falling as a proportion of all financial flows, and the primary sector has reduced its participa-

10 One of the most misunderstood of the demands of the Zapatista rebellion is the demand for local autonomy, as a means of strengthening their regions, and in this way contributing to a stronger national society.

tion in the FDI, certain investments have been increasing, notably in the forestry sector, where recent legislative changes have encouraged plantations of rapidly growing species to be harvested for cellulose. Similarly, investment in orchards and other commercial crops have also shown a resurgence. As a result, the efforts by local communities to find their own alternatives and directly engage in marketing and distribution arrangements offer a new approach that may effectively restrict the scope of action of foreign investors. This development might be a productive area to support as a way of reinforcing local efforts to find profitable means to engage in environmental management.

The significance of international financial flows for sustainable development

The present model of economic development, based on export-oriented production, low wages and rapid urbanisation, is not consistent with the accepted precepts of sustainability. The two areas discussed above illustrate the enormous impact of globalisation in aggravating environmental problems and limiting the opportunities for grass-roots groups to undertake initiatives that would benefit society as a whole. The inability of the new productive structure to create sufficient employment is a serious deficiency that is compounded by the obstacles that rural communities confront in attempting to forge their own small-scale alternatives based on the sustainable management of natural resources and diversified production. Local models that promote a blending of traditional crops for local consumption with innovative marketable goods and services, offer a promising avenue for reducing emigration and raising rural welfare, while building an improved capacity for providing essential environmental services.[11]

Although Mexico has constructed a modern legal framework to implement a regulatory mechanism, compliance is low and enforcement remains deficient, for lack of funding and well-trained people. Very few industries have the financial ability or technical capability to move from 'end-of-the-pipe' solutions to more integrated approaches to correcting the environmental impact of present productive systems. In the current period of intense international competition, high costs for domestic credit and highly concentrated structures of power and wealth, more attention must be accorded to mechanisms for public oversight of private efforts. This involves creating channels for greater accountability and better training of local groups to understand the trade-offs and complementarities between economic growth and environmental quality; this is the starting point for a constructive discussion about defining realistic limits on the exercise of power by financial capital. The industry groups themselves are searching for mechanisms by which to improve their public image of corporate responsibility, and they should be assisted in this task by efforts to better inform their employees and designers about the differences between remedial and preventative measures for environmental quality.

11 For a critical evaluation of this approach see Barkin 1998: ch. 4 and Barkin and Pailles 1998.

Poverty and lack of commitment to comply with environmental norms for production and natural resource use complicate remedial efforts. The serious efforts of the environment ministry must continually confront the challenges of those promoting growth without concern about resource degradation and its consequences for individual wellbeing and collective survival; there are innumerable instances of well-known flagrant violations of local and national norms, including those committed by official organisations. Conflicts within the government are as frequent as those with the corporate community. For example, the sale of permits to hunt a rare species of bighorn sheep for $350,000 directly contravened instructions from the SEMARNAP, while contracts to build toxic waste containment and processing facilities ignored legal provisions for local consultation and Environmental Impact Assessments.

Perhaps one of the most important lessons to be gleaned from the analysis is the urgency of a discussion of growth management. While especially important in the border areas, the issue is of significance throughout the country. In what ways can public discussion be directed to promote a better-informed evaluation of the dangers of unbridled growth? Is it possible to design programmes that will face the needs for greater employment of existing social groups while addressing the needs for improving infrastructure and reversing the trends in environmental indices? More serious still is the prevailing attitude among the members of the (presidential) economic cabinet of 'the environment be damned': they explicitly argue that a favourable climate for foreign investment to promote employment and growth must take precedence over all other considerations. Even when they are willing to admit the need for the application of existing rules about emissions and waste, there is no possibility of opening a fruitful dialogue on the subject of growth management or the possibility of alternative strategies for natural resource management and productivity in critical regions of the country.

The situation has improved in recent years, as the global discourse on environmental issues has become sharper. The Commission for Environmental Co-operation, created by the NAFTA, is becoming more effective in promoting a constructive relationship between private industry and government. Similarly, the environmental NGO community has become increasingly effective in making its voice heard, sometimes by ignoring local authorities and rising directly to international organisations where they can, ironically, often find a more sympathetic hearing. In Mexico, these changes have become especially important in intensifying the pressures for a fuller consideration of the environmental consequences of official policies. In the ultimate analysis, however, the political leadership is still convinced that economic growth is primary, and that the market will have to be the tool for imposing environmental responsibility on the community: a dismal prospect in a highly polarised society, where people and natural resources are still significantly devalued.

2 FOCUS ON BUSINESS

5

The Effect of Environmental Regulations on Industrial Competitiveness of Selected Industries in Developing Countries *

Ralph (Skip) Luken

A DEFINITION OF ecologically sustainable industrial development (ESID) is essential in considering how best to achieve it and in identifying interventions that could contribute to its achievement. The definition proposed for this investigation is the one endorsed by the UNIDO Conference on Ecologically Sustainable Industrial Development (UNIDO 1992). ESID is defined as patterns of industrialisation that enhance the contribution of industry to economic and social benefits for present and future generations without impairing basic ecological processes. These new patterns would increase economic development over time while efficiently utilising non-renewable resources, conserving renewable resources and not exceeding the waste-assimilative capacities of ecosystems; and they would differ depending on a country's resource endowments and stage of economic development.

The conference proposed three criteria that a particular pattern of industrialisation must satisfy if it is deemed ecologically sustainable, either absolutely or in comparison to other patterns:

- It must protect the environment.
- It must contribute to, or at least not hinder, the competitive development of industry.
- It must promote social equity.

---

* Paper prepared for the Fifth International Conference of the Greening of Industry Network, *Global Restructuring: A Place for Ecology?*, Heidelberg, 24–27 November 1996.

Conventional wisdom holds that at least two of the criteria—protection of the environment and promotion of competitive industry—are incompatible. Protection of the environment usually increases production costs, reduces outputs and results in lower profits. Imposition of environmental regulations reduces the ability of industry to compete in the domestic and export markets in which it might have had a competitive advantage due to lower costs of production.

This argument has been questioned, most notably by Michael Porter (1990). He argues that tougher environmental regulation leads to improved industrial performance because it induces innovation and upgrading and has identified many examples of this effect on industrial competitiveness. His assertion, in turn, has been questioned, most recently by Simpson and Bradford (1996), who make a plausible theoretical argument that this is not the usual case. In most cases, the negative direct effect of increased production costs would not be offset by the indirect effect of lower variable cost by spurring innovation. In the aggregate, environmental regulation would reduce output and would result in lower profits, thus reducing the ability of industry to remain competitive.

The trade-off between environmental regulation and industrial competitiveness for developing countries, two of the three dimensions of sustainable industrial development, can also be addressed with a less dubious assertion than the one made by Porter. Instead of claiming that environmental policy will enhance industrial productivity, a more believable argument is that environmental regulation would have only a minimal impact on industrial productivity. This would be the case if the direct effect of environmental regulations would result in only a small change in production costs. If this would be the case, then there would be only a small, perhaps not even measurable, reduction in industrial output and lowering of profits that are necessary to sustain a competitive industrial sector.

This chapter examines the potential cost impact of increasingly stringent environmental regulations on the costs of industrial production. It first estimates the costs of compliance with environmental regulation from a macro (industry-wide) perspective and it finds the magnitude of the costs to be small in comparison to the costs of production. However, this macro perspective masks several types of situation in which the costs of compliance can significantly affect the costs of production. The fragmentary micro (firm-level) data that is available from developing countries suggests that the cost impact varies depending on, among other things:

- The nature of the regulatory regime: the priority assigned by government and industry to pollution prevention versus end-of-pipe compliance strategies
- Type of industry: resource-intensive versus light manufacturing
- Size of firm
- Degree of openness of the economy
- Availability of technical assistance to cope with environmental regulations

The following sections of this chapter review data, primarily within the UN system, that address the macro and micro impact of environmental regulations on production costs of industry in developing countries. The next section of the chapter reviews the potential macro impact and the third section reviews the potential micro impact. A concluding section suggests measures that developing countries could take to ensure that environmental regulations in developing countries are not only effective, but also have the least cost impact on industrial production costs.

Macro effects

There are no empirical studies similar to those for the US and selected European countries of industrial expenditures for compliance with environmental regulations in developing countries. This is probably due to the fact that environmental regulations have only recently begun to be effective in developing countries and that no developing country is yet collecting systematic and economy-wide data on the cost of environmental compliance as part of their national statistics.

The World Bank (1992a) estimated that, by 2000, the investment by industry that would be needed in order to be in compliance with emission controls equivalent to those of OECD countries by 2030 would be in the range of US$ 10–15 billion per year (in 1990 prices). The World Bank did not specify the mix of end-of-pipe and pollution-prevention measures that would constitute this investment, nor did it estimate the annualised costs of compliance (annualised capital [depreciation plus interest] and operation and maintenance), which is the critical variable for determining the impact of pollution control costs on overall production costs. Generally speaking, annual operation and maintenance costs are approximately equal to the annualised capital costs of pollution control; the latter would be equal to the level of investment once industry is in compliance with environmental regulations assuming zero growth. This would mean that the annualised costs of compliance would be in the range of US$20–30 billion.

For this chapter, the author estimated the percentage of production costs that would be attributable to pollution control based on the experience of developed countries. This estimate should be on the high side, as industrialised countries, for the most part, particularly the US, have relied on uniform application of performance standards and the use of end-of-pipe technology to achieve environmental norms. With hindsight, achievement of ambient standards aimed at protecting human health and welfare—which should be the goal of environmental protection—and a more judicious mix of prevention and abatement measures would have resulted in a lower level of expenditure.

In order to make this estimate, it is first necessary to estimate the likely level of expenditure of industry in developing countries to comply with environmental regulations. One approach for making an estimate is to assume that the percentage of GDP spent on industrial pollution control in developing countries will be in the long run approximately the same as that spent in developed countries. The percentage of GDP spent for environmental compliance is, on average, 1.6% of GDP in developed countries (OECD 1986). Of that, one-quarter is spent on industrial environmental compliance and three-quarters are spent on municipal, transport and other sectors. The GDP of developing countries in 1991 was US$4.2 trillion, and is projected to be US$6.0 trillion in 2000, in 1990 prices (UNIDO 1996). Assuming that developing countries will spend in the extreme 1.6% of their GDP on environmental compliance and that one-quarter of that will be for industrial compliance by 2000, then the annual expenditure for industrial compliance would be approximately US$24.0 billion.

Another approach to making an estimate is to assume that the percentage of manufacturing value added (MVA) spent on industrial pollution control in developing countries will be, in the long run, approximately the same as that spent in developed countries. The average percentage of MVA spent on industrial compliance is only known for the US, where it has been estimated at 1.74% (EPA 1990). No similar estimates are available for Western Europe or Japan, but the overall investment of those countries is most certainly lower. The MVA of developing countries in 1991 was US$750 billion, and is projected to be US$1.1 trillion in 2000 (UNIDO 1996). Assuming that they spend approximately 1.75% of their MVA to comply with industrial environmental regulation, the annual level of expenditure would be US$19.0 billion.

A comparison of the estimated cost of coming into compliance would appear to fall in the range of US$20–25 billion, and the estimated magnitude of industrial production costs of US$2.7 trillion suggests that the cost of industrial compliance will be approximately 2% of production costs. Across all industrial sectors and all countries, this level of expenditure would not be an onerous burden and certainly would not significantly add to production costs.

The general conclusion about industry-wide effects of environmental regulation on production costs is supported by fragmentary survey evidence from some of the country studies conducted by UNCTAD (1995a). In the Philippines,

> pollution abatement costs as a percentage of total costs were less than one per cent for the majority of the sectors studied. The only sectors where these costs exceeded two per cent were case crops, livestock and livestock production and electricity. Apart from these sectors, it appears that domestic environmental standards would not have a significant impact on overall industrial competitiveness.

In Colombia, a survey of exporting firms showed that only 16% had experienced major competitiveness effects, whereas 64% said that the competitiveness effects were insignificant. In Argentina and Brazil, despite exports being natural resource- and energy-intensive with high pollution abatement costs, the UNCTAD studies claim that competitiveness impacts have not been significant because of the inherent dynamism of the industry.

Micro effects

Nature of regulatory regime

In 1997 it is possible to imagine that developing countries could adopt a different and less costly approach to reducing industrial pollution than the one implemented by developed countries. To the extent that developing countries allow their industries to take maximum advantage of more resource-efficient process technology as a way of achieving compliance with environmental regulations, their industries, particularly pollution-intensive ones (chemicals, iron and steel, non-ferrous metals, non-metallic minerals and pulp and paper) will not experience to the same extent the economic difficulties encountered by similar firms in developed countries.

There are several documented case studies of the potential for cleaner production to lower the costs of compliance as well as production costs in general and thus the impact of environmental regulations on profitability. Just a few of them are cited below to illustrate the difference between a regulatory regime that would allow plants the time and flexibility to implement cleaner production options and one that would force the use of end-of-pipe technology in order to meet a deadline or to show a visible sign of compliance with environmental regulations (Luken and Freij 1996).

India: agro-based pulp and paper

A joint study by the National Productivity Council of India and UNIDO investigated the potential for waste minimisation in three sectors: agro-based pulp and paper, pesticide formulation and textile dyeing and finishing. Before the investigation, one of the agro-based pulp and paper mills (30 tonnes per day) had prepared an estimate of the cost of meeting discharge standards based on end-of-pipe technology. As a result of implementing preventative measures, the mill achieved the following:

- Reduced its capital investment cost for end-of-pipe equipment by 25% and its annualised operating and maintenance costs by 35%
- Reduced the discharge of various pollutants by 20%–40%
- Increased annual output by 22%, improved the quality of the paper produced (specks were reduced) and made a new product (secondary fuel for brick kilns from the primary clarifier)
- Hired nine more employees to cope with increased production capacity
- Reduced off-site secondary pollution by reducing the consumption of sodium hydroxide and of energy (less suspended particulate matter and sulphur dioxide)

To achieve these results, the mill implemented 28 preventative measures at a capital cost of US$100,000 and an operating cost of US$40,000. The total savings from these measures were US$400,000, giving a payback period on capital investment of less than four months.

Tunisia: lead-acid battery manufacturing

The Environmental Pollution Prevention Programme of the United States Agency for International Development funded a two-year programme in Tunisia. One of the first demonstration projects was a waste reduction audit in a lead-acid battery manufacturing plant to identify pollution prevention options that would reduce the quantity of toxic chemicals, raw materials and energy used in the manufacturing process. As a result of implementing preventative measures identified by the audit, the company achieved the following:

- Reduced its capital investment cost for end-of-pipe equipment by at least 35% and reduced the costs of treatment chemicals by at least 66%
- Reduced employee exposure to lead dust
- Reduced energy and water use per unit output
- Reduced the amount of lead purchased
- Reduced lead-acid-contaminated waste-water
- Improved product quality by increasing service life

To achieve these results, the plant is implementing 19 pollution prevention options that will save over US$2.2 million in the first 24 months, for an investment of US$0.4 million. Options include several no-cost actions, such as capturing spilled raw materials and re-using them in the production process, as well as actions that require the purchase of capital equipment (a liquid lead atomisation mill) to reduce lead particle size and therefore waste.

China: fine chemicals

A recent cleaner production project in China, funded by the World Bank and implemented by the Industry and Environment Office of the United Nations Environment Programme (UNEP) and the Environmental Research Institute (IVAM) of Amsterdam University, looked at the potential for cleaner production at seven companies. One of the plants is a major manufacturer of fine chemicals in China, specialising in the production of additives for the processing of high-polymer materials. As a result of implementing preventative measures, the mill achieved the following:

- Reduced its capital investment cost for end-of-pipe equipment by 25% and annualised costs by 15%
- Reduced water use by 80% and chemical oxygen demand by 95%
- Increased output by 25%
- Increased the expenditure for labour by 40%

To achieve these results, the plant has implemented nine low-cost options and it is now considering four high-cost options. The investment needed for implementing the first batch of nine cleaner production options was less than US$1,200. The annual savings due to increased efficiency and decreased materials and water consumption was US$30,000, giving a payback period of less than two weeks. The investment needed for the four high-cost options would be US$520,000. The annual savings will be US$750,000, giving a payback period for the capital investment of less than nine months.

Size of firm

The effects of environmental regulations will have a more significant impact on the production costs of smaller firms than on larger firms because the smaller firms cannot take advantage of the economies of scale in end-of-pipe pollution control equipment, nor can they afford to install process technology that would allow them to meet environmental regulations.

One example of the effect of firm size occurred in the pulp and paper sector in Argentina (Chudnovsky *et al.* 1995). Alto Parana, along with Papel Prensa, are the two major companies in this sector in Argentina. Recently, it invested US$8.0 million, which is 8% of the value of its capital stock, in cleaner production technology to reduce organic and dioxin effluents. According to the firm, this investment did not significantly affect the profitability of the firm, which is oriented towards exporting to developed countries. On the other hand, a small pulp and paper firm in the same area could not afford to invest in cleaner technology and the only way it could comply with environmental norms was to cease production.

Another example of the effect of firm size from Argentina occurred in the leather sector (Chudnovsky *et al.* 1995). The larger firms, those primarily engaged in export, have built effluent treatment systems. Just a few of the approximately 35 firms in this group found any difficulty in meeting this requirement. The smaller firms, those primarily producing for the domestic market or as subcontractors for the larger firms, have not been able to build effluent treatment plants due to the lack of finance and sufficient space. Two of the firms that attempted to comply have recently declared themselves bankrupt. A third example of the effect of firm size is the impact of the European Union and German ban on the use of pentachlorophenol (PCP) for the conservation of leather and the use of dyes containing formaldehyde and benzidine (Wiemann *et al.* 1994). Larger tanneries in India, with access to imported leather and a labour cost advantage, were the least affected in terms of the export market by this ban. Smaller units with backward technologies and located in urban areas were the worst affected because they were unable to import equipment and process chemicals to reduce effluents and to maintain product quality.

Type of industry

Some types of industry, primarily the resource-intensive ones (chemicals, iron and steel, non-ferrous metals, non-metallic minerals and pulp and paper), should encounter more difficulties in complying with environmental norms than assembly industries because of the high initial investment costs in both cleaner production processes and end-of-pipe equipment. Unfortunately, the author did not find any quantitative case studies, of which some certainly exist, to include in this chapter.

A case study of the interaction of trade and environmental policies in Colombia states that some Colombian industries, the more pollution-intensive ones, will most likely be negatively affected by a strengthened environmental policy (Garcia 1994). Because industrial goods account for only 25% of the total exports, a strengthened industrial pollution control programme is not expected to alter Colombia's international competitive position. However, the following export-oriented, pollution-intensive industries may be affected to some degree: petroleum refining, leather, metallurgy, chemical, chemical substances and textiles.

Availability of technical assistance

Without technical assistance, industry often does not know how to comply with environmental regulations and will lose export markets, and in the extreme case will be forced to close. With technical assistance, industry often has the potential to comply at a reasonable cost with environmental regulations.

One example of the importance of technical assistance in reducing the adverse impact of environmental regulations was the assistance of the Government of India and the Government of Germany (GTZ) to the tannery sector, which had to respond to the above-cited ban on the use of pentachlorophenol (PCP) for the conservation of leather and the use of dyes containing formaldehyde and benzidine (Wiemann *et al.* 1994). The initial problems of the leather industry occurred mainly due to the lack of testing facilities to determine PCP content and the lack of PCP substitutes. These problems took a few months to resolve until testing centres were set up and the Indian tanneries obtained information on where to get substitutes. In order to facilitate the import of substitutes (such as TCMTB and PCMC), the Indian government reduced the import duty from 150% to 50% *ad valorem*.

Another example of the importance of technical assistance was one of private-sector co-operation between Chilean fishery enterprises and a Norwegian enterprise (Ezquerra 1994). In the late 1970s, the Chilean fisheries faced environmental challenges for new demands of more specialised markets requiring better-quality and more differentiated products and from environmental pressures exerted by local communities where the processing plants are located. The fishery association, whose products are fish meal and fish oils, had, in conjunction with the Norwegian enterprise, developed a number of cleaner technologies that met both environmental and cost-minimising goals. Among the environmental benefits obtained from the new technologies were lower levels of suspended solids in liquid effluents, fewer or no emissions of malodorous gases, energy savings and optimal use of raw materials. In addition, the processes developed enabled the fish processors to adapt better to market demand and obtain better prices and, at the same time, to produce better-quality fish meals differentiated in accordance with needs of their users.

Openness of the economy

The openness of the economy, in this case the degree of import restrictions, can have an influence on the cost and even the ability of industry to implement environmental regulations. Import restrictions can increase the costs of acquiring equipment and supplies that would allow industry to comply in a least-cost manner with environmental regulations.

The above-cited example on the ban of PCP is a good example of the potential effect of trade liberalisation policies. The ability of the Indian leather industry to respond to the ban was initially restricted by a high import duty on substitutes for PCP, and it was necessary for the government of India to lower the import duty for the industry to be able to afford the substitutes. In contrast, the Argentinean leather industry did not face the initial problems as a result of the PCP ban to the same extent as the Indian industry because the liberal trade policies already in place in Argentina made imports more accessible (Chudnovsky *et al.* 1995.). Apparently, the introduction of PCP substitutes was made without serious consequences and without increase in costs.

Another point to be made under this topic is that the share of pollution-intensive industries as a share of overall industrial output can be affected by the recent trends to make economies more open. Trade liberalisation can result in both an increase and decrease in these industries. In the case of Indonesia, the liberalisation of the 1980s promoted a surge in assembly industries reversing the pattern in the 1970s of more rapid growth in the pollution-intensive resource-processing industries (World Bank 1994a). In the case of Poland, the trade liberalisation of the 1990s has worked in the opposite direction. As of 1994, Poland is now importing more manufactured goods whose production is not pollution-intensive and is increasing its exports of manufactured goods whose production is pollution-intensive, such as fuel-energy, metallurgy, chemicals, minerals and pulp and paper. Similarly, in the case of Chile, the trade liberalisation started in the 1970s has resulted in a significant increase in pollution-intensive resource-processing industries for timber, fish and fruit (Instituto de Desarrollo Ademando 1994).

Potential measures to minimise impacts

The above sections suggest that there is an integrated effort on the part of government and industry to respond to the potential, but limited, effects of increasingly stringent environmental regulations on the costs of industrial production. Ways to minimise these costs would include (Kumar 1995):

- Assignment of priority to pollution-prevention measures over end-of-pipe measures to achieve compliance with environmental norms
- The wider use of economic instruments as complements to command-and-control measures to encourage compliance with environmental regulations
- Promotion of special programmes and support systems to improve the overall competitiveness of small-scale enterprises, including their environmental performance
- Elimination of government policies, such as import restrictions, that prevent or discourage industry from utilising least-cost measures to comply with environmental norms

Conclusions

The limited data found in preparing this chapter indicates that more empirical work is needed in this field in order to clarify the extent to which environmental regulations will add to the costs of industrial production in developing countries. This type of information is needed not only to address the concerns of those who claim that environmental regulations will have a significant cost impact, but also to design policies to assist those industrial sub-sectors and those categories of industry of a size that will encounter difficulties in achieving compliance with environmental regulations, particularly on the need for and effectiveness of government interventions.

This review suggests that the impact of environmental regulations on industrial competitiveness in developing countries will be much the same as it was in industrialised countries during the period 1970–90. At the industry level, the impact of environmental regulation appears to be limited and insignificant—somewhere around 2% of production costs. However, difficulties are being encountered by pollution-intensive industries in the investment phase of complying with environmental regulations, and some categories of industry, such as small firms in urban areas, are unable to remain competitive and at the same time comply with environmental regulations. These circumstances need to be addressed by changes in government policy and are yet another indication of the need for international transfer of environmental management experiences and environmentally sound technology.

6

Multinational Corporations' Environmental Performance in Developing Countries

The Aluminum Company of America

Dennis A. Rondinelli and Gyula Vastag

THE FLOWS OF INVESTMENT CAPITAL into developing countries have changed significantly over the past two decades. Nearly 86% of the financial resources flowing into developing countries in the mid-1990s was from the private sector, a dramatic reversal of patterns from the 1970s and 1980s when poorer countries depended primarily on official foreign aid. Foreign direct investment in developing countries increased from about $44 billion in 1990 to more than $243 billion in 1996 (Cavanagh and Anderson 1997). The growing influence of private investment and trade on the economies of developing countries brings with it a growing concern that multinational corporations (MNCs) are seeking locations for their facilities in developing countries with weak environmental laws and lax enforcement of environmental regulations. Korten (1995: 12-13) argues, for example, that, through mergers, acquisitions and strategic alliances, transnational firms are making the world more dependent on technologies that are socially and environmentally destructive, allowing rich countries to 'pass their environmental burdens to the poor by exporting both wastes and polluting factories'. He contends that the spread of market capitalism and MNC investments in developing nations are 'destroying livelihoods, displacing people, rendering democratic institutions impotent, and feeding on life in an insatiable quest for money'. The Worldwatch Institute, an international environmental organisation, claims that foreign investors are 'all too often an accomplice to environmental degradation on a massive scale', and that the mobility of international capital allows multinational firms 'to seek out the most hospitable home—which may well be a place with weak or unenforced environmental laws' (French 1997: 12, 10).

If, as critics contend, MNCs are simply seeking pollution havens and exploiting resources in developing countries, the impacts of increasing private investment flows to developing countries could have catastrophic consequences in the future. But little evidence supports the wholesale condemnation of MNC environmental performance in developing countries. Although critics can always find some multinationals that misuse human and natural resources in developing countries, a series of studies going back to the early 1980s confirm that highly polluting industries do not generally migrate to developing countries to take advantage of lax environmental regulations. MNCs seek locations in developing countries for reasons far more crucial to their competitive success than exploiting weaknesses in environmental laws. The Conservation Foundation concluded in the mid-1980s that most US-based MNCs' foreign direct investment in developing countries was not in pollution-intensive industries (Leonard 1984). A survey conducted by the United Nations (1992a) in the late 1980s and early 1990s found that the share of 'pollution-intensive' industries (chemicals, pulp and paper, petroleum, coal and metal) in the total outward investment stock of industrialised countries was relatively low—17% of France's, 19% of Germany's, 8% of Japan's, 13% of the United Kingdom's, and 19% of the United States'—and that many of these industries had begun to adopt more effective environmental management practices.

A United Nations study of Asian countries that had weak environmental laws found no significant relocation of pollution-intensive industries to those countries as the result of environmentally induced factors (ESCAP 1988). Because of their visibility, multinational corporations had far better environmental performance records in Asia than did local firms. Analyses of multinational corporations' environmental practices in Brazil in the mid-1980s also concluded that, because MNCs were more open to scrutiny by host-country politicians and journalists than many local companies, they responded more quickly to requests to correct environmental problems (Pimenta 1987). Harrison's (1994: 10) analysis of foreign investors in Mexico, Venezuela, the Ivory Coast and Morocco also uncovered no evidence that multinational firms in 'dirtier sectors' sought out locations in these countries or made investments designed mainly to take advantage of weak environmental laws or lax enforcement of environmental regulations. Indeed, the study concluded that multinationals investing in these four developing countries were 'much more efficient than domestic firms and also use cleaner types of energy'.

Other research found that neither national environmental standards nor environmental cost differences have been major determinants of the flows or shifts in the location of foreign direct investment. The United Nation's (1992b: 227) Transnational Corporations and Management Division points out that MNCs can and do have positive impacts on environmental conditions in developing countries because they not only have access to clean technology . . .

> developed in response to stringent environmental protection among industrial countries, but they possess the skills in the safe handling, transport, storage, use and disposal of hazardous materials, and in the development of pollution abatement technology itself.

Since the early 1990s many of the largest MNCs have adopted environmental policies that far exceed local requirements for their facilities in developing countries. This chapter assesses in detail the international impacts of the environmental policies of one MNC, the Aluminum Company of America (Alcoa). We first describe the global forces that are requiring MNCs to integrate environmental management policies into their overall business strategies and how Alcoa adapted to these requirements. Alcoa's experience provides rich insights into how MNCs with progressive environmental policies improve their manufacturing facilities, the lives of their workers, the communities in which they locate and the developing economies in which they invest.

Multinational firms and environmental management

Wholesale criticism of the environmental impacts of MNCs' operations in developing countries is misleading because it overlooks the fact that many multinational firms often bring significant improvements in environmental performance to the factories they build, acquire or control—and other positive economic and social benefits as well. A variety of global forces pressure MNCs to adopt more responsible environmental practices (Berry and Rondinelli 1998) (see Fig. 1.) Investors who clearly see the relationships between business performance, financial performance and environmental quality demand that MNCs reduce their environmental risks and operate in socially responsible ways (Cohen *et al.* 1995; Hart and Ahuja 1996). Increasing civil and criminal liabilities, the costs of repairing corporate image, the demands of customers, the wrath of disappointed shareholders, and the difficulty of obtaining capital from risk-averse financial institutions are making MNCs more aware of the need to prevent environmental disasters before they happen (Piasecki 1995; Vastag *et al.* 1996). The trend towards proactive environmental management is being accelerated by public pressures on governments almost everywhere to assure a cleaner environment. But, more importantly, there is growing evidence that firms that adopt proactive environmental management strategies become more efficient and competitive.

Progressive corporations are now looking at environmental performance from a very different perspective from that of the past (Schot and Fischer 1993). Beyond complying with increasingly stringent regulations, they must protect or enhance their ethical image, avoid serious legal liabilities, satisfy the safety concerns of employees and customers, respond to government regulators and stockholders, and develop new business opportunities in order to remain competitive in world markets. Market and business factors play the most important roles, but the adoption of global standards by international trade and investment organisations also encourages the adoption of proactive environmental management strategies by firms seeking to become globally competitive. International competition motivated more than 127,000 companies in 99 countries to become certified by 1996 under the ISO 9000 series guidelines for quality management. Total Quality Management has strongly influenced how MNCs manage their operations and has encouraged many to improve their environmental performance (Symonds 1996). Business leaders' growing recognition of the importance of environmental protection to their firms' international competitive advantage has

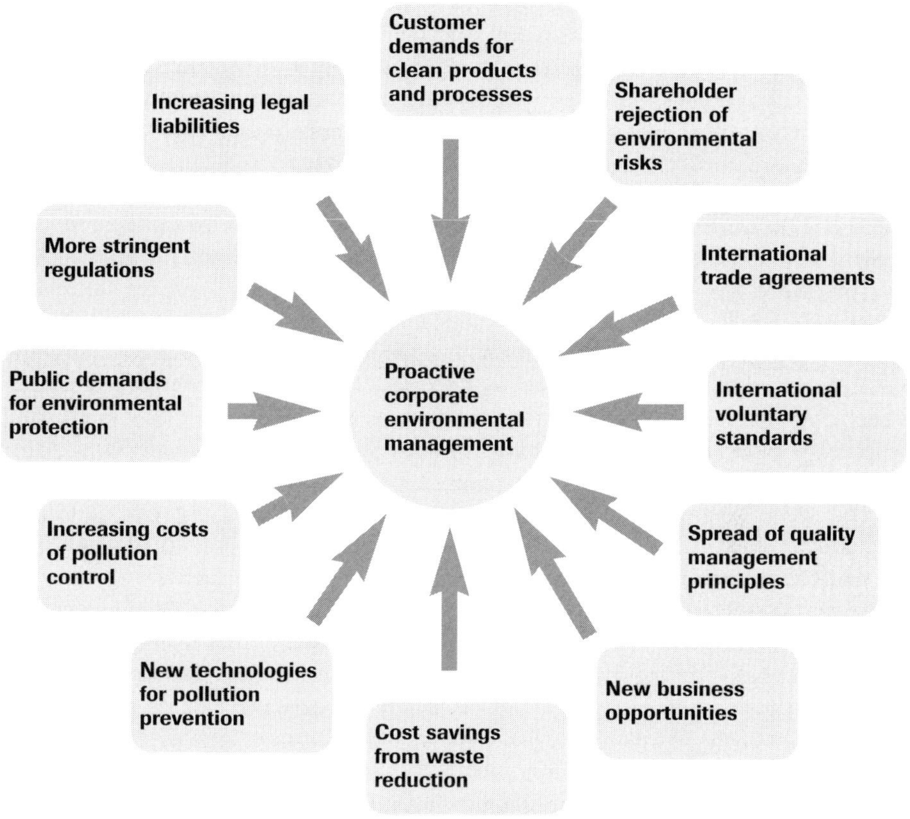

Figure 1: FORCES DRIVING PROACTIVE ENVIRONMENTAL MANAGEMENT

led to new rounds of voluntary standards emphasising the integration of environmental management and corporate strategy. The guidelines of the American Society for Testing and Materials (ASTM), which is standardising environmental auditing, assessment and criteria for investment and insurance, and of the British standard BS 7750, which is an industrial response to the adoption of the 1990 Environmental Policy Act in the UK, are being widely adopted internationally. The European Community expects member nations to implement the Standard Eco-Management and Audit Scheme (EMAS). And the ISO 14000 series is becoming the international standard for environmental management systems (Tibor and Feldman 1996; Jackson 1997). Although these standards differ somewhat in their requirements and criteria, they all seek to explicitly encourage corporations to integrate environmental and corporate management systems.

Many MNCs have adopted policies similar to 3M's pollution prevention programmes, Dow's waste reduction campaign and Chevron's toxic reduction strategies, which focus the attention of managers, employees and the public on environmental protection. These MNCs set clear environmental goals and measurable targets for pollution reduction in their worldwide operations (Rondinelli and Berry 1997). Between 1986 and 1996, for example, Baxter International (1997) reduced its per unit air toxic and chlorofluorocarbon emissions by 94%, its non-hazardous waste by 45% (75 million kg) and its hazardous waste by more than 48%. The firm recycled 128 million kg of materials in 1996 alone. From 1990 to 1996 the 3M Corporation reduced its air emissions by 70%, its water releases by 52% and its solid waste by 32% in its worldwide operations. Since 1991 Dow Chemical (1997) cut its emissions of compounds by 53% (more than 112,000 kg) in its facilities around the world. Xerox reduced hazardous waste generation by 50% between 1990 and 1995. Nortel, the Canadian-based telecommunications MNC, established specific targets for the years 1993 to 2000: a 50% reduction in pollutant releases, a 50% reduction in solid wastes, a 30% reduction in paper purchases and a 10% improvement in energy efficiency (Kerr 1995).

Moreover, the increasing cost of emissions control is pushing internationally competitive firms, such as the major automobile makers, to adopt pollution-prevention measures in sourcing, production and distribution (Hemenway 1996). These measures have become easier to apply with the proliferation of new technologies and processes that allow firms to reduce or eliminate waste rather than struggle with end-of-pipe pollution control (UNCTAD 1993). Many firms have also adopted pollution-prevention policies and integrated environmental management into their overall business strategies because they have found significant cost savings from waste reduction or elimination and new business opportunities in clean products and production technology (Ehrenfeld and Howard 1996). Philips Electronics, for example, now uses eco-design principles to develop new products that are cleaner to produce, use and dispose of, such as 'Philips Green TV', which reduces energy consumption and eliminates hazardous materials, and low-mercury fluorescent lamps that increase energy efficiency and eliminate toxic hazards in disposal (Pizzorusso 1998). Almost all MNCs in the chemical and petroleum industries have committed themselves to operate worldwide at government or company standards—whichever is more stringent—and to abide by the 'Responsible Care' principles adopted by the members of the Chemical Manufacturers' Association (Bond 1996).

Applying international environmental management standards: the case of Alcoa

For a variety of reasons, the Aluminum Company of America had no choice but to adapt to these changing international forces. In 1997 Alcoa had $13.3 billion in revenues and earned nearly $805 million in profits from 180 locations in 28 countries. About 46% of its sales came from outside the United States and more than 60% of its 81,000 employees worked in Europe, the Pacific Rim and Central and South America (Alcoa

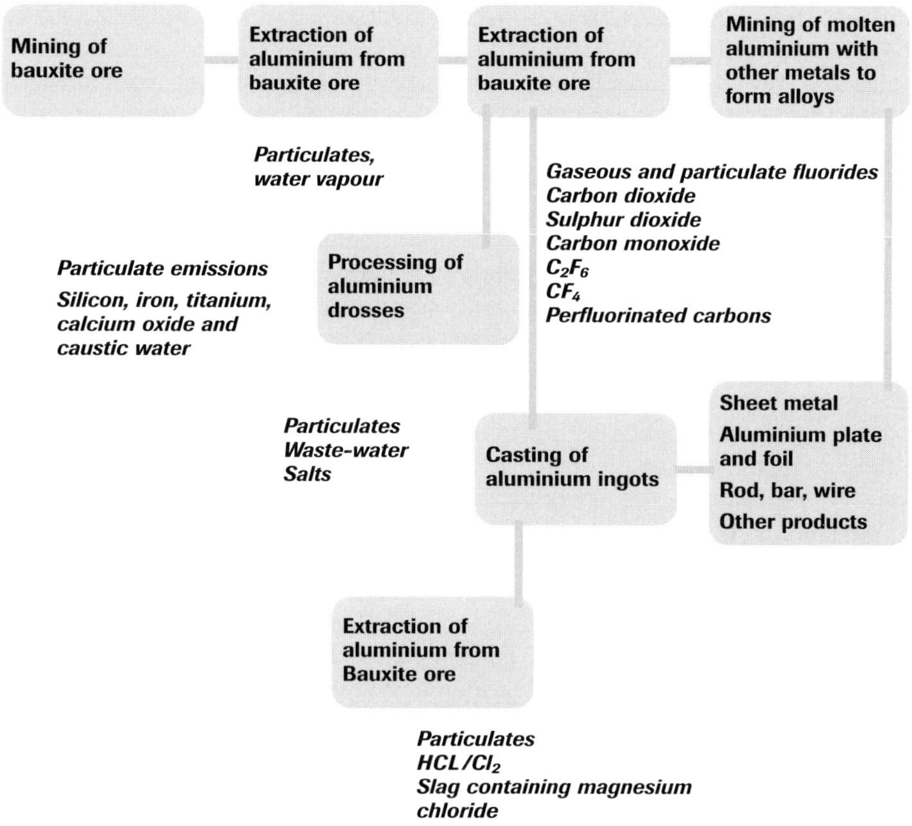

Figure 2: ALUMINIUM PROCESS AND POLLUTION OUTPUTS

1997a). In 1998 Alcoa acquired another large aluminium firm, Alumax, increasing its workforce to 100,000 employees in 250 operating locations in 32 countries.

Aluminium production is a potentially polluting industry. Alcoa is one of the world's largest integrated aluminium producers—it mines and processes bauxite ore, derives alumina from bauxite, melts aluminium scrap and processes aluminium dross (a by-product of melting operations), produces ingots as feedstock, and manufactures a wide variety of products for the packaging, automotive, aerospace, construction and other fabricated- and finished-products markets. All stages of aluminium operations can have potentially negative ecological and environmental impacts (see Fig. 2). Ore-mining operations can degrade the physical and natural environment. Bauxite refining and smelting processes use large amounts of energy and can pollute ambient air with particulates as well as surface and groundwater with residues containing caustics, silicon, iron, titanium and calcium oxides (EPA 1995). Smelting can pollute the air with fluoride, carbon dioxide, sulphur dioxide, carbon monoxide and perfluorinated carbons. Secondary scrap melting releases particulates and HCL/Cl_2 and produces slag containing magnesium and chlorides. Aluminium plants and mining operations have impacts on regional air quality and contribute to global ozone depletion. Moreover, aluminium companies must carefully manage bauxite residue, dispose of spent potlining, and manage waste-water and salts.

Alcoa publicly recognised the potential impacts of its plants on the environment and the need to protect the health of its employees and the safety of its operations (Alcoa 1996). In the face of serious competitive challenges in international markets and global forces pressing for progressive environmental management in the late 1980s and early 1990s, Alcoa's top management began to fashion a strategy by which the company would seek to shape its own fate (O'Neill 1996).

Although Alcoa's major thrust in environmental protection came in the early 1990s, during the 1960s the company pioneered a closed-loop process for capturing and recycling more than 99.9% of the fluoride of collected fumes from its aluminium-smelting process gases and dusts (which were found to be harmful to vegetation and livestock), re-using them in aluminium production. Alcoa executives recognised that a company so dependent on using natural resources, water and energy in its worldwide operations could not afford a reputation as a 'dirty industry'. The board of directors approved a formal environmental policy in 1975, revised it in 1985, and strengthened it substantially in 1991. Alcoa's (1995a: I-2) policy is 'to operate worldwide in a manner which protects the environment and the health of our employees and of the citizens of the communities where we have an impact'.

Alcoa committed itself to comply with all environmental laws, regulations and permits in all its locations worldwide, but also to use more stringent standards in places where that would be necessary to conform to corporate policy. Moreover, Alcoa pledged to anticipate environmental issues and take actions to prevent environmental problems in advance of legal or regulatory requirements and to work with host-country governments and other organisations to develop effective environmental regulations. In 1996 the corporation developed nine basic principles to assist in the implementation of the policy (Alcoa 1995a: I-4), committing Alcoa to:

1. Support sustainable development
2. Practise responsible use of natural resources
3. Use energy wisely
4. Practise sound environmental management
5. Provide training and information to employees, suppliers, customers and the public
6. Audit its operations and report findings
7. Sponsor activities to improve the science of environmental protection
8. Develop and adhere to the highest worldwide environmental standards and best practices
9. Report on its activities annually to shareholders and the public

Implementation of environmental policies in emerging markets and developing countries

Since 1990 Alcoa has invested between 8% and 10% of its annual capital expenditures on environmental, health and safety improvements. In 1997 alone, the corporation invested more than $94 million in these areas (in addition to the operating costs of existing facilities) and anticipated investing more than $102 million in 1998.

Each of Alcoa's business units is required to formulate an annual action plan for environmental management and to set specific targets. Alcoa had undertaken environmental auditing since 1982, but substantially revised its system in 1992. The updated system requires an environmental audit of all 170 facilities worldwide at least once every three years. The audits—conducted by multifunctional teams of central-resource experts, business-unit managers and external representatives—identify environmental problems or deficiencies and make recommendations for improvements.

Alcoa corporate headquarters developed detailed audit guidelines for every major environmental activity at its sites worldwide. These guidelines use the same structure to assess the environmental activities at all of the sites. Environmental audit guidelines for air, for example, include assessments of the following sets of items (Alcoa 1995b):

1. Understanding of management systems
2. Emission-source identification and characterisation
3. Registration and air-emission permit applications
4. Conformance with air emission standards
5. Monitoring and reporting
6. Identification of new sources
7. Emission standards for hazardous air pollutants
8. Ozone-depleting substances
9. Gasoline-dispensing operations
10. Fuel-burning equipment
11. Air pollution alert and emergency plan
12. Past operational practices

The teams provide a thorough diagnosis of a site's environmental conditions and identify unsatisfactory conditions that require improvements. Following the audits, facility managers must provide an analysis of the nature of the deficiencies, outline corrective action that will be taken in a detailed 'Audit Response and Action Plan', and submit quarterly progress reports. Sites with unsatisfactory ratings have a follow-up audit conducted one year later.

Continuous auditing and reporting have had a positive impact on Alcoa's operations. In 1993, the audits found that 80% of the facilities assessed had satisfactory environmental performance; that rate increased to 85% in 1994. In 1995,

Alcoa conducted environmental audits at 50 facilities—24 in the United States and 26 overseas—and 92% were found to have satisfactory performance. In 1996, 39 sites were audited, and 95% received a satisfactory or better rating.

In 1995, Alcoa consolidated its environmental, health and safety (EHS) policies into a unified comprehensive management system. Its EHS management system provides guidance policies, positions, guidance materials and 'informational toolboxes' for all its business units and operating locations. EHS became the responsibility of Alcoa's executive vice-president and general counsel, who is a member of the company's 11-member executive committee and reports directly to the corporation's chairman. The EHS advisory board, composed of business-unit presidents, offers advice on environmental, health and safety policy.

Every business unit—independently managed stand-alone enterprises with their own financial and non-financial objectives—is responsible to Alcoa's senior management for environmental performance in accordance with corporate guidelines. In addition to operating guidelines, Alcoa also developed a set of positions on key environmental issues to help managers understand and respond to environmental issues such as biodiversity, managing carbon dioxide, groundwater contamination, marine pollution, hazardous waste disposal, energy conservation and cleaner production (Alcoa 1995c). Each business-unit president is required to participate in quarterly reviews of business performance that include environmental, health and safety measures. Facility managers work closely in defining environmental concerns and needs with stakeholders, including business units, primary customers of Alcoa's products and services, employees, local community groups, neighbours, local resource users, other Alcoa facilities and industry or trade groups (Alcoa 1995a).

Alcoa's managers and employees worldwide have access to information on state-of-the art business practices and technologies for environmental, health and safety issues through the Alcoa Intranet and EHS home page. In 1995 Alcoa invested $150 million in a joint venture with Microsoft and Hewlett Packard to develop its own information superhighway connecting more than 15,000 computers in Alcoa's international network (Haapaniemi 1996). Knowledge transfer from one location to another is made possible through a large benchmarking 'knowledge warehouse' and by links to related environmental documents, many of which are available in Dutch, German, Italian, Spanish and Hungarian languages as well as English. Through the EHS home page, all of Alcoa's worldwide locations can download policies, standards, guidance documents, training materials, instructors' guides and presentation materials to allow EHS managers to provide on-site environmental training courses.

Components of Alcoa's international environmental management policy

Although Alcoa's environmental management system is comprehensive, the following components illustrate how this multinational firm has applied its practices in developing countries.

Environmental innovation awards

Alcoa managers and employees around the world began developing innovative approaches to environmental conservation and protection in response to the corporation's EHS strategies. The company provides annual 'Alcoa Environmental Excellence Awards' to teams of employees at locations that implement innovative ways of protecting the environment. The highly regarded awards, presented by the company's chairman and CEO, are given in four categories of environmental management: leadership, cultural change, technology transfer, and integration of environment, health and safety management systems into business operations. The programme to recognise environmental innovation was expanded in 1996 to include EHS Excellence Awards and Progress Awards as well as recognition of improved environmental performance.

Community environmental projects

Many of the award winners include community environmental projects such as Alcoa's refinery and smelter in São Paulo, Brazil, which developed a 4500-acre native-forest environmental park within the plant site. The park protects more than 200 species of birds, animals, insects and plants and is open to employees and their families, scientists and people from the local community. Alcoa's smelting plant in Victoria, Australia, created a wildlife habitat research, education and recreation area on the plant's site, where vegetation is fertilised by treated waste-water from the facility. At its bauxite-mining areas at Poços de Caldas, in Brazil's state of Minas Gerais, Alcoa restores the natural environment, after ore extraction, to its original topography and vegetation (*Revista do Alumíno* 1992).

New product development

Alcoa is also aggressively developing products that have positive environmental impacts. It is producing aluminium bodies and parts for cars and trucks in its plants in Germany, Hungary, the United States, Mexico, Ireland and Brazil. It is working with Audi, Chrysler and General Motors to lighten the weight and improve the performance of automobiles by replacing steel components with aluminium. Alcoa Automotive Structures is working with a dozen automobile manufacturers around the world on projects that use aluminium. The environmental implications are significant: every 10% reduction in vehicle weight increases fuel economy by about 7% and reduces emissions even more.

Transfer of environmental management systems

The impacts of Alcoa's environment, health and safety measures in developing nations and emerging-market countries, where it acquires existing companies or builds new operations, can be seen clearly in the transfer of corporate environmental policies after its acquisition of the state-owned aluminium company Köfém, in Székesfehérvár, Hungary.[1] Alcoa formed a joint venture with Hungalu, the parent company of Köfém,

1 We are grateful to the following people from Alcoa-Köfém for their time and assistance in providing both written information and interviews during our field research in Hungary: Mr

and the Hungarian Privatisation and State Holding Company by purchasing a 50.1% interest in January 1993. In 1996 Alcoa acquired the remaining shares of the joint venture, which had been renamed Alcoa-Köfém. Alcoa also moved its closure systems, aluminium truck wheel production and auto components businesses to Hungary (Rondinelli and Vastag 1998).

Although Hungalu's air, water and hazardous waste disposal problems were far less serious than those of other state-owned industrial enterprises, Alcoa carried out an environmental audit of Köfém as part of its due diligence analysis before acquiring the company in 1993, and another in 1995 of Alcoa-Köfém prior to acquiring full ownership. In 1993, 65% of Köfém's activities were satisfactory by Alcoa standards. By 1995, 72% of Alcoa-Köfém's activities complied with or exceeded Alcoa's standards, while 28% were generally satisfactory, and none required substantial improvement. Alcoa headquarters and Alcoa-Köfém's American general manager nonetheless applied the full range of environmental, health and safety requirements in the Hungarian operations.

Despite the fact that Hungarian laws at the time did not require it, in 1994 Alcoa began an extensive asbestos abatement project at Köfém. Alcoa environmental and safety guidelines required the application of the US standards for the removal and replacement of all asbestos, which had been used extensively for insulation at Köfém, from buildings, pipelines and process equipment. In 1994, Köfém began an extensive programme to separate and dispose of hazardous and non-hazardous wastes. With Alcoa's guidance, Köfém's EHS department developed a programme for collecting, separating and re-using wastes, and disposing of those that were not recyclable. More than 100 million Hungarian forints (HUFs), or about US$5 million, were invested in revamping Köfém's incinerator. An afterburner was added and a dust trap was installed in the stacks. Alcoa insisted that Köfém retained responsibility for hazardous waste after it left the plants until its final dumping or disposal. In order to prevent Alcoa-Köfém's wastes from causing environmental damage anywhere in Hungary, the company now stringently controls contractors by verifying its permits, insurance, financial reliability and technical competence, by making visits to disposal sites and by monitoring contractors' transport records.

Because Köfém uses more than 700 different types of chemical—mostly in its laboratories—Alcoa imposed strict guidelines for hazardous chemical use at Köfém. It required that all chemicals must be purchased, used and disposed of according to Hungarian environmental laws or Alcoa guidelines, whichever were more stringent. As part of its overall environmental management at Alcoa-Köfém, the company's EHS department monitors air quality on its plant site, follows Alcoa guidelines with regard to combustion inspections and maintenance, and uses natural gas as its main energy

---

Ralph Matera (general manager), Mr Tamás Horváth (EHS manager), Dr Béla Forgó (director of finance), Mrs Tünde Somogyi K. (environmental manager), Mr Péter Kovács (EHS co-ordinator), Dr István Miniska, MD (head of Occupational Health Service), Ms Beatrix Molnár (industrial hygienist), Mr Frank Geuens (TQM manager), Ms Márta Fatér (quality manager), Mr László Illés (energy supply manager), Mr Gyula Maár (central engineering manager) and Mr Isván Avramucz (senior mechanical engineer). We also appreciate the help of Mr John F. Kromberg, former plant manager, Alcoa Wheel Products Europe Ltd, and Mr István Janó, deputy director, Central Transdanubian Environmental Directorate, Hungary.

source to reduce pollution and improve efficiency. Köfém also reduced air pollution at its ingot facilities by cutting its use of cleaning salts and by switching to more environmentally friendly materials in production. The company terminated the purchase of ozone-damaging materials and of chemicals in spray-type packaging containing chlorated hydrocarbon. Upgrading of the on-site incinerator also reduced air pollution (Alcoa-Köfém 1996a).

In 1996, Köfém separated its water systems into potable water and industrial water components. Waste-water was separated through company canal systems into sewage, storm-water and drain components. Controls prevent: pollution from oil or grease, salt and other contaminants from industrial water system overflows; oil, grease, and floating materials from company roads; oil and salt from the flat rolling plant drain system; and oil and chemicals that might be spilled on accidents on company roads (Alcoa-Köfém 1996b).

Environmental and occupational health programmes

Alcoa places strong emphasis on environmental and occupational health in its facilities around the world. In 1997, Alcoa arranged with the Yale University School of Medicine to work with the firm's medical and occupational health staff in extending occupational and environmental health services throughout the corporation. But prior to this alliance with Yale University, Alcoa had been active in upgrading the environmental and health services for employees in the factories that it acquired internationally. In 1995, for example, Alcoa invested more than $5 million in a state-of-art occupational health services complex in the Alcoa-Köfém plant, which is comparable with Western European facilities, and in a programme that focuses on prevention as well as treatment. It hired two physicians, two nurses, a laboratory assistant and an industrial hygienist; provided emergency treatment services, and access to 24-hour ambulance services with connections to local hospital emergency rooms; and trained employee first-aid crews. Medical programmes were based on Alcoa worldwide protocols. The company prepared a noise survey and noise map and provided hearing tests for at-risk employees (Miniska 1997).

Materials recycling and re-use

Alcoa actively encourages the recycling and re-use of aluminium cans and containers in countries where it operates. In one of its Brazilian facilities, a 12-member employee team identified ways of recycling and re-using more than 400 tons of solid waste from the site's anodising effluent treatment station and of excavating for re-use more than 6,000 tons that had been landfilled (Ashton 1996). Employees in Alcoa-Fujikura's Cuidad Acuna plant in Mexico were able to reduce oily waste-water discharge by 80% in 1994 by adapting a water evaporative technology originally designed for another industry. The technology eliminated the need to discharge waste-water, and the oil residue was recycled (Alcoa 1994).

Integration of environmental and quality management

Alcoa's environmental management policies are being integrated into overall quality management systems in many of its international plants. In Alcoa-Aluminio, SA, based in São Paulo, Brazil, environmental, health and safety policies were integrated with total quality management in its Alumar refinery and smelter plants in northern Maranhão state and its casting and rolling mill in Itapssuma, near the coastal city of Recife (Manas 1995). Well before the Brazilian government strengthened its EHS regulations, the business unit president of Alcoa-Aluminio pushed for the integration of Alcoa's environmental, health and safety policies with the Brazilian subsidiary's productivity and quality management systems. He pursued ISO 9000 certification at a time when other Brazilian state-owned and private enterprises were relying on the traditional belief that the government would not enact more stringent regulations and would not enforce them even if it did. Alcoa-Aluminio combined an aggressive programme of benchmarking, planning, process control, customer satisfaction, asset utilisation and employee empowerment and recognition using ISO 9000 standards with 'eight pillars' of quality strategy. The quality strategy focused on:

1. Environment, safety and industrial hygiene
2. Administration
3. Initial control
4. Quality maintenance
5. Planned maintenance
6. Autonomous maintenance
7. Specific improvements
8. Training and education

Employees organised into teams to meet regularly for training, information exchange and discussion. Those who developed new ideas about how to contribute to quality, productivity and environmental protection and safety were given extra compensation based on the value of the contribution to Alcoa-Aluminio's financial savings. Employees could develop their own training programmes to implement new ideas and procedures. Environmental, financial and production targets were updated regularly and posted throughout the plants so that employees could easily gauge their performance.

Impacts

The impacts of Alcoa's international EHS management systems are wide-ranging. Between 1993 and 1996 Alcoa reduced its environmental, health and safety compliance penalties from nearly $1 million to less than $100,000 (Alcoa 1997b). By 1995, Alcoa had reduced ozone-depleting substances in the United States by 66% from the 246,913 kg that were released in 1988. It lowered its worldwide generation of spent potlining from smelting operations by 20,000 metric tonnes between 1992 and 1996. The 1995–96 waste cost-reduction targets of 10% were met, and waste volume declined by more than 100% over target. Employees in individual business units and facilities focused on environmental targets specific to their operations. For example, Alcoa's

Aerospace and Commercial Rolled Products unit sought to eliminate ozone-depleting chemicals—especially 1,1,1-trichloroethane, chlorodifluoromethane (HCFC-22), and TRI (Toxic Release Inventory) chemicals—from its processes. Alcoa, like many other multinational corporations, is integrating its environmental, health and safety standards into its overall business strategy throughout its international operations. Rather than seeking 'pollution havens' or exploiting weaknesses in regulatory standards in emerging markets and developing countries, Alcoa pursues a progressive set of standards because they contribute to overall quality and productivity and enhance Alcoa's competitive position. Even where the transfer of Alcoa's environment, health and safety standards temporarily reduces an overseas plant's revenues and profits—as was the case with Alcoa-Köfém in Hungary—business unit presidents act on the understanding that the investment will result in long-term gains (Rondinelli and Vastag 1998).

Alcoa has learned that it is more cost-effective to take preventative measures than to clean up environmental damage later. By reducing its liabilities, improving the company's environmental image, engaging employees in developing innovative solutions, minimising waste, re-using materials, and enhancing the quality of the environment in the communities in which its plants are located, Alcoa has found 'win–win' solutions to potentially damaging and costly environmental problems in emerging-market countries. In taking the initiative through progressive environmental management, Alcoa and other MNCs can reduce the high costs of environmental regulation and clean-up for governments in the countries where they invest.

In 1996, the World Environment Centre (WEC) gave Alcoa its 'Gold Medal for International Corporate Environmental Excellence'. The award praised the company for creating 'an exemplary environmental policy, globally uniform application of that policy, and international environmental leadership extending beyond traditional corporate boundaries' (Jones 1996: 5). Alcoa was also included in the United Nations' 'Global 500 Roll of Honour' for environmental excellence in its mine rehabilitation programmes in Western Australia (the first mining company ever to receive that honour) and has received numerous international, national and local awards for its environment, health and safety policies.

Conclusions

Although some firms will seek to exploit weaknesses in the countries in which they operate, many multinational corporations such as Alcoa make substantial contributions to human and natural resource development. They do so through forward-looking environmental management policies and global business strategies that commit them to long-term investment and operation in emerging-market countries. Blanket condemnations of MNCs' operations in developing and emerging-market countries must be tempered by the recognition that global corporations must increasingly operate by international environmental standards if they are to remain competitive. Firms such as Alcoa recognise the competitive advantages of progressive environmental management and they integrate corporate environmental, health and safety objectives into their business strategies and operating procedures around the world.

Alcoa's success in applying its progressive environmental, health and safety policies in its facilities in developing and emerging-market countries derives from strategic decisions about how it will conduct its businesses worldwide:

- Commitment and support for good environmental management comes from the top of Alcoa's corporate structure. Alcoa's chairman and CEO, board of directors and executive committee advocate and implement strong EHS policies. Alcoa's chairman and CEO Paul O'Neill (1998: 1) has given Alcoa a leadership role in defining the issues of global climate change: for example declaring that 'we are environmentalists first and industrialists second'. He has signalled to the entire corporation Alcoa's determination to reduce energy consumption and atmospheric emissions.
- Alcoa's policies are translated into specific and detailed principles and guidelines that managers and employees around the world can understand through audit and assessment documents, policy statements and the corporate intranet. These principles are implemented throughout the corporation.
- Business-unit presidents, although independent in the management of their units, are held accountable for integrating and implementing Alcoa's worldwide environmental, health and safety objectives and for adapting EHS guidelines to local conditions and needs. The corporation's commitment to these objectives was demonstrated in 1996 when Alcoa forced the president of Alcoa Fujikura Ltd in Acuna, Mexico, to resign after it was discovered that he failed to report three environmental and safety incidents in the plant two years earlier in which workers had to be treated for exposure to carbon monoxide and butane gas (Laabs 1996).
- Alcoa sets verifiable targets for environmental, health and safety performance and monitors and measures the results through regular audits that focus on diagnosis and improvement.
- Alcoa invests in EHS-improvement facilities, equipment, processes and training even when such investments may have short-term negative impacts on profits. Alcoa strongly signals through its communications systems, priorities and investments that the company is serious about implementing its proactive environmental, health and safety policies. Corporate headquarters strongly supports its business units and facilities around the world with state-of-the-art information through its intranet and EHS home page. Its communications network provides EHS managers with around-the-clock access to technical and managerial assistance, training materials and sound EHS standards. It encourages Alcoa's EHS managers around the world to share information, ideas and proven methods to improve performance. It enables site managers to offer continuing EHS training to employees.

- Alcoa rewards success through its personnel-evaluation systems and by offering visible recognition for accomplishment and innovation through its EHS Excellence Awards and Progress Awards.

Alcoa is not the only multinational corporation adopting beyond-compliance environmental management systems for its global facilities. A survey of 169 multinational firms based in Asia, North America and Europe by the United Nations Conference on Trade and Development (UNCTAD 1993) found at the beginning of the 1990s that 43% had already published international environmental management statements that committed them to at least complying with all national and local environmental laws and regulations of their home and host countries and many of them pledged to adopt environmental practices that went beyond compliance. About 75% of the MNCs had environmental policies in place that went beyond the requirements of national regulations. Priority areas included research and development programmes for energy-efficient production (70.7%), policies for conserving non-renewable resources (54.4%), programmes for recycling materials (84.5%), and worker health and safety programmes (67.5%). More than 62% of the MNCs adopted environmental health and safety policies in their international operations that reflected the requirements of their home-country laws and regulations, which were usually more stringent than those of their host countries. As with Alcoa, nearly 80% of the MNCs in the UNCTAD sample reported that environmental, health and safety programmes were initiated by top management.

Not all multinational corporations have adopted proactive environmental management practices and some may not even be in compliance with environmental regulations in some of the developing countries in which they operate, but a growing number of MNCs are recognising the importance of social responsibility and integrating environmental management into their overall business strategies. Blanket condemnations of the environmental impacts of MNCs' investments and operations in developing countries are neither accurate nor constructive. In order to encourage and support progressive environmental management practices by multinational corporations, governments in developing countries must adopt policies that are conducive to sustainable development and more stringently enforce environmental laws and regulations. The United Nations Centre for Transnational Corporations recommends that governments in developing countries adopt clear policy objectives for sustainable development, remove price distortions arising from government policies on natural resources, adopt and enforce polluter-pays laws, and mandate accounting procedures that require transparent financial reporting (United Nations 1992b). International voluntary standards such as ISO 14001 help MNCs to transfer proactive environmental management policies by encouraging them to certify their plants and by stimulating corporations such as IBM, Ford Motor Company, General Motors and Chrysler to require their suppliers around the world to develop and certify their environment management systems by ISO 14001 standards. The transfer of environmental technology and clean production processes from MNC operations in more developed nations to their facilities in less-developed countries can also improve environmental conditions. Governments in developing countries can also play important roles in providing incentives for both national and multinational corporations to adopt 'beyond-compliance' environmental practices and in working with progressive MNCs to adapt and transfer strong environmental management systems to host-country firms that are part of their worldwide supply chains.

7

ISO 14001: The Severe Challenge for China

An Overview of the Problems China Faced in the Implementation and Certification of ISO 14001

Di Chang-Xing (Mike)

THE PROMULGATION of the international environmental management standard ISO 14001 has only been taking place for two years. Within this short period, there has been an upsurge of interest in implementing ISO 14001 and acquiring certification via a third-party certification or verification institution. Developed countries and multinational corporations (MNCs) have been particularly aggressive in this movement. According to the most recent census from the Federal Environmental Agency of Germany (Fig. 1), up until June 1998 there were 973 organisations that had obtained ISO 14001 certification in Japan. This brought Japan to the top of the list, with the highest number of ISO 14001-certified companies in the world, followed by many EU countries. These countries, such as the UK, France and Ireland, have always been proactive in implementing EMS, having established their own national standards for EMSs long before the development of ISO 14001. The European Eco-Management and Audit Scheme (EMAS), the European EMS standard, is built on the unification of the environmental management standards among the EU countries and, to date, this remains the most stringent standard in the world. Although the international environmental management standard ISO 14001 has already been promulgated and implemented, the unified European standard EMAS has not been abandoned. However, the implementation of ISO 14001 has surpassed EMAS, even though EMAS was implemented a few years before ISO 14001. By June 1998, there were more than 2,000 companies with ISO 14001 certification. The UK is in the lead within the EU, with 650 ISO 14001-certified companies. Germany is next, with 630 companies, the Netherlands 230, followed by Norway 145, France 104, Finland 90, Austria 80, Ireland

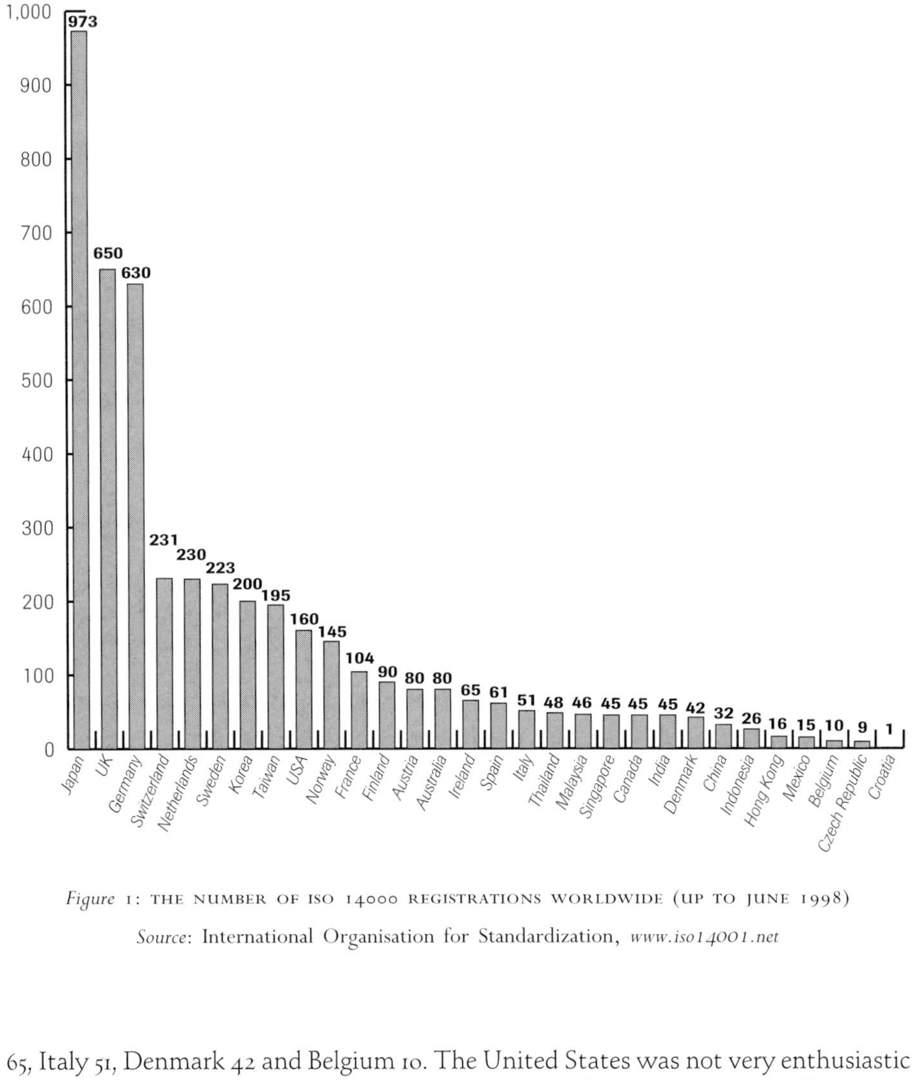

Figure 1: THE NUMBER OF ISO 14000 REGISTRATIONS WORLDWIDE (UP TO JUNE 1998)

Source: International Organisation for Standardization, *www.iso14001.net*

65, Italy 51, Denmark 42 and Belgium 10. The United States was not very enthusiastic about ISO 14001 initially, but has made rapid progress after a slow start, and has come from initially being behind China to having 160 companies certified by June 1998.

On the other hand, as illustrated by the census, none of the developing countries has more than 50 ISO 14001-certified organisations. Even large countries such as China and India have only 32 and 45 certified companies, respectively. Other developing countries have even fewer, such as Mexico, 15 companies, Indonesia, 26 companies and Croatia, 1 company. A significant number of developing countries are yet to begin implementing ISO 14001. Among the developing countries, China is one of the most aggressive advocates of ISO 14001 in the Asia-Pacific region. As of June 1998, the official figure for the number of ISO 14001-certified companies in China was 32. For a large nation such as China, this rate of progress is not commensurate with its size. A point to note is that, of these 32 companies, the majority are MNCs (70%), with the remaining 30% represented by Chinese local enterprises; the number of ISO 14001-certified Chinese SMEs is even smaller.

An interesting fact is that numerous MNCs from developed countries have included in their environmental policies a requirement that their subsidiaries and branch offices obtain ISO 14001 certification within a certain time-frame. ABB Corporation, Baxter Corporation and Xerox Corporation, for example, have made such a commitment. This implies that the number of ISO 14001-certified companies in developed countries will grow exponentially. This has been reflected by the situation in China. For example, the headquarters of ABB requires all its subsidiaries throughout the world to pass the ISO 14001 certification before the end of 1998.[1] In addition, Philips Electronics from the Netherlands and Rhône Poulenc from France both announced in Europe during early 1997 that their ventures in China will have to obtain ISO 14001 certification by 2000.[2] MNCs from Japan are even more aggressive. If the commitment of the MNCs from Europe for their local operations in China can serve as a sign of encouragement, then the commitment of the MNCs from Japan looks less like a promise and more like a command. For example, Sanyo instructed its 22 enterprises to obtain ISO 14001 certification before the end of 1998 fiscal year, and National Matsushita Group required its 32 enterprises in China to pass the ISO 14001 certification by March 1999. Among the pilot programmes in China, the majority of them are within Japanese companies. Besides National, Sanyo, Canon and Ricoh, other major MNCs have also taken the lead in obtaining ISO 14001 certification.

In contrast, even though China started off at around the same time as developed countries, and, even though the Chinese government is supportive of ISO 14001, the growth and development of ISO 14001 in China cannot match that of the developed countries. If the rate of implementation of ISO 14001 remains slow, China will soon be lagging far behind developed countries and MNCs. It is not difficult to see that, while developed countries and MNCs are extremely active in advocating ISO 14001, developing countries are experiencing many obstacles in pushing forward and making progress with ISO 14001. Therefore, a few questions arise:

- Where are the obstacles challenging Chinese enterprises in implementing ISO 14001?
- Is ISO 14001 beneficial to developed countries and MNCs or is it beneficial to China and SMEs?
- What is the impact of ISO 14001 on the economy of China?
- What is the stand that should be taken by China?

In this chapter, through extensive investigation, research and interviews with the ISO 14001-certified organisations, it has been found that the standard favours

1 Interview with EHS representative of ABB China.

2 Interview with Mr Salamitou, EHS manager of Rhône Poulenc and Mr Raymond van Ermen, executive director of EPE (EPE Infoservice 1997: 9).

developed countries and MNCs. For example, the level of difficulty in implementing ISO 14001 for Chinese enterprises is much greater than for developed countries and MNCs. Some of the challenges faced by Chinese enterprises in implementing ISO 14001 include: greater cost; the bigger steps involved; the non-tariff trade barrier imposed on Chinese enterprises by ISO 14001; difficulties caused by low environmental awareness; incentives; and excessive government intervention for the voluntary standard.

This chapter attempts to research and analyse the negative aspects of the above issues from the standpoint of China. There have been numerous reports on the positive effects of ISO 14001 implementation in China, so these positive effects will not be included in this chapter. The purpose of this chapter is to remind China and other developing countries not to pursue the new system blindly, but to acquire a comprehensive understanding of the circumstances, and tailor the application of ISO 14001 to the needs of local situations. The ultimate goal should be to seek the proper use of ISO 14001 in China so that it can be a useful environmental management tool for achieving sustainable development. This chapter hopes to promote further interactions and valuable feedback from all interested parties. The detailed problems and challenges that Chinese local enterprises face are presented below.

The difficulties of implementing ISO 14001 for local Chinese enterprises are greater than for MNCs in developed countries.

During the two years of the pilot programme in China, it has been proved that local enterprise has had much greater difficulties in implementing ISO 14001 than MNCs in developed countries. First of all, many MNCs have already had certain kinds of EMS in place, some of which are more stringent than ISO 14001, whereas local enterprises in China have had to start from scratch. EMS in China is a new concept, therefore exacerbating the difficulty of implementing this international standard. For example, initial environmental review is not mandatory for companies in developed countries, because they would have conducted it during the inception of their own EMS. Since the establishment of the world's first national EMS standard, BS 7750 in the UK, many companies in developed countries have established their own EMS based on BS 7750. The British standard required the execution of an initial environmental review. ISO TC 207 did not include an initial environmental review in the ISO 14001 standard, which was probably an accommodation to the needs of developed countries. In addition, MNCs in developed countries usually include a complete system of Environmental Impact Assessment, risk assessment and various audit schemes, so identifying and evaluating these aspects is regular practice for these MNCs. However, for most local enterprises in China, an initial environmental review is a prerequisite in the construction of the ISO 14001 system and this is not an easy job for them. Huge efforts are made in training their staff, inviting in outside consultants and experts, investigating past activities, collecting current applicable environmental regulations, etc. Chinese enterprises do not usually have complete records for their past activities and they are often also unfamiliar with the legislation and requirements; these record and information systems are readily available in developed countries. Therefore the process of investigating past activities and compiling the required information is a significant task for many Chinese firms.

Subsidiaries of MNCs in China, although also unfamiliar with the relevant current Chinese environmental regulations, face fewer difficulties than do Chinese enterprises. They usually have access to financial and technical assistance from their mother companies. Most of the MNCs in China have attained ISO 9000 certification and their document system is relatively complete. This issue is crucial. The 'start-up' costs of ISO 14001 implementation for MNCs in China could be far less than for Chinese enterprises of comparable size. They can usually draw on corporate documentation and systems methods and share joint resources that will reduce their cost of systems implementation and registration. For example, Canon, National, Sanyo, Johnson & Johnson, Xerox, Bristol Myers Squibb, ABB, BASF and Philips all provided assistance to their subsidiaries in China. Chinese local enterprises often experience the dual pressure of obtaining certification for both ISO 9000 and ISO 14001. By starting the process from the very beginning, a significant amount of time and effort is needed in writing and editing the documentation. Some of these enterprises even travel thousands of miles so that their documents can be reviewed and modified by external consulting companies.[3] The detailed cost issue will be discussed in the following section.

The cost of implementing ISO 14001 for local Chinese enterprises is higher than for MNCs.

Surprisingly, the cost incurred by local enterprises implementing ISO 14001 is higher than for MNCs operating in China. One important factor is, as mentioned earlier, that Chinese enterprises have to start from zero and they need the whole package of consulting and certification services from external parties. Therefore, the implementation and certification costs are higher than for MNCs in China. Another important factor is that Chinese enterprises also need to invest in the extremely expensive environmental 'hardware'[4] to comply with the regulatory requirements. The details of the consulting and certification fee structure as well as the environmental 'hardware' investment of Chinese enterprises are discussed below.

Overview of consulting and certification fees in China

Since ISO does not specify the fee for consultation and certification, and there is no regulated international reference, the ISO 9000 consulting and certification fee structure is used, which is RMB 3000 per day per person (about US$360).[5] On the surface,

---

3 This is because only one company was allowed to carry out the ISO 14001 consulting and certification work at that time.

4 Environmental protection facilities and equipment.

5 The Chinese unit of currency; at the time of writing, US$1 = RMB 8.3.

Item	Description	Day rate	RMB	US$ (1:8.3)	UK£ (1:12)
Internal auditor training	Establish and audit EMS	2–3 people for 5 days	30,000–45,000	3,615–5,422	2,500–3,750
Initial environmental review	Identify and evaluate environmental aspects	2–3 people for 1–2 days	6,000–18,000	722–2169	500–1,500
Guidance on documentation	Design, policy, manual, procedure	2–3 people for 1–2 days	6000–12,000	722–1,446	500–1,000
Review documents	Policy, manual, procedures	2–3 people for 1–2 days	18,000–24,000	2,169–2,892	1,500–2,000
Assist internal audit	Planing to action	2 people for 2–3 days	12,000–18,000	1,446–2,169	1,000–1,500
Pre-assessment	Like formal	3–4 people for 2–4 days	18,000–48,000	2,169–5,783	1,500–4,000
Travel cost	Flight/train average single trip is RMB 700	At least 4 return journeys	12,600–14,000	1,518–1,687	1,050–1,167
Entertainment	Hotel, meal, etc. (RMB 150 + 100 per day)		6500–12,000	783–1,446	542–1,000
Total			109,100–191,000	13,144–23,014	9,092–15,917

Table 1: CONSULTING COST IN CHINA FOR MEDIUM-SIZED ENTERPRISES

this price does not seem to be high but, in practice, it can be enormous. For those enterprises participating in the pilot programme in particular, the average consultation fee comes to around RMB 109,100–191,000 (US$13,144–23,014) (see Table 1) and the certification fee is around RMB 37,600–79,400 (US$4,531–9,566). This cost is not a problem for most of the MNCs in China, but for local Chinese enterprises, especially the SMEs, it is a heavy burden.

Consultation fee

The consulting package in China in the early stages includes the following components: EMS awareness training, internal auditor training, initial environmental review, guidance on documentation, reviewing and modifying documentation, assisting in the internal audit and pre-assessment of the system. The total consulting fee is based on the calculation of the whole consulting package. EMS awareness training is usually a half-day and, in the early pilot programme, EMS awareness training was usually free to an organisation that showed interest in ISO 14001. However, the travel cost, hotel expenses and meal costs for the trainer is paid by the organisation. In China the internal auditor training and external auditor training are almost exactly the same. They use the same training materials and training content and method. However, many companies in the pilot programme sent people on both of these training courses. The standard internal auditor training course is usually five days, but in some cases can be longer—the training for the Guangzhou Hua Ling Refrigerator Company went on for 10 days. For Chinese enterprises, this five-day internal audit training cannot be waived, and it will normally cost around RMB 30,000–45,000 (see Table 1), excluding instructor's transportation, accommodation and meal expenses.

The initial environmental review is usually conducted straight after the internal auditor training course. Normally the trainers stay for a few more days to help the enterprises to identify and evaluate their environmental aspects, so the cost also depends on how many trainers they send and how many days they stay after the training. Naturally, the weekend expenses in between are also paid by the enterprises.

The documents normally need to be edited two or three times. The pre-certification audit is similar to the preliminary audit conducted by the certification body. Although it is not necessary to perform the pre-certification audit, most consulting firms will insist on doing it because pre-certification audit experience is accepted by the Chinese government as auditing experience for the purposes of being registered as auditors. For a typical SME, an approximate breakdown of the consulting fees is shown in Table 1.

Assistance from headquarters of mother companies is not available to Chinese local enterprises. For example, ABB China corporation organised an internal audit training course collectively for its ten ABB companies in China and, in doing so, has saved the training fees of the nine courses required if each company had its own internal auditor training course. US Xerox Corporation has sent specialists to offer training to their two branch companies in Shanghai and Suzhou and obtained ISO 14001 certification without the help from external consulting firms. The US Lucent Technology China operation also conducted internal EMS training courses for its branch companies. Most headquarters of the Japanese firms also offered guidance to their subsidiaries in China on the construction of their environmental management system. Most Japanese companies in China can get document templates from their mother companies, which reduces the workload considerably.

Environmental 'hardware' cost

In order to be able to comply with relevant environmental laws and regulations, some Chinese SMEs need to invest in environmental protection equipment and facilities 'hardware'. This is a situation particular to China and the cost can be very high. Henan Xinfei Refrigerator is a state-owned enterprise that acquired ISO 14001 certification in July 1998. In the course of developing the ISO 14001 EMS, the investment was significant. The cost of the waste-water treatment facility was RMB 1.12 million (US$135,266) and the cost of importing sound insulation materials from Italy was RMB 800,000. In addition, construction of noise barriers, a water re-circulation system and an energy-saving system has also incurred substantial expenses. Changling Refrigerator is another local enterprise in China, which is quite well equipped with environmental protection facilities. However, during the implementation of ISO 14001, it invested RMB 10 million for the boiler facility to mitigate its atmospheric discharge. Guangdong Kelong is another example. In the process of implementing ISO 14001, it spent more than RMB 20 million on its waste-water treatment facility, noise control equipment, re-engineering its generator, etc. This company was among the biggest investors in 'hardware' for the purposes of ISO 14001 certification.

Certification fee

The ISO 14001 certification fee rate is also RMB 3,000 per person per day, but the total cost is relatively fixed. Similar to consultation, even though the certification fee is not too high compared to developed countries, the number of people involved and the duration of the certification process are unreasonably high in the early pilot programme. Due to lack of experience, the Chinese certification bodies tend to send more personnel than necessary and the time management is not as efficient as that of international certification bodies. While international certification bodies can complete the certification in two days with two people, local certification firms may take as long as four days with three to four people. The local enterprise usually has no references to draw on and will agree to the terms set by the certification body. This is a fair portrait of the market conditions during the early stages of introducing ISO 14001 in China. A major difference between certification and consultation is that the cost of playing host to certification personnel is higher than that for consultants. Since the certification outcome directly affects the fate of enterprises, they would usually treat the certification personnel very well, with entertainment, gifts and sightseeing tours. The expenses for such events can be significant. An approximate breakdown of the certification fees is shown in Table 2.

The pressure of environmental trade barriers faced by local enterprises in China is much higher than for MNCs in developed countries.

Although ISO 14001 has clearly stated that the standard is not for the creation of non-tariff trade barriers, in its actual implementation the potential trade barrier is manifested through the acquisition of ISO 14001 certification. The pressure of the trade barriers faced by local enterprises in China is much higher than for MNCs in developed countries. The standard requires the organisation to have an influence over its contractors and suppliers, which implies that organisations are encouraged to place a requirement on their corresponding contractors and suppliers to establish an EMS and obtain ISO 14001 certification. As a result, suppliers and contractors will be on the passive side of the market. Since local enterprises in China are less environmentally aware compared to enterprises from developed countries, this type of control becomes one-sided and biased. In other words, developed countries can place their

Item	Description	Day rate	RMB	US$ (1:8.3)	UK£ (1:12)
1st stage assessment	Documents, site check, system check	2 people for 2–3 days	12,000–18,000	1,446–2,169	1,000–1,500
2nd stage assessment	Documents, site check, system check	3–4 people for 2–4 days	18,000–48,000	2,169–5,783	1,500–4,000
Travel cost	Flight /train		5,600–8,400	675–1,012	467–700
Entertainment	Hotel, dinner etc.		2,000–5,000	241–602	166–417
Total			37,600–79,400	4,531–9,566	3,133–6,617

Table 2: CERTIFICATION COST IN CHINA FOR MEDIUM-SIZED ENTERPRISES

restrictions on enterprises from developing countries, but developing countries cannot control enterprises from developed countries in the same way. This is one of the constraints faced by China and other developing countries. At present, a number of MNCs from Europe, the United States and Japan have already established internal standards for their suppliers. Some European companies such as Siemens, Nokia and the Ciba Geigy Corporation (Shao 1998) have already required their suppliers to have ISO 14001 certification. The same situation can also be seen in China. For example, IBM has issued a global letter to all its suppliers, including its Chinese suppliers, requesting ISO 14001 certification. Hewlett Packard has also asked Dalian Canon office suppliers to obtain ISO 14001 certification for its inkjet printer production and Xiamen ABB has requested its five suppliers in China to acquire ISO 14001 certification. It is obvious that there is a growing trend for MNCs to enforce restrictions on suppliers. The laws and regulations from developed countries cannot impose direct restrictions on export enterprises from developing countries, but, if developed countries decide to use only suppliers with ISO 14001 EMS, then this will have a devastating impact on local Chinese enterprises.

Chinese local enterprises have to take a bigger step in their actual environmental performance than MNCs do in the implementation of ISO 14001.

Another challenge for Chinese enterprises is that their efforts to improve their environmental performance are relatively greater than those of MNCs operating in China. There are two important points here.

First, as we know, ISO 14001 does not set an absolute requirement for environmental performance. The standard only requires organisations to apply the applicable local regulatory requirements. The flexibility of this standard enables MNCs who already have attained high environmental performance to acquire ISO 14001 certification easily. Therefore, MNCs in China can enjoy the prestige of having ISO 14001 certification while operating with a relatively lower environmental performance than in their own countries. In other words, although ISO 14001 is an international standard, in reality the 'double standard' still exists between MNCs and Chinese local enterprises in terms of absolute environmental performance. To local enterprises in China, ISO 14001 is a stringent standard that is difficult to attain. In contrast, to MNCs in China, ISO 14001 is a very basic standard that is even lower than their corporate environmental performance standard. Companies such as GE, Ciba Geigy, Rhône Poulenc and Baxter all believe that their corporate EMSs have more stringent requirements than ISO 14001.

Second, it is common practice for MNCs not to put the international treaties or sector code of practice that they should be obeying into their environmental policy. This is a result of the unclear term 'applicable local requirements' in the standard. Even though MNCs may be committed in their home countries to certain international treaties or sector codes of practice, they may not include these since the Chinese government does not require it. In theory, international treaties should be incorporated into national laws and regulations. However, countries that are not party to a treaty would not apply. In this case, these international environmental treaties apply to governments, not organisations. Moreover, China has established many industrial development zones to attract foreign investment, and has given foreign companies bonus schemes and incentives, including lowering the environmental standards and requirements. Some of the government requirements for sound environmental practice may not even apply to MNCs in these zones, so MNCs may not comply with them. Therefore, the term 'conform to applicable laws and regulations' is very limited and affords significant leeway to MNCs in lowering their environmental performance.

In the implementation of ISO 14001, China and developed countries are on different levels, and the effect will be different.

In the global implementation of ISO 14001, since the environmental 'green' market differs between developed countries and China, the environmental concept, the environmental regulations and the mitigation costs are also different. Hence, the effect of implementation differs between developed countries and China. Some of the positive results of implementing ISO 14001, such as relief of pressure from consumers and reduction in costs of production, are more pronounced in developed countries, and may not be obvious in China or other developing countries, at least not in the short term. For example, in developed countries, if the enterprise does not implement ISO 14001, it will feel the pressure from the market, and consumers may choose another product with ISO 14001 certification. This is because consumers are more environmentally aware, and a 'green' market already exists in developed countries. However, in China, such an effect may not exist, because consumers in general neither know nor care about ISO 14001. So the effect of implementing ISO 14001 may not be visible. As in the case of CFC-free refrigerators, Chinese consumers do not know the background, and are not aware of the relationship between refrigerators and the stratospheric ozone hole. Their only concern is the price, so the development of a 'green' market in China will still take a considerable amount of time.

As for cost reduction and increased competitiveness in the implementation of ISO 14001, for enterprises in developed countries, the effect can be very obvious. First, the penalties for poor environmental performance in developed nations are high; second, the mitigation costs such as those for waste-water treatment and solid waste treatment are costly. Therefore, the savings in production costs are obvious during the implementation of ISO 14001 in developed countries. In China the situation is different; environmental regulations are not well enforced, the penalties are relatively low and the investment required for ISO 14001 is too heavy, so the effect of implementing ISO 14001 will not be obvious, especially in the short term.

As a result, many Chinese enterprises, especially the state-owned enterprises and SMEs, are not so active with regard to ISO 14001 certification. They generally feel that the benefits of ISO 14001 are marginal, the costs too high, and that environmental protection is not their top priority for the time being. They generally do not feel the demand from the market to implement ISO 14001. Furthermore, for some of the high-performance local enterprises or large enterprises, although they are reluctant to implement ISO 14001, the local EPB (Environmental Protection Bureau) has recommended them for certification. This type of recommendation usually has a compulsory implication. Therefore, these enterprises dare not defy the recommendation, as they are afraid of hurting their relationship with the local EPB. Shanxi Caihong enterprise is one such example. There are other companies that have started the application process, but have had to withdraw due to lack of funds or other reasons. This was more pronounced in the second and third pilot programme stage. For example, Changchun car factory, Wuhan steel company, Ermei semiconductor, Tianshan boiler factory, Guangdong Wanbao electrical appliances, Jinjiang Fengzhu knitting and dye factory, Fuzhou synthetic board factory, Fuqing City Mingwei cutlery, Qiqihaer paper and pulp, Longzhong cement, Jingtu enterprise, Dalian silk and carpet, Lasa leather factory have all participated in the second and third pilot programmes and have withdrawn due to financial problems and other reasons.

Local Chinese enterprises are currently undergoing recession due to the Asian economic crisis; many companies have not even obtained ISO 9000 certification, and now they are faced with the pressure of obtaining ISO 14001 certification. Since most local enterprises in China are SMEs, they are unable to compete with MNCs financially, and at present China does not offer any bonus scheme or incentives for implementing ISO 14001. Under these circumstances, Chinese SMEs are faced with a severe challenge in implementing ISO 14001. In the long term, the inability to implement ISO 14001 may result in the elimination of local SMEs in the market by competing MNCs. This might be something that the Chinese government should pay close attention to.

Excessive governmental interventions have created more burdens for Chinese enterprises in implementing ISO 14001.

One of the fundamental characteristics of ISO 14001 is that it is a non-governmental, market-based standard and excessive governmental intervention will make the market-driven standard less effective. Unfortunately, China serves as a typical showcase of excessive governmental intervention on the implementation and certification of ISO 14001. This happened from the very beginning. Several ministries involved in this issue all wanted to control the market in favour of their own interests, so they did not take the interest of the country and many Chinese enterprises fully into consideration. The following demonstrates a few examples.

During the first two years of the pilot programme (early 1996 to mid-1998), China only had one organisation that could deliver the certification service of ISO 14001. There are probably many reasons for this, but the main reason was the monopoly of NEPA (National Environmental Protection Agency) and disputes between various ministries. This made the promotion of ISO 14000 in China fall below the initial equal footing with the rest of the world. This delay will affect Chinese firms in their international trade business if trade barriers occur. Another example is that, when a company is ready to acquire ISO 14001 certification, no certification body is allowed to conduct an audit without approval from local EPBs. However, the cost for the approval is substantial. A company has to prepare four documents: (i) Environmental Impact Assessment (EIA) statement; (ii) 'Three Synchronisation' certificate (see below); (iii) certificate for meeting total emission standards; and (iv) proof that the enterprise had no environmental fines before certification. In addition, all the certification bodies have to inform the local EPBs of the initiative and invite their representatives to participate in the assessment as observers (China Accreditation Committee 1998: 11).

On the surface, the above requirements may appear to be reasonable but, in reality, they represent typical governmental interference and monopolistic behaviour. The real purpose is to control the ISO 14001 certification market within the SEPA[6] system. A detailed analysis of SEPA's four additional requirements shows that there is a severe lack of understanding of the essence of ISO 14001. The aim of ISO 14001 is to encourage all organisations to implement the system no matter where they start. In other words, they can start from different levels and make their own continuous improvement. Thus, two organisations carrying out similar activities but having different environmental performance may both comply with the requirement. In other words, ISO 14001 is not a standard for environmental performance but rather a management model, which emphasises continuous improvement regardless of the starting point. The underlying rationale is that, if every business establishment improves from its current level, the earth would be a better place to live in.

This is particularly significant in China where the starting point is low for most enterprises. Most local Chinese SMEs have not conducted a proper EIA and 'Three

6 State Environmental Protection Administration, formerly NEPA.

Synchronisation' certification before starting their operation owing to management inadequacies in China. This is the reality. Unless they are forced to close, they should be given an opportunity to improve their environmental performance, and the ISO 14001 aims to achieve precisely that. So, for existing companies, obtaining the above-mentioned certificate is meaningless. Taking 'Three Synchronisation' as an example, it is obvious that the real purpose of certification is to achieve market monopoly.

In China, the Three Synchronisation policy is called *San Tong Shi*, meaning 'triple concurrent processing'. The policy requires that environmental protection treatment facilities (any equipment used to reduce discharges under water, air and noise regulations) be designed, constructed and operated in tandem with design, construction and operation of industrial projects. The Three Synchronisation programme is one of the effective tools by which the People's Republic of China regulates pollution discharges, because it is able to force compliance with EPB requirements through the *yanshou* (inspection) certification. Through the *yanshou* process, the EPB can stall full-scale production of the factory indefinitely until pollution control requirements are met. However, in practice, this policy has several problems and drawbacks. Primarily, the policy is limited by a lack of formal approval processes in the design and construction stages. Without an official certification procedure in the first stage, regulation is only practical during the operation phase where effluent is already being discharged. If the factory does not achieve *yanshou* certification, the EPB is authorised to shut down the facility completely. However, this appears to be a rare occurrence, and non-compliant discharges will generally continue until *yanshou* is achieved. In addition, after *yanshou* is granted, the enforcement of the goals of the Three Synchronisation policy is weakened. The policy's effectiveness is also limited by its application only to new and expanding industries. A more serious weakness, though, lies in the fact that the policy is rarely applied to township village enterprises due to their lack of investment resources and the general lack of attention paid to pollution problems in rural areas. Problems also occur when the policy is applied to joint venture facilities where the joint venture and the EPB may have agreements regarding the responsibilities of the foreign and local partners. In some joint venture operations, the local partner has responsibility for complying with all Chinese environmental regulations but may not have access to the necessary capital to install treatment technologies and obtain *yanshou* certification.

From the above, we can see that, in reality, a lot of projects are set up without appropriate Three Synchronisation certification and it is not possible to repeat the process. Whether the enterprises can obtain the certificate or not depends on their relationship with the local EPB, and this not only encourages enterprises to try to conciliate the EPBs through back-door deals but also gives the local EPB special privileges to control the other certification bodies. If the non-SEPA-controlled certification bodies, including international bodies, want to undertake certification in their area, they will not award the enterprises the certificates easily. The enterprises usually dare not offend the local EPBs. The enterprises that obtain certification do not necessarily meet the requirements of Three Synchronisation but have completed the paper exercise. And the enterprises have to pay for getting this certificate. The same applies for the other three additional requirements outlined above. The requirement for proof of no environmental fines does not reflect the spirit of ISO 14001. First, ISO 14001 does not say that a company must not have been fined before certification. Second, if it were fined RMB 200,000 previously but, during the establishment of ISO 14001, an additional fine of only RMB 200 was imposed by the local EPB, what does that indicate? It indicates that its system is working and is achieving continuous improvement. However, according to the Chinese government, these organisations cannot apply for ISO 14001. The requirements are problematic in themselves since they place emphasis on paying fines rather than improving actual environmental performance. The requirement that all the certification bodies have to inform the local EPBs of the initiative and invite their representatives to participate in the assessment as observers is another example of direct monopolistic behaviour (China Accreditation Committee 1998: 11). This requirement is not to ensure the quality of the certification, but to control the non-NEPA certification bodies and international certification bodies.

In general, the real meaning of NEPA's additional requirements for enterprises is not the four documents themselves but to keep the market under NEPA's control. These additional requirements keep many Chinese enterprises, especially SMEs, away from ISO 14001. Many SMEs adopt a wait-and-see attitude unless the local EPB forces them to participate in the pilot programme. This is not a sensible initiative for China itself because it will hinder the speed of development in China and, in turn, may make Chinese firms uncompetitive with potential trade barriers to face in the international market.

Conclusion

From the above discussion, we can see that Chinese enterprises are facing many severe challenges in seeking implementation and certification to ISO 14001. ISO 14001 is designed to fit into the existing management systems of MNCs in developed countries and the difficulties of implementation for local Chinese enterprises are much greater than for MNCs in developed countries. Due to the different starting point and lack of international consulting and certification practice, the financial investment of Chinese enterprises in seeking ISO 14001 implementation and certification is too high. Chinese enterprises are under more pressure from the potential trade barrier than are MNCs. There are 'double standards' regarding the efforts to implement and achieve certification under ISO 14001. The efforts of Chinese enterprises towards the improvement of environmental performance are relatively greater than those of MNCs. The economic gain for Chinese enterprises in implementing ISO 14001 is lower than for MNCs in developed countries due to different starting points. Excessive governmental intervention has made it more difficult for Chinese enterprises to implement ISO 14001. These challenges put Chinese enterprises in an economically disadvantageous situation. If the Chinese government does not pay enough attention to these issues, it could result in the massive failure of Chinese enterprises to maintain global competitiveness. Under such a situation, what stance and approach should be taken by China? What will be the future of ISO 14001 in China? And what is the significance to other developing countries? These issues are discussed below.

Recommendations

1. China should open up the market for ISO 14001 consulting and certification as soon as possible and should not only open it to Chinese consulting and certification bodies but also to international ones. When all those domestic and international consulting and certification companies can provide their services officially in China, there will be more organisations certified with ISO 14001. Also, through this increased competition, the cost of implementation and certification will be greatly reduced and the quality of the service will be greatly improved. Otherwise, Chinese enterprises will continue to suffer high costs and face the risk of trade barriers in entering international markets.
2. The Chinese government needs to provide assistance to Chinese enterprises in implementing ISO 14001, especially for SMEs and encourage as many as possible to certify with ISO 14001. First, the government needs to make a policy to provide financial support for Chinese firms seeking ISO 14001 certification. Some countries already offer financial assistance for SMEs and the Chinese government needs to do the same. Second, the government needs to help Chinese firms to reduce their costs as much as possible in ISO 14001 implementation and certification. The government could produce guidance books, organise joint training and promote low-cost ISO 14001 software to reduce the consulting service cost and help SMEs share environmental protection facilities, etc. In its broadest vision, this would achieve a result where national businesses are globally competitive and therefore contribute to national economic development and, at the same time, reduce negative impact on the environment.
3. The concept of 'self-registration' needs to be introduced to Chinese SMEs so that they do not have to seek external third-party certification. Establishing an EMS according to ISO 14001 and making a self-declaration is also a good approach for SMEs at present. However, this concept has never been introduced to Chinese enterprises for commercial reasons. It would not be a bad thing if SMEs established an EMS according to ISO 14001 requirements and, when conditions are ready, go for certification.
4. ISO 14001 is not perfect, especially for developing countries. China needs to analyse the standards and think carefully before acting. It is clear, at this stage, that China cannot expect Chinese firms to make environmental improvements with the same amount of effort and money as developed countries. Therefore, China needs to negotiate with ISO and try to put forward its own position. If the Chinese government can recognise and pay enough attention to the problems, then I am sure the correct approach will be easily identified.

The future perspective of ISO 14001 in China

The future perspective of ISO 14001 implementation and certification in China depends on many factors. The most crucial one is that the government institutions responsible for ISO 14001 need to acquire a comprehensive understanding of the standard and the circumstances in China, and tailor the application of ISO 14001 in accordance with the needs of local situations. If they continue to pursue ISO 14001 in China without such understanding, it will impede the speed of implementation. China should recognise the challenge and vulnerable position of Chinese firms and try to correct these problems and create more favourable conditions for SMEs to implement ISO 14001. For example, the government should open the market, provide financial assistance and introduce the self-registration concept. When huge numbers of SMEs are willing to implement ISO 14001 and can afford implementation, ISO 14001 will have a real bearing on progress towards sustainable development. Otherwise, China will continue to remain far behind the developed countries.

The significance for other developing countries

Figure 1 indicates that other developing countries are also slow in implementing ISO 14001. However, in developing countries, SMEs constitute a major part of national economies. The high costs involved in implementing an EMS may prove to be unattainable for SMEs and this could result in economic failure. The potential benefits from ISO 14001 in developing countries may not be as visible or measurable in terms of savings or gains as in developed countries. It is clear that ISO 14001 will become a potential market trade barrier. If companies in developing countries are not certified to ISO 14001, they will lose markets or potential markets. However, the economic consequences of ISO 14001 on developing countries are still not completely known, but the challenges that Chinese enterprises face may help other developing countries to learn from China's problems and experience.

8

Environmental Management, Crime and Information

A Russian Case Study

Alexey A. Voinov, Irina P. Glazyrina, Bruno Pavoni and Nadezhda A. Zharova

THERE IS MUCH EVIDENCE of environmental degradation and mismanagement in Russia and throughout the Former Soviet Union (Pryde 1991; Feshbach and Friendly 1992; Mnatsakanian 1992). The poor state of the environment inherited from the Communist past has been well documented and information has continued to come to light since the beginning of the *glasnost* period. It could be anticipated that the new information provided and increased environmental awareness of the public, in conjunction with the new democratic mechanisms of rule, would result in environmental clean-up, or at least would reverse the trends and offer some hope in the future. Unfortunately, this does not seem to be the case in Russia.

Contrary to expectations, the 'Westernisation' of the Russian political and economic landscape has done nothing for the improvement of environmental conditions; in many cases, they have actually deteriorated further. This Westernisation has proved to be mostly cosmetic, while in essence not much has changed. None of the basic attributes of a market economy has yet been put in place, property rights are not defined, and mechanisms for free competition and equal access to resources are not developed and are not enforced (see Chapter 10). The economic and political decentralisation in a vacuum of power and under demagogic democracy has provided an excellent substrate for criminal groups to flourish. Whereas most of the environmental degradation during Communist rule was due to negligence, lack of responsibility, mismanagement and abuse of power, the more recent ecological disasters and misappropriations of natural capital are closely related to certain criminal activities. The abuse of nature in the old era of the centralised economy was hardly ever translated into inputs into bank accounts and personal fortunes: personal benefits, if any, were somewhat indirect (titles, awards, jobs, but rarely cash). The new 'free' economy offers a direct link between natural capital and personal income. This has made natural resources a lucrative area for criminal management.

Crime has become an important factor in economies of many countries in transition. It seems to be playing an especially prominent role in countries that are rich in natural resources. There is a staggering correlation between the amount of natural capital available and the level of integration between state and criminal structures. Since natural capital appears to be most readily available for export and offers rapid returns, it is particularly appealing to the criminal sector. An abundance of natural resources seems to stimulate the growth of criminal behaviour. Reciprocally, under the dominance of criminal mechanisms of management, it is unlikely that any reforms to promote fair competition, access and distribution would be implemented. In this way, the criminal scenario creates a vicious circle of environmental abuse that is extremely hard to break. The following examples and case studies drawn from recent developments in Russia illustrate this. They also show that some of the paradigms of environmental management that are commonly accepted in the West do not function properly in Russia.

Mismanagement and abuse of natural capital

Experience over recent years of Russia in transition provides numerous examples of voluntary and involuntary mismanagement of resources and the environment. Russia is a country of tremendous resources and potential where today 'the largest sale in history is going on' (Glinkina 1998). The apportioning of these significant resources occurs under conditions of legal uncertainty, which immediately triggers an outbreak of corruption. According to a recent study of corruption in 85 states, Russia is placed tenth from the bottom, followed only by such countries as Paraguay, Honduras, Tanzania and Nigeria (Fedyanin 1998). Russian natural resources are among the most enticing targets, the value of fossil fuels alone being estimated at $30 trillion (trillion $= 10^{12}$). There are no estimates of the value of forests, water resources, etc. The whole evaluation process is hindered and obstructed since this makes it much easier to privatise resources at significantly lower prices. Most criminal activities become centred on natural resources, because in many cases they are the easiest to develop and to sell, especially abroad.

In 1996–98 the Russian government adopted several acts on the conversion of 'first-group' forests into the category of non-forested lands. First-group forests, according to Russian law, are those with important ecosystem significance and which provide important environmental functions. These acts were prepared by officials from the Federal Forest Service and have been adopted under pressure from stakeholders who were interested in using these lands for business purposes. These lands were often located close to cities and industrial centres, where they could play an especially important environmental role. The total area of these doomed forests is more than 32,000 ha. According to the acts, these forests can be clear-cut and the land can be used for any economic activities not connected with forestry and performing an entirely different environmental function. These acts contradict Russian legislation, which requires ecological expertise at a federal level in such cases. There was no impact assessment analysis performed and the Federal Environmental Committee, which is responsible for ecological expertise, did nothing to prevent these illegal activities.

In 1997 several environmental NGOs initiated public action against this practice. After many fruitless appeals to governmental bodies, more than 50 well-known scientists and NGO activists, with support from the federal Duma (parliament), appealed to the Russian Supreme Court in an action against the acts. On 17 February 1998 the Supreme Court recognised these acts as contradictory to existing Russian legislation and annulled them. However, most of the forests were already cut before this late 'victory' for the environmentalists. Decisions of the Supreme Court are not subject to appeal. Nevertheless, the Forest Services staged a media campaign discrediting the court's decision. This example highlights the existing practice of ignoring environmental legislation, even at federal level, and definitely serves as grounds for pessimism. On the other hand, it also demonstrates that public activity can lead to environmentally sound decisions. It shows that open society institutions are appearing in Russia and may become influential in environmental management.

According to the Russian mass media, a significant portion of extracted gold goes directly onto the black market (estimates range from one-third to one-half for different regions). This means that gold companies do not pay full royalties and, as a result, this highly polluting industry contributes an artificially small amount to the state budget.

Certain criminal bodies focus their activities on illegal forest cutting and export of timber. One of the centres of illegal timber cutting is in the northern Caucasus. The most valuable woods are harvested here—oaks, chestnuts and beeches—and delivered to ports on the Black Sea and sold abroad. The illegal cuts take place almost everywhere in Russia, but in the Caucasus this became a sphere of interest of well-organised crime groups which act in concert with regional governmental services. In such a situation no environmental legislation is fulfilled, and no one appears to care about reforestation (*Forest News* 1998).

A staggering example of mismanagement is the so-called VSM (*Vysokoskorostnye Magistrali*) project on high-speed railways. The project was announced with much press coverage and excitement back in 1991, when it was backed by Yeltsin's decree. The first stage of the project was to build a high-speed railway line between Moscow and St Petersburg, which would allow trains to carry passengers and cargo between these two Russian cities at speeds of over 350 kmh. In the future the line was to be extended to reach the Black Sea. The whole project was described as the start of the rebirth of the Russian economy. State funding was guaranteed, special investment funds were created and work has begun. As usual, no adequate environmental assessment was provided, which is no surprise, since, according to the project, the route was chosen in such a way that a large forest of significant importance for water protection in the Upper Volga area was to be clear-cut on the territory of the Valdai Natural Reserve. The project was so environmentally devastating that it was quite obvious that no ecological expert would ever agree with it. Yet it took more than two years of concerted efforts by the Federal Committee of Environment, Environmental

Committee of the Duma, NGOs and scientific and local communities to literally stop the train. Another presidential decree of late 1998 concluded the saga. The construction started in 1996 and was stopped just recently. During this time state funding—a total of three billion roubles—was channelled to the investment funds and spent on purposes that are now almost impossible to account for. Maximov (1998) claims that the project was environmentally absurd from the very beginning and there is good reason to suspect that the whole affair was masterminded as another extortion scheme. The environmental community in this case seems to have been used as a pawn in the game. The 'management' of this project has been most effective.

Oil and gas were always important export commodities in the USSR. Therefore, oil and gas industries, in addition to access to a valuable resource, also feature a well-established infrastructure for export (oil and gas lines, sea terminals). Since oil and gas have traditionally provided the largest hard-currency profit for the USSR, this piece of the pie was the most keenly sought and was the first to be divided among the newly formed élite. It also became the source of all major fortunes made after the fall of the USSR. Although definitely criminal by nature, the oligarchies that were created and currently control all the oil and gas industries are so closely interwoven into the governmental web that, by admitting that they are criminal, we may as well declare the whole government criminal.

This was proved by the recent scandal of the privatisation of Purneftegaz, a subsidiary of Rosneft, the largest and the richest oil concern in Russia. Purneftegaz was an especially lucrative piece of property because it possessed the most valuable and productive oil fields which contributed up to 60% of Rosneft production. When Rosneft failed to pay its debts last summer (in spite of its huge profits!), its most liquid assets—the Purneftegaz shares—were sold at an auction to four other Russian companies. This is when the scandal broke, because, apparently, the 'wrong' companies had bought Purneftegaz. Prime Minister Primakov, acting on a written order from the President, cancelled the sale. Why would the President get involved in business interactions that were found totally legal by several courts? It has been reported that the firm that lost in the auction, Sibneft, is controlled by B. Berezovsky and R. Abramovich, the latter known as the holder of the accounts of the Yeltsin family (Ukhtomskiy 1998). Environmental management is unlikely to flourish in a climate where stakes are so high and the stakeholders are the President and his family or the like.

Not surprisingly, the oil and gas industries also offer a record of environmental abuse that is hard to match. Following the Komi oil spill in 1994, where, according to various estimates, 14,000–318,000 tonnes of oil were spilled, Russia probably achieved the world record for spilled oil. The abandoned oil and gas fields are so polluted that it will be centuries before anything can possibly grow there, especially in the climatically severe conditions of the tundra. It seems that the environmentally concerned community gave up in their struggle with the oil barons, which is only to be expected since the criminal connections in this field reach to the highest echelons of power.

In a scenario of responsible environmental management, the arrangement would be as follows: if certain oil and gas companies pollute more than the others, because they use a huge amount of national natural capital and are closely controlled by the government, it would be reasonable to expect these companies to pay more to the state budget, to finance reform in other spheres. The fact that this is not the case makes for a popular subject for political discussion on television, but reform remains wishful thinking. It is also clear that any regional or local decisions are totally ineffective with respect to these companies and the environment. In order to define the relationship between these companies and other parts of society, it is necessary to show political will at the highest levels of power, prior to deciding on rules of decentralised regulation of environmental management.

The coal-extraction industry is another criminalised sector. After the powerful miners' strikes in Siberian Kuzbass during summer 1998, the federal government identified that there are more than a hundred criminal organisations that act as middlemen in sales of coal. They pay no money to the coal-extracting enterprises, so miners do not get paid for many months. *Izvestiya*, a well-known newspaper, published a series of articles on this in July–December 1998. Who would dare to suggest the implementation of the polluter pays principle (PPP) in such a situation, or insist on even a minimal environmental restoration programme for this highly polluting industry, when workers are not paid their wages, and the enterprises are on the verge of bankruptcy. It should be emphasised that this whole situation has been well known at a regional level for several years: the governor was well informed, but could not or would not do anything to fix the problem and prevent social unrest. Only with the intervention of the federal power structures and law enforcement units has the situation slowly started to improve.

The criminal sale of Russian natural resources is readily supported at international level. This is perfectly illustrated by the close co-operation between Russian and Japanese criminal structures that control the Far East fisheries (Reznik and Golovnin 1997). Millions of dollars are misappropriated and paid as bribes to local and state officials. Each illegal quota and permit has a price that is paid in cash to inspectors from various local and state organisations. The web of connections, kick-backs, bribes and services links many hierarchical levels in Russia and Japan (Fig. 1) with the only common goal being to extract as many resources and profits as possible while avoiding any responsibility, taxes or fines. Under this arrangement, scientists from the Pacific Institute of Fisheries and Oceanology (TIPRO) also receive their share to keep their eyes shut when necessary and to issue the required permits and quotas.

Any mineral resource and any extracting industry one may care to think of in Russia is probably controlled by the criminal world, which makes sure that the short-term profits are maximised to the highest possible extent, at the expense of taxes, environmental conservation and restoration and social justice. Environmental management in this context turns out to be a fight against crime and the Mafia, something the usual environmental bodies, state and local environmental committees and NGOs are hardly equipped or trained to do.

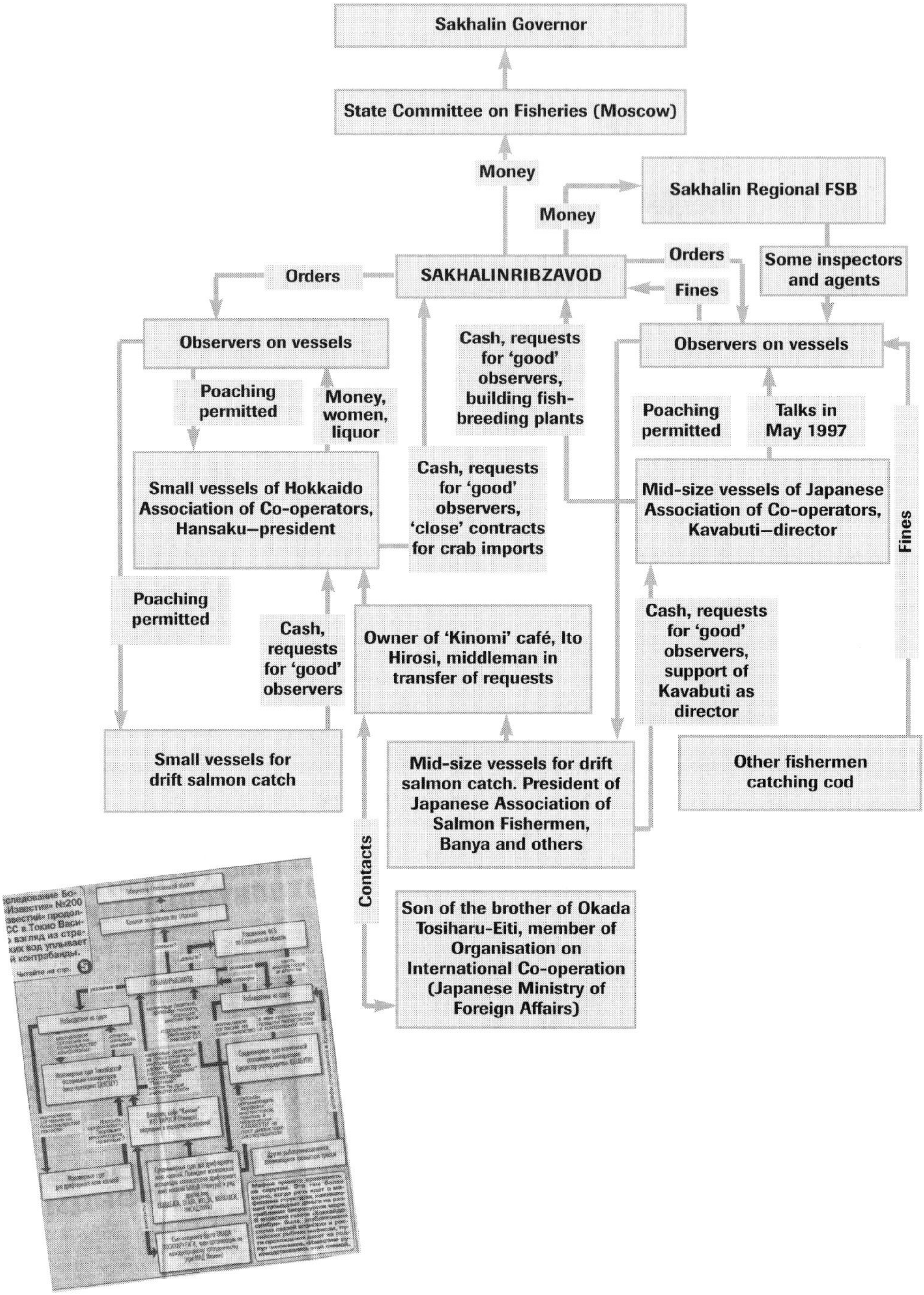

Figure 1: THE MAFIA IS USUALLY COMPARED TO A SPIDER'S WEB; THE DIAGRAM SHOWS THE STRUCTURE OF LINKS AND AGENTS INVOLVED IN ILLEGAL FISHING IN THE PACIFIC.

Source: © *Izvestia* 202 (1998)

Figure 2: WHILE THE PRESIDENT WAS MOSTLY CONCERNED WITH FIGHTING THE GHOSTS OF COMMUNISM IN RUSSIA, VERY LITTLE WAS DONE TO TREAT THE MOST IMPORTANT PROBLEMS OF TODAY, AMONG WHICH CRIMINALISATION AND CORRUPTION ARE PROBABLY THE MOST SERIOUS.

Source: © *Nezavisimaya Gazeta* 4.20-21 (1998)

Uneducated democracy

It should be noted that, formally, Russia could claim to have a democratic constitution, state and society. The constitution provides for free and democratic elections and offers all the necessary freedoms of a democratic state. However, it is apparent that democracy cannot be declared and introduced overnight: it needs a lengthy period of education and assimilation in order to be adopted and understood by society. Otherwise it easily becomes distorted and can compromise its own basic principles.

Democracy in Russia may be fairly described as uneducated and naïve. Even in the most democratic society, if a power vacuum occurs, it is quickly occupied by the structure that is the best organised at the time. The most well-organised structure in Russia used to be the Communist Party (CP). However, it was injured during the period of *glasnost* and *perestroika* and was dealt some severe blows later, delivered by Yeltsin and his entourage. The KGB, which was probably the best-organised substructure within the CP, was entirely dismantled. The next-best-organised structure turned out to be the criminal world with its organisations and hierarchies (Fig. 2).

The criminals managed to adapt to the new democratic conditions probably faster than anybody else. They attempt to seize real governmental and legislative power and very often succeed. The state and local parliaments (Dumas) offer the most desirable positions because of the immunity from prosecution automatically granted to the elected deputies. It is currently estimated that at least 50 deputies in the state Duma have a criminal past.

Probably the most scandalous recent democratic outcome was the result of the mayoral elections in Nizhniy Novgorod, where the criminal record of one of the contenders was known at the time of the election, was widely discussed, and yet nevertheless he won. In this case we are not talking about political crime; the newly elected mayor, Klimentyev, has served his sentence for theft and pornography. A presidential decree was required to declare the elections invalid which, strictly speaking, was not quite democratic.

The Federal Law on Protection of the Environment was adopted in 1992. It gives all Russian citizens the rights to a healthy environment and information about the state of the environment. But ordinary people, especially in remote regions, have no or little experience in exercising their legal rights. Many projects involving natural resource use turn out to be detrimental to the environment no matter whether they were adopted at national, regional or local levels. Very often companies and governmental agencies have presented distorted or simply false information about the consequences of the project.

This uneducated democracy appears to be a very conducive milieu for shadow, illegal and semi-legal structures to gain more control. There seems to be a peculiar correlation between crime, mismanagement of natural capital and effective reform. Goble (1999) observes that political and economic reforms are proving to be more important than location and natural resources in creating favourable conditions for both local businessmen and outside investors.

> Those countries and regions that have carried out such reforms have out-performed those that have not—even when the latter have the edge in resources and other traditional foundations for economic growth. And this gap between the reformers and the non-reformers seems likely to grow in the years ahead. The most dramatic example of the impact of reform on economic performance is provided by an Economist Intelligence Unit survey of business conditions in Russian cities outside Moscow that was published in December. The EIU survey concludes that the six best cities for business in Russia—Nizhnii Novgorod, Samara, Saratov, Yekaterinburg, Perm and Velikii Novgorod—have two things in common: one, their leaders are committed to economic and political reform; and two, they lack the natural resources that many, both inside and outside the region, had expected would be 'Russia's saving grace'.

However, if we bring into the picture the evident interest of criminal groups in natural resources, especially in the mineral ones to which Goble is probably referring, which can be easily extracted and exported requiring relatively little investment, it may well be that the commitment of local leaders and the speed of reform also result from the lack of natural resources. If a region is rich in natural capital, which is easy to extract, it inevitably becomes lucrative for criminals. In a situation of uneducated democracy and lack of appropriate legislation and enforcement mechanisms, criminal groups can easily become dominant in regional governance. They do not have to take office themselves: the story of Klimentyev only proves that it may be much wiser for criminals not to become conspicuous, but instead to control local governments via bribes and threats. With criminal dominance in a region, market reforms are extremely unlikely to move forward. No matter how committed a leader is, he or she will not be allowed to foster a climate of open access to resources and free competition, as this runs counter to the interests of the criminal groups. Any leader attempting such reforms will either be eliminated or become part of the plot.

Recent developments in the Krasnoyarsk Krai offer an interesting case study in this respect. In the summer of 1998, General Lebed was elected governor of the province. It may not be strictly true to describe Lebed as an active proponent of market reform in the Western sense; however, he is unlikely to be susceptible to bribes and corruption. Krasnoyarsk Krai is a resource-rich region. Recently it has been reported (Newsline 1998) that Anatolii Bykov, director of the Krasnoyarsk aluminum plant, warned Lebed that he may well be removed from office because 'Lebed's young and inexperienced team mistreat the local élite.' On 17 December, directors of large plants, factories and coal-mining companies followed Bykov's lead by announcing that Lebed's policies were leading the region towards catastrophe. *Izvestiya* newspaper argued that Lebed must hand power over to the local élite or his government 'will be finished'. It added that gathering enough signatures for an impeachment referendum could be easily accomplished: the uneducated democracy in full swing.

In such a context, any hope of a move towards sustainable, or even stable development, based on extraction of natural resources seems naïve, if not dangerously deluded. This idea has been repeatedly pronounced both by scientists and officials. In the *Proceedings of the NATO Advanced Research Workshop* we read:

> The Lake Baikal Region is extremely rich in natural resources . . . This region possesses an abundance of energy resources . . . That is why the mineral resources here could and should be utilised with a high economic efficiency. Only on this condition can the sustainable development of this territory be ensured (Konnikov *et al.* 1996).

In reality, focusing on resource extraction tends to hinder economic development. Worldwide the economically most advanced nations happen to be the ones that are the least dependent on natural capital. On the other hand, witness the small settlements in eastern Siberia (e.g. Baley in the Chita *oblast* [district]) where many tons of gold have been extracted over many years. Now that the source of natural capital has been depleted, we find these areas in very poor condition, with extremely low (even for Russia) living standards and a catastrophic state of the environment. The easy harvest has been taken and nothing is left behind. The challenge is for other areas of Russia to avoid going the same way.

There is no possibility of environmental management becoming ecosystem management rather than management over resource extraction until effective legal and institutional mechanisms are developed to enforce citizens' rights to information about the state of the environment. With the arrival of *glasnost*, there was much hope that finally the time of free access to information had come. To a certain extent this has indeed happened. Now numerous publications and media reports are available about the poor state of the environment and violations of basic environmental laws and acts. Unfortunately, there is no tradition of prosecution and legal enforcement through courts for these laws. Moreover, there are obvious state- or criminal-imposed limits to the amount of information that can be disclosed.

One fresh example is offered by the widely known Nikitin case. Radioactive waste, nuclear materials and technology is another sphere in which state and local, criminal and citizens' interests clash. Substantial areas of Russia are contaminated by radioactivity from Chernobyl fallout, dumping of spent nuclear fuel from submarines, electric power stations and nuclear weapons, mishandling of nuclear materials in industries and the army. In addition, Russia is currently importing radioactive waste from a number of European countries. Alexander Nikitin, a former Russian army officer has co-operated with the Bellona Foundation and provided valuable data on the contamination of the North Sea from the nuclear submarines stationed there.[1] According to the Russian Minister for Atomic Energy, Yevgeniy Adamov, 'Aleksander Nikitin disclosed state secrets and inflicted colossal damage on our [Russian] national security while preparing the Bellona report.' Nikitin was imprisoned and went on trial. On 29 October 1998, the judge dismissed the indictment against Nikitin in St Petersburg City Court, sending the case back for further investigation; thus the process against Nikitin continues. On 4 February 1999, the Russian Supreme Court considered the case, but, despite the international attention and involvement, it was still not closed and was adjourned for additional investigation. Whatever the final judgement, the case has already lasted for over three years and Nikitin has probably been punished quite severely. Also, an important message has been sent to other environmental activists and citizens.

Can information technology help?

The last example shows that access to information is an extremely important issue for environmental management. One tool that may be useful is the development and implementation of new efficient information technologies. In this context technology should not be viewed as a panacea that can cure all the problems of environmental degradation and resource depletion, but rather as a means of understanding, educating and resolving conflict.

Among other examples of innovative technology, Internet communication seems one of the most promising for the goals of ecosystem management; its advantages for dissemination of information and ecosystem management are probably hard to match (Voinov and Costanza 1999). The consensus-building power of the Internet and the World Wide Web (WWW) has certainly been underestimated. We argue here that there are a number of features that make the Web an exceptionally important tool for watershed management in particular, and for regional management in general. The WWW is:

1 *http://www.bellona.no/e/*

- **Open.** The Internet is one of the most readily available and reliable media providing information across geographical, administrative, social and economic boundaries. It is relatively cheap and can be accessed by all stakeholders in a region and outside of it. Direct access to all the necessary information and, reciprocally, the ability to disseminate the facts of concern to particular stakeholders are important prerequisites of ecosystem management.

- **Interactive.** It is most important for management purposes that the user has the option of interacting with the provider of information and with other stakeholders. With the Internet this can be accomplished either via e-mail or directly through forms that can be filled in on the web pages and transmitted to the server. In this case, information is not only passively received, as with traditional media (radio, press, newsletters, etc.), but it also stimulates direct feedback. Moreover, users can modify the content and format of existing pages by ordering excerpts from databases or providing scenarios for model runs and thus creating their own output to be viewed immediately. They may also submit additional information in response to published requests or as an expression of their own findings and concerns.

- **Fast**. Communications via the Internet are probably the fastest and the most economical, since they do not require any intermediate carriers (as with ordinary mail) or materials (paper or printers, as with faxes). Once the information is updated on the server it becomes immediately available for further use and processing. The feedback in many cases can be handled automatically and be directly channelled to the appropriate web link or interest group.

- **Spatially distributed.** Internet access is offered over telephone lines and therefore covers almost the entire planet. The various nodes on the Internet can correspond and represent the spatially distributed data of different stakeholders on the watershed and outside. Web tools allow information to be linked together; search engines exist to find the necessary information and data. In this way, concerns and awareness can be shared across different geographic localities. This gives a broader picture of the region within the framework of external systems and concerns.

- **Hierarchical.** The hierarchical structure supported by web design allows organisation of data in logical and efficient ways, where various branches of the Web may present specific fields, domains and interest groups. Links on web pages can stitch the whole structure together offering cross-references and alternative views whenever necessary. The watershed hierarchy of subwatersheds and sub-subwatersheds (see Chapter 10) can be easily mirrored on the web with specific groups of pages representing each of the particular levels. The hierarchical structure also offers levels of protection for the information, allowing certain domains to be completely open to all users, others being only read-permitted, and others being accessible only to limited users and interest groups, providing the necessary extent of privacy and discretion.

All the important features and tools to augment and improve ecosystem management seem to be present on the Internet and it becomes a matter of using them efficiently. Interestingly, in Russia, probably because of a relatively high level of computer literacy, web communication is developing rapidly and spreading across the whole country. For example, during the 1991 coup, when the media was blocked and when, amid all the excitement and anxiety, television was broadcasting the Swan Lake ballet, the Internet remained the only reliable source of information about developments.

The development of open institutions is proceeding apace in Russia. More and more NGOs, scientific and professional organisations are trying to become involved in environmental decision-making and in environmental management. The key issue in this respect is access to information about the state of the environment, about real consequences of business and political initiatives. At all levels of the governmental hierarchy, there are always some authorities who may choose to conceal certain information, in spite of citizens' right to know, as declared by federal law. The Internet as an alternative source of information becomes even more important as other sources of mass media are privatised and eventually controlled by the same criminalised groups that already control large sections of industry and trade.

Means of access and involvement become especially important in enforcing personal responsibility of governmental officials for the performance of governmental bodies at all levels. Currently, this responsibility is very 'fuzzy' in Russia and can be best characterised by the term 'collective irresponsibility', inherited from the socialist past. This needs to be replaced by a 'hierarchy of responsibilities' both for decision-making and access to environmental information. Such a hierarchy is a necessary condition for 'education of democracy' in order to provide public control over environmental management. It is also an extremely important factor for the effectiveness of all open society institutions in their influence on governmental services and for future decentralisation of environmental management.

Conclusions

As Polterovich (1998) notes, 'criminal economic structures emerge faster than mechanisms of competitions that could block them. The base of criminal bodies is corruption'. Corruption now is such a significant factor in the Russian economy, that it became one of the foci of basic research in economics (see references in Levin and Tsirik 1998).

Economic decentralisation is more of a favourable than a limiting factor in this process of criminalisation. The resource-rich regions and businesses dealing with natural resources have turned out to be the most criminalised and corrupt. Most of the profits are dispersed; as a result, efficiency remains very low, there is little or no re-investment in production, innovative technologies are ignored (no 'greening of economy'), and production processes remain polluting and environmentally unsound. It distorts the financial flows for environmental management and ultimately leads to total deterioration of ecosystems. Criminal economy has no incentive for reform, therefore a vicious circle is created that has little chance of being broken without strong external influence.

Since criminal organisations often operate at national and international levels, it is hopeless to fight them at a regional or local level, on the basis of decentralised decisions. Effective legal enforcement mechanisms should also be implemented at all levels: local, regional and national. It should be stressed that, at this point, law enforcement seems to be even more important than new legislation. Lawyers from the Ecojuris Institute claim that the necessary legal basis already exists for efficient environmental management (Bezlepkin 1998). The problem lies predominantly in poor enforcement and the lack of tradition and experience of citizens.

Dissemination of information, promotion of environmental education and public awareness become crucial for the preservation and management of natural resources in Russia. These are also important components for the development of democracy and institutions of open society. If the current generation of bureaucrats and managers is already spoiled by corruption and amorality, there is still a chance of educating future generations in the best traditions of sustainability, intergenerational equity and ecological morality. The public needs to become accustomed to direct participation in the decision-making process, and needs to be offered tools and methods to process available information and to learn to make the right decisions based on what they learn.

3 NATIONAL FOCUS

9

Driving Forces and Barriers to the Implementation of Sound Environmental Management in the Andean Region of Latin America

Percy Garcia, Julia Gonzalez and Dixon Thompson

LATIN AMERICAN COUNTRIES and multinational corporations operating there are developing new strategies to protect the natural environment and to compete, as important international markets change and globalise. The incorporation of environmental concerns into the decision-making process is affected by driving forces that create a need and promote change, and by barriers to implementation.

Environmental management can be defined as that dynamic part of the overall management system that sets environmental policies, goals and objectives, selects and implements appropriate means of reaching objectives, and provides feedback on success.

This chapter identifies and assesses a set of driving forces and barriers and provides recommendations to companies doing business in the Andean Region of Latin America.

Driving forces

Twelve driving forces to environmental management were identified: financial institutions, foreign direct investment, investors and insurance, regulatory requirements, government policies, increased public awareness, non-governmental organisations, international agreements, co-operation programmes, international standards, markets, and globalisation (Table 1). The driving forces, which create a need for improved environmental management and promote change, are one tool in a set of environmental management tools (Kirkland and Thompson 1997, 1999).

1.	Financial institutions
2.	Foreign direct investment
3.	Investors and insurers
4.	Regulatory requirements
5.	Government policies
6.	Increased public awareness
7.	Non-governmental organisations
8.	International agreements
9.	Co-operation programmes
10.	International standards
11.	Markets
12.	Globalisation

Table 1: TWELVE DRIVING FORCES

Understanding driving forces is important for three reasons: (i) they are used to convince decision-makers that improved environmental management deserves attention; (ii) the driving forces affect the design and implementation of the environmental management system (EMS); and (iii) they facilitate determination of benefits to be derived from the EMS (Kirkland and Thompson 1999).

The description of driving forces that follows can be used by corporations operating in the Andean Region to determine which factors may be significant in their particular circumstances, so that they can introduce appropriate changes to their EMS. Governments must understand these driving forces to ensure that regulations, practices and policies facilitate appropriate changes in government and the private sector rather than hinder those changes.

There is very little information in the literature specifically about driving forces in Latin America, so a generic list of driving forces identified by Thompson (1997) and Garcia (1998) was used as the basis for designing a literature search and for interviews in Andean Latin America with key informants. Those driving forces have caused change in the implementation of environmental management in North America and Europe and are starting to cause change in Andean Latin America. It is very difficult to quantitatively assess the impact. However, because most of them have a strong international component, which puts them largely beyond the control of individual corporations and governments, they will be difficult to resist.

Financial institutions

Financial institutions such as the World Bank and Inter-American Development Bank have established operational policies incorporating environmental requirements into their lending agendas, based on the assumption that countries and companies with bad environmental performance pose a high financial risk (Schmidheiny and Zorraquin 1996). As environmental sustainability became the theme for environmental management policy-making, the World Bank strengthened and modified its lending policies to address environmental concerns in the international development scheme. Being the lead financial institution for policy advice and appraisal of national investment for socioeconomic development, the World Bank adopted a development strategy similar to Agenda 21 (World Bank Group 1995).

Among the most notable trends in the Bank's active lending portfolio was the increase in projects with primarily environmental objectives, particularly since the Earth Summit in Rio de Janeiro in 1992. Bank-financed environmental projects emphasise:

- Capacity-building for environmental management (i.e. training, staffing, monitoring and policy studies)
- Loans to enterprises and agencies for improved environmental management
- Direct investment in pollution prevention and treatment facilities
- Support for research on new technologies and improved policy design (World Bank Group 1995)

The Green Alliance has published the results of a survey of 26 international banks which signed the Statement by Banks on Environment and Sustainable Development in Rio in 1992.[1] The report identifies initiatives and leading-edge practices (Hill *et al.* 1997).

Foreign direct investment

The increase of foreign direct investment (FDI) in Latin America, as a consequence of globalisation, has stimulated stricter environmental management policies in legislation. Currently, Andean Latin American countries not only recognise the economic gains generated from foreign investment, but also the potential environmental benefits that could result from the implementation of cleaner extraction, production and disposal methods in the major industrial sectors (i.e. manufacturing, oil and gas, mining). Colombia, for instance, brought forward fair and favourable legislation that encourages and protects investment. One of its components emphasised the potential that the mining sector represents for future economic development, intending to re-structure the precious metal mining sub-sector by implementing innovative environmental management practices and technologies (Minerales de Colombia 1998).

In Peru, sectoral reforms have proved to be successful in attracting foreign exploration to the region. Peru was ranked as the first country in the world in terms of mining exploitation expenditures in 1994/95. Further, in January 1998, President Fujimori announced the implementation of the Law on Incentives for Mining Investment (Ley de Incentivos para la Inversión en Minería, D.L. 818). The biggest

1 *http://www.gn.apc.org/gralliance/*

gold-mining investment in Peru in 1998 will be Barrick Gold in the Pierina Mining Project (Flury 1998). Foreign investment, however, is also being channelled into other mining sub-sectors. The Antamina megaproject in Ancash constitutes the biggest investment in copper and zinc (Instituto de Ingenieros de Minas del Peru 1998).

Investors and insurers

Investors and insurance companies are becoming important sources of pressure that influence the implementation of environmental management practices. Investors consider environmental costs and the potential environmental liabilities associated with companies and the way in which these affect share performance (Schmidheiny and Zorraquin 1996). Insurers are incorporating environmental requirements into their coverage policies after paying elevated costs for claims against liabilities for environmental damage in countries such as the United States. Environmental risks are becoming important to insurance policy valuation and the pricing structures of insurance premiums (Schmidheiny 1992).

In Peru, for instance, investment in the oil and gas and mining sectors has stimulated environmental spending. It has been estimated that privatisation of La Pampilla Refinery owned by Perupetro will result in an investment of approximately US$150 million for plant retrofitting purposes. In addition, the new buyers of Lote X, also formerly owned by Perupetro, have committed to invest close to US$100 million to improve production processes and environmental quality at the site (Aquino 1998).

Regulatory requirements

Increasing environmental regulations are forcing companies to change their practices. The risks of failing to comply with these regulations have taken on new meaning in countries where penalties are large and enforcement is effective. Penalties for environmental infraction have even moved beyond civil litigation to criminal sanctions that affect directors, officers and employees throughout the organisation (Epstein 1995).

In their attempt to improve and organise the environmental regulation system for the oil and gas industry, government bodies were created in the early 1990s. For example:

- Ecuador established an environmental division within its Ministry of Energy and Mines, and placed the responsibility for environmental regulation of the petroleum industry in the hands of that office (known as National Directorate of Environmental Management).
- Colombia and Venezuela formed environmental ministries with broad responsibilities, including administration of environmental regulation of the petroleum industry (Arthur D. Little 1996).

Countries in the Andean Region of Latin America are still in the process of developing and implementing regulatory systems. Arthur D. Little (1996) has stated that current environmental regulations in the oil and gas industry in the Andean region of Latin America are characterised by (i) overlapping authority, and (ii) frequent regulatory change.

Government policies

Governments often have policies that are not enshrined in legislation, but which are, nonetheless, goals and objectives that the governments want to meet. Such policies would include:

- National goals for employment
- Economic development
- Health promotion by reducing pollution
- Improved quality of life
- Meeting international agreements

Macroeconomic liberalisation policies are redefining the role of the government in the petroleum and mining sectors, and markets are being deregulated. Increasingly, the private sector is participating in a more competitive environment. These changes in policy development have stimulated growth of environmental management within Andean Latin America; therefore those interested in pursuing ventures in these countries will need to understand growing environmental concerns and increased regulations which affect the feasibility of those ventures (Arthur D. Little 1996).

Increased public awareness

Increased public awareness of environmental issues arose during the 1980s, as a result of spreading knowledge of the negative effects associated with resource-based activities. The Gallup International Institute (1993) published *Health of the Planet*, which surveyed 24 major nations, and was designed to assess environmental and economic development concerns. The main findings were that people are very concerned about air pollution, water pollution, contaminated soil, loss of species, loss of rainforest, global warming, and loss of ozone, regardless of the state of development or economy.

With the diffusion of information, for instance, the Latin American public have learned about the damages left after mining or oil and gas development, if the necessary precautions are not taken and clean-ups carried out. Corporations that learned from the experience and faced strong public concerns about their operations, are now leading better environmental practices. For instance, Shell Prospecting & Development of Peru (SPDP), a subsidiary of Royal Dutch/Shell Group, had carried out an extensive Environmental Impact Assessment programme in the first stage of its operations in Camisea, Peru (see Chapter 21). This approach to sound environmental management practices could be the result of its parent company's operations in Nigeria, where problems attracted international attention.

Non-governmental organisations

NGOs exert pressure on governments to improve environmental quality. In the Andean Region, NGOs are increasingly mobilising against harmful industrial practices and for more responsible resource extraction and processing.

In Ecuador, for instance, in the 1980s, a broad array of local and international environmental groups began to protest against the impacts of oil and gas development in remote areas of the Ecuadorian Amazon. In particular, two oil and gas multinationals, Conoco and Texaco, have received scrutiny from environmental NGOs. Responses against Conoco's development spanned continents and ranged from radical, outright opposition to any drilling to more general concerns regarding the environmental impacts. Among the most active groups were three Ecuadorian environmental groups: Fundación Natura, Acción Ecológica and Cordavi, and two US counterparts: Rainforest Action Network and the Natural Resource Defense Council (Hall and Williams 1993).[2]

Actions against Texaco took the form of a $1.5 billion lawsuit in the federal court of New York in 1993. Through this lawsuit, indigenous and colonist residents accused Texaco of negligence, public and private nuisance, strict liability and trespass. Having received extensive coverage in the Ecuadorian press, the lawsuit has generated enormous interest among Amazonian organisations such as the Federation of Comunas Union of Natives of the Ecuadorian Amazon, Indigenous Organisation of the Cofán Nationality of Ecuador, and Organisation of the Huaorani Nationality of the Ecuadorian Amazon (Kimerling 1996).

International agreements

Examples of international agreements affecting Andean and overall Latin American governments' environmental decision-making include, the Free Trade Area of the Americas (FTAA), the Southern Common Market (Mercosur) Agreement, the Earth Summit and Agenda 21 (Rio 1992), Declaration of Santa Fe de la Sierra, Kyoto Protocol and the Buenos Aires Conference of the Parties.

The FTAA[3] initiated at the First Summit of the Americas in 1994 in Miami and formally negotiated at the Second Summit of the Americas in 1998 in Santiago, Chile, seeks to unite the economies of the Western Hemisphere into a single free-trade arrangement. After the completion of the San José Declaration in 1998 by the trade ministers of the 34 participating democracies, commitments were made to establish the free trade zone by the year 2005. These included commitments to strengthen their national, hemispheric and international efforts to protect the natural environment and achieve sustainable development goals (Inter-American Development Bank *et al.* 1999).

---

2 Their work is described in their websites (Accion Ecológica: *http://habitat.aq.upm.es/bpal/pgu-lac/exp/e010.html*; Cordavi: *http://lanic.utexas.edu/la/region/news/arc/lasnet/1995/0650.html*; Rainforest Action Network: *http://www.ran.org/ran/*; Natural Resources Defense Council: *http://www.nrdc.org/nrdc/*).

3 *http://www.ftaa-alca.org/*

The Mercosur Agreement, signed by the Argentina, Brazil, Paraguay and Uruguay in 1991 to establish the free transit of production goods, services and factors between member states, imposes environmental trading requirements on countries and companies (Andorno 1997). These requirements, apart from forcing participants to strengthen their environmental management practices, could also be used in the development of environmental provisions under the FTAA. As a result, Mercosur has the potential to affect environmental management in the Andean Region. Environmental requirements under Mercosur include: vehicular emissions, pesticides, energy and environment policies, and hazardous materials transportation.

The Earth Summit in 1992 witnessed the signing of two international agreements, the Rio Declaration on Environment and Development and Agenda 21 (Williams and Petesch 1993). By offering policies and programmes to achieve sustainable balance between consumption, population and development, Agenda 21 influenced Latin American countries to incorporate environmental considerations into their industrial activities. With minor exceptions, essentially all countries in Latin America are in the process of ratifying these agreements.

Another important agreement that encourages Latin American nations to improve their environmental management practices is the Declaration of Santa Fe de la Sierra in 1996, by which countries committed themselves to prioritise the adoption of sustainability principles into development schemes.[4] Moreover, the Kyoto Protocol, later ratified at the Fourth Conference of the Parties in Buenos Aires in November 1998, established an action plan that was approved by 160 countries. Argentina became the first developing nation to commit to voluntary emissions reduction (Worldwatch Institute 1998).

In 1997, Canada and Chile carried out negotiations to establish a bilateral agreement much like the North American Free Trade Agreement (NAFTA), which had a environmental parallel accord. The Canada–Chile negotiations included detailed discussions of environmental aspects that would meet the conditions of the environmental parallel accord to NAFTA.[5]

Co-operation programmes

Countries of the Andean Region are part of co-operative agreements with developed nations to strengthen environmental management structures, policies and practices. The following Canadian examples illustrate these efforts at building capacity, especially in education.

The government of Colombia signed the Memorandum of Understanding with the Canadian International Development Agency (CIDA) in 1997 (CERI 1998). This agreement focuses on advice, training and institutional strengthening in the environment, hydrocarbons and mining sectors for a period of five years (CERI 1998). The Peruvian government signed a five-year co-operation project in 1998 with Canada to

4 *http://www.summit-americas.org/*
5 *http://www.infoexport.gc.ca/section4/ agreement-e .asp*

improve the country's environmental policies and practices in the hydrocarbon sector. This project, called the Perú Petroleum Regulatory Assistance Project, is being carried out by the Canadian Institute for Petroleum Industry Development.

A similar agreement with Canada and Peru established an environmental science programme, which has a strong focus on Environmental Impact Assessment, at the University of Ancash, Peru, in partnership with the University of Calgary. The Latin America Energy Organisation (OLADE) and Canada have also signed a co-operation agreement to teach a University of Calgary Masters Degree in Energy and Environment in Quito, Ecuador.

These are just a few Canadian examples of the many international co-operation programmes that are building capacity for environmental management in Latin America. With time, such programmes will provide the necessary skills, knowledge and expertise.

International standards

In 1987 the International Organisation for Standardization (ISO) established the ISO 9000 series of standards for product quality control. After ten years, there were more than 225,000 certificates in 129 countries, an increase of about 40% over 1996. A similar environmental quality standard (ISO 14001) was established on 1 September 1996. By the end of 1997 there were more than 5,000 ISO 14001 certificates in 55 countries—after only 16 months. Given the time and expertise required to gain certification for ISO 14001, it is surprising how rapid the utilisation of the standard has been. Only a few companies in Latin America have been certified for ISO 14001, but this probably reflects the difficulty of meeting international environmental management standards in such a short period of time. The rapid adoption of the ISO 9000 and ISO 14000 series is expected to continue.[6]

Markets

A large number of companies invested in the emerging markets of Asia and Latin America early in the 1990s. The Asia-Pacific region and Pacific Latin America countries represent a market of US$5.5 trillion (trillion = 10^{12}), with a combined population of almost two billion. All of the emerging markets have taken steps to increase market access to foreign competition (Lemaire 1996). If companies of the Andean Region wish to compete internationally and gain new markets, they will have to comply with international market requirements (such as ISO 14001 or the equivalent).

Furthermore, governments in these nations are introducing market-based incentives to achieve sound environmental behaviour through market mechanisms (e.g. charges, taxes, subsidies) and those economic instruments are used in a complementary manner to command-and-control measures in some cases (World Bank 1996a).

---

6 *http://es.epa.gov/partners/iso/iso.html*

Globalisation

Globalisation is a process that introduces similar conditions in all countries around the world. Part of the process is the technical standardisation demanded by telecommunications, international transportation, manufacturing for international trade, and standards for measurements, etc. However, the technology-based global linkages have cultural, social and political consequences which lead to global homogenisation. Globalisation is caused by a combination of factors, including some of the driving forces that create a demand for improved environmental management.

Marshall McLuhan's 'Global Village' (McLuhan and Fiore 1967) is becoming a reality for environmental managers due to factors such as: global environmental problems and the response of the international community; global communications; global markets; international banking and investments; international standards and guidelines; and civil lawsuits for environmental damages that cross national boundaries. While it may be difficult, if not impossible, to quantify the impact of these factors on environmental management in the Andean Region today, these factors will have an impact and will be impossible to ignore (Table 2).

Global environmental problems have led to a long list of international agreements on global warming (Kyoto and Buenos Aires), depletion of the ozone layer (Montreal), hazardous wastes, biodiversity, etc. Many counties have signed these agreements and are in the process of ratifying them, and there is increasing pressure to sign exerted on those who have not.

Media analyst Marshal McLuhan has noted the homogenising effects of communications and trade: 'Any community that wants to expedite and maximize the exchange of goods and services has simply got to homogenize its social life' (McLuhan 1964: 204). The nature of the media—electronic technology—reshapes and restructures patterns of social interdependence. Global communications, especially the Internet and television, are major factors in reducing the world to a global village. Argentina launched a communications satellite in 1967, and groups in Brazil, Panama, Mexico, Peru, Dominican Republic and Guatemala are using the Internet. Although the number of Internet host computers in Latin America was less than 1% of the number in North America (5 per 10,000 population compared to more than 500) the number of Internet host computers in Latin America is increasing at the same rate as in Asia. (Brown *et al.* 1998: 99). Detailed knowledge can be disseminated very rapidly through the Internet without requiring the resources of a major organisation. It is no longer possible for

1.	Global environmental problems
2.	Global communications
3.	Global markets
4.	International banking and investments
5.	International standards and guidelines
6.	Civil lawsuits for environmental damages that cross national boundaries

Table 2: FACTORS CONTRIBUTING TO GLOBALISATION

a major environmental problem to remain hidden because it is in a remote location, whether it be major spills from tailings ponds, or pollution from cyanide or petroleum. The reputation of major multinationals is affected and investors and regulators take notice.

Expanding global markets through international trade and international trade agreements mean that those wanting to export into the wealthiest markets, especially the European Union, must understand and be able to meet the environmental requirements of those markets. Corporations and governments are increasingly requiring suppliers to meet environmental purchasing guidelines. At the regulatory level for example, the take-back legislation that started in Germany and is now on the books in 28 countries, requires that manufactures join and pay fees to a collection organisation, or take their own packaging back (*EM* 1999: 18).

The Japan External Trade Organisation held the second in a series of seminars on international standards in Canada and Japan in March 1999. The seminar discussed advice on increasing investment opportunities, why the ISO 14000 series is considered to be so valuable in Japan, and how registration can improve a company's marketability. There has been no official announcement, but observers of international standards have speculated that this could be interpreted as a move that could lead to a requirement for ISO 14001 registration for trade with Japan.

International standards and guidelines such as the ISO 9000 and ISO 14000 series facilitate trade and improve environmental management. Agenda 21, the Canadian Chemical Producers' Association, and the United Nations Environment Programme (UNEP) Committee on Banking and the Environment urge companies to use the standards of the country of origin as the basis for their operations abroad. Because environmental management systems include a provision for continual improvement, improved systems can be expected in Latin America, as these standards and guidelines are followed (Gleckman and Krut 1997). Davy (1997) provides a realistic perspective on the future for the ISO 14000 series in developing countries. He predicts that, although current global trends tend to push the implementation of international standards such as ISO 14000 in Latin America and other less developed countries, more co-operation and assistance from developed countries, aid agencies, environmental NGOs, and the private sector are required to establish the necessary infrastructure for their implementation.

International investments and the international mechanisms to provide loans, to protect lenders, and to manage the globe's finances can have a greater impact on local economies than domestic circumstances (Myers 1999: 3). International currency speculation, the International Monetary Fund and demand for protection of international investments have been criticised for adverse financial and social impacts in the countries they are supposed to be helping. Beck (1998) predicts that this influence will change because of the Asian Crisis and the G7 discussions about a new regulatory body to regulate global capital flows.

Civil lawsuits for environmental damages caused by companies based in the US have been facilitated by that country's Alien Tort Victims Act. US companies operating chemical plants in India (Union Carbide), or oil fields in the Amazon (Texaco and Chevron), are sued for damages in US courts where US environmental standards would be applied, and US levels of compensation could be awarded. Therefore, some US companies are using US domestic environmental laws as the standards they set internationally. Other multinationals are following similar practices, even if based in countries without legislation similar to the Alien Tort Victims Act.

Globalisation has led to the implementation of reform policies among Latin American countries. These policies assign high priority to the liberalisation and/or privatisation of public utilities to create new saving and investment strategies by introducing incentives to:

- Deregulate the economy
- Open up national economies to foreign trade
- Liberalise domestic financial markets
- Downplay the role of the state, particularly by privatising public corporations, including utilities (Economic Commission for Latin America and the Caribbean 1997)

Experience in the Andean Region and worldwide demonstrate that globalisation is improving environmental management practices in those countries by:

- Stimulating the transfer of cleaner technologies and best management practices
- Forcing markets to demand high-value, natural products
- Shifting environmental management to become self-regulated through the adoption of voluntary codes of practice (Bragd *et al.* 1998)

Barriers

Eight barriers affecting sound environmental management have been identified: socioeconomic factors, national priorities, multiple stakeholders with conflicting interests, absence of clear environmental policies, lack of enforcement, avoidance of the unknown, lack of expertise, and lack of information and communication (Table 3).

The barriers listed were determined by starting with a generic list for North America (Kirkland and Thompson 1997, 1999) and adapting them to the Andean Region through literature reviews and key informant interviews. The list was also analysed and criticised by Garcia (1998) and two classes of graduate students in the University of Calgary Energy and Environment programme at OLADE in Quito. It is important to have some understanding of barriers that might slow or stop corporate activities, in order to make appropriate changes to the environmental management system (EMS), and to review government legislation and policies to reduce or eliminate barriers where appropriate.

Socioeconomic factors

Socioeconomic factors such as uneven distribution of income greatly hinder the implementation of sound environmental management in Andean Latin America. Most

1.	Socioeconomic factors
2.	National priorities
3.	Multiple stakeholders with conflicting interests
4.	Absence of clear environmental policies
5.	Lack of enforcement
6.	Avoidance of the unknown
7.	Lack of expertise
8.	Lack of information and communication

Table 3: EIGHT BARRIERS

Latin American countries are organised into centralised governments; thus, income received from resource extraction practices is not equally distributed between rural and urban areas. In Peru, for instance, the regions of Pasco, Huancavelica and Ilo, which contribute to the national economy by extensive mineral exploitation, do not receive capital to develop and improve environmental practices. In other regions, such as the Ecuadorian Amazon, which produces very significant revenue from petroleum, the same applies.

Consequently, inter-regional development disparities, generally described as centre–periphery inequalities, affect the implementation of sound environmental management in oil and mining activities. The centre, the metropolitan area, is linked to international markets, absorbs and concentrates the most qualified human resources, and controls the flow of information and business opportunities. The periphery, the scene of oil and mining operations, can generally be characterised as having low levels of education and technical training, a weak economic base, low productivity, weak government institutions and non-existent or poor environmental management (Angulo and Chelela 1994).

National priorities

National priorities divert environmental expenditures to the payment for items that take precedence. Governments in the Andean Region, for instance, struggle to strike a balance between conflicting needs (i.e. health, education, housing, poverty, infrastructure, etc.). In doing so, they tend to spend aid funds trying to provide these necessities, often at the expense of environmental expenditures. Health and education, for instance, are given priority over environmental issues, as governments make efforts to improve social conditions, while neglecting environmental factors. However, it should be obvious that it is easier to fight poverty and improve health in a clean, undegraded environment that in a polluted, degraded one.

Another competing expenditure is infrastructure. With a lack of basic infrastructure and the constant threat of natural disasters (i.e. earthquakes, hurricanes, floods and droughts), governments are forced to spend significant amounts of capital to repair damages. With the 1997–98 el Niño climatic phenomenon, affected nations such as Colombia, Ecuador and Peru used funds to reconstruct infrastructure and provide assistance to affected people.

Multiple stakeholders with conflicting interests

The presence of multiple stakeholders with conflicting interests hinders governments from incorporating effective environmental management into their institutional structures. Latin America in general has a diverse mixture of races and cultures divided by social, economic and political differences. These groups are often ideologically fragmented, particularly in countries experiencing political instability. In Colombia, for example, with the civil war that began in 1948 and escalated into the 1990s, society has been so polarised that it has been difficult for the government to establish a more open participatory process regarding environmental concerns. As a result, decisions on the implementation of sound environmental management practices have been merely left to individuals in power.

Absence of clear environmental policies

Andean Latin American countries are in the early stages of defining environmental goals in the form of quality standards. Most countries in the region still do not have standards in place. Furthermore, where such quality standards exist, they are usually general sets of values adopted from the World Health Organisation (WHO), the Food and Agriculture Organisation (FAO) or the US Environmental Protection Agency (EPA). These foreign recommendations are often applied to Andean circumstances without much consideration of the local conditions. Those values can serve as a first approximation but need to be elaborated as more national background information becomes available (World Bank 1996a). Moreover, many of these countries have a number of diverse ecosystems within their borders and it seems appropriate to set different environmental goals for different regions.

Lack of enforcement

Environmental supervision in the Andean Region is carried out either by a central environmental agency (Venezuela), a number of sectoral and regional institutions co-ordinated by a central environmental agency (Chile, Colombia), or a ministry/ secretariat (Peru). A central environmental agency can work satisfactorily (Chile) but in many countries it functions less effectively due to bureaucracy, shortage of technical expertise, and the lack of contact with and understanding of resource-based activities (i.e. oil and gas, mining). This makes environmental enforcement weak and slow. On the other hand, leaving environmental responsibility with a ministry implies a risk of lax control due to conflicts of interest (World Bank 1996a).

In Peru, for instance, the implementation of PAMAs (environmental improvement and management programmes) for energy, mining and electrical projects has not been effective in providing acceptable environmental protection. PAMAs are designed to reduce contamination to maximum permissible levels. A major drawback, however, is that the PAMA regulation is very lenient, allowing for long time-lapses for environmental improvement. In the case of oil and gas, the deadline for companies to improve their environmental quality is seven years, whereas in mining it is five years for activities not including smelting, and up to ten for activities including smelting. In addition, the procedures followed to determine applicable sanctions of fines for contamination are not very consistent (Varillas 1998).

Avoidance of the unknown

There is reluctance among government officials to implement new environmental management practices. This perception is often attributed to factors such as institutional culture. Culture refers to the identifiable set of assumptions, social habits and behaviour traits that characterise a given group of people (Plas 1996: 91). Institutional culture in Latin America has compromised decisions pertaining to environmental management. Government officials in charge of regulating environmental policies often view environmental protection goals as secondary to increased economic development. This mind-set results in the establishment of lenient environmental policies which, instead of promoting compliance to environmental standards, seem to accommodate the interests of resource-based corporations.

Lack of expertise

Factors related to lack of expertise such as inadequate skills and personnel pose great constraints on environmental management in Latin America. Adequate staffing is the backbone of any institution. The availability of educated and trained professionals, with sufficient scientific and management capabilities, is extremely limited in these countries. Individuals working in Latin American public and private sectors often do not have the required skills to solve environmental problems. One of the main reasons for this lack of knowledge is related to the fact that environmental concerns are relatively new issues and the majority of post-secondary academic institutions are only starting to offer environmental education within their curricula.

Lack of information and communication

The implementation of effective environmental management requires large amounts of baseline data on natural conditions. In the Andean Region, information regarding baseline conditions is limited, and extremely scarce in some countries. There is an urgent need for resources and foreign expertise to develop local research capabilities and to obtain national and regional environmental data. Without this information, individuals responsible for setting environmental criteria are unable to develop relevant standards. Absence of communication between government bodies, practitioners and researchers is a common constraint on environmental management. This results from lack of co-ordination and overlapping of function and jurisdiction, and causes delays to environmental permits and licences.

Conclusion

The pressure for improving environmental management in Latin America due to the driving forces is likely to increase. This is in part because the driving forces originate from a broad range of sources, not just one or two points. Further, many of the driving forces are international or have an international component, so they do not come from one particular nation. The driving forces are largely voluntary. Any country can choose not to act and there are no enforceable sanctions. The driving forces are also largely positive. That is, benefits can be obtained by responding effectively to them.

It is important to be realistic about how quickly long-lasting, well-designed changes in environmental management can be achieved. It would be unfortunate if unrealistic expectations for change were not met and that led to a pessimistic outlook. The anticipated changes will require skills and knowledge. The foundations for providing the required expertise are being set in academic institutions throughout Latin America. The achievement of improved environmental management also requires realistic analysis of the benefits to be derived, and the costs that would be incurred if improvements are not made.

The barriers that have been described are largely domestic and, therefore, to some extent under local control. They are manageable in the longer term, particularly if irreversible damage is minimised. Because of the desire for access to resources and opportunities for investment, developing countries are in a strong bargaining position to select those partners for development who assist with capacity-building by providing financial resources, access to advanced technologies and improve the capacity of countries to train and educate their citizens.

Two attitudes or perceptions might be particularly difficult to overcome. The first is the policy that economic development must come first, and then environmental considerations will be introduced. That policy rests on the mistaken assumption that environmental degradation will not affect efforts to improve quality of life in other aspects and that the costs to reverse environmental degradation can be covered, if the degradation can be reversed at all. The second perceptual problem is that good environmental management is expensive. That is only true if the benefits to be derived are not counted. Careful selection of partners for development can help overcome both of these problems.

The driving forces represent strong incentives for change, but the barriers hinder the entire process. Identified barriers, however, could be overcome if Andean countries adopt appropriate strategies that account for:

- Identification of driving forces affecting public and private sectors
- Education and communication on issues pertaining to environmental management
- Design of environmental management practices matching governmental and industrial goals
- Sharing of resources

- Use of established international standards such as the ISO 14000 series
- Selection of partners in development by examining corporate policy strategies with respect to environmental management

10
Environmental Management in Uncertain Economies

*Alexey A. Voinov, Irina P. Glazyrina, Bruno Pavoni and Nadezhda A. Zharova**

ENVIRONMENTAL MANAGEMENT may be conducted in two ways that differ quite significantly.

1. It may be built into the framework of traditional economy and be limited to natural resource management. The management goal in this case is to provide resources to economic development. Concerns about the environment *per se* are secondary and have little weight as long as the resources are supplied in a non-limiting fashion.
2. As an alternative, environmental management may be implemented at a level no less significant than economic management, within the framework of ecological economics paradigms that stress the importance of environmental integrity and ecosystem health as prerequisites of any further economic development. The ecosystem management or watershed management approaches have been formulated along these lines.

Of these two management strategies we are mainly interested in the second, as a more integrated and advanced approach to management of both economic and social development. Ecosystem management embodies the 'greater-ecosystem' concept (Grumbine 1990), which broadens the ecosystem definition beyond its original biological and physical meaning. The fact that ecosystem management is based on the principle of preserving ecosystem integrity while maintaining sustainable benefits for human population (Norton 1992) implies that the decision-making process should be fundamentally restructured in order to take into account all the subsystems

* The authors are very grateful to Dr Tatiana Strizhova, Professor Peter Soderbaum and Professor Vitaliy Shabanov for useful and stimulating discussions.

in their entirety and all the stakeholders with all the diversity of their potentially contradicting interests and concerns. In addition to scientific research and data acquisition by what Slocombe calls 'substantive methods' (Slocombe 1993), there is demand for new 'process methods' that refer to working with people, communities and businesses in describing, planning and managing ecosystems.

Lackey (1998) identifies five general characteristics for the ecosystem management problems:

1. Public and private values and priorities are in dispute, resulting in mutually exclusive decision alternatives.
2. There is political pressure to make rapid and significant changes in public policy.
3. Private and public stakes are high with substantial costs and risks (some irreversible) to some groups.
4. The technical, ecological and sociological facts are highly uncertain.
5. Policy decisions will have effects outside the scope of the problem.

He concludes that 'solving these kinds of problems in a democracy has been likened to asking a pack of four hungry wolves and a sheep to apply democratic principles to deciding what to eat for lunch' (Lackey 1998: 4). The latter remark seems to be even more appropriate to feeble democracies and structurally undeveloped economies and governments as in the Commonwealth of Independent States (CIS). Is there a chance for ecosystem management in uncertain economies and shaky democracies?

The concept of ecosystem management has made its way to the front line of environmental research very much in conjunction with the concerns about sustainability and sustainable development. Sustainability is a systems property and it requires economic concerns to be considered within the framework of available ecological options, and values of the society to be brought into harmony with the carrying capacities of the environment. Is sustainable development possible in today's uncertain economies? What should be done to promote it, and should it be promoted in such conditions?

Watershed analysis and management inherits all the main paradigms of ecosystem management. The watershed management approach has emerged as a holistic and integral method of research, analysis and decision-making at a watershed scale. It certainly implies more than just a regional scale of analysis. The method stresses the need not only to integrate physical and biological factors, but also political and socio-economic processes. The watershed boundary delineates a physical boundary and not a political one, creating the need for methods that allow management and communication between many administrative entities such as towns, counties and states. Clearly, existing administrative and sociogeographic boundaries and institutions are not really designed to take into account both the socioeconomic and the ecological features of systems. Watersheds seemed to be a reasonable alternative to administrative/political boundaries. But then the existing administrative hierarchies need to be supplemented by appropriate institutions that could operate in a flexible way over alternative regional divisions. Although the concept seems to be very appealing, there are, perhaps, just a few examples of successful implementation of this design in the West. Can the uncertain economic conditions contribute to the creation of such institutions and laws? Is there any chance for such developments in the CIS?

These are some of the questions we analyse in this chapter.

Sustainability and renewal

> The great cycle of the ages is renewal (Virgil).

Ever since it has been brought to the centre of socioeconomic and environmental debate by the World Commission on Environment and Development (WCED 1987), the notion of sustainability has generated tremendous interest and an avalanche of publications, even though (or maybe because) it has never found an agreed definition.

Most sustainability definitions originate from the relationship between humans and the resources they use. Wimberly (1993: 1) states that:

> to be sustainable is to provide for food, fiber, and other natural and social resources needed for the survival of a group—such as a national or international society, an economic sector, or residential category—and to provide in a manner that maintains the essential resources for present and future generations.

Norton (1992: 25) argues that

> sustainability is a relationship between dynamic human economic systems and larger, dynamic, but normally slower changing ecological systems, such that human life can continue indefinitely, human individuals can flourish, and human cultures can develop—but also a relationship in which the effects of human activities remain within bounds so as not to destroy the health and integrity of self-organising systems that provide the environmental context for these activities.

Costanza (1992: 240) leans on the systems properties, stressing that 'sustainability . . . implies the system's ability to maintain its structure (organization) and function (vigor) over time in the face of external stress (resilience)'. Solow (1991) says that the system is sustainable as long as the total capital of the system is equal or greater in every next generation. Costanza and Daly (1992) argue that sustainability only occurs when there is no decline in natural capital.

Whatever may be the specifics of different definitions, there is one common component in all of them. The words used may be different, the applications may vary, priorities may differ, but in all cases there is something about maintenance, sustenance, continuity of a certain resource, system, condition, relationship; in all cases there is the goal of keeping something at a certain level, of avoiding decline. Costanza and Patten (1995: 193) formulate this straightforwardly: 'a sustainable system is one which survives or persists'.

However, up till now this kind of behaviour does not seem to be intrinsic to either natural ecological or man-made economic or social systems. Instead of maintaining a certain state or condition, living systems tend to go through a life-cycle. This was observed for ethnic systems by Gumilev (1990). Holling (1986, 1992) generalised this cyclic behaviour for ecological and socioeconomic systems. Thermodynamics of very similar cycles at the cellular level have been documented by Zotin and Zotina (1993). In all cases, the renewal cycle assumes that a system goes through a series of stages, starting from growth, followed by conservation (inertia and homeostasis, in Gumilev's terms), then release (obscurity) and finally renewal.

Sustainability in these terms may be interpreted as the goal of breaking the cycle, of extending a certain stage in the system life pattern. According to different visions of sustainability, it is the growth or the conservation stages that are to be extended, and it is the delay of release and renewal that would be sought. Sustainability assumes extension of existence of a certain system. Renewal assumes the release phase, when the system components are disintegrated and set free to recombine. Therefore the goal of sustainability of a system contradicts with renewal. The phase of release is the end, the collapse of a system *per se*. The released components may recombine to perform again as a similar system but the system itself would be different (Voinov 1998). Renewal allows for readjustment and adaptation. But it is the next hierarchical level that benefits from this adaptation. Renewal in components helps a system to persist. Therefore, for a hierarchical system to extend its existence, to be sustainable, its subsystems need to go through renewal cycles. In this way, death of subsystems contributes to sustainability of the supersystem, providing material and space for re-organisation and adaptation. We would expect more sustainability from a system made of components that are readily dissipated and re-organised, rather than from one made of durable and persistent blocks that have no potential for such change in their organisation.

Therefore, in the development of proper institutions to maintain life-support systems on this planet we certainly need to emphasise the global priorities and first of all test our policies and strategies against the sustainability of the biosphere, rather than the regional or local interests of stakeholders, representing particular localities, communities, districts or countries. Interestingly, in the report *Our Common Future* (WCED 1987), the document that paved the way for the term 'sustainable development' and which actually generated so much attention to the issues of sustainability, we can hardly find any discussion of types of sustainability other than the global one. The whole purpose of the report was focused primarily on designing scenarios of global sustainable development, recognising that the local level offers no solutions to the global problems and, although most of the action is available at the local level, it is the global level that should be of major concern and be the ultimate goal. The original essence of the concept seems to be in the unified vision of the development of this planet as a whole, and it would be a pity for this integrating mission of sustainability to be eventually torn apart and grounded in local declaratively 'self-sufficient' and 'self-centred' efforts. Probably other terminology would be more adequate for the local and regional levels. It could be 'co-evolution' or 'harmonic development' or 'adaptive development', while 'sustainability' should be reserved for the global level, for the biosphere as a whole.

Evolution of sustainability

There are not many regional systems for which sustainability is feasible. Systems in transition in the developing countries or in the CIS are not ready to embrace sustainability because, by definition, they are disposed towards change rather than maintenance; they are either in the release or renewal stages which one would hardly want to sustain, or have just entered the growth stage, when it is still hard to start thinking in terms of stable state economy (Daly 1977) and sustainability. Economic transition assumes wide shifts in social and political institutions. These shifts and adjustments become possible as a result of discontent and rejection of the status quo by the majority of the population, while sustainability is based on social contentment and agreement.

Sustainability is certainly enticing for the developed economic systems, which have reached the conservation phase, and would rather endure this stage for as long as possible. In this case there is a clear goal for maintenance and sustainable development seems to be desirable and realistic. Unfortunately, there is little awareness of the fact that in most cases sustainability can be ensured only by borrowing energy, resources (capital) and adaptive potential from outside of the system, or by decreasing the sustainability of the global system. Sustainability of a subsystem is achieved only at the expense of the supersystem or other subsystems.

Quite ironically, 'sustainability' has been translated into Russian as 'stability', bringing a totally different flavour to the concept. 'Stable' development is mostly understood as continuous economic growth. Apparently, this linguistic twist resolved the controversy between growth and development (Daly 1992; Goodland 1997) entirely in favour of growth. The notion of sustainability has reached the highest echelons of power and became an issue of a 1994 presidential decree on 'stable development'. Again, according to that decree, by the end of 1994 all regions were supposed to produce a *regional* plan of *stable* development for their particular *region*. Naturally it was assumed that such 'sustainable' regional development would result in sustainability at the national level as well (Parfenov 1996).

'Stable development' became a hot issue for wide political speculation, and almost every political party and movement has used 'stable development' in its documents and propaganda, in most cases its interpretation having little or nothing to do with the original concept and its goals. (See a review of how sustainability is interpreted by different parties and leaders in Rosenberg *et al*. 1998.) In some aspects, the goal of sustainability seems to be close to the goal of communism: both require radical changes in human moral and behaviour patterns, both assume concerted efforts for the whole world or at least over substantial territories, both are theoretically very desirable and beneficial. However, both currently seem equally unrealistic and Utopian.

People tend to define sustainability in the ways that suit their particular applications, and often use the term with no explicit evidence and recognition of the exact meaning being implied. Just like biodiversity (Ghilarov 1996), sustainability became more of a political issue than a scientifically supported concept. This only proves that sustainability can be a good buzz-word, but it can hardly become an ecologically and environmentally useful concept, especially in the local understanding that currently prevails. It is certainly inappropriate for systems undergoing rapid transformation, such as in Russia or other developing countries. There it quickly becomes skewed and misinterpreted to suit the short-term needs of groups, regions, parties or individuals. Russia at this time needs renewal, rather than sustainability.

It should be also noted that Russia has great potential for becoming a part of a truly sustainable world. The stock of natural resources is immense and, if managed properly, it can greatly contribute to the world sustainable order. The population is educated and the achievements of science and technology are matchlessly high for the level of economic development of the country. There are still many territories that are ecologically healthy and can provide important biosphere functions. Besides, Russian philosophical thought offers a lot of ideas that readily contribute to the sustainability concept (Glazyrina and Glazyrin 1997), creating an excellent background for the public to adopt the sustainability paradigms.

The concept of sustainable development may be related to the idea of 'noosphere' which was developed by Vernadsky (1945) in the 1930s. Similar concepts have been studied by Teilhard de Chardin (1927). The noosphere assumes a new stage in the development of the biosphere, when human intellect becomes a major driving force in the biosphere. This development goes on along with a rise of new institutions, 'which adjust the co-evolution and rules of interaction between them to other governmental and public bodies' (Gofman and Ryumina 1994). The way to sustainable development is a purposeful process of creation and improvement of the hierarchical structure, which consists not only of institutions but also of 'tools of interaction' between nature and society. The tools of environmental management should play an important part in this 'co-evolution structure'.

The noosphere creation extends the boundaries of scientific activities *per se*. Concrete sciences study the laws of nature and societies. According to the Russian philosopher N. Berdyaev (1916), they are included in the 'kingdom of necessity', which is determined by these laws. Intellectual efforts in search of new ways for the development of mankind must break away from these limits and restrictions. The 'scientific objectivity', which is indifferent with respect to good and evil, is no longer to be of prime importance. Values, as well as personal and social responsibilities, become prioritised. This does not preclude the significance of scientific knowledge, which is still a necessary component of human creativity in the process of the noosphere development. Yet, being necessary, it should no longer be considered sufficient. Berdyaev's vision was that of a new creative epoch, when the main goal of human intellectual work will not be the search for new tools and methods, but rather it will be focused on the creation of a 'new heaven and new earth' (Revelations 21.1).

Interestingly, this original philosophical thought has already found support and some forms of implementation in Russia. One trend towards sustainability that is worth mentioning is found in a community not far from Minusinsk (Turovskiy 1998). On a voluntary basis, people moved to villages and started a new life based on local organic farming, production and trade within the community. There is no crime in the community, and health standards and life expectancy are steadily growing. People were driven by the teachings of Vissarion, whose vision of the future is very reminiscent of the sustainability concept. There are currently more than 2,000 households in the community and it is still growing. It should be noted that faith

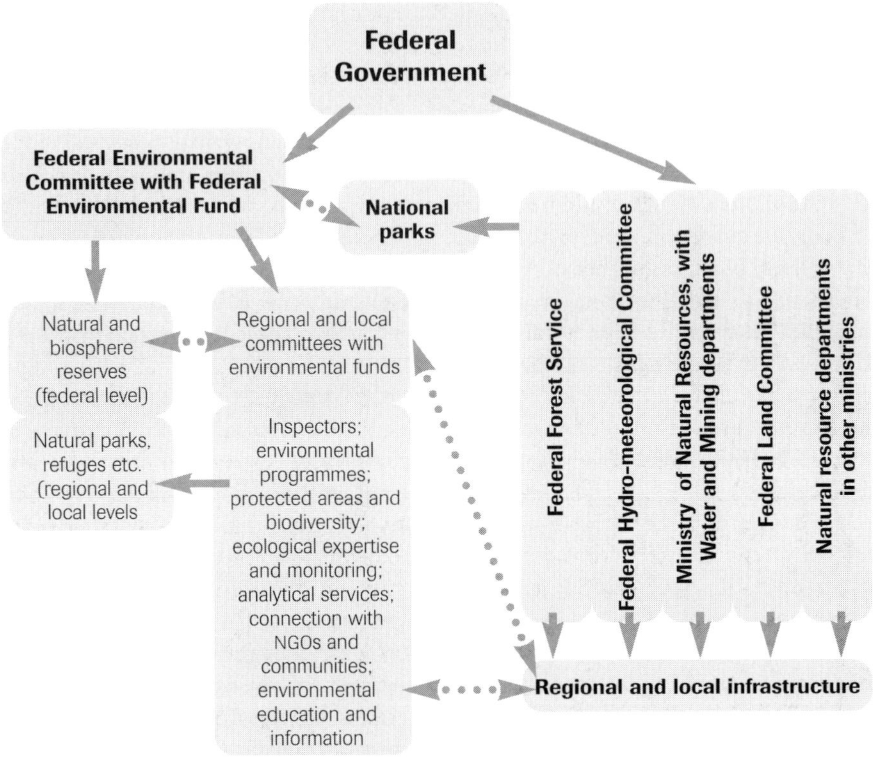

Solid lines indicate subordination; dotted lines show interaction and co-ordination

Figure 1: GENERAL STRUCTURE OF ENVIRONMENTAL MANAGEMENT INSTITUTIONS IN RUSSIA

played an important role in bringing people to this lifestyle. Faith seems to be an important component of all Utopias, if they are to be realised.

Systems analysis of environmental management

Applying some of the principles of systems analysis can help in understanding the peculiarities of the environmental management process in the CIS. Systems analysis requires that we identify the system we are to study, the main connections between its elements, the processes and feedback that regulate these connections, and the internal and external controls that may regulate these processes. The existing structure of environmental management in Russia (Fig. 1) is fairly complex and cumbersome. In addition to the federal–local contradictions, there are also several federal bodies related to management of particular natural resources that often cannot co-ordinate their decisions at the federal level. Since these federal bodies have their own local hierarchies attached, the federal dispute inevitably translates into additional uncertainty at the local level. Parallel to the decision-making hierarchy, there is also a hierarchy of environmental funds which is well described in an OECD report (OECD 1998). The two are not necessarily co-ordinated, so that many management decisions are made with inadequate or no funding provided.

The systems hierarchy for environmental management is not well defined. One possible approach is to build management mechanisms on the watershed principle. This has been advocated in numerous studies (Perciasepe 1994; Montgomery *et al.* 1995). Clearly, there are a number of advantages in this approach. The system boundaries associated with a watershed approach are objective. Instead of being the result of some historical, subjective, often unfair, voluntary or contradictory process, they are totally based on certain geographical characteristics such as relief, which is difficult to change and makes little sense to dispute. In this sense, a watershed is a perfect geographic unit around which to build consensus among the multitude of administrative, legal and public bodies located within. The flow of water serves as an indicator of the relief and landscape characteristics, on the one hand, and as an integrator of many of the processes occurring within the watershed, on the other. The watershed approach is not supposed to replace existing borders and regions, but rather it offers a superadministrative viewpoint to exercise consensus across economic, social and administrative bodies.

Well-defined boundaries are an important feature of a management object. A hierarchical context is another crucial component of successful management schemes. The implied hierarchical structure of superwatersheds and subwatersheds is instrumental for upgrading and downgrading, zooming in and out, changing resolution, depending on the type and scale of the managerial problems to be resolved. This hierarchical approach adds flexibility to management, breaking the usual rigid connection between policy and scale. Whereas in most cases the scale becomes driven by the policy problem, and it is usually unclear who should formulate the policy question and over what scale, with the hierarchy provided by the watershed approach the scale of the targeted management object becomes less crucial, as long as it is presented as an element of the whole hierarchical structure. The smaller watersheds are embedded into the larger ones, and various policies formulated can be treated at the appropriate level.

This was well understood in the USSR as early as the end of the 1980s, when work was started on the River Basin Agreements for some major watersheds in Central Russia, such as the Oka and the Volga rivers. In 1992 the 'Agreement on Joint Use and Protection of Water Resources in the Oka Basin' (Oka Watershed Council 1992) was drafted and was supposed to be signed by all the interested stakeholders, which included representatives from all 17 administrative regions on the Oka watershed, the Federal Ministry of Ecology and Natural Resources and the Moscow–Oka Basin Water Resources Union. The agreement included important provisions on co-ordinated monitoring of water quality and quantity, and decided on quotas of water consumption, use and pollution. It was based on the polluter pays principle and decided on the funding mechanism for environmental protection that was to be shared between all the stakeholders involved.

It was realised at that time that the watershed approach was not supported by appropriate legal and governmental institutions and a first priority was to develop appropriate legal and institutional support. However, at this stage, the process already stalled because of a lack of co-ordination between the regional, local and state levels. Instead of being viewed as a compromise or an alternative to the existing territorial divisions, which are already contradictory on issues of environmental management, the watershed approach was repulsed by the state level, where there were too many concerns about loss of control over regions, and by the local level, which was afraid of too much control from the top. In addition to that, the dissolution of the Moscow parliament (Duma) and the shelling of its building in 1993 brought this work to a complete halt.

During 1998 the Federal State Duma failed to work on almost any environmental laws. The only exception was the 'Law about Lake Baikal Preservation'. This was also one of the first attempts to establish environmental management based on the watershed approach. The early draft of this law was initiated in 1994 by regional administrations, scientific and public environmental groups from territories that belong to the Lake Baikal basin. Originally, the concept of this law was based on the ecosystem approach, expressed in the principle of responsibility for the integrity of the Lake Baikal ecosystem. It contained a proposal to create an institutional structure in order to achieve this goal and the mechanism of financial support. However, during the long procedure of discussion it had lost many of its provisions. The dramatic history of this law highlights the fierce resistance of central authorities to creation of any power-sharing mechanism. When, after four years of debates, the final (largely cut and imperfect) version was finally adopted by the Duma, the President simply vetoed the law at the end of 1998. Lack of desire to develop appropriate mechanisms for decentralisation of natural resource management seems to be the main reason for this decision.

Therefore we see that the boundaries and the hierarchical structure of the management system remains quite uncertain. The uncertainty in the division of power between the local and state levels results in undecided management hierarchies, which are hard to co-ordinate. These problems cannot be resolved locally, because they involve much larger scales than the local ones, and there is no desire to resolve them at the state level, which cannot decide on the power-sharing mechanisms.

If we look at the elements of the management system, we may observe similar disagreements between the local and state levels. Even though it has been reported that there is no direct correlation between property rights and success of resource management (Smith and Voinov 1996), it is obviously crucial that the property rights are at least defined and enforced. Unfortunately, in the CIS, property rights on natural resources (natural capital) are not quite established or legally supported. The federal state is the owner of almost all natural resources (this is described in a few laws adopted in 1992–97): forest, mine deposits, and main water resources all belong to the state. However, there are almost no efficient mechanisms to manage these resources according to the interests of society in a decentralised economy. Besides, for such a significant resource as agricultural land, the definition of property rights is not complete. The Duma failed to adopt a new land code over the last three years, the focal point of disagreement being the privately owned land.

A state owner is significantly different in its behaviour from private owners. It does not necessarily aim at maximising such objective functions as utility, if it represents consumers' interests, or profit, if it acts as a producer. The state is not very sensitive to changing economic conditions represented by production functions and marginal abatement costs for pollution. Privatisation of natural resources is often considered as a promising approach for effective management. Private companies are more sensitive to economic incentives than are public bodies. However, Russian experience in the privatisation of enterprises gives good reason to be extremely cautious in the privatisation of natural resources. The majority of new owners ('in the first generation') seem to be much more concerned about their personal accounts in banks rather than the performance of plants and factories they own. They attempt to extract all liquid resources from their own enterprises to add to their personal short-term income. Artificial bankruptcy is a common method used, stimulated by imperfect legislation and corruption of civil servants. The main reasons for such behaviour are the uncertain future ('they will come back . . .'), lack of a tradition of private ownership ('uneducated ownership') and weak government. Foreign owners turn out to be very much the same. Since the risk of investments in uncertain economies and under political instability is always higher, they prefer short-term bargains to long-term responsible activity. Such ownership leads to depletion of natural resources, deterioration of the environment and irreversible changes in landscape and biological diversity. This is a strong argument against the rapid privatisation of natural stock.

Another important attribute of the environmental management structure is the access to natural resources and environmental goods and services. One cannot expect economic instruments to be efficient if access to scarce natural goods and services is not controlled within the framework of social and regulatory control. Russia has inherited a tradition of centralised distribution of goods. It is still not uncommon at present when even financial resources from the state budget are allocated to certain commercial bodies with no competition involved. This is done in spite of the President's decree (Yeltsin 1997). The tradition of centralised distribution has deep roots, which are very hard to change. The market economy needs to be extended to provide for competitive access to natural resources. This is a necessary condition for the introduction of economic tools into environmental management. It is especially important for goods in common property, because as Godard (1998) notes, the so-called 'tragedy of the commons' is simply a 'tragedy of free access'.

Under these conditions and peculiarities of the Russian transitional economy, when the market hardly exists at all, an immediate introduction of economic instruments for environmental management seems to be quite inappropriate. On the other hand, it makes little sense to wait for the full development of market economy since there are some essential opportunities offered by economic transition itself. 'Mixed' forms of regulatory systems which combine administrative approaches with economic tools and 'third-generation' instruments (dialogue, consultation, persuasion, covenants, voluntary agreements) might be more appropriate. However, incentive compatibility of regulatory rules and institutional regimes has critical importance for the cost-effectiveness of policies (Godard 1998).

To become an effective owner, the state needs a comprehensive system of regulation, which contains both economic and institutional mechanisms at federal, regional and local levels. At this stage of economic transition, the most urgent need is to solve a whole series of legal problems. First of all, the institutional instruments of state property rights need to be legally stipulated and enforcement mechanisms need to be introduced. Second, rules of law must be established, which can guarantee access to scarce natural goods and services within a free competitive market.

Both of these measures can be introduced only at the federal level and on a centrally based approach. Early decentralisation is most likely to result in regional and local resource oligarchies. We can observe this process clearly in today's Russia. Local authorities are very often personally interested to benefit from natural resource use and are responsible for biased allocation and distorted prices for natural resources and taxes for pollution. The era of decentralised decision-making in environmental management can begin only after these two crucial steps are accomplished.

We can observe that the system of environmental management does not seem to function properly in today's Russia. The spatial organisation mostly follows traditional administrative divisions and can hardly cope with the challenges of the ecosystem management approach. The elements of the system are poorly co-ordinated and the management hierarchy is not enforced.

Conclusion

Most of the Western recipes for environmental management are designed for decentralised market economies and democratic societies with comparatively strong and accepted enforcement of regulatory control. How can they be applied to Russia and the CIS? The economy in Russia has by now certainly been decentralised. However, it is far from being a market economy. Consider some of the main features of a market economy, according to Godard (1998):

- 'Property rights on scarce goods are strictly defined and legally enforced by the rules of the law.' As we have shown above, this is certainly not so in Russia. Some property rights are not defined at all (agricultural land in Russia), law enforcement is weak and easily overridden by criminal methods.
- 'Each agent is given the opportunity to fully exploit his own property rights.' In Russia even the state often cannot exercise its rights, because of inadequate legislation, corruption and lack of responsibility.
- 'Each agent, at the same time, strictly respects the property rights of others.' This is not the case, for reasons similar to those above.
- 'Economic agents aim to maximise an objective function.' In Russia the only function that seems to be maximised is the personal profit of the executive, which seems to be quite subjective. Even when the economic agent is a

company or the state, the executive that represents it is primarily concerned with his or her private profit, potentially at the expense of the body represented.

With certain modifications, the same applies to most of the other CIS countries. In some cases, for example in Belorussia, there are little or even no claims for a market economy. In other cases, such as in the Ukraine or Kazakhstan, there is considerable rhetoric about the introduction of elements of market economy. However, none of the above principles is implemented, and the economies are driven by informal personal relations ('crony capitalism' in terms of G. Soros), rather than free competition and rule of law. The conclusion is clear: there is very little evidence of a market economy in the CIS. Orientation on Western types of legislation, which were supposed to create new efficient market institutes, failed in Russia (Polterovich 1998) and in other CIS countries.

Accordingly, it makes little sense for the CIS to try to apply the environmental management concepts that have been designed for market economies. The economic uncertainty creates a vacuum of power, which contributes to environmental abuse and hinders effective management. In these conditions, any definite choice of the development pathway, no matter which one, would be better for environmental management, than no choice at all. The economic agents that benefit most from this uncertainty are the criminal elements in association with corrupt governmental officials (see Chapter 8). Sustainable development, ecosystem management and environmental stewardship can hardly become priorities under economic turmoil and rapid degradation of living standards. In theory, there are chances that mechanisms of ecosystem management can be effectively built into the structure of the newly emerging economies and democracies. In this respect, there may be certain benefits in rebuilding the economy and the society at a time of increasing environmental awareness and concern worldwide. However, there is yet very little indication that this integration between ecology and economy can indeed happen in practice in one of the less-developed countries.

The success of ecosystem management will very much depend on dissemination of information, promotion of environmental education and public awareness. It becomes clear that fast 'Westernisation' can hardly be the solution to economic turmoil in the CIS, and that the path to genuine democracy and social welfare is a rather long and difficult one, requiring patience and responsibility from authorities, citizens and communities. 'Society as a whole appears to be involved in a cooperative learning process concerned with the problem faced' (Soderbaum 1998). It well might be that some innovative yet unknown management concepts and paradigms would be found on the way. In any case, it is already clear that promotion of transparent policies and public discussions as part of economic and environmental decision-making are more important than the rapid privatisation of natural resources and decentralisation of environmental management.

11

Just Green Marketing?

State, Business and Environmental Management in Egypt*

Jeannie Sowers

MANY ADVOCATES of market reform expected that economic liberalisation in developing countries would also yield environmental benefits. Until recently, the International Monetary Fund (IMF) and World Bank considered more efficient economies to be the greatest contribution developing countries could make to improving local environments. The expectation that all good things might go together, that economic reform would make environmental improvements likely, was also an attempt to address the seemingly intractable problem of widespread non-compliance with formal environmental laws. Despite extensive legislation regarding such issues as pollution, public health and occupational safety, the gap between laws and practice was surreally apparent in most developing countries.

The economic logic was and is compelling. At the firm level, privatisation was to result in investments in newer, cleaner technologies, thereby reducing pollution loads. At the sectoral level, marketisation was expected to reallocate resources out of unproductive and often environmentally wasteful sectors into more economically productive ones. At the level of the state, market reforms should allow the state to divest itself of production functions, making resources available to perform supervisory and regulatory tasks. The inefficient former Soviet economies and their attendant environmental problems, more fully revealed after the 1989 democratic transitions, added fuel to the idea that reforming economies would reform patterns of environmental degradation.

* This research was supported by the Institute for the Study of World Politics Dissertation Fellowship and the Center for International Studies, Princeton University, USA. I am very grateful to all those in Egypt who facilitated this research through their generous gifts of time and information.

Market reforms in many developing countries, however, have not produced the expected environmental benefits. More precisely, the process of marketisation was shaped by several factors which received inadequate consideration from the more strident market reformers. The first of these was the continued dominance of the state apparatus in a variety of economic activities, often maintained by incumbent regimes for strategic and political reasons. The second, related, factor was the importance of formal and informal networks between state agencies and powerful economic actors. These ties restricted the growth of competitive markets and mediated the impacts of global trends. Third, market reforms did not require substantive political reforms, and in many countries economic liberalisation accompanied political 'deliberalisation', as limited civil freedoms were further circumscribed. Political stagnation or regression meant few opportunities for publicly pressured environmental reforms. These patterns—which in many developing countries might be crudely summarised as a combination of state capitalism, persisting authoritarian political relations, and the remaining structures of centralised planning—meant that the links between market efficiency and environmental accountability were more problematic than often acknowledged.

This is not to say that continuing state-led industrialisation was either preferable or feasible for most countries. But all too often the particular interests of regimes and their allies were overlooked in favour of homogenised adjustment recipes that worked only under certain conditions. As argued by Hellman (1998), based on the Eastern European and Russian experiences, the more the benefits of economic reform were concentrated in the hands of a few, and the more these élites were insulated from electoral accountability, the more the 'winners' of economic reform had the economic and political clout to block further reform in areas that threatened their lucrative streams of income. These income streams were often concentrated in short-term speculative investments and boom-and-bust-style developments.

For countries facing the collapse of state structures, entrenched political–economic élites, or emerging new strongmen, the environmental implications have been sobering. At the firm level, romancing private investors often meant glossing over private-sector pollution, and, without an established regulatory presence, private-sector companies had little incentive to incorporate environmental considerations if and when restructuring. Sectorally, investments often focused on short-term profits or extraction rather than long-term productive capacity of natural resources. Economic activities that exhibited environmental entrepreneurship, such as adopting innovative technologies, pursuing low-impact activities, or acquiring environmental management systems, often had little place in tumultuous, speculative and uncertain markets. Finally, continued political exclusion of the public has meant that national environmental priorities continue to be set by élite groups in many states. This suggests that the idea that economic efficiency could be elided with environmental quality emerged from contexts where the politically engaged public had already set limits to local environmental degradation.

Market and state in Egypt

Like many other regimes that married state controls over the economy with authoritarianism, the Egyptian regime tried to embrace market liberalisation without jeopardising its own stability. Market liberalisation, initiated by President Sadat in 1974, was thus partial, gradual and selectively contained. Consequently, the country was relatively insulated from both the large influxes of foreign direct investment and the financial turmoil that recently engulfed many emerging markets. As state controls were lifted, well-connected businessmen faced fewer restrictions in extorting direct and indirect subsidies from the state (Sadowski 1991). By the time President Mubarak entered office, the image of businessman and state bureaucrat colluding at public expense had become the popular understanding of Sadat's *infitah* ('opening') policies.[1] As the state accelerated its reforms in the past several years, private-sector actors have become more numerous and diversified, although the most influential remain closely tied to the regime. Both the lower classes and the so-called 'state bourgeoisie' created by state-led industrialisation have been marginalised, while élite networks have been reshaped to accommodate a re-emergent private sector with many public-sector connections.

In many ways, these state–market relations were a variation on an older theme in Egyptian history. Nasser's policies in the 1960s did not destroy an earlier competitive market system, but rather nationalised colonial-era 'circles of collusion' between local business conglomerates, international capital and the colonial state (Vitalis 1995). The shift to import-substituting industrialisation, concentrated in basic industrial and strategic sectors, occurred in already oligopolistic markets in such commodities as fertilisers, cement and construction.

This chapter suggests that the kind of partial marketisation pursued thus far has improved the environmental performance of some firms but that these gains have thus far been outweighed by several countervailing trends. While a few dominant firms selectively employed corporate environmental strategies, the majority of their activities were unregulated, protected from competition by their political connections to the regime and Egypt's relative insularity from international markets. New and smaller firms, often more likely to be at the cutting edge of employing, creating or diffusing environmentally friendly models, were limited in their access to credit, policy-making and state-sponsored projects. The state continued to channel large investments into projects that are statutorily exempt from Environmental Impact Assessments. Finally, the regime's policy of political 'deliberalisation' over the last decade has further limited the ability of civil society to engage the state on issues of public concern. Thus, some of the most pressing environmental problems in Egypt, about which there is considerable public awareness, remain largely unaddressed, while a few with much less relevance to the needs of most Egyptians are pursued vigorously.

---

1 Although Sadowski focuses primarily on the agricultural sector, his conclusions about endemic 'crony capitalism' apply to the Egyptian political economy as a whole.

Environmental entrepreneurs?

While discussion of environmental issues emerged among small circles of Egyptian scientists in the early 1970s, it was only in the 1990s that a few Egyptian companies began to see possibilities in the environmental sector. This prior lack of interest was well founded. With the most polluting enterprises owned by the state, no enforcement of environmental regulations, few institutionalised mechanisms for public participation, and little international market competition, there was little pressure for environmental improvements and consequently little demand for environmental services.

Several factors, however, began to change the calculation of corporate interests in the 1990s. An influx of donor funding specifically for environmental projects raised the profile of environmental investments and issues (Al-Baradei 1998). The expanding presence of multinationals, particularly in infrastructure projects, also alerted their Egyptian counterparts to external trends in environmental accountability. Some international contracting and construction firms began to require that domestic subcontractors and consortium partners have an environmental management system. For instance, a representative of Osman Ahmed Osman's Arab Contractors, the largest contracting company in Egypt and the recipient of the lion's share of all government contracts, complained that the company was sometimes excluded from bidding on consortium projects because it did not have any environmental management system.[2]

Lastly, and perhaps most influentially, although few formal preparations have been made to comply with Egypt's signing of the GATT agreements, Egyptian exporters were concerned with the stricter environmental requirements of the European Union. Some attempted to obtain ISO 9000 series certifications in the belief that these will be required for entry to developed markets. In the process, awareness of the 14000 series on environmental management also increased. These certifications sometimes served another purpose as well: to counter popular concern about industrial hazards. For example, the Egyptian Environmental Affairs Agency and Alexandria Carbon Black, a subsidiary of Union Carbide managed by the India-based Birla Group, often cited the company's ISO 14000 certification to the media to downplay pollution-related petitions filed by small farmers cultivating nearby plots. Several cement factories initiated the process as well, as their dust emissions provide perhaps the most visible air pollution target in urbanised areas.

In addition to market changes, environmental regulatory pressures were increasingly publicised in the second half of the decade. The Egyptian Environmental Affairs Agency announced in 1998 that it would begin to implement some provisions of the 1994 Law #4 for the Environment through several donor-funded projects. Although the agency had a restricted legal mandate (under Egyptian law the agency had only a co-ordinating status with other agencies), publicising these projects prompted some

2 Interview with Dr Abdou Islam, head and sole employee of the Arab Contractors Environmental Division, 15 June 1998.

response among businessmen since the agency administered donor funds for industrial restructuring and also had the authority to close plants temporarily in co-operation with local government authorities.

The first project asked companies to voluntarily gather information on pollution loads and prepare 'action plans' which would help bring them into compliance with the law. In exchange, participating firms would receive an extension of time before they would have to fully comply with the law. Although the Egyptian Cabinet later refused such extensions, removing the incentive to complete action plans, several hundred firms had completed them before extension approvals were suspended. The second regulatory initiative attempted to impose some conditions on development near protected parks and coral reefs. Despite often inadequate impact assessments and the fact that no development was halted completely, some proposals were modified to be less destructive.[3] In a few cases, investors were taken to court for violations, although the penalties levied were only symbolic.

Aside from the limited scope of these regulatory and market changes, the companies that positioned themselves for environmental business opportunities and environmentally based marketing were often the largest and most powerful in Egypt. In other words, corporate environmentalism was a luxury they could afford, one that could be selectively employed for international and donor audiences but which often had little impact on their routine activities. There were exceptions to this, among businessmen convinced of the economic value of pollution prevention, who found that simple investments generated considerable savings in terms of water and power consumption. However, the most prominent companies fit the pattern described above.

For instance, ORASCOM, a large private contracting and construction company, marketed one of its Red Sea luxury developments as environmentally friendly. In addition to formal negotiation of approval for the project's marina with the Environmental Affairs Agency's Protectorates Department (although no formal EIA was submitted), the management also brought *zabaleen*, people who traditionally collect, sort and recycle Cairo's rubbish, to the development as a more environmentally responsible way of coping with solid waste problems. While this development was arguably more responsible than others in the area, this laudable action did not translate into environmental management practices for the variety of other economic activities undertaken by the family-held conglomerate. ORASCOM, however, acquired a reputation as environmentally responsible, valuable in this case because of its overseas activities, contracts with international firms and ability to receive loans from such institutions as the International Finance Corporation of the World Bank.

The catalytic converter coup

The introduction of catalytic converters to the Egyptian market revealed even more clearly how corporate environmentalism derived from, and reinforced, the position

3 Although the actual numbers of investment projects in the Gulf of Aqaba exceeded even the targets set by the Ministry of Tourism, these targets were revised upwards rather than slow the pace of coastal development (EEAA and EU Delegation 1998).

of influential firms within the private and public sector. With the introduction of unleaded petrol to the Egyptian market in 1997, it became possible to require the use of catalytic converters on domestically assembled and imported cars. As the Egyptian automobile fleet grew by 13% between 1994 and 1997 alone, it represented an increasingly important market (Fiana & Partners 1999). The issue of converters was first publicly raised at a workshop sponsored by the 'Association of Enterprises for Environmental Conservation', a semi-governmental forum whose members were a variety of public and private Egyptian companies. In practice, the principal financial sponsor was Osman's Arab Contractors.[4]

In 1998, with no further public discussion and no legislative consideration of the issue, the Ministry of Industry issued a decree requiring the use of converters in all imported and domestically assembled cars. At the time, only the Osman Group, the private wing of the Osman family empire, had acquired a licence to import catalytic converters from Johnson Matthey, one of the largest manufacturers of catalytic converters worldwide. The Osman Group had already begun negotiating exclusive distribution agreements with Egyptian representatives of international car manufacturers. According to a company manager, representatives of the company met with the Ministers of Industry and Environment several months previously to push for the ministerial decree, which helped explain the unexpected timing and lack of prior public discussion.[5] However, implementation of the decree was delayed, as domestic vehicle assemblers used their own political connections to persuade the regime that implementing the decree immediately would cause them undue hardship.

The second company to enter the catalytic converter market by January 1999 illustrated the continuing presence of the public sector, and particularly that of the military, in Egyptian economic life despite market reforms. The Minister of Industry announced that 'as for the possibility of manufacturing the converters locally, it is possible to do so in our factories with high efficiency, and a diesel engine converter will be manufactured by the National Authority for Military Production' (Al-Ahram 1998). The National Authority administers approximately 25 companies, producing an eclectic mix of civilian and military products including chemicals, fans, landmines and televisions. Several of these companies have moved into producing environmental technologies, including incinerators, compost plants, water treatment plants and industrial hazardous waste treatment systems. At least seven have been certified for an ISO 9000 series standard, although, to my knowledge, no military factory has been certified for the environmental series.[6]

Requiring catalytic converters will help slow declines in urban air quality, but at a higher cost to consumers than if competitive bidding and transparent politics had prevailed. Other policy innovations with potential air quality impacts, such as

---

4 My thanks to John Sfakianakis, School of Oriental and African Studies, for first alerting me to the Osman family's interest in catalytic converters.

5 Interview no. 58, Cairo, 3 May 1998.

6 These numbers were compiled by comparing known military factories with lists of ISO recipients provided by local affiliates of international certification companies. The figures are provided to illustrate the importance of the military sector in acquiring international standard certification and should not be considered to be absolutely accurate.

designated bus and taxi lanes (as in the congested cities of Athens and Cubatao, Brazil) did not receive the same priority from corporate actors, perhaps because these measures did not directly benefit these firms.

Environment in Egypt is thus becoming a business opportunity, but not all corporate entities are created equal when it comes to participating in this new arena. Access to this sector, as in many other economic activities, depends in part on the firm's linkages to parts of the state. The two firms that tried to create a demand for catalytic converters illustrated well the kind of 'partial marketisation' undertaken in Egypt thus far. The private Osman Group was owned by the same family that managed the public-sector Arab Contractors, while the National Authority for Military Production showed a public-sector company attempting to diversify into environmental technologies. The next section explores how the formal privatisation of public-sector companies did not necessarily translate into more environmentally accountable management practices.

Pollution, privatisation and the public sector

Privatisation of publicly owned assets was one of the central tenets of most market liberalisation strategies. Yet many of the first-wave privatisations carried out in Egypt and other emerging markets did not result in more accountable management styles, more efficient production practices, substantive private ownership, or environmental improvements. Instead, a range of factors helped perpetuate 'partial marketisation' and environmental degradation.

Privatisation via the stock exchange often resulted in majority ownership in the hands of state entities, particularly through shares held by public-sector banks, insurance companies and pension funds. This ownership structure often retained the same board of directors and chief executive officers as before privatisation. In the case of Misr Chemicals, a chlorine plant on the north coast of Egypt, this kind of intra-public-sector asset acquisition persisted, even though the firm's majority privatisation was a prerequisite for donor financing of new production lines.

Misr Chemicals was an attractive investment for environmentally oriented donor programmes because of the grave public health hazard posed by the plant's use of mercury in its production process. Founded in 1959 to ensure a national supply of chlorine for drinking water, the plant discharged mercury-contaminated effluent into the Mediterranean for 35 years until the production lines were shut down in December 1996. Mercury contamination of soils around the factory itself exceeded World Health Organisation standards by a factor of 12,000 (Mechede 1997). The German development bank Kreditanstalt für Wiederaufbau (KfW) therefore agreed to finance new mercury-free production lines if the company was privatised.

Accordingly, an initial stock offering of 29.9% of Misr Chemicals was sold in 1994, with a second tranche to reach 51% later. Bank Misr, one of the four large state-owned banks, bought 18% of these shares, while other public entities acquired another 2%. The state-owned Chemical Holding Company retained 49% (Fiana & Partners 1998).

Thus only 31% were held in formally private hands, and the existing management structure remained unchanged.

This kind of privatisation was not exceptional in Egypt, but has been the norm. Only 12 of the 84 large companies privatised since 1991 were sold to anchor investors (IBTCI 1998: 1). Privatisations of 31 companies included a variety of state-owned or affiliated buyers, especially public-sector banks (IBTCI 1998: 19-23). Acquiring shares in other public-sector entities was a variation on pre-privatisation linkages, as both banks and companies had been expected to carry large sums of outstanding debt to each other. The cumulative debt owed by public-sector companies was estimated at $21 billion dollars by 1996, while figures for debt owed to individual companies by the government was rumoured to be equally staggering (Waterbury 1993). As the privatisation process continued, however, this intra-state acquisition was criticised by market observers, and therefore the regime increasingly sought anchor investors.

Despite this shift in emphasis, many anchor investors were simply not interested in the worse-off public-sector companies. In addition to the reasons often cited for lack of investor interest—obsolete production processes, outstanding debts, overvaluation of company worth, excess employment, and uncompetitive products—several other factors, some directly related to environmental liability, emerged in the Egyptian context.

First, as in many other developing countries, a significant portion of Egypt's public sector was concentrated in pollution-intensive basic industries. Before the privatisation programme began in 1991, the 314 companies listed for privatisation represented 70% of the Egyptian industrial sector (American Chamber of Commerce in Egypt 1997). The Egyptian Environmental Affairs Agency claimed that 80% of all industrial pollution in the country was emitted by 20% of the firms, and that the majority of these were state-owned. In an additional twist, since these companies had been founded or nationalised in order to extend state control over strategic industries, sometimes the main competitor of a newly privatised company was another unprivatised company. In the case of Misr Chemicals, its sole competitor in chlorine production was a military factory in the Cairo suburb of Abu Rawash, which, according to the CEO of Misr Chemicals, consistently undersold his products.

Second, the state was able to collect rudimentary information on public-sector pollution loads through existing bureaucratic networks, in contrast to the almost complete lack of available information on private-sector companies. As a former top official at the Egyptian Environmental Affairs Agency noted, 'We had no information on pollution from the private sector.'[7] Thus companies with linkages to the public sector were seen as more likely to receive state regulatory intervention than their private-sector counterparts. In the spring of 1998, the newly appointed Minister for Environment, Nady Makram Abeid, promised to shut down factories discharging untreated pollutants to the Nile. In the first set of 31 firms identified for priority monitoring and inspection, most were public-sector companies.

7 Interview no. 2, Egyptian Environmental Affairs Agency, Cairo, 21 May 1998.

Finally, the government had no formalised mechanisms in place to reassure investors about future environmental liability claims. Although the Ministry of Industry's Public Enterprise Office asserted that no company was sold if potential liability existed, offering chemical and cement companies on the stock market with well-known pollution problems belied this claim.

Bringing citizens back in

In order for privatisation to produce environmental improvements, it is not sufficient that ownership be shifted from the public sector to the private sector, or that anchor investors replace diffused shares in the stock market. Private markets remain competitive and accountable only through state-structured mechanisms empowering citizens and consumers. In contemporary Egypt, an individual has neither a citizen's rights nor a consumer's range of choice. The case of Misr Chemicals provides an example of how incentives for environmental improvement did not stem from legitimised popular participation, but from interest by donors and firms.

Mercury contamination at Misr Chemicals was a largely unknown hazard to the plant workers and the surrounding communities. But chlorine emissions from the plant to nearby informal housing areas were frequently protested, through a series of complaints filed with the local police station. As a top manager in the chemical company pointed out, these complaints were of little concern because of the company's public status. He noted:

> People went to the police station because of course, if they came to us [the chemical company], we would say there is no problem. So they would go to the police, and the police would call us, and we would say, 'do you have the authority to close us?' And the police would realise that of course they didn't.[8]

Thus the impetus for pollution controls was not popular concern, but the company's desire to install new production lines with greater capacity, and an international donor's commitment to treat a long-term hazardous waste threat, one largely imperceptible to the families living nearby.

As part of the refinancing agreement, KfW insisted on decontaminating the old plant and landfilling the remains in a secure desert landfill, over the initial objections of the company's CEO.[9] The press, hampered by lack of access to objective information, published a series of increasingly alarmist articles about the purpose of the landfill.

---

8 Interview no. 6A, Misr Chemicals Company, Amriya, 15 February 1998.

9 Gaining the required permissions for the landfill illustrated the preponderance of military agencies within the state apparatus. Although the EEAA granted approval of the site in May 1996, construction did not start until November when permission was received from the Department of Chemical Warfare (Cairo), Military Command North (Alexandria), the Military Operation Agency (Cairo) and the Third Military Brigade of Mubarak City.

These articles asserted that the landfill was a 'burying ground' for nuclear waste imported from Germany.[10]

Official response to these press accounts set in motion a process common in many conflicts in Egypt over industrial pollution. Since centralised decisions are taken with no public input and no defined guidelines for decision-making, there is widespread suspicion that decisions are made for reasons other than those publicly stated. Therefore, state authorities typically summon a committee of experts and ministers to assure the public that the decision was taken on technical and scientific grounds, not corrupt favouritism. The cabinet of ministers then approves the reports of the committee. In this case, the technical committee was made up of delegates from the same public agencies that had *already* formally granted permission. The predictable conclusions of the committee validating the previous permissions were then carried in the major state-owned newspapers.[11]

The style of handling public discontent demonstrated above is endemic in Egypt. The attitude of the regime, as one professor noted, is 'to create a reality and then expect that people will adjust to it'.[12] This has been the governing approach to both market reforms and environmental degradation. The ability of less privileged social groups to demand equitable distribution of environmental goods and public services has continued to be limited by what one analyst termed Egypt's political 'deliberalisation' (Kienle 1998). New restrictions on civil liberties to contain Islamic opposition groups and head off discontent with market reforms have made the general political climate more repressive. While public awareness of environmental issues is increasing, owing to severe localised pollution and sustained media coverage (Hopkins *et al.* 1998), fewer 'avenues of participation' are legitimised by the state than in the previous decade. Three potential avenues of élite influence into national environmental policy-making—non-governmental organisations, independent media and scientific expertise—are circumscribed by formal limitations on their activities, the selective co-optation of individual leaders into state-sanctioned organisations and, ultimately, the threat of arbitrary arrest and detention, the fate of an estimated 13,000 people at present.

Despite this, several environmental organisations have pursued first-ever court cases on environmental grounds, including suits over factory location, rehabilitation of public tram lines, quarrying in a natural preserve and preservation of historic buildings. An urban environmental group in Alexandria, Friends of the Environment (*Asdiqa' al-Bi'a*) generated considerable public sympathy by suing the governorate in two of the cases mentioned above. Neglect of the tram lines and tearing down historic buildings

10 See, among others, Fikry 1997a, b; Said 1997a; Al-Akhbar 1997. These reports played on Egyptian concerns that industrial wastes were being dumped in Egypt and other developing countries by the industrialised countries. These fears gained credence when Greenpeace Mediterranean reported that Italy and Germany had sent used plastics and batteries to Lebanon. A campaign to have the countries of origin take back the materials met some success in 1997, when the German government agreed to transport 36 containers of plastics back to Germany from Lebanon (*Greenpeace Mediterranean Quarterly* 1997).

11 Among others, see Gweida 1997; Riad 1997.

12 Personal communication with N. Hopkins, American University in Cairo, January 1999.

were seen by the association's middle class constituency as emblematic of the presidentially appointed governor's disregard for the city and its heritage. The association included not only middle-class professionals, but also several of the most powerful private-sector individuals in the city. Although the association successfully won its cases against the governorate, the organisation's support declined when the governor was simply replaced by another presidential appointee. Business leaders' support turned out to be based more on antipathy to the former governor, whom they saw as hostile to the private sector, than an interest in creating durable institutions in civil society. Middle-class support also waned as the new governor unilaterally undertook several beautification projects which, however cosmetic, convinced many that a new regime had begun in the city. The association, without substantial roots in disadvantaged communities still excluded from public services, saw its support decline.

Recent social science research has highlighted the importance of instances of 'state–society synergy', or constructive engagements between civil associations, political parties and state agencies, in providing public goods such as urban environmental quality (Evans 1997; de Mello Lemos 1998). In many states, opportunities for such engagements, both conflictive and co-operative, occurred when activities of social movements were at least semi-legalised by political reforms. In Egypt, however, market reforms have proceeded in the absence of political openings, undermining the natural constituencies for environmental regulatory actions.

A coterie of state and business élites in Egypt continues to define what is a pressing environmental problem and how it should be addressed. The claim that marketisation would revitalise civil society overlooked the continued crucial role of overlapping public agencies in controlling business activities, as well as the kinds of formal and informal linkages between the state apparatus and public/private-sector businessmen explored in this chapter.

State-linked monopolistic business circles will increasingly face external pressures, as Egypt tries to access European markets and conform to GATT trade rules. Thus far, however, external pressures for environmental reform have been limited and domestic ones contained. Marketisation as implemented in Egypt and other developing countries contributed to this situation, as constituencies with interests in environmental equity were not included in governing coalitions, and corporate interests, both public and private, were given priority. Without legitimised avenues of state–society engagement, environmental protection has so far been relegated to the realm of voluntary corporate environmentalism and well-publicised but ineffective state initiatives.

Environmental measures undertaken as a business opportunity, as in the case of the adoption of catalytic converters, or as a donor-sponsored project, as in the example of mercury decontamination at a chemical company, did not translate into a commitment to environmentally sound business strategies. Corporate environmentalism has an important but limited role in addressing fundamental issues of environmental protection; it is an insufficient guarantee that collective environmental goods will be provided. Efforts at improving environmental management in Egypt should be part of a broader agenda to foster mechanisms of accountability and avenues of participation, whether these are through public agencies or through the market. For public authorities, substantive political reforms, including legitimate elections of local officials and freedom of association for non-governmental associations, is a requisite first step. For the market, reformers should focus on the policy reforms necessary for creating more competitive markets, and not focus on the simpler task of privatising public assets. In the absence of these kinds of considerations, globalising market reforms may simply replace domestic capital with foreign capital, but without substantive improvements in environmental quality or services for broad sectors of the population.

12
Environmental Management in Thailand

Achievements, Barriers and Future Trends*

Mandar Parasnis

THE RAPID GROWTH of industrial and agro-industrial sectors in Thailand in the 1980s and early 1990s transformed Thailand from a mainly agrarian economy into an economy dominated by the manufacturing and service industries. The rapid expansion of the manufacturing industry was followed by the rapidly increasing rates of air, surface water and ground pollution, mostly concentrated in the Bangkok Metropolitan Region (BMR) (see Box 1).

One important feature of Thai industry and economy is the dominance of small and medium-sized enterprises (SMEs), which have an estimated contribution of up to 90% of the total Thai industrial output and hence of the economy. The SMEs have traditionally been operating as family-owned job shops, without changing much with time. Further, the Thai SMEs represent the typical Asian SME scenario, namely, lack of technical know-how, obsolete and polluting production technologies and an overall lack of awareness about productivity- and pollution-related issues. Naturally, in Thailand too, SMEs constitute a major source of industrial environmental pollution.

* The author wishes to record his heartfelt gratitude to Dr Chaiyod Bunyagidj, Vice-President of TEI, for all his encouragement and valuable insights and experiences as this chapter was developed. It has been prepared based on the available and cited references. TEI neither guarantees nor does it authenticate the data presented. Further, the opinions presented in this chapter do not necessarily reflect those of the Institute.

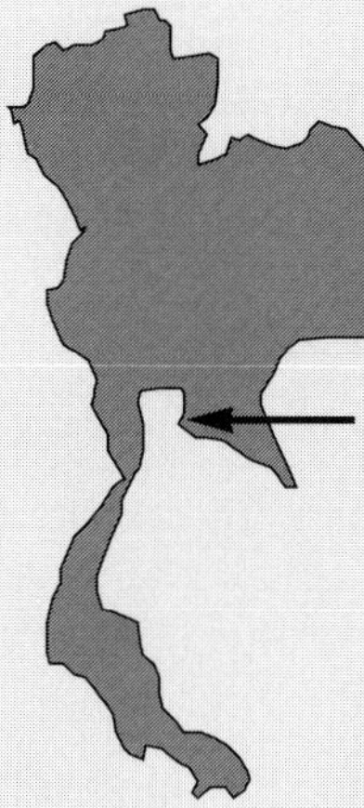

THE Bangkok Metropolitan Region (BMR)—which includes Bangkok and the surrounding five provinces and is home to approximately 16% of the population—is both the centre of government and the centre of economic growth. With approximately 75% of Thai manufacturing output located in the BMR, this region has been at the hub of the growth in Thailand's manufacturing sector.

Samut Prakam, along with Nonthaburi, Pathumthani, Samut Sakhon and Nakhom Pathon, is one of five provinces forming the urban fringe around Bangkok. With an area equivalent to approximately 1,000 km^2, Samut Prakam is situated roughly 25 km east of Bangkok on the mouth of the Chao Phraya River. Within the BMR, Samut Prakam is experiencing the most rapid industrial growth, as well as a rapid increase in all types of industrial pollution problems. As such, this region is the target beneficiary for many projects on augmenting current pollution control and abatement activities and the promotion of sustainable environmental management practices.

Box 1: THE BANGKOK METROPOLITAN REGION (BMR)

State of Thailand's environment

Water pollution

Water quality in principal rivers has followed a continuously downhill trend during the 1980s and the 1990s, particularly in areas of the lower Chao Phraya river and Thachin river. Water quality in these areas has degraded to Class 4 surface water quality standards (for consumable water), namely: dissolved oxygen (DO) less than 2 mg/l, biochemical oxygen demand (BOD) over 4 mg/l and total coliform bacteria over 20,000 MPN/100 ml. The water sources and principal rivers in other regions are also vulnerable to degradation. Water quality in many provincial rivers becomes periodically deteriorated and polluted, especially during the dry season.

Groundwater has begun to become contaminated by waste-water from solid-waste deposits and the toxic residues of agrochemicals. Coastal water quality at many popular tourist destinations such as Chonburi, Pattaya and Phuket is lower than the acceptable standards for swimming: with total coliform bacteria over 19,000 MPN/100 ml (standard = 1,000 MPN/100 ml).

Air pollution

The problem of air pollution is primarily predominant in the large communities and in rapidly developing areas, where industry, transportation and construction activities are prevalent; and in the areas where power plants are situated. The problematic air pollutants that do not meet acceptable standards include dust and carbon monoxide. Dust is a serious problem especially in crowded communities with traffic congestion, being 3–5 times above the standards. Other pollutants include lead, sulphur dioxide and nitrogen dioxide; however, their levels remain below prescribed ambient air quality standards.

According to air quality data for 1995, the quality of air alongside the roads in BMR was lower than that in the residential areas. It is, however, reported that the air quality in other provinces has not become a serious problem except in some areas such as Saraburi, where dust from rock extraction is a major problem. At present the government addresses air pollution problems by designating ambient air quality standards, emission standards, fuel quality standards, lubricant quality standards or by promotion of the use of unleaded petrol.

Solid waste and sewage

The amount of solid waste generated by communities nationwide according to the 1995 data was 34,000 tons per day (TPD), which increased to 36,000 tons per day in 1996. Solid waste produced in BMR totalled 7,000 tons; the remaining waste is produced by communities within municipalities and sanitary districts nationwide. Almost 100% of the total solid waste produced in BMR was collected and disposed of. Approximately 5,000 tons was disposed of in landfills and 1,100 tons was composted to produce organic fertiliser. While the municipalities and sanitary districts are also able to collect and dispose of increasing amounts of solid waste, the methods of disposal are still not hygienic.

For municipalities and Pattaya City, although they have the capacity to collect and transport 80% of the solid waste produced (or 4,500 TPD), only 600 TPD was properly disposed of in sanitary landfills. The remainder is left to decompose by itself. As for sanitary districts and surrounding areas, solid waste is openly dumped and is left to decompose naturally, which is unhygienic and is the source of pollution and the cause of nuisance. The result is that more surface and groundwater sources become contaminated by leachate.

In Thailand, the septic tank system is used for sewage collection. Some sewage is disposed of directly into sewers or is transported and dumped into rice paddy fields or public areas. This is the cause of the pollution of water bodies and the spread of pathogenic organisms. Bangkok metropolis has two sewage treatment plants, which treat only 600 m^3 per day, and uses the sludge for organic fertiliser production. In the case of municipal districts, only 30% of all municipal districts are able to dispose of sewage properly.

Solid waste and sewage management problems are becoming more serious, with increasing environmental contamination and health risks, especially in peripheral provinces of BMR, the eastern seaboard, and other provinces where the generation of solid wastes tends to increase annually, but the implementation of solutions addresses only immediate problems.

Waste type	Hazardous waste quantity (tons per year) 1986	1991	1996	2001
Oils	106,372	188,254	332,779	589,508
Liquid organic residues	187	311	522	876
Organic sludge and solids	3,737	6,674	11,951	21,533
Inorganic sludge and solids	11,655	19,163	31,858	53,696
Heavy metal sludge and solids	302,316	536,322	946,565	1,658,192
Solvents	19,760	36,163	66,532	124,306
Acid wastes	18,505	31,432	53,793	46,105
Alkaline wastes	5,769	9,839	16,846	29,019
Off-spec. products	12	25	52	107
PCBs	0	0	0	0
Aqueous organic residues	116	242	499	1037
Photo wastes	8,820	16,348	30,398	57,809
Municipal wastes	7,231	11,787	19,090	31,093
Infectious wastes	46,674	76,078	123,219	200,699
Total	531,154	932,638	1,634,104	2,813,980

Table 1: HAZARDOUS WASTE COMPOSITION

Source: TDRI 1997

Hazardous materials

Thailand has been importing an increasing volume of hazardous materials over recent years for utilisation in the development of agriculture, industry and public health. Imported hazardous (organic and inorganic) chemicals increased from 1.31 million tons in 1988 to 2.79 million tons in 1993. For the most part, the chemicals are inflammable, explosive, toxic and corrosive in nature, are not properly utilised, and are used rather irresponsibly without realisation of the inherent dangers.

Hazardous wastes

The problem of hazardous waste pollution is serious and is expected to worsen in the future due to rapidly increasing generation of hazardous waste from various activities throughout the country including industry, agriculture, communities, businesses, services, ports, hospitals and laboratories.

In 1992, the Pollution Control Department under the Ministry of Science, Technology and Environment (MoSTE) in collaboration with the Department of Industrial Works (DIW), prepared some realistic estimates of the volumes of hazardous waste generated in Thailand by type, which are presented in Table 1. In 1995, the hazardous waste produced nationwide amounted to 1.5 million tons (an estimated 13% increase from the previous year), which came from various sources; this is presented in Table 2.

Industry	1,100,000
Commercial and service sectors	126,150
Hospitals and laboratories	122,400
Ports and sea transport	121,950
Households	18,900
Agricultural activities	10,800

Table 2: SOURCES OF HAZARDOUS WASTE IN THAILAND (TONS)

The task of monitoring hazardous waste is further complicated by international 'trade' in hazardous materials and waste. Thailand is, more often than not, the recipient of waste from both industrialised and developing nations. During 1990–93, an estimated 4,446 tons of hazardous waste entered Thailand in the form of raw waste (i.e. solids, sludge, slag) and spent consumer products (e.g. batteries) from Australia, the UK and the US. Although approximately 40% of the imported waste materials can be expected to be recycled, Thailand is claimed to be the terminal disposal site for many kinds of hazardous waste.

Management of hazardous waste

For a number of reasons, hazardous waste management has become an issue of growing concern in Thailand. Facilities for the treatment and disposal of wastes arising from existing industries are inefficient. They are not able to provide sufficient services and are able to treat only certain types of hazardous waste. Hazardous wastes can be treated in only two stations: Samae Dam station, and at a landfill in Ratchaburi province. Moreover, mechanisms, standards and practices for control at all levels, including collection, transportation, stockpiling, separation, treatment and final disposal, are not well established at this time, particularly for wastes from communities. Government and private hospitals (a total of 24,000 of them), which are important generators of hazardous wastes, with potentially serious implications, are operating without proper infectious waste disposal systems.

Due to inadequate hazardous waste treatment facilities in Thailand, in the early 1990s the Ministry of Industry (MoI) strongly encouraged all factories classified as hazardous waste generators to have on-site storage facilities, where hazardous wastes could be stored until treatment facilities were constructed. Many industries responded by storing the waste at landfills on-site and in storage facilities. Other firms either sent their waste to the Samae Dam treatment facility or disposed of it using small on-site incinerators. Unfortunately, reports of hazardous waste dumping on public land (i.e. municipal landfills or close to public parks) are not uncommon.

Legislative and regulatory framework for environmental management in Thailand

Since the early 1970s, successive Thai governments have proclaimed their commitment to environmental protection, and have responded to the increasing pressure on the environment through regulatory measures. National development plans have emphasised the need to manage environmental quality, and the environment has been the cornerstone of the 7th and the 8th national development plans.

There are four major laws that affect industrial environmental practices. These are:

- 1941 Public Health Act and its 1992 amendment
- 1967 Poisonous Substances Act and its 1992 amendment
- 1969 Factories Act (FAC) and its 1992 amendment
- 1975 Enhancement and Conservation of National Environment Quality Act (NEQA) and 1992 amendment of NEQA

The focus of the Public Health Act is on the public sphere and some of the sections of the Public Health Act provide legal authority for the prevention and abatement of water, air and noise pollution. The Poisonous Substances Act controls the import, export, manufacture, marketing, storage, transport and use of poisonous substances and is an important set of regulations affecting the use of dangerous substances and responsibilities for their effects.

Factories Act (1969) and its 1992 amendment

The Factories Act provides the legal basis for regulating industrial plants, and makes the DIW in the MoI responsible for:

- The establishment and operation of factories through mandatory factory licensing at three-year intervals
- Industrial safety and pollution control
- Setting and enforcement of industrial emissions standards
- Monitoring of waste-water and hazardous waste treatment facilities

Government-owned factories and other facilities are exempt from the provisions of the Act.

Enhancement and Conservation of National Environmental Quality Act (1992)

The Enhancement and Conservation of National Environmental Quality Act (NEQA) is the primary law relating to Thailand's environmental protection measures. The 1992 revision of NEQA addressed the weak structure of environmental management

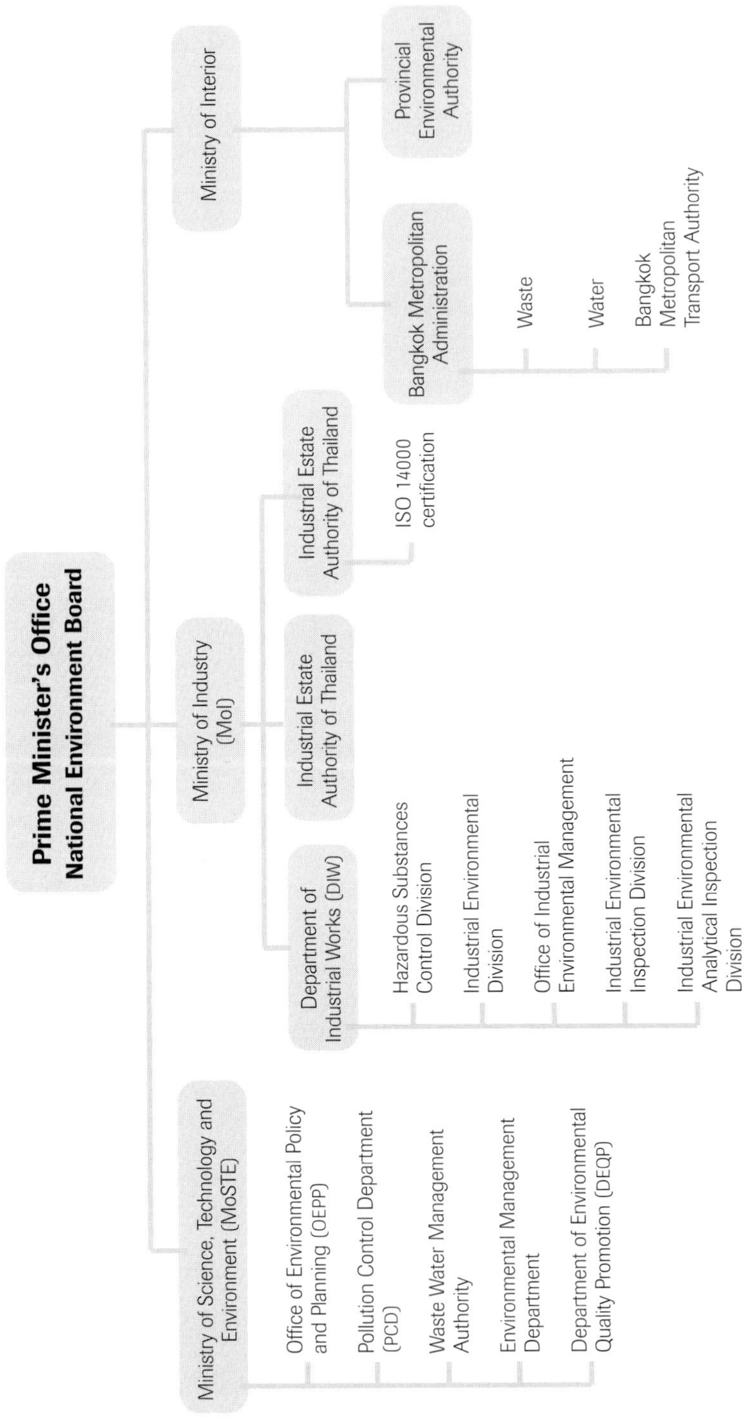

Figure 1: REGULATORY FRAMEWORK FOR ENVIRONMENTAL MANAGEMENT by creating MoSTE with a standard-setting and enforcement authority and a new cabinet-level National Environment Board (NEB) representing all major ministries and headed by the prime minister. NEQA is conceived as the framework legislation for environmental management and control in Thailand.

A key provision of NEQA concerns implementation of the Environmental Impact Assessment (EIA) requirement. EIAs are prepared for a specified list of projects with somewhat different procedures for government and private projects. NEQA provides for punitive measures (fines) against companies in case of non-compliance with environmental regulations. On the other hand, the Act also provides for tax incentives for companies' activities concerned with environmental protection and for the possibility of government financial support to private-sector projects concerned with environmental quality.

Institutional mechanism for the implementation of environmental legislation

Responsibility for industrial pollution control and monitoring is primarily divided between a number of public institutions. A schematic representation is depicted in Figure 1. The government's monitoring and enforcement duties with respect to industrial pollution abatement, labour safety and occupational health hazards are vested in the DIW under the MoI. DIW has the responsibility for approval and monitoring of the industrial environment within enterprises' premises. DIW has been vested with the power to issue the annual operating permit (mandatory factory licensing) required for factories of all sizes in Bangkok and for large-scale factories all over the country. DIW sets standards for emissions from industrial point sources, monitors emissions coming from industrial plants and carries out inspections at industrial plants. Furthermore, DIW is concerned with safe transport, treatment and disposal of hazardous material generated by industry including the physical planning and installation of hazardous treatment facilities.

MoSTE is responsible for three state enterprises and nine departments, three of which are directed by NEQA to carry out functions that may be added to by NEB. The latter three are:

- The Office of Environmental Policy and Planning (OEPP), which is responsible for the formulation of environmental protection policies
- The Pollution Control Department (PCD), which is responsible for the 'external' control of industrial pollution (outside the premises of the industry). It sets ambient water and air quality standards and monitors air and water quality in the different regions of Thailand.
- The Department of Environmental Quality Promotion (DEQP), which primarily conducts public education and awareness programmes. It also oversees relations with and helps build the capacity of environmental NGOs.

MoSTE also manages the Environment Fund on behalf of NEB, which can be used by the municipalities and local governments for constructing the central waste treatment facilities.

The Industrial Estate Authority of Thailand (IEAT) under the MoI constructs, owns and operates most of the industrial estates in Thailand. According to the Thai regulations, the power to control individual plants within an industrial estate has been passed from DIW and PCD to IEAT, and DIW and PCD have direct control only on the emissions from the estate as such. IEAT, the waste-water treatment plant operator imposes the pre-treatment level on the individual plants located in the estate.

Barriers and problems in environmental management practices

Traditionally, the focus of environmental management in Thailand has relied heavily on the command-and-control (CAC) approach. However, the success of the CAC approach has been limited, primarily due to enactment of very stringent environmental standards beyond the ability of existing industries or certain industrial sectors to comply with these standards.

This overly regulated situation is compounded by a generally weak monitoring and enforcement regime that is the result of insufficient manpower and training. This is further complicated by the lack of co-ordinated management of the environment sector. The responsibility for enforcement is unclear and spread across a variety of governmental bodies with conflicting jurisdictions. The proliferation of unenforced or unenforcable laws and regulations arising from a large number of agencies has created an atmosphere of tolerance that further hampers enforcement.

Costs to polluters, even if levied, are too low to induce investments in pollution control measures. As such, when factories can afford the fines and do not have to fear for their livelihood, the laws become a licence to pollute. Also, corruption in the public sector allows violators to avoid prosecution.

Enforcement is effective only in cases where public awareness and protests have created too much publicity for a case to be ignored, or where major companies adopt a corporate environmental policy. As a result of lax enforcement practices, new industries generate major quantities of air, water and solid waste pollutants. Loopholes in the laws are also incentives for some foreign investors who might not be complying with stringent domestic environmental laws.

Changing winds

The environmental pollution problems have indeed reached an alarming stage for Thai society and the government's efforts to control pollution have seen limited success. Nevertheless, environmental consciousness is growing: *inter alia*, as a result of efforts by NGOs and their community education and awareness programmes.

It is received wisdom that the current set of laws regulating environmental activities is incoherent, and that new regulations will have to supersede the diffuse and sometimes conflicting codes derived from diverse aspects of Thai law. It has also been recognised that laws are not enough to deal with new environmental stresses, and that enforcement is the main problem. There is consensus on, and open discussion of, the need to overhaul existing legislation and the institutional framework for monitoring and enforcing compliance.

Moreover, the Thai government is now placing an increasing emphasis on a participatory approach and voluntary measures and is encouraging industry to take the initiative on environmental issues. The government sees this as an area where Thai companies can gain international competitiveness and it also wants to encourage more self-regulation among the larger companies. To complement this, it is supporting programmes to assist Thai industries, particularly the SMEs that account for over half of the country's GDP and are responsible for more than three-quarters of the industrial pollution.

Changes at the policy level

The Eighth National Economic and Social Development Plan (1997–2001) endorses the principles of sustainable development and underscores the need for concerted actions on behalf of all Thai stakeholders. It calls for collaboration and co-operation among the various sectors of Thai society to translate its recommended strategies into action.

Thailand's current Policy and Prospective Plan for Enhancement and Conservation of National Environmental Quality (1997–2016) establishes several policies and guidelines encouraging the use of clean technologies and strategies to reduce pollution as supplements to traditional pollution control measures. The 20-year plan includes policies to promote and support private-sector participation in managing solutions to environmental problems. Emphasis is laid on collaboration among all sectors of Thai society, and numerous strategies to build capabilities in Thailand to use best environmental management practices through research, education and training are recommended.

Industrial Restructuring Plan (1998–2002)

In June 1998, the MOI and National Industrial Development Committee finalised the Industrial Restructuring Plan (1998–2002). The Industrial Restructuring Plan emphasises the need to strengthen human resource development efforts designed to increase knowledge and capability of factory personnel and of the organisations that interact with and support the industrial sector.

The plan also recommends actions to reduce production costs, streamline production and upgrade obsolete technologies and machinery. Factory evaluation and analysis systems and the use of incentives to improve industrial competitiveness are planned. The plan explicitly calls for the need for projects and activities to increase the use of cleaner technologies and improve environmental management. Industrial restructuring activities to support production process modifications, improved business management and increased product quality are some of the means proposed.

The budget requested to implement this plan is approximately US$1.2 billion. This budget consists of expenses for private-sector investment in acquiring technologies and machinery, factory relocation, industrial soft loans, hiring experts and other related expenses. This four-year proposed budget presents significant opportunities to achieve the mutual goals of industrial competitiveness and improvements in environmental quality.

Participatory approach to environmental management and clean-up in Samut Prakarn Province (1997–98)

Within the BMR, Samut Prakarn is experiencing the most rapid industrial growth, as well as a rapid increase in all types of industrial pollution. The objective of this recently concluded landmark project was to sustainably enhance environmental management in Samut Prakarn province through utilisation of a participatory approach to industrial pollution management. This project, supported by the European Commission (EC), was implemented by the Thailand Environment Institute (TEI) during 1997–98.

Specifically, a 'Participatory Environmental Management Committee' was formed, drawn from the major stakeholders (community, industry, government, NGOs, etc.) affecting environmental management in the province. The committee was charged with evaluating the current environmental situation and researching, planning, implementing and monitoring pollution control and abatement strategies. Emphasis was placed on adoption of the preventative or cleaner production (CP) approach as a tool to solve the environmental problems of the region. Demonstration projects, nominated by the committee and awarded by the EC, targeted 'typical' factories in specific industrial sectors and showcased a successful application of clean technology and pollution abatement technology.

As the donor support diminished, the committee evolved into Samut Prakarn Environment Society and has continued playing its key role in environmental management and clean-up in the province in tandem with the government agencies.

Samut Prakarn cleaner production industrial efficiency programme

Thailand has received a loan from the Asian Development Bank and the Japanese Overseas Economic Co-operation Fund to support funding of the Samut Prakarn Waste-water Management Project. The major focus of the project includes turnkey construction of a large-scale waste-water collection and treatment system. It also includes pollution control and pollution prevention measures as part of the overall effort to manage the rehabilitation of the water environment of the most industrialised province of Thailand.

The four-year programme aims to promote and develop CP and industrial efficiency (CPIE) among industry and businesses in Samut Prakarn. The essential features of the programme will include establishment of a resource centre, provision of advice on CPIE to local industry and demonstration of applied CP processes. The CPIE programme will also include industrial audits, and the development of a network within the local industry for collaboration on promoting CPIE and setting up the necessary institutional structure to enable the programme to continue beyond the contract duration.

It is important to note that the Samut Prakarn CPIE programme is the first CP programme financed directly through use of Thai government funds. Other programmes received supporting funds from international and bilateral donor organisations.

Economic instruments in environmental management

Polluter pays principle

A suggestion in the Seventh National Plan states that the development mechanism and environmental management should follow the polluters pay principle (PPP). Accordingly, the TEI study of suitable economic tools to be used by industries to deal with industrial pollution, *Development of Economic Tools in Industrial Environmental Management in Thailand*, which was supported by DIW and the German aid agency GTZ, was recently completed. The study focused on three main industries:, namely, tanneries, palm oil and canned tuna industries. A review of waste characteristics, the economic situation and market environment of the industries has been undertaken and type and level of charges analysed. To follow this, a feasibility study of applying a market-based instrument to specific type of industries will be carried out and the willingness to pay and acceptance of the scheme will be assessed. From the results of the study, a policy and implementation plan for each of the three industries and other industries in general is being developed.

Soft loans, subsidies and venture capital

The Board of Investment (BOI) in the Prime Minister's office is the primary agency that is responsible for providing fiscal and non-fiscal incentives. BOI is closely linked to MoI and MoSTE through the overlapping board memberships of government officials. Most recently, BOI's policy focused on high-technology industries, low-polluting or pollution-controlled industries, and the location of industry outside Bangkok. BOI offers special privileges such as customs duty exemption for equipment to be used in pollution control.

The Technology Transfer Centre under the MoSTE offers financial assistance for technology development/modification/upgrade to result in improved productivity and reduced environmental impacts. The National Science and Technology Development Agency (NSTDA) also offers a similar soft loan to the industries, particularly for SMEs for technology development and upgrading.

Private-sector initiatives and tools for environmental management

Thailand Business Council for Sustainable Development (TBCSD)

TBCSD represents a group of business leaders in Thailand interested and engaged in issues of environment and development. The main objectives of TBCSD are: (i) to encourage business to take a leading role in preventing and solving national environmental problems; (ii) to foster the business role in environmental policy formulation leading to sustainable development; (iii) to promote the spirit of corporate citizenship with business-supporting initiatives in enhancing the quality of the degrading environment; and (iv) to promote the concept of 'sustainable development' among business leaders through dialogues, activities and by disseminating information about clean technologies and sound environmental practices to business communities and the public.

TBCSD is a not-for-profit membership organisation whose work is funded by contributions from its members. Additional funds may be solicited from outside organisations for specific projects. The operating budget includes all the funds for the operation of TBCSD. TEI serves as the secretariat responsible for carrying out the activities approved by the Council.

A number of activities and projects are undertaken by the TBCSD. On the international level, it co-operates with the World Business Council for Sustainable Development (WBCSD) in addressing global environmental issues such as 'Internalising Environmental Costs' and 'Trade and the Environment'. On the regional level, TBCSD co-operates with ASEAN Chambers of Commerce and Industry (ASEAN-CCI), specifically with its Working Group on Sustainable Development (WGSD), to promote co-operation among businessmen in ASEAN countries in fostering sustainable economic growth in combination with sound environmental management.

On the national level, TBCSD activities focus on public awareness/educational programmes that aim at educating the public about various environmental issues in order to raise environmental awareness. Some of the TBCSD projects demonstrate collective corporate responsibilities in cleaning up the environment and in introducing a better lifestyle for the public at large. TBCSD also undertakes policy studies that strive to achieve the dual objectives of sustainable development and environmental conservation, looking from the business perspectives.

Cleaner production

CP concepts and practices are receiving increased recognition as one of the preventative environmental management tools in Thailand. This is particularly attractive for Thai industries at the time of recent economic crisis, since CP concepts and practices have proved that economic and environmental benefits can go hand in hand.

For the past ten years, there has been a number of international bi- or multilateral donor-supported projects in Thailand aiming at the promotion of the CP concept in Thai industries. Very recently, one such major project was concluded at the TEI and the Federation of Thai Industries (FTI) with support from Danish Co-operation for Environment and Development (DANCED). As a prominent outcome of this two-year project, advisory services are now offered by TEI and FTI to the industry on the implementation of CP.

Moreover, the government is keen to promote this concept widely and is looking at ways of integrating it into existing environmental legislation. Notably, the DIW under the MoI, also with support from DANCED, has initiated efforts to re-orient existing industrial policy to promote CP in Thai industries. Similarly, the PCD under the MoSTE is developing a comprehensive National Pollution Prevention Action Plan, which is expected to overhaul the environmental policies for all the sectors (agriculture, tourism, services, etc.) and orient them towards CP concepts and practices.

A national forum (Thai National Pollution Prevention Roundtable) is being constituted to bring together all the stakeholders and identify the means for concerted action towards CP promotion in Thailand. This is expected to greatly facilitate and accelerate the CP promotion efforts in governmental as well as non-governmental sectors.

Environmental management system (ISO 14000)

The government has promoted and supported the ISO 14000 series in Thailand by establishing the organisational framework and provision of financial and technical assistance to the industry. The MoI has overall authority over the introduction of these standards in Thailand through its Thailand Industrial Standards Institute (TISI). It has also established the National Accreditation Council for Environmental Management Standards (NACEMS) to set up the accreditation system for Thailand, including accreditation of the Thai-based certifying bodies as lead assessors and training bodies associated with ISO 14001. The MoI formed a committee to review ISO 14001 and to recommend the strategy for Thai implementation. Its members represent a cross-section of industry and government interests.

In terms of financial support from the government, there are two funding sources available. The National Science Technology Development Agency (within MoSTE) provides matching funds up to about US$10,000 for EMS implementation. The Thailand Productivity Institute (TPI) is also offering matching funds by paying for, or providing, consulting services.

Export-oriented Thai companies have been very interested in ISO 14000-based EMS and its certification, which many view as an important asset in global marketing. This is evident from the fact that more than 100 companies have been certified for ISO 14000-based EMS to date and this number is growing steadily. Details of the ISO 14000-certified companies in Thailand are available on the TISI website.[1]

Green label

The concept of the Thai Green Label uses life-cycle consideration and stresses certain high-priority national goals: e.g. waste reduction, and energy and water conservation.

1 *http://www.tisi.go.th*

This Green Label programme was initiated by the TBCSD, and project development was officially undertaken by the TEI in 1994 in co-operation with the TISI, MoI and MoSTE. Product selection and criteria are developed for the Green Label with regard to local capability to conduct the necessary testing and monitoring.

Green Label product criteria have been developed for around 20 product categories and, up to now, more than 125 product models have received the Green Label certification. This scheme has been modestly successful and hopes to be an effective tool for environmental management as consumer awareness increases in the future. Complete information about the Thai Green Label scheme can be found on the TEI website.[2]

Towards a cleaner and greener future

Over recent decades, Thailand has experienced serious environmental degradation problems consequent to its phenomenal economic growth in the 1980s and 1990s. The severity of these problems could not be satisfactorily addressed by regulatory means with limited governmental resources. As such, a number of complex and urgent environmental problems need to be solved. Moreover, there is increasing pressure from buyers in the Western world demanding improved environmental performance, which can even be translated to trade barriers for this export-based economy.

In the past few years, however, the Thai government has radically changed its perspective towards environmental problems, and keeping pace with the global trends has resulted in a more participatory, voluntary and market-based approach to control the problems of industrial pollution. Both short- and long-term measures have been pledged keeping in mind the lessons learned and perceived weaknesses of past and present systems. While one cannot expect dramatic changes in the national legislative and regulatory framework overnight, the changing trends and the initial steps are indeed promising.

One noteworthy ambitious effort—the 'Dawn Project'—initiated by the Ministry of Education, attempts to integrate energy and environmental issues into the entire education system in Thailand, from primary schools up to university level. Existing curricula have been extensively revised to include these issues for all levels. The success of this effort will be visible only after a few years, but it is indeed an appropriate and promising initiative, taking Thailand one step closer to a cleaner and greener future.

The direction adopted and the steps taken in environmental management in Thailand are appropriate considering the changing needs of the time. A clear shift away from CAC to more voluntary and market-based instruments and, importantly, an increasing emphasis on public participation are probably the important lessons that many other developing countries can learn from the Thai experience and adopt in their national policies and programme.

---

3 *http://www.tei.or.th*

Appendix: Internet resources on environmental management in Thailand

Ministry of Science, Technology and Environment (MOSTE)

Office of Environmental Policy and Planning (OEPP)	*http://www.deqp.go.th/oepp/index.htm*
Pollution Control Department (PCD)	*http://www.pcd.go.th*
Department of Environmental Quality Promotion (DEQP)	*http://www.deqp.go.th*

Ministry of Industry (MoI)

Department of Industrial Works (DIW)	*http://www.diw.go.th*
Thai Industrial Standards Institute (TISI)	*http://www.tisi.go.th*
Federation of Thai Industries (FTI)	*http://www.fti.or.th*

National Science Technology Development Agency (NSTDA)	*http://www.nstda.or.th*
Thailand Development Research Institute (TDRI)	*http://www.nectec.or.th/bureaux/tdri/*
Thailand Environment Institute (TEI)	*http://www.tei.or.th*

13

The Colombian Road to Environmental Management

Emilio Latorre

The legal framework for environmental management in Colombia

LOCATED IN A TROPICAL AREA at the northern end of the Andes, Colombia is recognised worldwide for its exceptional biodiversity. It covers an area of 1,141,000 km^2, five times bigger than that of the UK, and has a population of approximately 38 million. Its economy has changed in recent years to include not only the primary economic sector, but also a developing industrial sector, and has increased trade with other countries. A country once known only for its coffee production, Colombia now exports not only primary products such as oil, coal and bananas, but a great deal of manufactured goods such as sugar, leather articles and textiles.

Since 1972 the country has had a set of established regulations for the production sector; however, the environmental management of production activities in Colombia was then primarily a question of trying to meet legal requirements established by the government. Because the environmental authorities lacked legal power, the actions of the private and public productive sectors towards environmental management depended mainly on the willingness of individual companies, and were therefore insufficient.

In general, the government's control of environmental pollution has been very limited. Only in the more socioeconomically developed regions has the control of water and air pollution been achieved with some degree of success. The Cauca Valley in the south of Colombia was, in 1954, the first region to establish a coherent policy towards water pollution, thanks to the creation of a regional body, the Corporación Valle del Cauca (CVC), emulating the creation of the Tennessee Valley Authority in the United States.

For many years the control of environmental damage was managed at municipal level by way of laws and government regulations concerning air and water pollution and solid waste management. Legislation was very weak in land management, noise pollution, the use of hazardous materials and the protection of wildlife. Only large cities had land use regulations; rural regions had no land management structure apart from the river basin planning in the area of the CVC, which was only a recommendation rather than mandatory legislation in terms of land use.

But in 1991 a new constitution was established with clearer intentions as far as environmental protection was concerned. In 1993, following the constitution, a new law was passed by Congress (Law 99 of 1993) which established national environmental goals, and created the Ministerio del Medio Ambiente (Environment Ministry) which was to be supported at the regional level by the Autonomous Regional Corporations (one in each political department) and the Sustainable Development Corporations (located in areas of important biodiversity). This structure is also supported by the environmental authorities of the four largest cities in the country, all of which have a population of over one million. At the base of this pyramid are the municipalities with very little authority in the matter of environmental protection.

One of the most important goals of Law 99/93 is to encourage the protection of the environment as a joint effort between the state, the private sector and non-governmental organisations (NGOs). Thus, environmental management becomes not only the responsibility of the state, but also an issue that concerns the private sector directly.

The government's 1994 environmental plan

In 1994, the new government established a development policy called 'The Social Leap', and, following the United Nation's new approach to environmental issues, this development plan was subtitled 'Towards Sustainable Human Development'. The plan not only had an important chapter that dealt with environmental goals and actions to be taken, but was based on ideas of sustainable human development. It represents an important change of focus, because in the past all development plans were concentrated on economic and social development.

The plan stated that the strategic ecosystems[1] of the country were in a state of extreme deterioration: 30% of the natural forest has been destroyed, 23% of the population has no access to clean water, 8.5% of the land has erosion problems, and only 5% of the cities operated sewage treatment plants (Republica de Colombia Ministerio del Medio Ambiente 1995: 6-9).

In 1995, the National Planning Department published the first paper that described the industrial pollution situation for the entire country (Sanchez Triana and Uribe Botero 1994). This book was the result of several years of research and evaluation in

1 Those with a great biological interest, and those that are essential to the development and wellbeing of the country.

Colombia's most important industrial centres. Unfortunately, this publication does not take into consideration other areas of the productive sector which are non-industrial, yet which have an important effect on the environment, such as mining activities, cattle farming, agriculture (including Colombia's most important export product, coffee), and the exploration, extraction and transportation of oil. Thus, there appears to be a bias towards pollution problems, concentrating on the industrial sector and ignoring other productive activities which are potentially more harmful to the environment.

This publication on industrial pollution demonstrates the reality of the environmental impact of the industrial sector:

> Even though information on Colombia's air quality is very limited, data show that the levels of air pollution in Barranquilla, Cartagena, Santafe de Bogotá, Cali, Medellín and Sogamoso are higher than the permitted regulatory levels. In the six cities studied there are 2,870 stationary sources of industrial contamination considered to be high-level air polluters (Republica de Colombia Ministerio del Medio Ambiente 1995: 5).

In terms of industrial waste, the figures are equally limited and unreliable; however, in 1991 the daily amount of solid industrial waste in urban areas was 6311 tons (Republica de Colombia Ministerio del Medio Ambiente 1995: 135). This waste comes mainly from thermoelectric power plants, basic metal-producing companies and food industries. An estimated figure of 541 tons of potentially dangerous solid industrial waste is produced in the country every day. Much of this waste is considered toxic, particularly that from mining and oil exploration (Republica de Colombia Ministerio del Medio Ambiente 1995: 49). In Colombia daily BOD (biological oxygen demand) and COD (chemical oxygen demand) production by the industrial sector is 514 tons and 780 tons, respectively.

To counteract the above and other environmental problems, the national proposal contained the following five environmental goals:

1. To promote a new culture of development
2. To improve quality of life
3. To promote cleaner production
4. To establish sustainable environmental management
5. To direct population growth and migration

These goals were implemented through seven different programmes: promoting the protection of strategic ecosystems; safe water; clean seas and coasts; forest development; better cities; population control policies; and cleaner production.

The programme involving cleaner production was conceived as a way

> to introduce an environmental dimension to the production sectors and to reorient them towards management strategies and the use of technologies which are environmentally friendly, increasing efficiency in the use of energy and water resources, involving the substitution of raw materials, and optimising processes,

modifying products and reducing the production of waste (Republica de Colombia Ministerio del Medio Ambiente 1995: 23).

The 1994 national plan also established objectives for cleaner production in each of the following sectors:

1. Energy
2. Mining
3. Transport
4. Manufacturing industry
5. Agriculture and cattle farming
6. Fishing
7. Health sector (particularly the production of solid wastes and pathogenic materials)
8. Tourism

Clearly the plan marked a very significant shift in the government's attitude towards environmental problems, in stark contrast to its previous efforts and written statements. Before the foundation of the Environment Ministry, the national environment authority was a secondary level institute that was part of the Ministry of Agriculture.

In terms of land management, the government has proposed a Law for Territorial Ordering (land-use planning, in English terminology) which has been approved by Congress. This law sets each one of the approximately 1,000 municipalities in the country an 18-month deadline to work out a land-use plan.[2]

The public sector and the promotion of cleaner production

The implementation of the 1994 plan in the area of cleaner production followed the following topics (Republica de Colombia Ministerio del Medio Ambiente 1998):

1. Integration with other governmental policies
2. Institutional strengthening
3. Clean production agreements
4. Environmental licences
5. Economic instruments

2 The land use plan has to be completed by the end of 1999.

6. Technical assistance and training
7. Environmental quality follow-up and monitoring
8. Environmental policies and regulations
9. Environmental management systems
10. International co-operation agreements

The above subjects are described below.

Integration with other government policies

One of the key tasks of the Ministry has been to secure the involvement of other state bodies in the environmental effort. Thus, several inter-administrative agreements have been made with the following groups: Ministry of Economic Development, Ministry of Defence, Ministry of Agriculture and Rural Development, Ministry of Mines and Energy, Ministry of Education, and the National Road Institute.

Institutional strengthening

Thirty-one Corporaciones Autonomas Regionales, which are the organisations in charge of the environmental policy at regional level, have been provided with monitoring equipment, and 19 environmental laboratories have gained more support. The effort has also included the design and mounting of environmental quality monitoring networks in the main cities of the country. The Ministry of the Environment has undergone a reform which includes the creation within the Ministry of the Sustainable Development General Direction to encourage the clean production policy. This entity consists of four working groups: sector activity, policies and regulations, compliance management, and urban environmental activity.

At urban level, there is an initiative called 'Institutional Strengthening for Urban Environmental Management' which has obtained a loan from the World Bank for US$20 million. This programme supports environmental initiatives in the main cities: Bogotá, Cali, Medellín, Barranquilla, Cartagena and Sogamoso. The Environmental Unit of the Ministry of Mines and Energy has also been created (1994), as well as the Environmental Subdirection of the National Road Institute (1995) and the Environmental Management Unit of the Ministry of Agriculture (1996).

Clean production agreements

As part of the stated goals and objectives of the 1994 National Development Plan, on the 5 June 1995[3] the government publicly announced its approval of the 'Cleaner Production Agreement'. This agreement defines a new national approach towards environment as a combined enterprise with the private sector.

3 This is Environment Day worldwide.

The agreement was signed by the most important private bodies in the country such as the National Industrial Association, the Coffee Growers' Association, the Association of Traders, the National Agricultural Association and more than 20 other important organisations, representing the majority of the country's private sector. The agreement outlines a set of goals and methods for cleaner production to be adopted by the government and private sector, it establishes a permanent committee to follow up the agreement, and sets up the general outline of what should be done to involve environmental management in the country's private sector. The agreement opens the way to regional and industrial-sector agreements that may be elaborated upon, approved and put into practice, in order for the ideas to be put into effect.

In 1996, the COMIS (Comité Interinstitucional de Producción Limpia—Clean Production Interinstitutional Committee) was created with the purpose of applying the above agreements. This committee is an advisory group set up to guide and co-ordinate initiatives to apply the agreement. It consists of two representatives from the Ministry of the Environment and one representative from each one of the following industry groups: the National Industry Association, the Colombian Construction Chamber, the Colombian Mining Council, Acoplasticos, the Marketers' Federation and the Colombian Grower Society.

As well as this basic agreement, several other more specific ones have been signed:

1. With industries in the area of the Cartagena bay (1995)
2. With industries in the eastern part of Antioquia, a very important industrial region near Medellín (1995)
3. With small gold miners (1995)
4. With cane-sugar growers and sugar producers in the western part of the country, principally in the Cauca Valley Department (1996)
5. With the coal production sector (1996)
6. With Antioquia pig breeders (1996)
7. With Antioquia flower growers (1996)
8. With the oil producers (1997)
9. With industries from the region of Sogamoso (brick manufacturers and limestone quarry) (1997)
10. With the electricity sector (1997)
11. With palm oil growers (1997)
12. With pita fibre producers (1997)
13. With pesticide producers (1998)
14. Brick and clay by-product producers (1998)
15. With industries in Barranquilla (1998)

Each one of these agreements has an operative committee to follow up its implementation. Some results of such agreements are as follows:

- Cartagena industries agreement (Mamonal): BOD 38% reduction, 20% suspended solids reduction, and 91% grease and oil reduction
- Industries in the western region of Antioquia: 54% reduction in BOD and 67% reduction of suspended solids
- Sugar cane grower agreement: reduction of burning in 11,400 ha (from the 180,000 ha currently grown)
- Agreement with flower growers: 85% removal of the following agrochemical products from sewage: malathion, diazinon, furadan and clorpyrifos

Apart from these major agreements, others have been secured in various regions of the country, some under the lead of the Environment Ministry, others under the lead of the Autonomous Regional Corporations.

In order to produce a signed agreement, a specific process has to be followed. The institutions involved in this process are: the Environment Ministry, the representatives of the firms involved, the regional corporation with jurisdiction in the area, and occasionally a representative of the environmental NGOs. After a series of discussions, the agreement is signed and a follow-up committee is established.

This system has been useful in the efforts to promote environmental management, although some have criticised (with good reason) the lack of significant participation by the community and by NGOs, in terms of knowledge and authority. Another criticism is that legislation has to be obeyed by everyone: thus there should be no need to sign agreements in order to make firms comply with environmental management plans; this should be mandatory under the existing laws.

Environmental licences

From 1994 to the first half of 1998, the General Direction of Sustainable Development granted 590 environmental licences. The environmental licence is a permit required by several projects and activities to allow their operation. The licence is obtained after the owner of the project or activity submits an environmental impact study. Of the 590 licences issued, 31% relate to infrastructure and 59% to hydrocarbons.

This activity has demanded much effort from the Ministry, but has been a good start to streamline studies and processes. Indeed, there are 51 models of reference terms for different projects and there are 12 more under preparation.

Economic instruments

The state has been working on several economic instruments to encourage environmental management. First, firms that contaminate waters are charged a retributory fee. A regulating decree was issued which provides that each environmental authority implements a charging system in its respective area. This process has been slow and only some authorities are observing it with any rigidity.

Likewise, some measures indicated by Law 99 of 1993 have not been applied, such as a charge for using water from rivers, lakes and underground sources, with the purpose of rationalising water use and to finance environmental management. In this sense, the Ministry has been reluctant to issue a standard to regulate this charge.

On the other hand, the Tax Reform Law of 1995 provides for exemption from sales tax payment on national and imported equipment and devices destined for: construction, installation, mounting and operation of environmental control and environmental monitoring systems; recycling and waste processing; scrubbing or sewage treatment plants; atmospheric emissions or solid residues; and recovery of rivers and basic sanitation. From 1995 to June 1998, 297 companies obtained a tax reduction, for approximately $9 million.

Technical assistance and training

In May 1996 the Environment Ministry organised the first international seminar on cleaner production in Cartagena.[4] This was an important opportunity to gain an insight into the current situation in Colombia (and worldwide) as far as cleaner production is concerned. It also highlighted projects being developed within the Ministry with international co-operation (primarily with the governments of Canada, Germany and the Netherlands) in certain areas of cleaner production. In April 1998 a second international seminar was organised by the Ministry.

In March 1998 the Environment Ministry created the National Center for Cleaner Production and Environmental Technologies (CNPMLTA) in Medellín. This centre will provide technical assistance services on clean technologies and has the support of 39 founder members among state entities, companies, groups, universities and some bodies from other countries.

Environmental quality follow-up and monitoring

Fourteen environmental regional entities were provided with regional environmental laboratories, 31 authorities were provided with environmental monitoring equipment, four air quality monitoring networks were designed and became operational in Bogotá, Medellín, Cali and Bucaramanga and eight air quality monitoring networks were put in operation in other regions. In addition, actions have been taken to accredit laboratories in the country to operate within the National Environmental System.

Environmental policies and regulations

From 1994 to 1998 policies on the following aspects were formulated: cleaner production, solid residue integral handling, and water and pesticide integral management.

The regulations have not worked as expected, as the Ministry has been slow in issuing standards, mainly due to private-sector pressure. Some of the standards issued

---

4 Cartagena is a city on the Caribbean coast of Colombia and has been declared a World Heritage Site by UNESCO.

are still to be regulated with more accuracy, particularly with respect to air contamination control. The main standards already approved are for: air contamination control, retributory tax payments for regular liquid spillage, water rationing and efficient use, environmental licence procedures, hazardous wastes[5] and construction residues.

Environmental management systems

The Environment Ministry and the Ministry of Economic Development have been working on a joint basis in order to establish a national accreditation and certification system for environmental management systems pursuant to ISO 14001. The entity in charge of such accreditation and certification is the Superintendency of Industry and Commerce. Up to now, two industries have been certified; however, an increase is expected in the next few years.

The 1999 development plan and cleaner production[6]

In August 1998, the newly elected government began to work on the cleaner production issue, by appointing a known environmental defender who had been linked to an important NGO in the country. It can be said that, with respect to cleaner production, the previous government had already prepared the way in 1994 and 1998 and therefore that the same policy was only being maintained.

In May 1999 the Congress approved the new development plan called 'Environmental Collective Project'.

> The purpose of the environmental plan is to make a collective work around the construction of a sustainable development model, based on the nation's social and environmental potential, and based on a participative process, that establishes respect for ecological patrimony and preserves the environment, as a source of national and world wealth for present and future generations.

In this plan, water is the key element, a strategy that is complemented by education and environmental awareness and with the participation of Colombia in the environmental perspective at international level.

The programmes proposed in the new plan are as follows: water, biodiversity, forest, urban quality of life, endogenous productive process sustainability, cleaner production and green markets. The cleaner production programme continues very much as it had been developed by the previous government, with no significant modifications. This has been possible thanks to the continuity of personnel at the Environment Ministry.

---

5 Colombia is a signatory of the Basilea Agreement on hazardous wastes.
6 Republica de Colombia Ministerio del Medio Ambiente 1995.

The policy includes elements concerning land-use planning, particularly in mining areas and hydroelectric projects. The oil sector is also considered as a critical player, and therefore '. . . control of significant indirect impacts generated by these activities and which are ultimately the cause of the colonisation' are proposed. Cleaner production agreements also contemplate the establishment of specific goals which, once adopted, are compelling, as currently goals are either not established or are not complied with. Small and medium-sized companies (SMEs) are also encouraged towards cleaner production practices.

Issuing environmental licences should also be a quicker process, and the productive sector should become a self-regulating agent, although the latter is not sufficiently detailed in the plan. Other regulating and economic measures will be adopted, although there is little clarity in this respect.

Business initiatives for environmental management

While the government has been trying to negotiate with the private sector to produce a set of objectives and agreements, several organisations have been following their own paths in establishing environmental management systems.

In 1990 the National Association of Industries (ANDI) set up an environmental programme at both national and regional levels which requires each regional branch of ANDI to create an environmental committee that promotes environmental planning among its members. A brief was drawn up containing recommendations on how these committees should be organised, how they should function, and how they should produce results. In 1996 ANDI organised courses on ISO 14001 and environmental auditing, and a course on input–output and industrial metabolism models.

Another private initiative that started in Canada but which also has roots in Colombia is 'Responsible Care'. This approach to environmental management works on the basis of ten guiding principles and six codes of management practice, mainly in the chemical sector. Several of the country's industries belong to this programme, including one of the largest paper industries in the Cauca Valley. In April 1998, 51 companies in Colombia were adhering to the Responsible Care programme (Responsabilidad Integral 1997).

In 1993 a group of major Colombian firms created the Colombian Council for Sustainable Development (CECODES), intended to find a solution to the problem of generating continuous economic development offering opportunities to a great number of people, while protecting the environment and making efficient use of natural resources. The group decided to set the following goals: economic growth, social equality and environmental protection, within the framework of 'responsibility' (CECODES 1995).

CECODES is the Colombian branch of the World Business Council for Sustainable Development (WBCSD) and its purpose is to implement an environmental project in each one of the 23 member firms and to develop a set of environmental indicators to evaluate the environmental performance of each firm. CECODES also shares its research

Activity	Company
Sugar production association	ASOCANA
Coal extraction and export	EL CERREJON
Flower production association	ASOCOLFLORES
Banking	OCCIDENTE and FUNDACION FES
Computer production	COMPAQ
Cement	ARGOS and SAMPER
Ceramic floors	CERAMITA
Insurance	BOLIVAR and DE LIMA
Iron and steel production	CONSTRUCEL
Importing of machinery for industry	IMOCON
Design and construction of water treatment systems	INDECO
Personal cleaning products	INEXTRA
Wood products	PIZANO
Polypropylene production	POLIPROPILE
Cardboard and paper	SMURFIT CARTON DE COLOMBIA
Home cleaning products	VARELA
Bricks	SILICAL
PVC pipes and accessories	PAVCO

Table 1: COMPANY MEMBERS OF CECODES THAT HAVE UNDERTAKEN ENVIRONMENTAL MANAGEMENT PROPOSALS

Source: CECODES 1997: 11-60

and findings with other firms in the country. The approach of this group is based on the idea that competition has to be increased on a national and international level. The vision of competition is founded on three main goals which each firm must seek to obtain in a dynamic and balanced way to assure its viability in the long term. These goals are: economic efficiency, social equality and efficient management of natural resources.

In 1995 the member companies of CECODES published a paper requiring that their activities should be oriented to the achievement of the three above-mentioned goals. These companies are detailed in Table 1 under their relevant activity. By way of example, an industry member of CECODES that produces ceramic floors and has been involved in cleaner production can offer the following figures: daily water consumption of 600 m^3 with 500 m^3 of recycled water; air emissions of 30 mg/m^3 (whereas regulations stipulate 100 mg/m^3 from each chimney); and 100% reprocessing of solid wastes (CECODES 1995: 26).

In 1997 CECODES submitted a report showing economic, social and eco-efficiency performance indicators for most affiliated companies, thus following the proposed model (CECODES 1997).

The standardisation of environmental regulations in Colombia

Colombia's standardisation organisation is called ICONTEC. It is a private organisation supported by private and public firms, whose role is to establish a system of standards in the country. In so doing, ICONTEC has approved many standards concerning environmental matters.

ICONTEC is a member of the International Organisation for Standardization (ISO) and, as such, played its role in the recent discussion of the ISO 14000 series standards. In Colombia ISO 14001 and 14004 have been approved after they were defined at an international level in September 1996. The organisation has also been publishing and distributing the regulations and giving courses on their use, through training in France. Furthermore, ICONTEC co-ordinates the efforts of seven working groups that have been established country-wide, in accordance with their definition by Technical Committee 207 of ISO. Colombia established the accreditation group for ISO 14000 in the Ministry of Economic Development (Superintendencia de Industria y Comercio), as was done with ISO 9000.

Environmental management, research and education in Colombia

One of the most important problems faced by environmentalists in Colombia is the lack of training at various levels in the country's education system. A decade ago, environmental problems were only the concern of 'sanitary engineers' or 'chemical engineers'. As the problems continued to grow, a new approach was needed; yet only after the creation of the Environment Ministry in 1993 did a new series of graduate careers appear, as well as a great number of postgraduate courses, masters and PhDs.

But, even though the effort has been significant, the orientation of actions towards environmental protection have centred around the public sector and not on the private sector. The areas studied most include environmental impact analysis, river basin management plans, water pollution control and treatment plants, air pollution and basic ecology. Only recently have subjects such as industrial environmental management, environmental audits and enterprise and environmental management appeared.

The Universidad del Valle in Cali, Colombia has been working for several years on water treatment systems and recently organised an International Workshop on Cleaner Production (October 1998) in co-operation with the Institute for Hydraulics and Environment (IHE) in the Netherlands. Other courses have been introduced on business and environmental management at undergraduate level in industrial engineering in this same university and in graduate courses in other universities in Cali, Cartagena, Bogotá and Barranquilla. Universidad Pontificia Bolivariana in Medellín has been working on air pollution control for several decades and has been helping the industrial sector in the area to control their emissions. The Universidad Nacional de Colombia

	Manizales	Pereira
Total (industry)	980	1,152
Total (commerce)	4,470	8,138
Other firms	3,504	2,518
Total	**8,954**	**11,808**

Table 2: NUMBER OF REGISTERED FIRMS (INDUSTRY AND COMMERCE) AT THE CHAMBER OF COMMERCE IN MANIZALES AND PEREIRA, COLOMBIA, 1995

Source: Cámara de Comercio de Manizales, 1995; *Cámara de Comercio de Pereira,* 1996.

in Bogotá has also been working on solid waste control. Obviously, in many universities all around the country, courses are being taught on specific areas of pollution control and environmental management.

There are several institutions that are working with industries to assess their environmental impact. One of them is ACERCAR in Bogotá, which has published several guides for environmental systems in the industrial sectors of chemical production, textiles and graphic arts and others concerning productivity and responsible water and energy use in SMEs.

Environmental management at local level

Recent research carried out by the author in two of Colombia's medium-sized cities shows how environmental management is being undertaken in the country at local level. The two cities concerned are Manizales with 327,000 inhabitants and Pereira with 387,000, both located in the central coffee-producing region of the country, a region of relatively important economic development (FESCOL 1997a, b). The study acknowledges that, to obtain good results in the area of environmental protection, a system must be created that links together the different 'elements' involved. There is a need to create a synergetic effect through the co-ordination of the elements. It was found that no such system exists and that efforts remain somewhat isolated.

The 'elements' involved in the study were the firms, the environmental authorities[7] (including municipal), the education and research institutions (universities) and the consultants and laboratories that give support in identifying environmental effects (emissions, effluents, noise, hazardous materials, food, etc.). Table 2 shows the total number of businesses located in each city that are involved in environmental management in their day-to-day operation. This gives an idea of the kind of job that has to be done to promote environmental management in a city from the point of view of the productive sector.

7 In Manizales, Corporación Autónoma Regional de Caldas and, in Pereira, Corporación Autónoma Regional de Risaralda.

It was found that in both cities the organisation that has made the greatest efforts to implement environmental management is the National Association of Industries (ANDI). In both cities there is an environmental committee with representative members from the firms and from the universities. In Manizales there has been a significant effort to organise courses in ISO 14000 and there is a medium-term plan, proposed by the ANDI, to integrate the municipality, the universities and the Environment Ministry. In Pereira, a conference is held every month to discuss the impact of environmental aspects on management. Nevertheless, industries in general are still struggling to comply with the regulations and there is still a lack of action in implementing environmental measures in the private sector, although there are some excellent exceptions, especially in Pereira.

In Manizales one of the most polluting industries belongs to the regional government. The public sector contributes enormously to the pollution of the country. The municipalities do not treat their waste-water or their solid waste, and roads and public services are provided with limited environmental impact analysis. In both cities it was found that there is a lack of high-quality consultants to help the firms in setting up environmental programmes. Many of the firms limit their actions to legal compliance, mainly in water pollution and air emissions, but are not working towards the comprehensive approach suggested by the ISO 14000 series, Responsible Care or other integrated models. Also, there is a lack of laboratory support for the identification of environmental effects and for monitoring. Pereira is trying to set up an information system on environmental quality through the use of environmental indicators over a period of time.

From the point of view of the environmental authorities, both cities are trying to set up systems to control and evaluate environmental effects and quality, but are still a long way from having control over the situation. This is due to the flexibility that the environmental authorities have shown towards the private sector in the past, in terms of the violation of environmental regulations. Little has been done to educate the private sector, by whom the environmental authorities are still viewed as 'punitive' bodies. Also, there is little control or law enforcement in the public sector for political reasons, because in general the environmental authorities are part of the local political power. Any help received from the Environment Ministry is scarce and the funds for local action have to be obtained through part of a property tax.

Although the universities in both cities offer undergraduate and graduate careers and environmental studies, they are still state-oriented, or treatment-oriented without an integrated approach. Such an integrated approach has to involve a multidisciplinary effort that includes environmental management as a result of administrative, economic, technological and social considerations combined with the different 'elements' to produce a sustainable result.

The conclusions of this study are important in that they show that there are actions being taken to work in environmental management, that the private sector is open and working towards this objective, but that there is still a long way to go in order to have firms acting as responsible agents with a sustainable operation. The environmental authorities also have a long way to go in terms of their real control over the situation; furthermore, they do not have a support group to help enterprises work towards cleaner production, they act merely as 'control' agencies and not as organisations that promote environmental management.

Another study carried out by the author in Cali in 1994 regarding the concrete sector showed that there are great differences between industries in their approach to environmental management. At that time Cali was undergoing one of the most important construction booms in its history but, at the same time, with the recently created Environment Ministry, more controls were being implemented. An evaluation of 13 concrete plants belonging to five different companies, showed that the land-use regulations were so weak that one could locate a concrete plant in a residential area. Some of the concrete plants were using technological advances to control their environmental effects (such as filters for total suspended particles, waste-water control systems from the washing of the mixer vehicles, machines for reclaiming raw materials, and landscape design), but other plants were constructed and operated with practically no consideration for the environment or for workers' health.

The environmental plan that was proposed, although approved by the five directors of the companies, needed the approval of their boards. Unfortunately, the change in local government and the recession that hit the construction industry in Cali changed the prevailing political and economic conditions of the study, and the implementation of the plan was undertaken primarily by one or two companies that were already working in environmental management.

The study developed a system called the 'balance method', much the same as life-cycle assessment, but following a systems approach method. One of the important conclusions reached was the need to 'open up' the system or industry being studied and relate it to raw material production and transportation on one hand, and to transportation and product consumption on the other. This methodology clearly showed the need to integrate environmental management efforts all along the productive chain—in this case, from the producers of sand and gravel, the cement industries and the companies that transport these raw materials to the concrete plants, to the concrete production plants and finally the construction companies.

Conclusions

If one had to place Colombia somewhere on the road to environmental management from the point of view of the productive sector, we would have to admit that it is still at the beginning. The country has the legal and administrative bases to support the process, but it lacks a real commitment both from the private sector and the government to continue the journey. In general, there is a lot of work being done, especially by the large firms that have the financial resources to work in the area of environmental management. Some of them, particularly multinational companies, have come a long way and are working in accordance not only with Colombian legislation but also with their own requirements. Several examples of technological actions involving environmental considerations have been identified.

The lack of political focus by the environmental authorities, their limited control, and their insufficient resources prevent them from becoming leaders in the process, although in the period between 1997 and 1998 a lot of efforts were channelled into the cleaner production programme. But the change is more likely to come either from the firms themselves or from their organisations, through the application of voluntary agreements and the establishment of working groups.

Universities have an important role to play in this issue, and one would expect a change in their orientation from environmental state management towards the productive sector and the introduction of environment management aspects in graduate areas such as management, economics, engineering and architecture. The lack of a network of laboratories to help the process of identifying environmental problems and monitoring is also a serious handicap that needs much investment but, recently, the government has been working on the idea of laboratory certification.

However, there is an awareness in the productive sector that environmental management is a one-way road with no return. In the future it will be an integral part of every business and not an option but a necessity.

4 TRADE AND ENVIRONMENT

14

Trade Liberalisation and the Developing World

The Environmental Impact of the Uruguay Round

Matthew A. Cole

THE URUGUAY ROUND is the name applied to the most recent round of World Trade Organisation (formerly GATT) trade negotiations, completed in April 1994 after eight years of discussions. Over one hundred countries took part in the negotiations and the final agreement achieved a significant degree of trade liberalisation by committing its signatories to reductions in both tariff and non-tariff trade barriers. The final agreement is predicted to have a significant impact on global production levels and trade patterns, with a notable impact on the developing regions. François *et al.* (1995), for example, predict that the developing world will experience 57% of the estimated increase in global production levels, equivalent to an increase of approximately US$120 billion.

With such an impact on global GDP and trade patterns, the Uruguay Round agreement can be expected to have implications for the health of the environment. In general terms, there are three ways in which a trade agreement of this nature can affect the environment. First, by providing greater access to foreign markets the agreement is likely to increase the scale of economic activity. This *scale* effect will generally prove damaging to the environment. Second, following trade liberalisation, a nation may change its production techniques. This may occur either as a result of greater access to 'cleaner' production technologies or in response to increased environmental legislation, the demand and resources for which generally increase with income levels. This effect is referred to as the *technique* effect and is likely to prove beneficial to the environment. Third, the reduction in trade barriers may mean that it is no longer profitable for countries to produce certain goods, while the production of other goods now becomes profitable. Thus, the Uruguay Round is likely to change the composition of a nation's industry, with the associated environmental impact depending on which sectors expand and which contract. This effect is referred to as the *composition* effect.

This chapter estimates the impact of the Uruguay Round in terms of these three effects, on five air pollutants, for China, East Asia, South Asia, Africa and Latin America. Estimates are also made for the USA and the European Union (EU), allowing a distinction to be made between the nature of the environmental impact in developed and developing regions. Monetary estimates of the resultant pollution damage are also made. The impact on pollution emissions is estimated using the results of François *et al.* (1995), who estimate the impact of the Uruguay Round on GDP and sectoral production levels, together with sectoral pollution intensities from Hettige *et al.* (1994). These are then used in conjunction with estimates of the relationship between per capita pollution emissions and per capita income (GDP).

Methodology[1]

Estimating scale and technique effects

Using the results of François *et al.* (1995), who estimated the impact of the Uruguay Round on regional levels of GDP, the impact on regional levels of *per capita* GDP can be calculated.[2] This increase in income is likely to affect pollution emissions via scale and technique effects; that is, through the increase in the actual scale of GDP and through changes in the techniques of production which may arise with increasing incomes. These two effects can be captured through the estimation of the relationship between per capita income and per capita pollution emissions. For many pollutants, this relationship forms an inverted-U shape, known as an environmental Kuznets curve (EKC), as shown in Figure 1.

Figure 1 illustrates the increase in pollution emissions that occurs due to the increasing scale of economic activity, up to the turning point. Beyond this point, the scale effect is overcome by the technique effect which arises as increasing incomes provide greater resources for environmental legislation, while the demand for such legislation increases with income as individuals find that their more basic needs have been met. EKCs therefore combine scale and technique effects and are econometrically estimated for each pollutant using panels of cross-country time-series data for per capita income and per capita emissions. Further information regarding the estimation of the EKCs can be found in the appendix to this chapter, while Cole *et al.* (1997a) provide a thorough discussion of the nature and estimation of EKCs.

Having estimated EKCs for each pollutant, with an intercept for each region, it is possible to apply the estimated levels of per capita income in the presence of the Uruguay Round (from François *et al.* 1995) to provide the resultant level of per capita emissions, for each region. Multiplying by the level of population then provides the

1 Further details of this methodology can be found in Cole *et al.* (1997b, 1998).
2 François *et al.* (1995) estimate the impact of the Uruguay Round on the pattern of world production and on the world level of income (GDP) using a 19-sector, 13-region computable general equilibrium model of the world economy.

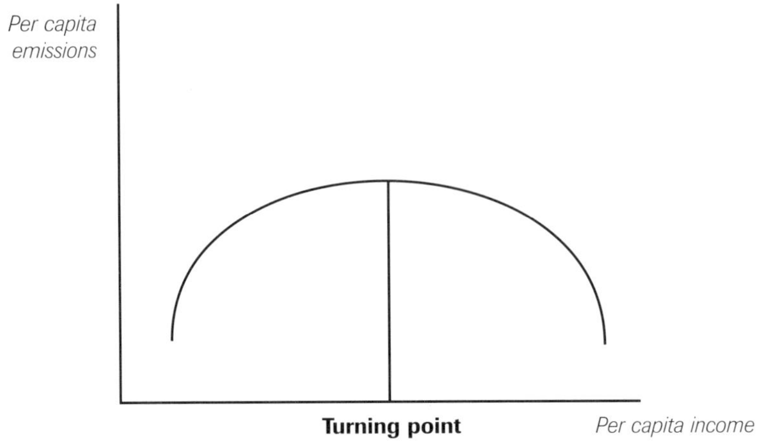

Figure 1: AN ENVIRONMENTAL KUZNETS CURVE

total level of emissions resulting from combined scale and technique effects. This can then be compared with the total level of emissions in the absence of the Uruguay Round.

Note that scale and technique effects are estimated for two scenarios. The first scenario estimates emissions for 1990 if the full Uruguay Round Agreement had been in place and compares this with 1990 emissions in the absence of the Uruguay Round. The second scenario estimates emissions in 2000 if the initial 1990 impact on GDP had 'grown' for ten years and if this growth rate was also 0.5% higher than World Bank (1994) per capita GDP growth rates as a result of the Uruguay Round.[3] These emissions are then compared with emissions in 2000 in the absence of the Uruguay Round. UNEP (1993) population forecasts are used to obtain total emissions for 2000 from per capita emissions.

Composition effects

François *et al.* (1995) also provided estimates of the regional change in production levels, for International Standard of Industrial Classification (ISIC) industrial sectors. Hettige *et al.* (1994) provided the average level of pollution emissions, for each air pollutant except carbon dioxide, per million US dollars of total output, for each ISIC sector. Applying these estimated sectoral pollution intensities to the estimated sectoral output changes provides an estimate of the composition effect, for each region and each pollutant. Hettige *et al.* (1994) provided pollution intensities only for the USA. However, for the purposes of this chapter, these US intensities have been scaled for

3 The choice of a 0.5% addition to the rate of growth is not intended to be an estimate, but merely serves to illustrate the impact on the pollutants of a change in the rate of GDP growth.

different regions according to the difference between the *total* pollution intensity in the USA and in each region. For example, if the total sulphur dioxide intensity of GDP (total sulphur dioxide emissions/GDP) is 50% higher in China than in the USA, then each US *sectoral* intensity has been increased by 50% for China. Although this assumes that sectoral pollution intensities are uniformly higher or lower in each country compared with the USA, it was felt that this approach was preferable to the application of US intensities to other countries without modification. The estimated EKC equations were rearranged to provide regional pollution intensities for each pollutant.

The pollutants

The impact of the Uruguay Round is estimated in terms of five of the most prevalent air pollutants in developed and developing countries alike. Nitrogen dioxide, sulphur dioxide, carbon monoxide and suspended particulate matter (SPM) all have a direct impact on the locale in which they are emitted, and hence have been classified as local air pollutants.[4] In contrast, carbon dioxide is believed to contribute towards global warming and does not have a direct local impact. It has thus been classified as a global pollutant.

Local air pollution

Emissions of sulphur dioxide and SPM stem largely from the burning of coal and oil, while the use of motor vehicles is largely responsible for emissions of carbon monoxide and nitrogen dioxide. Concentrations of sulphur dioxide and SPM are particularly high in the developing regions and especially in large urban areas. Indeed, WHO/UNEP (1992) report that the 15 largest cities in the developing world are all exceeding World Health Organisation guidelines for SPM concentrations, by more than a factor of two in many cities.

All four local air pollutants cause respiratory difficulties and other health problems, and poor health and nutrition in developing countries are likely to make their populations more susceptible to these effects. The adverse health effects associated with SPM are perhaps proving to be the most problematic, however, with the World Bank (1992a) estimating that, if average levels of SPM were to stay within WHO guidelines, between 300,000 and 700,000 premature deaths per year could be avoided in the developing world.

Global air pollution

Carbon dioxide is the principal 'greenhouse gas' and is believed to contribute to global warming. It is released through the burning of fossil fuels and has the effect of

4 Nitrogen dioxide and sulphur dioxide also have a transboundary impact since they are responsible for acid deposition in lakes, rivers and forests.

preventing heat from escaping into the upper atmosphere. It is therefore widely believed that any increase in carbon dioxide concentrations will cause the earth's surface and lower atmosphere to become warmer, with social, ecological and economic implications. The magnitude and geographical distribution of these impacts is still far from certain, however.

Results

The impact on pollution emissions

Table 1 provides the estimated composition effects and scale and technique effects for each pollutant, for the developing regions. These effects are then aggregated to provide the total impact of the Uruguay Round on each pollutant, in each region. Since composition effects could not be estimated for carbon dioxide, scale and technique effects alone are reported for this pollutant.

With regard to composition effects, François *et al.* (1995) suggested that the phase-out of the Multi-Fibre Arrangement (MFA) will be the largest cause of changes to industrial composition. Under the MFA, a large proportion of clothing and textile exports from developing countries to industrial countries was subject to quotas. The liberalisation of the MFA is therefore predicted to cause the textile and clothing production sectors in the developing world, and particularly in Asia, to expand. This is likely to occur at the expense of the heavy industrial sectors such as steel and non-ferrous metals. Since the textile and clothing sectors are far less pollution-intensive than the latter sectors, the Asian regions are predicted to experience a reduction in air pollution as a result of compositional changes. Latin America does not experience the contraction of the industrial sectors and compositional changes are therefore expected to generate an increase in air pollution. For Africa, the direction of the changes in compositional air pollution varies depending on the pollutant. In contrast to the Asian regions, the developed regions are expected to see a contraction of textile and clothing sectors and an expansion of the heavy industrial sectors. As Table 2 illustrates, these compositional changes have the effect of increasing air pollution.[5]

The impact of scale and technique effects on the developing regions is unequivocally to increase pollution. Per capita GDP levels in each developing region are below those estimated at the turning points in the EKCs. Table 6 (page 218) provides these estimated turning point per capita income levels for the five air pollutants. These turning points indicate the point at which, on average across the different regions and across the time-series considered (1970–92), emissions are estimated to have started to fall, or are predicted to start to fall. Since income levels in the developing regions are below the local air pollution turning points, the regions are positioned on the upward sloping portion of the curves. The increase in per capita GDP resulting from the Uruguay Round therefore serves to increase per capita pollution emissions and hence total emissions.

5 Cole *et al.* (1997b) provided the full compositional effects, for each pollutant, for 9 regions and for 17 separate industrial sectors. The compositional effects reported in Tables 1 and 2 are aggregates of the pollution changes in these 17 sectors.

	Composition effect (%)	Combined scale and technique effect (%)		Total impact (thousand tonnes and %)			
		Scenario 1 1990	*Scenario 2 2000 + 0.5%*	*Scenario 1 1990*		*Scenario 2 2000 + 0.5%*	
Nitrogen dioxide							
China	-0.3	1.6	6.3	*118*	1.3	*1,179*	6.0
East Asia	-0.1	2.0	4.0	*60*	1.9	*218*	3.9
South Asia	-0.5	1.0	6.6	*9*	0.5	*237*	6.1
Africa	0.2	2.0	7.8	*21*	2.2	*160*	8.0
Latin America	0.6	0.9	3.7	*59*	1.5	*232*	4.3
Sulphur dioxide							
China	-1.8	2.1	7.0	*18*	0.3	*1,026*	5.2
East Asia	-3.1	1.8	3.8	*-190*	-2.2	*79*	0.7
South Asia	-0.6	1.3	8.0	*31*	0.7	*729*	7.4
Africa	-0.08	2.8	9.7	*57*	2.7	*486*	9.7
Latin America	0.5	0.7	1.9	*124*	1.2	*317*	2.4
Carbon monoxide							
China	-0.1	1.8	8.5	*569*	1.7	*5,322*	8.4
East Asia	-1.9	1.9	5.3	*9*	0.03	*521*	3.4
South Asia	-0.5	1.3	8.9	*67*	0.7	*1,467*	8.4
Africa	-0.05	2.4	10.1	*107*	2.4	*963*	10.0
Latin America	0.2	0.8	2.5	*184*	1.0	*588*	2.7
Suspended particulate matter							
China	-0.9	2.0	10.0	*21*	1.1	*325*	9.1
East Asia	-3.0	1.7	3.7	*-26*	-1.3	*36*	0.7
South Asia	-0.4	1.4	10.0	*10*	1.0	*201*	9.6
Africa	0.02	2.7	10.7	*15*	2.7	*130*	10.8
Latin America	0.4	0.6	2.4	*31*	1.0	*92*	2.8
Carbon dioxide							
China		1.4	6.2				
Rest of Asia		1.7	8.9				
Africa		1.8	7.4				
Latin America		1.0	4.6				

Table 1: THE ENVIRONMENTAL IMPACT OF THE URUGUAY ROUND ON THE DEVELOPING REGIONS (THOUSAND TONNES [ITALICISED] AND PERCENTAGE OF TOTAL 1990 EMISSIONS)

Source: Cole *et al.* 1998

It can also be noted that the scale and technique effects are generally larger than the composition effects so that the direction of the former dictates the direction of the total impact. East Asia is the exception to this rule, however, since, for sulphur dioxide and SPM, the predicted fall in pollution as a result of compositional changes is larger than the increase in pollution from scale and technique effects in scenario 1. This has resulted in an overall predicted reduction in these pollutants in East Asia.

	Com-position effect (%)	Combined scale and technique effect (%)		Total impact (thousand tonnes and %)			
		Scenario 1 1990	*Scenario 2 2000 + 0.5%*	*Scenario 1 1990*		*Scenario 2 2000 + 0.5%*	
Nitrogen dioxide							
China	-0.3	1.6	6.3	*118*	1.3	*1,179*	6.0
EU	0.1	0.2	0.9	*36*	0.3	*145*	0.9
USA	0.1	0.05	-0.3	*23*	0.1	*-60*	-0.2
Global	0.04	0.5	2.6	*349*	0.6	*2,267*	2.6
Sulphur dioxide							
EU	0.3	-0.4	-4.4	*-8*	-0.1	*-602*	-4.1
USA	0.4	-0.7	-5.4	*-103*	-0.3	*-1,473*	-5.0
Global	-0.3	0.2	0.5	*-64*	-0.1	*343*	0.2
Carbon monoxide							
EU	0.2	-0.3	-3.9	*-129*	-0.1	*-1,951*	-3.7
USA	0.1	-0.6	-4.4	*-590*	-0.5	*-5,007*	-4.3
Global	-0.05	0.1	0.4	*158*	0.1	*1,151*	0.4
Suspended particulate matter							
EU	0.2	-0.3	-3.6	*-7*	-0.1	*-143*	-3.4
USA	0.2	-0.8	-7.1	*-45*	-0.6	*-426*	-6.9
Global	-0.1	0.1	0.3	*-2*	-0.0005	*56*	0.2
Carbon dioxide							
EU		0.4	2.4				
USA		0.3	1.8				
Global		0.5	3.3				

Global estimates are aggregates of the seven regions reported in this chapter, together with Japan and Eastern Europe.

Table 2: THE ENVIRONMENTAL IMPACT OF THE URUGUAY ROUND ON THE DEVELOPED REGIONS (THOUSAND TONNES [ITALICISED] AND PERCENTAGE OF TOTAL 1990 EMISSIONS)

Source: Cole *et al.* 1998

Pollution changes for scenario 2 can be seen to be considerably greater than those for scenario 1. Furthermore, the difference between pollution emissions in 2000 with and without the Uruguay Round was also estimated under the assumption that the Uruguay Round *did not affect* the GDP growth rate. For reasons of space those results are not reported here, although estimated pollution changes were generally of a very similar magnitude to those estimated for 1990 (scenario 1). The impact of the increased growth rate is therefore notable.

Africa is predicted to experience the largest relative increase in emissions for the four local air pollutants as a result of the Uruguay Round; emissions of carbon monoxide and suspended particulate matter are predicted to increase by over 10% in this region if the GDP growth rate is increased by 0.5%. The largest absolute increase in emissions as a result of the Uruguay Round is predicted to occur in China. For the developed regions, per capita income levels now exceed the estimated turning point per capita income levels for sulphur dioxide, carbon monoxide and suspended particulate matter, resulting in a predicted reduction in these pollutants as a result of scale and technique effects. Furthermore, these effects outweigh the composition effects, thereby resulting in a negative total impact. For carbon dioxide and nitrogen dioxide, emissions are predicted to increase in the developed world, with the exception of scenario 2 for nitrogen dioxide in the USA. Although the results for carbon dioxide stem only from scale and technique effects, the results in Tables 1 and 2 illustrate that, for the four local air pollutants, it is the increase in GDP originating from the Uruguay Round that determines the direction and broad magnitude of the environmental impact, rather than the changes to the composition of industry. Emissions of sulphur dioxide and SPM in East Asia are the only exception to this. Thus, scale and technique effects generally dominate the composition effects.

The total impact of the Uruguay Round is very different for developing and developed regions for three of the local air pollutants (sulphur dioxide, carbon monoxide and SPM). In the developing regions, the Uruguay Round is likely to increase these pollutants, quite significantly if the Uruguay Round also increases the GDP growth rate. In contrast, these pollutants, which are already falling in the developed regions, are expected to fall further in these regions as a direct result of the Uruguay Round. The global impact on emissions of these pollutants is therefore relatively small since the increase in emissions in the developing world has been offset by falling emissions in the developed regions. Emissions of nitrogen dioxide and carbon dioxide, however, are predicted to increase in developing and developed regions alike, as a result of the Uruguay Round, with the exception of nitrogen dioxide in the USA for scenario 2. These changes have resulted in a predicted global impact that is larger than that estimated for the other pollutants.

In many developing countries, the continued reliance on the burning of oil and coal for cooking and heating has meant that emissions of SPM and sulphur dioxide, in particular, have increased steadily in recent years. This reliance on oil and coal, together with the lack of resources generally available to tackle environmental damage, means that any significant expansion of industrial output, such as that originating from the Uruguay Round, is likely to prove environmentally damaging. In the developed world, a change from domestic coal burning to electricity and natural gas for cooking and heating, together with the introduction of strict air quality legislation, has meant that emissions of many local air pollutants are now falling. For such pollutants, technological fixes are generally available, providing sufficient resources exist. Any increase in GDP in the developed world is therefore likely to further reduce emissions of these pollutants. Nitrogen dioxide emissions have continued to increase even in many developed countries, however, largely due to steady increases in traffic volumes. The recent introduction of three-way catalytic converters in the developed world has now seen nitrogen dioxide emissions from transport begin to stabilise and in some cases fall. The growth of carbon dioxide emissions is a problem common to developed and developing regions alike. Although energy use per unit of GDP is now falling in many developed countries, the growth of GDP itself has been sufficient to ensure that energy use (and hence carbon dioxide emissions) also continues growing, albeit at a decreasing rate. In many developing countries, *both* GDP and energy use per unit of GDP continue to increase, resulting in rapidly escalating levels of energy use and carbon dioxide emissions.[6] As a result, the increase in GDP associated with the Uruguay Round is predicted to increase emissions of carbon dioxide in developed *and* developing regions, with emissions increasing by a greater proportion in the latter.

Monetary damage estimates of the change in pollution emissions

Having estimated the impact of the Uruguay Round on pollution emissions, rough monetary estimates of the costs/benefits associated with these changes in emissions can now be made. Fankhauser (1995) and Pearce (1993) provide monetary estimates of the damage resulting from one tonne of nitrogen dioxide, sulphur dioxide, carbon monoxide and SPM in terms of factors such as the costs of illness among individuals exposed to the pollution, damage to buildings, etc. Fankhauser (1995) estimates the damage from one tonne of nitrogen dioxide and sulphur dioxide to cost $5,000 and $2,500, respectively, while Pearce (1993) estimates the damage cost of one tonne of carbon monoxide and SPM to be $15.23 and $14,283, respectively. These costs are undoubtedly subject to much uncertainty and, furthermore, are based on the costs incurred in developed countries. Therefore, following Fankhauser (1995), these costs are scaled according to differences in income to obtain estimates for developing regions.[7] Fankhauser (1995) also estimates the marginal social cost associated with one tonne of carbon dioxide to be $20.30. Since the impact of each tonne of carbon dioxide is globally distributed, the source of the emissions is not relevant. As a result, the same figure of $20.30 is applied to carbon dioxide emissions in all regions.[8]

Table 3 illustrates that the developing regions may suffer a monetary cost of many millions of US dollars as a result of increases in air pollution brought about by the Uruguay Round. The developed regions are also predicted to suffer costs due to increases in emissions of nitrogen dioxide and carbon dioxide, but to also enjoy monetary benefits due to reductions in sulphur dioxide, carbon monoxide and SPM, as shown in Table 4. The fact that the monetary costs have been scaled according to income means that, for the local pollutants at least, the estimates for the developed regions are significantly larger than those for the developing regions even though emissions changes are often larger in the latter. As a result, global estimates tend to be heavily influenced by the costs/benefits predicted for the developed world.

---

6 Although increasing more rapidly in developing regions, per capita levels of both energy use and carbon dioxide emissions remain substantially lower compared with those in developed regions.

7 More specifically, damage costs in middle-income and low-income regions are taken to be one-fifth and one-tenth of those in developed regions, respectively. Latin America and East Asia are classified as middle-income regions and China, Africa and South Asia are classified as low-income regions. Scaling according to income, in this manner, assumes that the per capita damage costs incurred in all countries form an equal proportion of each country's per capita income.

8 The interpretation of the monetary costs associated with carbon dioxide emissions should be different from those from the other, local, air pollutants. For carbon dioxide, a region's monetary cost does not represent the cost incurred by that region, but rather that region's contribution to global costs. This stems from the fact that damage from carbon dioxide emissions is likely to be shared globally.

	Scenario 1 1990	Scenario 2 2000 + 0.5%
Nitrogen dioxide		
China	59	590
East Asia	60	218
South Asia	4	118
Africa	10	80
Latin America	59	232
Sulphur dioxide		
China	5	257
East Asia	-95	40
South Asia	8	182
Africa	13	121
Latin America	62	159
Carbon monoxide		
China	1	8
East Asia	0.03	1.6
South Asia	0.1	2.2
Africa	0.2	1.5
Latin America	0.6	1.8
Suspended particulate matter		
China	30	464
East Asia	-75	104
South Asia	14	287
Africa	21	186
Latin America	90	263
Carbon dioxide		
China	125	1177
Rest of Asia	286	2249
Africa	63	527
Latin America	55	388

Table 3: THE MONETARY COST/BENEFIT ASSOCIATED WITH THE CHANGE IN AIR POLLUTION EMISSIONS FOR THE DEVELOPING REGIONS (US$ MILLION, 1985)

Source: Cole *et al.* 1998

Table 5 provides the total pollution cost/benefit experienced by each region. It can be seen that, for scenario 1, all regions experience a monetary cost except the USA which experiences a substantial monetary benefit. Globally this results in a moderate monetary cost. For scenario 2, the developing regions all suffer monetary costs totalling several billion US dollars. However, the EU, and the USA in particular, experience a monetary benefit of many billions of US dollars, resulting in a substantial global benefit. Table 5 therefore indicates that it is the developing regions that will incur pollution damage as a result of the Uruguay Round. However, in monetary terms, Table 5 also indicates that all regions benefit from the Uruguay Round since the estimated monetary costs under scenario 1 form only a small proportion of the estimated financial benefits from the Uruguay Round, estimated by François *et al.* (1995) for 1990 had the Uruguay Round been in place.

	Scenario 1 1990	Scenario 2 2000 + 0.5%
Nitrogen dioxide		
EU	180	724
USA	117	-302
Global	553	1,890
Sulphur dioxide		
EU	-19	-1506
USA	-257	-3682
Global	-240	-4668
Carbon monoxide		
EU	-2	-30
USA	-9	-76
Global	-11	-110
Suspended particulate matter		
EU	-105	-2038
USA	-647	-6090
Global	-721	-8317
Carbon dioxide		
EU	77	567
USA	107	672
Global	747	6287

Table 4: THE MONETARY COST/BENEFIT ASSOCIATED WITH THE CHANGE IN AIR POLLUTION EMISSIONS FOR THE DEVELOPED REGIONS (US$ MILLION, 1985)

Source: Cole *et al.* 1998

	Scenario 1 1990	Scenario 1 as a % of GDP gains	Scenario 2 2000 + 0.5%
China	220	1.25	2496
East Asia	33	0.1	1489
South Asia	169	1.65	1714
Africa	107	1.0	916
Latin America	267	1.32	1044
EU	131	0.41	-2283
USA	-689	1.9	-9478
Global	328	0.15	-4918

Table 5: TOTAL REGIONAL POLLUTION COST/BENEFIT (US$ MILLION, 1985)

Conclusion

As a result of the Uruguay Round, the environment of the developing regions is likely to suffer from increases in all five of the air pollutants considered in this chapter. Although these increases are reasonably small, they become as large as 10% of 1990 emissions if the Uruguay Round increases GDP growth rates by 0.5%. In the developed world, the Uruguay Round is predicted to benefit the environment by reducing emissions of three local air pollutants, but the environment may be harmed through increasing emissions of nitrogen dioxide and increasing emissions of carbon dioxide from developed *and* developing regions.

In the developing regions the increased local air pollution stemming from the Uruguay Round is likely to have a detrimental social impact, resulting in greater incidences of smog, respiratory problems and premature death. Furthermore, it is now widely believed that increasing carbon dioxide emissions will contribute towards global warming with potential social, ecological and economic implications.

Trade liberalisation, however, and the economic growth that it generates, will undoubtedly increase income levels thereby relieving poverty and providing potentially immense social benefits. Many social problems experienced in developing countries require financial resources to remedy them and access to clean water, sanitation, education and healthcare has typically only improved in regions experiencing income growth. Indeed, in the last 25 years, across developing countries as a whole, per capita income levels have increased by 70% while at the same time life expectancy has increased from 51 to 63 years, and primary school enrolment rates have reached 89% (World Bank 1992a). Although these improvements have not been evenly spread, the potential social benefits of economic growth for developing countries are clear to see. Poverty is also responsible for many environmental pressures currently faced by developing countries. Population growth is often highest in regions experiencing acute poverty since children can provide security and farm labour, while poverty also places pressure on families to cultivate unsuitable, and often ecologically fragile, land. Poor, undeveloped regions also lack the resources necessary to tackle environmental problems. The fact that emissions of most local air pollutants are now falling in the developed regions illustrates that *some* environmental problems can be mitigated with financial resources.

In the developing world, the social benefits stemming from the Uruguay Round are likely to exceed those costs resulting from increased environmental damage. Indeed, in strictly financial terms this analysis indicates that *all* regions will benefit from the Uruguay Round since GDP gains are significantly larger than the estimated pollution damage. This pollution damage should not be underestimated, however, since it is likely to have a detrimental impact on health and since financial gains may not be able to compensate for irreversible damage to ecosystems. There is therefore a clear need for any industrial expansion to occur with efficient use of resources and using technologies that are less environmentally damaging. Environmental legislation is also required. While the source of the funding necessary to implement such high-technology equipment and environmental legislation is obviously problematic, and beyond the

	Turning point	Data source
Sulphur dioxide	$5,200	UNEP 1993
Nitrogen dioxide	$20,300	UNEP 1993
Carbon monoxide	$9,900	OECD 1993, 1995
Suspended particulate matter	$7,300	OECD 1993, 1995
Carbon dioxide	$62,900	Marland *et al.* 1994

Table 6: ESTIMATED TURNING POINTS AND DATA SOURCES FOR THE FIVE AIR POLLUTANTS (US$ 1985)

Source: Income data from Summers and Heston 1991

remit of this chapter, the role of the industrialised countries may need to be significant.

Finally, it should be pointed out that this analysis provides only a very partial estimate of the environmental impact of the Uruguay Round, considering only five air pollutants at the expense of many other environmental indicators. It is therefore likely that the environmental costs and benefits estimated in this chapter considerably underestimate the total environmental impact.

Appendix: Environmental Kuznets curves

EKCs are obtained by estimating the following reduced form equation using generalised least-squares regression analysis and using cross-country/region panel data:

$$\ln e_{it} = (\lambda + \kappa_i F_i) + \eta \ln y_{it} - \theta(\ln y_{it})^2 + \varepsilon_{it} \qquad (1)$$

where: e_{it} denotes the pollutant in per capita form in country/region i, year t; y_{it} denotes per capita income in country/region i, year t; F_i denotes effects specific to country/region i; $i = 1, \ldots, n$ countries; $t = 1, \ldots, T$ years.

Table 6 provides the turning point per capita income levels for each pollutant, estimated from equation (1). To put these turning points in context, in 1992 per capita income was $17,945 in the USA, $12,724 in the UK, $6,253 in Mexico, $1,282 in India and a mere $408 in Chad (Summers and Heston 1991).

15

Reaping the Benefits

Trade Opportunities for Developing-Country Producers from Sustainable Consumption and Production

Nick Robins and Sarah Roberts

IN TODAY'S globalising world, export success is one of the major routes to economic progress for developing countries. But the conditions for success are changing as producers face rising environmental expectations in key export markets, resulting from tightening regulations, new corporate practices and changes in consumer values and lifestyles. These new expectations reflect the growing recognition that current patterns of consumption, particularly in the richer, industrialised world, are environmentally unsustainable. As the world moves into the next century, profound changes in the ways in which goods and services are produced, traded and consumed will be required both to reduce the burden on the global environment and to ensure that a growing population has the resources to meet its needs.

The primary responsibility for taking the lead in making these changes lies with the industrialised economies of North America, Western Europe and East Asia. For developing-country producers seeking to succeed in these markets, sustainable consumption presents a number of new and often complex challenges. For those that can adapt to these requirements and start moving to anticipate trends, there could be new opportunities to capture market share, generating financial, environmental and social benefits in the process. Across the developing world, a small number of pioneering companies are gaining premium prices and increased market share by providing goods and services that meet these new expectations. This chapter looks at the lessons to be learned from these pioneers to ensure that sustainable consumption moves out of the margins and into the mainstream.

Setting the Agenda

Sustainable consumption and production came of age as an international policy priority at the United Nations Conference on Environment and Development (UNCED) in June 1992—the 'Earth Summit'. After strenuous bargaining, during which the US had declared that 'the American way of life is not up for negotiation', the Agenda 21 action programme agreed by the world's governments concluded that 'the major cause of the continued deterioration of the global environment is the unsustainable pattern of consumption and production, particularly in industrialised nations' (Agenda 21, Chapter 4).

The Earth Summit highlighted the deep divide in consumption and pollution between North and South, whereby the 20% of the world's population in the rich 'North' account for 50%–90% of consumption and pollution. To remedy this, Agenda 21 called on the industrialised world to take the lead in making the shift towards more sustainable consumption and production patterns. It also called for a new balance to be struck to make international trade flows, development needs and environmental sustainability mutually reinforcing.

In the five years that have passed since Rio, much attention has been focused on trying to understand the implications of changing production and consumption patterns for the global economy. Essentially, sustainable production and consumption present two sides of the same coin. The emphasis of sustainable production is on the supply side of the equation, focusing on improving environmental performance in key economic sectors, such as agriculture, energy, industry, tourism and transport. Sustainable consumption addresses the demand side, looking at how the goods and services required to meet basic needs and improve quality of life—such as food and health, shelter, clothing, leisure and mobility—can be delivered in ways that reduce the burden on the earth's carrying capacity.

Both sides are, of course, inextricably linked, and a life-cycle perspective is required to pinpoint where action can best be taken along the product chain to reduce environmental damage to levels within the earth's carrying capacity. Traditionally, most efforts have been directed at cleaning up the production process, particularly in industrialised countries. Now attention is shifting to finding new ways to change consumption so that the conventional links between meeting needs and improving the quality of life with pollution, resource use and waste can be broken. Doing this is, of course, highly complex, with many structural factors combining to make up the patterns of consumption, which then determine the choice and use of goods and services. Key factors include market dynamics, technological innovation, physical infrastructure, the regulatory framework and cultural values.

Experience has shown that sustainable consumption and production presents four critical challenges at the international level.

1. *Restructure the economy over the long term*

Given the current pressures being placed on the world's environment and the prospects of further expansion in both affluence and human numbers, there is a growing consensus in international policy circles that tough targets for environmental improvement will have to be achieved in the years ahead. The European Union has now adopted the goal first proposed by the Wuppertal Institut for a 'Factor 10' improvement in resource productivity and pollution reduction over the next 30 years; there is also growing enthusiasm for a more short-term 'Factor 4' improvement over the next decade (von Weizsäcker *et al.* 1997).

2. *Rethink core ethical values*

Much of the sustainable consumption agenda has been driven by citizens and non-governmental environment, development and consumer organisations promoting more sustainable lifestyles. Indeed, for many, sustainable consumption is not a scientific or a technical question, but is first and foremost a question of values, requiring a new 'ethic of living sustainably'. For environmental organisations such as Friends of the Earth, this means designing strategies for sustainable production and consumption on the basis that each person should have equal access to the natural resources required to meet his or her needs (FoEE 1996).

3. *Reform the policy framework*

The scale of change required means that action cannot be left up to market or voluntary efforts alone. Governments have a major responsibility for putting in place an assertive policy and regulatory framework that rewards producers and consumers whose actions contribute to long-term sustainability and penalises those that deplete natural capital (see Box 1).

4. *Renew international co-operation*

Shifting the global economy onto a sustainable path will require an unprecedented degree of international co-operation. The requirements of an open world trade system need to be carefully balanced with the imperatives of environmental sustainability and poverty reduction. Transitional support will be required to support developing countries in the move to sustainable production and consumption methods, providing a new role for development assistance agencies. Already, international agencies are also supporting both sustainable production initiatives and efforts to promote trade in more sustainably produced goods and services. These range from the network of national cleaner production centres, supported by the UN Environment Programme (UNEP) and the UN Industrial Development Organisation (UNIDO) in Brazil, China, India, Mexico, Tanzania and Zimbabwe to Germany's GTZ Biotrade initiative for promoting exports of organic agriculture from almost 20 developing countries.

To date, however, international policy efforts to address sustainable consumption have resulted in much frustration and suspicion. There are genuine fears in many developing countries that much of the environmental criteria adopted in richer countries is protectionism in another guise, implemented to reduce the competitiveness of developing-country exports. Globalisation, increasing trade liberalisation and the establishment of the World Trade Organisation have raised the stakes. Consumption patterns and their 'footprints' are now increasingly international, as are aspirations.

INDUSTRIALISED-COUNTRY policy-makers and regulators have been taking action in six main areas with impacts for developing-country producers.

1. Product regulation. Limiting and phasing out the use of toxic chemicals that have adverse health effects for consumers has remained a critical area of activity. A prominent example has been Germany's ban on the import of textiles and other products treated with potentially damaging azo dyes.

2. Waste legislation. Governments are now placing greater emphasis on the duties of corporations to reduce consumer wastes through the 'extended producer responsibility' approach. For example, Germany's new Closed Substance Cycle and Waste Management Act, which came into force at the end of 1996, will mean that whoever produces, markets and consumes goods is now responsible for the avoidance, recycling, re-use and environmentally sound disposal of waste.

3. Economic instruments. Between 1989 and 1994, the number of economic instruments used for environmental policy purposes, such as taxes, charges, deposit–refund systems and tradable permits, increased by 50% in the OECD. These include a new landfill charge on waste in the UK, a new energy levy in the Netherlands and federal taxes on ozone-depleting substances in the US.

4. Product information. Considerable heat has been generated by the growth in environmental labelling schemes in the industrialised world, notably the European Union's Eco-label scheme. For example, the EU's Eco-label criteria for paper have been attacked by developing-country exporters for placing too high a premium on recycled content and thereby making it almost impossible for them to gain the label for their products made from sustainably harvested wood (IIED 1996). Elsewhere, positive steps are being taken to improve the access of developing-country products to eco-labels. Building on its 20-year experience with the Blue Angel scheme, Germany's Federal Environmental Agency is now developing a new initiative to improve communication and co-operation with developing countries to produce goods with high environmental and social standards.

5. Public procurement. Governments in North America, Europe and Japan are moving to integrate environmental provisions into their purchasing programmes. In October 1993, President Clinton issued an Executive Order on Federal Acquisition, Recycling and Waste Prevention to guide government agencies in the choice and purchase of environmentally preferable products. All federal government agencies are now also required to purchase Energy Star computers, monitors and printers. In Japan, a 'Green Purchasing Network' was established in 1996, comprising 400 companies, 100 governmental bodies and 100 private agencies.

6. Trade policy. Trade policies are also being changed in the industrialised world to give positive encouragement to sustainably produced goods from developing countries. For example, when the European Union updated its Generalised System of Preferences agreement with Asian and Latin American countries in 1994, it included a special incentive arrangement to provide additional preferences to countries implementing international agreements on sustainable forestry management. Some governments are supplementing their formal trade policies with additional efforts to transfer information both on new environmental regulations and on clean technology. One notable example is the GREENBUSS database launched by the Dutch Centre for the Promotion of Imports from Developing Countries (CBI). GREENBUSS is accessible on-line via the Internet and is used by trade associations and export promotion agencies in developing countries to find the latest information on regulatory requirements throughout the European Union.

Box 1: POLICY INNOVATION FOR SUSTAINABLE PRODUCTION AND CONSUMPTION

Environmentalists fear that the current trade rules, which mean that countries cannot discriminate against a product on the grounds of the way in which it was produced, will reduce the impact of many hard-won environmental regulations, ultimately leading to the lowest common denominator of environmental protection in the name of open markets and free trade. Sunita Narain and Anil Agarwal from the Centre for Science and Environment in India set out the dilemmas clearly in Box 2.

Threat or opportunity for developing-country exporters?

An increasing number of businesses is viewing these changes in a positive light, seeing new growth markets opening up. The *Harvard Business Review* in its January/February 1997 edition described the business implications of a sustainable world as 'one of the biggest opportunities in the history of commerce'. For business, this means going beyond compliance with environmental regulations and engaging in pollution prevention in their factories, product stewardship for their goods and services and investing in the new generation of sustainable technologies. In Europe and North America, a small committed group of companies has been experimenting with new ways of producing and selling goods and services, which create new market dynamics for developing-country exporters and suppliers. Three sectors have been particularly affected to date: forestry, food and textiles.

THE CREATION of a global economy is taking place at a time when the ecological impacts of production and consumption are increasingly spilling over national frontiers. However, the world currently lacks a clear system for resolving the tensions that this creates. One thing is sure: sovereign nations alone cannot take decisions in the best interest of the global environment.

Recent disputes over trade and environment have exemplified this problem. Developing countries have strongly opposed efforts by developed countries to introduce new environmental regulations that seek to alter the ways in which exports are produced. Thus, in 1991, the US banned imports of tuna and tuna products from Mexico on the grounds that the numbers of dolphin killed were far greater than by the US fish industry. But under international trade law such non-tariff barriers dealing with production processes are not allowed, and so a GATT dispute panel ruled against the US. India and other developing nations have more recently challenged a similar US ban on shrimp imports that have been caught in ways that damage turtle populations. While, on moral grounds, it is hard for any country to argue that it has the right to develop its economy on an unsustainable basis, there is a real fear in developing countries that new environmental regulations could be used as a way of reducing market access and increasing production costs, thereby harming their competitiveness. Developing countries also argue that trade measures are inherently unfair, as they can be used only by the economically powerful against the economically weak: what trade instrument can be used by Bangladesh or the Maldives to ensure that the US does not export products that have been produced with very high carbon emissions?

Box 2: TRADE, SUSTAINABLE CONSUMPTION AND THE ENVIRONMENT

Source: Robins and Roberts 1997

Forestry

For over a decade, high-profile campaigns have been waged to highlight global deforestation, particularly in the tropical rainforests, with the aim of pressurising government to introduce effective regulation. Campaigners urged individuals and institutions in industrialised countries to cut their consumption of wood-based products and boycott tropical timber in particular. Protests were staged outside shops identified as selling unsustainable timber. In Europe, environmental campaigns have certainly been one factor in the recent decline in imports of tropical timber. But when it became clear that regulation could not deliver sustainable forestry quickly enough, the focus shifted to the marketplace.

One example is the establishment of the Forest Stewardship Council (FSC), set up by a global coalition of environmental and social interest groups. The FSC has developed principles and criteria for sustainable forest management, which producers can voluntarily use to certify their products. Simultaneously, the FSC has formed buyers' groups in a number of countries of companies who pledge to phase out all non-FSC-certified wood producers by a certain date. The FSC is thus using business concerns about reputation, risk management and customer loyalty to develop a new market in sustainable timber. Interestingly, one of the most fervent business supporters of the FSC in the UK is B&Q, a DIY chain previously targeted by environmental groups. With support from NGOs and businesses, some developing-country producers are tapping into the lucrative international market for sustainable wood, thereby gaining higher prices and secure livelihoods (see Box 3).

Food

Agriculture has long been the mainstay of South–North trade flows, but the long-term decline in the real price for many commodities and the volatility of the commodity markets has resulted in highly insecure livelihoods for many developing-country producers. Now, however, some are gaining higher prices and long-term income security by selling their products into environmentally friendly or fair-trade markets in the North.

Concern about the environmental and animal welfare implications of intensive agriculture combined with some very well-publicised health scares (e.g. pesticide residues; BSE) has led to soaring demand for organic produce in many Northern countries. The European Union market for organic goods was estimated to be worth nearly ECU 3 billion in 1993, over half of which is met by imports. In the US, demand for organic food is growing at over 20% per year, providing lucrative markets for developing countries who can make up the shortfall between demand and domestic production.

And organic markets can indeed be lucrative. Although yields can be lower and labour costs higher than for conventional production, food that is certified organic fetches premiums of between 50% and 200%. In total, it is estimated that Northern consumers currently spend US$500 million on organic produce from developing countries, over and above what they would pay for conventional foodstuffs.

Gaining international market advantage through certification

When PIQRO Laminated Flooring Company, originally set up by the Mexican government, was sold, its new owners saw exports as the key to their future success. The company began sourcing its wood from Plan Piloto Forestal, a nearby community forest project part of which had been FSC-certified, and became the first company to export certified tropical timber flooring to the US. It was sold through a number of independent distributors and, after a few months of marketing, PIQRO products were picked up by a national store due to their certification. This attracted the attention of a number of large flooring distributors, including International hardwood Flooring (IHF), the largest tropical flooring importer in the US. IHF, which was seeking to differentiate its position in the market, negotiated to buy and distribute all PIQRO's export-grade products. In exchange for this exclusivity, IHF is investing in PIQRO to enable it to meet world standards, essentially becoming a strategic partner in PIQRO, helping PIQRO complete the metamorphosis from an unprofitable state-owned company serving the regional flooring market to a world-class exporter of high-quality sustainable products.

European demand supports small producers in the Solomon Islands

Forests are being exploited at a wholly unsustainable rate in the Solomon Islands as foreign timber companies buy up communal logging rights. Communities were finding the incentives offered difficult to resist in a country with few employment options and services, until NGOs in the Solomons and Europe began working together to develop trade in timber which would offer communities long-term sustainable livelihoods while maintaining the forest resource. NGOs are working with producer groups in the Solomons to develop sustainable management systems for the forests and gain FSC certification. The timber that they produce is being sold through alternative trading organisations in Europe, where there is high awareness of the impacts of unsustainable logging and willingness from individual and institutional consumers to seek out alternatives and, in some cases, pay a premium for wood products that are guaranteed as coming from sustainable sources. Producers receive 40 times more per tree than if they had sold their logging rights and they are provided with a decent long-term income.

Box 3: DEMAND FOR SUSTAINABLE TIMBER CREATES MARKET ADVANTAGES FOR SOUTHERN PRODUCERS

Source: Robins and Roberts 1997

Latin American producers have been particularly quick to tap into these markets. The organic sector in Mexico is now estimated to be worth US$500 million and Argentina is making serious efforts to develop its organic sector with sales rising from US$1.5 million in 1992 to a projected US$20 million in 1996. This rapid development has been supported by efforts to overcome the bureaucracy surrounding EU recognition of imported organic goods. By requesting equivalency status for its certification system, Argentina became the first developing country to obtain a place in the EU provisional list, thereby gaining market advantages.

Organic certification is one of the most widely recognised and trusted labels and essential for consumer confidence and payment of premiums. However, certification can be a slow, laborious and relatively costly process and a particular challenge to small developing-country producers. A common solution is to form co-operatives to bring down the costs and to develop domestic certification systems. Costs remain, however, and national legislation is required for full compliance with the EU requirements which can be an insurmountable hurdle for many developing countries.

The fair-trade movement has been taking practical action to try to increase trade from developing countries for over 20 years, focusing on providing secure sales, fair

A NUMBER OF ORGANISATIONS have been working with coffee producers' groups in developing countries for many years to develop fair international trade in this commodity. In recent years, these efforts have received a major boost with the development of recognisable fair-trade marks and the development of brands of instant coffee which are sold in mainstream retailers.

Cafedirect is one such brand, developed by a partnership of four fair-trade organisations with the aim of building an instantly recognisable, generally available brand of fair-trade coffee to which buyers would find it easy to switch. It is now sold in 1,700 supermarkets across the UK and sales have increased dramatically over the last five years, with Cafedirect now accounting for 3% of the roast and ground market and 2% of the instant market. It has become the third-best-selling brand of coffee in Safeway's, one of Britain's leading supermarkets, despite being 10% more expensive than conventional brands.

Fourteen producer organisations from Mexico, Costa Rica, Peru, Nicaragua, the Dominican Republic, Uganda and Tanzania supply Cafedirect, and the farmers and their families have benefited from higher price and secure sales. For some producer organisations, fair trade has provided secure foundations from which to convert to organic production generating environmental benefits.

Box 4: FAIR TRADE COFFEE: AN INSTANT SUCCESS

Source: Robins and Roberts 1997

prices and decent working conditions for poor producers. Over the last ten years, a variety of organisations have developed independent certification processes for a number of agricultural goods. The provision of quality control and marketing support for producers, and easily recognisable fair-trade marks combined with some strenuous market development work, has brought certain fair-trade goods out of the margins of health-food shops and onto the mainstream shelves of the majority of supermarkets in many countries. The most well-known fair-trade commodity is coffee (see Box 4), but a more recent success story is the fair-trade banana, which has seized 12% of the Swiss market and 9% of the Dutch market since its launch in 1996 (Smith 1997).

Fair trade can also bring environmental benefits. Ethical trading organisations encourage the producers with whom they work to improve the environmental sustainability of their production and reduce the use of external inputs such as pesticides and fertilisers. A number of initiatives with the producers of other beverages, such as tea and cocoa, which originally aimed to improve their economic and social conditions, have also resulted in environmental benefits as these producers convert to organic production.

Textiles

Textiles is another sector where attention has been focused on the environmental and social issues associated with production, leading to changing market conditions for developing-country producers.

NGO campaigns on the conditions of Southern workers who produce goods for Northern retailers have led to a number of firms developing codes of conduct for their suppliers. Examples include Nike and Gap, who were both targeted after poor working conditions at their developing-country subcontractors were revealed and the code of practice negotiated between FIFA (International Soccer Federation) and international

PATAGONIA is a fast-growing outdoor clothing company, based in California, which has taken an assertive stance on environmental and ethical issues since its foundation. The company started to introduce organic cotton to its products in 1991 and, although it did not meet with much consumer interest, in 1994 the Board of Directors decided that the environmental impacts associated with conventional cotton were severe enough to justify requiring that Patagonia's entire cotton range should be organic by 1996.

Patagonia worked with their suppliers to help them make the change. One of these was a Thai company who had never used organic cotton before but were willing to try. According to Michael Brown, Head of Environmental Assessment at Patagonia, both sides gained from the changes: 'We've benefited from their sophistication and willingness to engage in development with us; they've developed expertise in organic cotton which may be marketable elsewhere.' Patagonia reports buoyant sales and, as the company's founder Yvon Chouinard says, 'it is possible to apply our environmental principles and be successful'.

However, they believe that their products have sold well primarily for the traditional reasons that people buy their products. 'Our customers wanted the value in our products that they had always sought from us: durability, performance, fit, timeless styling.' The message is clear: ethical products can be highly desirable, but they have to meet all the other product criteria as well.

Box 5: INCORPORATING ETHICS INTO MAINSTREAM COMPANY POLICY

Source: Robins and Roberts 1997

trade unions to improve conditions in the production of sportswear and footballs after the use of child labour in the manufacture of footballs was revealed at the time of the World Cup.

Most of these codes of conduct have tended to focus on labour conditions, but some include broader social and environmental issues. Levi-Strauss, the US clothing manufacturer, has developed 'Terms of Engagement' with its potential business partners, which include environment, ethical, health and safety, legal, employment (including child labour) and community development conditions.

Other clothing companies have implemented ethical policies despite little consumer interest or public pressure (see Box 5).

Government policy and regulation have also forced producers to make some significant changes to their production processes in order to keep their markets. A prime example of how industry innovation and government support turned a potential threat to exports into an opportunity for growth and environmental improvement is given by the Indian response to the German ban on azo dyes.

In 1994, Germany prohibited the import of textiles containing certain azo dyes on health grounds, which had direct repercussions for exporters to the German market, particularly in India, where textiles account for nearly half of all exports to Germany. Similar regulations have now been introduced by other European countries, such as the Netherlands, and in the future it is likely that the whole European Union will adopt such regulations. This is exactly the type of regulation that many developing-country producers fear, potentially requiring costly use of new materials and changes in production processes if they are to keep their export markets.

The Indian government responded in two ways. First, having decided that there were sufficient domestic health concerns, they matched the German restrictions on

CENTURY TEXTILES, India's largest textile producer, managed to turn the new requirements into a market advantage through early awareness of the development of the regulations, good relationships with their customers and independent certification. In 1994, one of Century's major German clients sent through details of the new standards that they required, which essentially meant that Century had to find substitutes for a number of their dyes and become Eco-Tex certified.

The chemical technology manager, Mahesh Sharma, declared: 'I went through hell, but then there were dividends.' These dividends included the optimisation of the dyeing process, so that, although most of the substitute dyes cost 10%–15% more than their predecessors, overall production costs only rose marginally, and significant market advantages ensued. Eco-Tex certification enabled Century to charge an 8%–10% premium and bought them new buyers, particularly from the US and UK who re-export to Germany, increasing their market by 10% in the first year.

Box 6: TURNING BANS INTO DIVIDENDS: THE CASE OF CENTURY TEXTILES

Source: Robins and Roberts 1997

azo dyes; and, second, they provided support in terms of information and technical assistance to small mills, who were likely to find it the most difficult to adjust. The industry themselves took steps to meet or surpass these new requirements. One company that managed to incorporate sustainability requirements and remain internationally competitive is Century Textiles (see Box 6).

Opportunities in other sectors

It is not just in traditional developing-country export sectors where Southern producers are benefiting from moves towards more sustainable production and consumption. In higher value-added manufacturing sectors, such as consumer durables and electronics, Southern producers are increasingly having to meet higher production standards and energy-efficiency targets if they are to access export markets.

Take the case of refrigerators. Under the Montreal Protocol, which regulates the production, import and export of ozone-depleting substances (ODSs), industrialised countries were required to phase out the production of CFCs by 1996, while developing countries have until 2006. However, for Southern refrigerator manufacturers to export to Northern markets, they need to meet the higher environmental standards now. For a number of companies, this accelerated schedule has provided the route for market development (see Box 7).

Sourcing from the South: lessons for the future

The Earth Summit +5 meeting in June 1997 concluded bleakly that 'Five years after UNCED, the state of the global environment continues to deteriorate . . . Marginal progress has been made in addressing unsustainable production and consumption patterns' (UNCSD 1997).

There is no doubting the truth of this statement, but there is much that producers and consumers can do that will immediately contribute to improving the sustainability

FRIDGEMASTER IN SWAZILAND is the largest manufacturer of refrigeration products in southern Africa and was instrumental in Swaziland becoming a signatory to the Montreal Protocol in 1992. By 1993, the company had become the first producer of CFC-free goods in Africa. Currently, its major market is regional, with the bulk of its products being sold through outlets in South Africa, but it also exports to Mozambique, Botswana, Zimbabwe and further afield to Mauritius, Malta, Dubai, Turkey and Russia. By phasing out CFCs long before the international deadline, FridgeMaster hopes to enhance sales in existing markets and access new markets, particularly in Europe.

Although converting to CFC-free production cost the company US$4 million in operating costs, 6% of turnover, this has been more than recovered through accelerated sales, and the company has expanded significantly since it switched to CFC-free production, with sales through its major South African retailer, Hyperama, trebling in one year. In order to reach its target of 15% growth over five years, FridgeMaster is investing close to 4% of its profits in R&D, seeing this as the only way to maintain its competitiveness in world markets. The company is also focusing on reducing the energy consumption of its products as a way of appealing to European consumers willing to pay a premium for energy efficiency. Thus, rather than being a barrier to exports, the high expectations of European consumers fits with FridgeMaster's ambition of tapping new markets and continually adding value to its products.

Box 7: GAINING NEW MARKETS FROM PROTECTING THE OZONE LAYER: FRIDGEMASTER, SWAZILAND

Source: Robins and Roberts 1997

of production and consumption. The more that both consumers and producers can benefit from such efforts, the greater the progress that will be made; and this means high-quality products produced, used and disposed of in a sustainable way. Business has an important role to play; and pioneering companies are already taking advantage of the new trade opportunities generated by changing consumption and production patterns in their export markets. The challenge now is to build on the practical lessons success and target policy and market action towards removing barriers to change and enhancing further innovation.

◿ *Pioneers can make a difference.*

Pioneering companies, such as those profiled above, demonstrate that sustainable production and profitability can be combined and that the potential threat of changing markets can be turned into a business opportunity. Their success has come from a combination of long-term commitment and the development of the necessary capacity to make the transition.

◿ *No one can do it on their own.*

However, few companies will be able to make this transition on their own. What has proved central to success is new partnerships along the product chain. Support from NGOs, government agencies or close relationships with their buyers in the North is generally crucial to support the transition to more sustainable practices. This is particularly important for small and medium-sized firms who may face considerable information, skills and resource gaps. However, as the fair-trade movement has illustrated, relatively small amounts of support at the initial stages can result in significant dividends in the future.

Combining quality with sustainability

One fundamental element that is required if sustainability is to be combined with profitability is the need to retain high standards of quality. Few people will buy inferior products in return for sustainability benefits. As Flip van Helden said of the sustainable timber project in the Solomon Islands: 'Sustainable timber is a beautiful concept but we cannot sell a concept only, we are selling a product.' Century Textiles cloth, FridgeMaster fridges and FSC-certified timber all demonstrate that sustainability can mean high-quality products that meet all usual buyer specifications as well as delivering environmental and social benefits.

Independent verification and performance guarantees

Central to the credibility of sustainable products is a trustworthy labelling system, particularly if premium prices are being charged. Independent certification schemes provide buyers with a guarantee that the claims about the product can be substantiated and these have proved central to the development of many markets, including organic products, sustainable timber, environmentally friendly textiles and fridges and fairly traded goods. However, the certification process can prove to be a severe managerial and cost burden. Initiatives such as the training of local inspectors and the development of group certification schemes are essential if certification is not to become a barrier to small producers generally and producers in developing countries.

Moving sustainability into the mainstream

Supplier codes of conduct and sustainable procurement criteria can help to ensure that more sustainable practices go beyond the certified niches and enter the mainstream of trade. Ultimately, all commercial and institutional buyers should implement supplier criteria that can be independently verified. Ideally, such codes of conduct should cover both environmental and social issues. It is essential that retailers work with their suppliers to help them improve their performance rather than simply dropping those who cannot meet the standards immediately. Initiatives such as the UK Ethical Trading Initiative, a partnership of companies and NGOs that is working to develop a common system of monitoring and verification, are important developments in making the use of these codes more widespread and credible.

A supportive policy framework

Positive policy choices can make a difference to the ease with which sustainable initiatives can emerge and spread. The response of the Indian government to the German legislation on azo dyes helped turn a potential threat into an export opportunity for their textile producers. Governments in export markets have responsibilities to ensure that their policy-making processes are transparent to exporting countries and that new regulations are phased in in such a way that producers have time to make the necessary changes. Government procurement criteria can help to develop the market for more sustainable products, as can support for practical mechanisms for implementing sustainable production and consumption. In her support for the UK Ethical Trading Initiative, Clare Short, the UK Minister for International Development, has stressed the importance of partnerships between governments, business, consumers and pressure groups and especially the role of business since private trade and investment now dwarfs aid flows. These types of partnership are likely to play an even more important role in the future.

16

Multinational Corporations' Impacts on the Environment and Communities in the Developing World

A Synthesis of the Contemporary Debate

Titus Moser and Damian Miller

GROWING CONCERN about the social and environmental impacts of multinational corporations (MNCs) operations in less developed countries (LDCs) has generated considerable debate about the role of MNCs in sustainable development. This emotionally charged and often acerbic debate tends to be driven by and concentrate on sensational and high-profile cases, with limited analysis of common themes and possible solutions. In an attempt to move beyond the existing debate, this chapter provides a thematic framework for understanding the recurring issues at stake, supported by a range of case studies, and concludes with a number of recommendations for promoting sustainable business practice in LDCs. The contents of this chapter derive primarily from the exchanges between non-governmental organisations (NGOs) and MNCs. A forum for such exchange was provided by a workshop held at Cambridge University under the title of 'Managing Sustainability Dilemmas' on 19 February 1997.[1] The views contained within are those of the major stakeholders as expressed at this workshop,[2] with case study material and analysis provided by the authors.

1 Organised by the Committee for Interdisciplinary Environmental Studies, Cambridge University, UK. Tel: +44 (0)1223 333366; e-mail: *jhs15@cam.ac.uk*.

2 'Chatham House' rules were applied at this workshop, in which statements are made in confidence, without attribution.

Background

MNCs play an increasingly important role in LDC economies. LDC governments have retreated from direct intervention in the management of their economies, to adopt more market-based policies that emphasise private-sector investment and free trade (Fairbanks and Lindsay 1997). Simultaneously, MNCs are increasingly attracted to LDCs, based on the size of potential markets, access to natural resources and lower production costs. These concurrent trends have resulted in record high foreign direct investment (FDI) to LDCs.

Between 1981 and 1996, private sources of investment to LDCs grew from $13 to $244 billion, increasing fivefold between 1986 and 1993, and growing at over 30% per annum in the first half of the 1990s (IIF 1997; UNCTAD 1995b). Of this total investment, the most important is FDI by corporations which in 1996 accounted for 40% of total private flows, increasing from $24 billion in 1990 to $129 billion in 1997 (French 1997; UNCTAD 1997). Moreover, the World Bank estimates that FDI to LDCs will grow between 7% and 10% per annum over the next decade.

This increase in FDI by MNCs comes at a time when there is growing concern about how economic growth in LDCs can be achieved in a more sustainable manner—specifically how economic growth can be combined with environmental protection and greater social equity (Cairncross 1992; Daly and Cobb 1994; Redclift 1994; WCED 1987). This has prompted considerable discussion about whether MNCs can contribute to the sustainable development of LDCs.

There are those that question whether MNCs can ever serve as agents of sustainable development. Some view the prevailing global economic system—characterised by free trade and deregulation of local markets—as being the main cause of unsustainable business practice in LDCs (Costanza *et al.* 1995; Daly and Cobb 1994). Others point more to the intrinsic characteristics of MNCs, and question whether their overriding pursuit of growth and profit enables them to behave in a sustainable manner (Korten 1995).

Those less critical argue that MNCs' international expertise in project implementation, access to the latest technologies and considerable financial resources provide them with a unique capacity to behave in an environmentally and socially responsible manner (Hadlock 1994, Harrison 1994; Schmidheiny 1992; Tahija 1993; Wescott 1992). In light of these considerable resources, MNCs are viewed as not only being capable of behaving sustainably, but capable of shaping more sustainable policy frameworks (Choucri 1993).

Given the growing expansion of MNC operations in LDC economies, much of the contemporary debate tends to focus less on whether MNCs have the potential to advance sustainable development and more on how they might do so. It accepts MNCs' presence in LDC society as a *fait accompli,* and concentrates on the necessary changes, both external and internal to the MNC, for the latter to fulfil its potential as an agent of sustainable development.

Today, MNCs face criticism regarding where they choose to invest and how they operate once located in an LDC. Those MNCs facing greatest pressure are high-profile companies involved in extractive industries, often operating in pristine environments and potentially inhabited by indigenous populations. MNCs involved in more downstream activities, such as chemical manufacturers, have also faced criticism over their impact on the broader environment. Finally, global consumer MNCs have more recently been criticised over their social policies, in particular their exploitative work practices in LDCs (Jackson 1997).

MNCs recognise that, as global players in a world of instantaneous communication, they must respond to these concerns. However, MNCs and their critics differ on how they and other stakeholders should respond.

Four 'Rs' in the current debate

Four central themes within the contemporary debate on MNC activities in LDCs are:

1. Responsibility for sustainable development
2. Repositories of power for sustainable development
3. Representation for sustainable development
4. Re-organisation for sustainable development

1. *Responsibility for sustainable development*

Although there is a wider discourse about the responsibility of business for social welfare, responsibility in this context centres on two key concerns. First, critics contend that MNCs have a responsibility to be selective in their investment decisions in light of the prevailing socio-political conditions in LDCs. Second, having invested in an LDC, it is felt that MNCs have a responsibility to apply the highest prevailing standards necessary for minimising their environmental and social impacts, whatever the context of operation.

The decision to invest in LDCs

Critics maintain that there are circumstances where business should, out of principle, not invest in an LDC. They further contend that, when an MNC invests in, or has prior investments in, an LDC with questionable human rights and democratic records, it has a moral responsibility, given its size and power, to pressurise the relevant authorities for democratic reform and respect of civil rights. For instance, many felt that Shell should have intervened in the case of Ken Saro-wiwa in Nigeria, or at a minimum should have terminated their operations, as Pepsi did in Myanmar.

MNCs have in turn responded that, while they have a duty to behave in an environmentally and socially responsible manner, they have neither the power nor the internal mandate to influence broader political change. Moreover, their attempts to influence political processes, however well intentioned, can be interpreted as undue interference in the country's sovereign affairs. MNCs further contend that, if they do not themselves invest in a country, other lower-profile and potentially less conscientious companies will do so.

The application of global standards

Furthermore, critics maintain that MNCs have a responsibility to apply the same environmental and social standards wherever they operate: be it in a developed- or less-developed-country context. MNCs contest this point, with some claiming that they already apply global standards and others admitting that they do not, as it is not deemed an appropriate strategy.

Some MNCs are adamant that, through their internal health, safety and environmental policies, as well as internal audits, they already apply global principles. These proclamations are, however, called into question. A number of cases, including Shell in Nigeria and Texaco in Ecuador, are used by critics to illustrate that, in practice, universal standards are not always applied. NGOs argue that MNCs behave far more responsibly in a developed-country context where there is tighter legislation and greater public scrutiny.

Other MNCs maintain that standards and regulations *should* be developed at a local, rather than a global level, since conditions vary the world over. These MNCs feel that the task facing business is now to 'think locally and act globally'. Needless to say, NGOs dispute this approach.

Of those MNCs that do not believe in global standards, a number contend that their responsibility should primarily be to comply with local regulations and expectations. For instance, Disney Corporation justifies the low wages given to Haitian workers by its compliance with all relevant local legislation, including that pertaining to the minimum wage (Cooper 1997). While compliance with local legislation is considered important, critics of MNCs do not see this approach as reflecting responsible business practice. In many cases, social and environmental legislation in LDCs is weak, and, even where strong, there is often an absence of enforcement mechanisms.

Moreover, critics argue that, where local regulation is weak, MNCs have a responsibility to lobby for legislation that protects both local communities and their environments. MNCs typically respond that they should not be considered 'agents of change' on issues such as strengthening weak environmental and social legislation. However, critics point out that, when in the *economic* interest of MNCs, they have shown themselves willing to exert considerable influence over legislation and policy. For instance, oil companies lobbied for the passage of the 1971 Alaskan Native Settlement Claims Act, which needed to be passed prior to oil extraction in the Prudhoe Bay area (Chance and Andreeva 1995).

2. *Repositories of power for sustainable development*

A second important theme in the contemporary debate concerns which agents have the power to advance sustainable development in LDCs.

Power at the host-country level

MNCs feel strongly that the national government is ultimately the repository of power for promoting sustainable development. They argue that NGOs have a tendency to overestimate the power of MNCs and underestimate the ultimate power of the state. For example, governments can at any time nationalise MNCs' assets as seen in the cases of ITT in Chile and the oil industries in Iran, Peru and Venezuela.

However, given the dependence of local economies on MNCs' investments and, more generally, international financial markets, NGOs contest that, in reality, host-country governments do not today retain the power to enforce sustainable business practices. They cite, for example, the case of Nigeria, where an overwhelming percentage of Nigeria's foreign exchange derives from oil, thereby limiting the government's power to intervene. In support of this claim, critics note that, although Nigeria's environmental laws are strong on paper, in practice a number of oil MNCs have ignored these laws without sanction.

It has also been suggested that other factors might, in practice, limit the powers of the host-country government. In a number of LDCs, critics maintain that legislation on environmental issues was and continues to be written in direct consultation with the very businesses whose interests are at stake. Moreover, they assert that business and government interests can become so aligned as to exclude the interests of local communities. For instance, it has been reported that representatives of the Nigerian government and Shell have routinely switched from one organisation to the other, making it increasingly difficult to differentiate between the state and the MNC. MNCs counter that their internal operating procedures weed out corruption, and that this provides an effective mechanism against undue influence on government decision-making.

Power at the level of the international community

Variations in environmental legislation between LDCs and developed countries has led NGOs to call for international regulation of MNCs. In an age of globalisation, it is argued that laws at the purely national level do not lead to sustainable business practice and that it is instead necessary to regulate MNC activity at the international level. NGOs lament that there are no international standards, let alone an international enforcement regime to regulate MNC operations.

The MNC position, however, is that the global economy has a number of incentives for sustainable business practices—notably that negative public relations changes in consumer buying patterns and discontented employees generate competitive pressures for responsible behaviour. MNCs maintain that, as a consequence of this pressure, they now equate good environmental and social policies with good business: particularly in a world of global media and instantaneous communications.

Power at the level of the home country

The NGO community feels that, in the absence of power at the level of the host-country government (where the MNC subsidiary operates) or the international community, there is scope for formal and informal enforcement at the home-country level (where the MNC headquarters are situated). They cite the precedents provided by Ecuador's indigenous peoples taking Texaco to court in the US, and the consumer campaign against Shell in Europe regarding the disposal of the Brent Spar production rig at sea.

Power at the local level

Critics of MNCs contend that local communities are typically excluded by their own governments from any meaningful participation in projects in their own territories, citing cases such as RTZ in Madagascar and Elf in Peru. It is strongly felt that, if the local community does not want a project, they should have the power to stop it, or, at a minimum, have an active involvement in its definition; this is the principle of prior informed consent. MNCs have responded that they accept the principle of prior informed consent, but are not explicit in explaining whether the power of veto rests solely with national government or includes the affected communities.

Even in those cases where consent has been obtained from local communities, NGOs point to the asymmetry in knowledge between the MNC and the local community with regard to the impacts of the project. Specifically, they question whether communities have adequate information and, critically, are able to understand this information in a manner that allows them to make an informed decision. MNCs, however, contend that, through the activities of NGOs and their lawyers, local communities now possess better resources to make informed decisions.

3. *Representation by sustainable development*

The limited representation of affected communities in the project development process is a recurrent theme in the debate. In this regard, NGOs speak of a 'democracy gap' at the local level.

Representation by the host government

NGOs contest that the host-country government often does not represent the local interests. This is particularly the case in those countries with non-democratic regimes and excluded minorities. More profoundly, some representatives of the NGO community note that a universal feature of the development process within the nation-state has been the sacrifice of local interests for the sake of the so-called 'greater good'.

Nigeria is often cited as a case in point where, regardless of whether Shell was conforming with host-country legislation, the government, being a military dictatorship, was not representative of local community interests. It has been asked rhetorically, 'Why was Shell dealing with a military dictatorship? Why was it not dealing directly with the local people?'

MNCs counter that NGOs are expecting too much of business to bypass the national government and deal directly with more local communities. It has been asked, 'Who is business to decide that the national government does not legitimately represent the interests of the local people?'

Representation by the MNCs' national subsidiaries

Critics further submit that in-country subsidiaries of MNCs do not adequately represent the interests of local communities. The case of RTZ Mining in Madagascar has been cited by members of the NGO and some members of the MNC community as an instance where the subsidiary did not adequately represent the views of the local community.

Furthermore, it is asserted that the restructuring and downsizing of many MNCs means that their subsidiaries have inadequate human resources to represent local-community interests. MNCs respond that, with slimmer subsidiaries, decision-making has become less bureaucratic and more efficient, and thus they are now better prepared to respond to and represent local community interests.

In their defence, MNCs explain that it can be difficult to identify the 'true' local interest, and who represents it. One MNC representative has asked rhetorically, 'Is it a question of who talks the loudest?' This dilemma was illustrated by the follow-on question of 'Who, for example, speaks for the local community on the issue of the Newbury Bypass?'[3]—the point being that, if you spoke to the local community in Newbury, you would probably receive widely differing views on the possible merits and disadvantages of the bypass. NGOs contend that, in situations of this complexity, the burden of responsibility lies with MNCs to communicate to *all* local stakeholders.

However, even within the NGO community, it is acknowledged that the above strategy is perhaps unrealistic: the question was raised as to whether business actually has the *time* to deal with the diversity of contrasting views at the local community level. Furthermore, the difference in values between the MNC subsidiary and local community may be so great as to block effective communication. The question remains: 'Can the distinct, possibly non-monetary, values of a local community be effectively represented within an organisation that values profit above all else?'

Representation by the NGO community

Finally, NGOs assert that, since local community interests in developing countries cannot find representation in either the national government or MNC, that it is ultimately left to NGOs to represent the views of the local community. A member of the NGO community has offered the example of Papua New Guinea, where an NGO arranged for legal representation of the affected community in the Australian courts.

4. *Re-organisation for sustainable development*

It is acknowledged by both MNCs and NGOs that there are a number of important organisational constraints that hinder MNCs' responsiveness to sustainable development in LDCs.

Issue prioritisation and incentives

Critics contend that MNCs' practices are geared to maximise profits and growth, and thus, in the course of doing business, local environmental and social interests are often sacrificed. MNCs themselves acknowledge that, traditionally, environmental and, in particular, social issues are not always given the priority that they deserve. This situation has led to an absence of internal incentives and performance-related indicators for these issues. MNCs have identified the lack of incentives as a constraint at both the headquarters and subsidiary level, where performance still tends to be measured in terms of traditional financial and production criteria.

---

3 The Newbury Bypass was one of a number of UK government road-building projects to alleviate congestion in city centres. These projects have generated public concern over their environmental impact as the proposed bypasses often run through ecologically sensitive areas.

In particular, MNCs acknowledge that equal priority is not yet accorded to the issue of social responsibility. In the words of one MNC representative, community relations has traditionally been viewed as 'wallpapering on the wall', where the community relations department plays a 'sweeper, clean-up role', usually after the situation has already deteriorated. It is also recognised that, relative to environmental issues for which there are often technological solutions, it is perhaps more difficult to define the social responsibility of business and relevant standards.

The lack of priority given to social and environmental performance has traditionally been reflected in the organisational response from MNCs. These issues have been dealt with by autonomous departments, who are viewed as putting the brakes on financial gain. Consequently, they have not received the necessary financial and human resources and have lacked senior management support.

Inter-firm communications

NGOs question whether the current communication channels used by MNCs limit their capacity to behave sustainably. It is contended that, in an effort to please headquarters, there is a tendency for MNC subsidiaries to be economic with the truth regarding social and environmental impacts. While MNC headquarters may have the best environmental and social intentions, the feedback they receive from the field may not provide an accurate picture of reality. Therefore, it is only after serious and sometimes irreparable damage has occurred that headquarters become aware of the situation, such as the case of Shell in Nigeria and Union Carbide in Bhopal, India.

Possible solutions

The previous section has identified four important themes in the current debate on sustainable business practice in LDCs. This final section seeks to explore a number of possible changes that could be made to advance the responsiveness of MNCs to their social and environmental impacts. These have been divided into solutions that are: (1) external; and (2) internal to the MNC.

1. *External to the MNC*

A number of critics of the global economy and the role of MNCs therein advocate international regulation of MNCs on environmental and social issues: as in the European Union, where environmental and social standards are in the process of being harmonised. This approach has been advocated since the 1970s and, in spite of various initiatives within the United Nations, has been unsuccessful. Indeed, even where international conventions exist—notably the International Labour Organisation's *Convention 169 Concerning Indigenous and Tribal Peoples in Independent Countries*—there has been inadequate compliance. In short, there would not appear to be adequate support from MNCs or governments—North and South—to establish and enforce international regulation.

In the absence of international regulation

In the absence of international regulation of MNCs, a number of international voluntary codes have been established—for instance, the 1976 OECD Guidelines for Multinational Enterprises (which does not explicitly address environmental and social issues), the Valdez Principles and the 1991 Business Charter for Sustainable Development established by the International Chamber of Commerce (Hagg 1984; Sanyal and Neves 1991; ICC 1994). Yet the critics of MNCs feel that, without sanctioning powers, these voluntary codes do not adequately protect local communities and their environment (Mayhew 1997).

MNCs feel that international market forces can provide the necessary competitive pressures for sustainable business practices. NGOs share this view, but contend that this is conditional on their efforts to expose recalcitrant MNCs and mobilise consumer interest in the North. Moreover, international market forces would only appear to be effective for high-profile MNCs, such as oil companies with up- and downstream operations and MNCs that rely on their brand names, such as Levi-Strauss, Gap, Nike and Disney.

Home-country legislation

NGOs propose that, without international regulation and with weak legislation in the host country, it should be possible to enforce responsible behaviour in the country of the MNC's headquarters. In this way, marginalised communities might find a voice in the courts of the North. NGOs point to the historic example of Ecuador's indigenous peoples taking Texaco to court in New York City.

Host-country legislation

There seems to be a consensus between NGOs and MNCs that there should be institutionalised mechanisms for representation and participation of the local community in the project development process. For this reason, the constitutional framework adopted by an LDC would seem highly relevant. In those countries where there are decentralised—as opposed to centralised—constitutional structures, such as Colombia and South Africa, affected communities are more likely to secure their rights through participation in the project development process.

Beyond the constitutional framework, the precise nature of environmental and social legislation appears to be important. LDC governments should enact laws that establish a strict set of environmental and social standards, but allow companies the flexibility to meet these standards as they see best. Second, governments should emphasise the compliance of industry with standards, and avoid mandating numerous studies on how industry will meet these standards. Third, governments should promote mechanisms that enable affected communities and NGOs to participate in the identification of environmental and social impacts, and ensure MNC compliance with relevant mitigating measures.

The entity or entities responsible for environmental and social issues should be adequately resourced. In particular, they need to possess the relevant managerial and technical competence. For instance, in Colombia, as part of its 1991 Constitution, a Ministry of Environment was established as an autonomous unit, with direct funding from central government, and has since created a competent team of trained environmental and social specialists.

Partnerships

In the wake of pressure to respond to their direct environmental and social impacts, as well as adopt a broader role in the development of their areas of operation, a number of MNCs have established partnerships with NGOs and local governments. MNCs have recognised that they often do not possess the necessary skills and human resources to meet these objectives. For example, MNCs have found that co-operation with local NGOs can be effective for independent environmental monitoring, for implementing community development projects such as education and health and for ensuring interested local communities are included in the Environmental Impact Assessment process.

2. *Internal to the MNC*

The first challenge facing MNCs is how to structure themselves to better meet the demands of sustainable development. At the headquarter level, it has been suggested that MNCs appoint non-executive directors who are explicitly responsible for sustainable business practice (PIRC 1997). It is further suggested and acknowledged by many MNCs that line managers be made directly responsible for environmental and social impacts, rather than delegating this responsibility to individual departments.

MNCs can also adapt their operating policies to better incorporate social and environmental issues. Senior management should be made aware that the failure to address environmental and social impacts can affect the MNC's bottom line, and thus need to be incorporated into traditional investment and operating decisions. To encourage this change, incentives should be developed that reward and sanction company employees and contractors on the basis of their environmental and social performance. MNCs can link bonuses directly to these performance indicators. For instance, one oil multinational has introduced a 'no surprises' policy, whereby senior management pay is linked to an absence of unreported social and environmental problems.

To measure their environmental and social impacts, MNCs can adopt relevant performance indicators. For instance, to monitor environmental impacts, they can adopt indicators that pertain to atmospheric emissions, spills, discharge into water supplies, recycling, use of toxic chemicals and overall environmental expenditure. On social issues, equivalent indicators are still largely to be developed, although MNCs such as The Body Shop are at the forefront of defining such indicators.

Traditional auditing techniques can largely be adapted to measure MNCs' environmental and social performance, as proposed by organisations such as Traidcraft and the New Economics Foundation for social issues. One means of assuring that auditing remains accurate is to establish parallel lines of communication with local communities. Under this arrangement, MNC headquarters would receive reports not only from their subsidiaries, but representatives of the affected communities. This could provide a form of independent external auditing of subsidiary activities.

Conclusion

The contemporary debate on how to promote more sustainable business practice among MNCs in LDCs has tended to be dominated by individual cases. This chapter has shown, however, that four common themes transcend the individual cases. Each theme encapsulates some of the major challenges facing MNCs and other stakeholders in the pursuit of sustainable development in LDCs, and could usefully serve as avenues for future research. This chapter has concluded with a number of possible solutions, external and internal to the MNC, in an effort to advance the debate and support the objective of more sustainable business practices in the developing world.

17

Logging versus Recycling

Problems in the Industrial Ecology of Pulp Manufacturing in South-East Asia*

David A. Sonnenfeld

AMONG THE MOST often-cited principles of industrial ecology are 'dematerialisation' and 'decarbonisation'—using fewer raw materials and contributing less to global warming (cf. Ausubel 1994). Environmentalists around the world have argued that pulp and paper manufacturing can become more ecological by using more post-consumer waste paper, logging fewer native forests and producing less waste (cf. Kroesa 1991; TWS 1992; WALHI and YLBH 1992; Smith 1997).

Until recently, South-East Asian paper manufacturers drew much of their fibre from waste paper and agricultural wastes (see Fig. 1). Encouraged by decades-old development policies of international development agencies such as the Food and Agriculture Organisation (FAO) of the United Nations (cf. ECAFE and FAO 1962), many South-East Asian pulp producers have now moved to embrace the dominant 'Northern' paradigm of wood-based pulp production.

Establishment and operation of new wood-based mills and fast-growing tree plantations have resulted in the clearing of millions of hectares of primary and secondary tropical rainforest in South-East Asia, with great impact on peoples

* Comments from Professor Reid Lifset, Yale University, and Ms Maureen Smith, UCLA, were very helpful in revising this chapter. The author also wishes to thank Mr John Stuart, Managing Editor, and anonymous reviewers for *Greener Management International* for their support and helpful suggestions. This article draws on the author's PhD research in South-East Asia, Australia and North America (Sonnenfeld 1996a; see also Sonnenfeld 1996b, 1998a, 1998b, 1999). Financial assistance has been provided by the Australian-American Educational Foundation (Fulbright Commission), the University of California Institute on Global Conflict and Co-operation, the Switzer Foundation, the Australian National University, the University of California, Santa Cruz, and Washington State University. Views expressed are the author's alone.

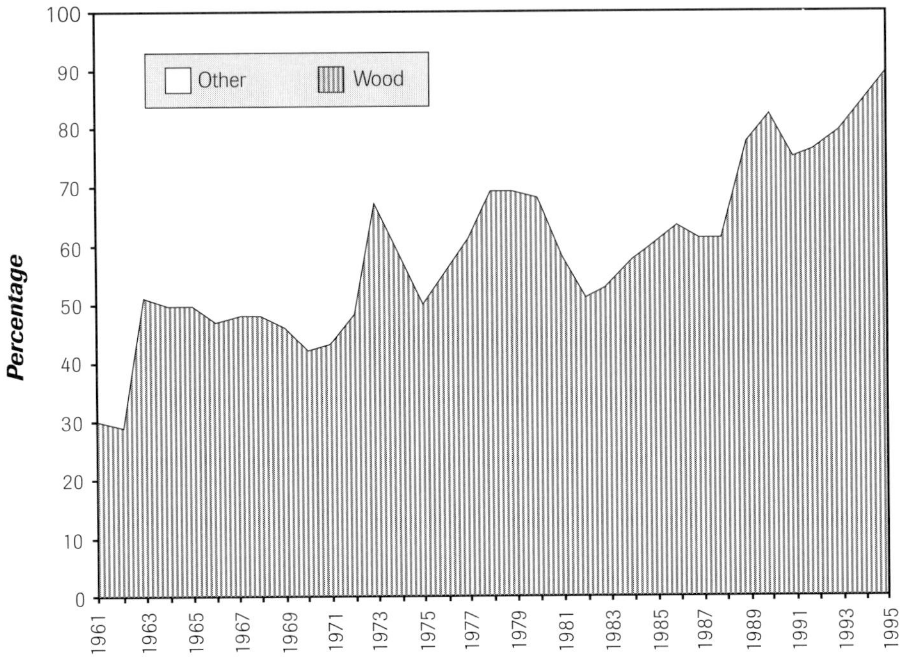

Figure 1: SOUTH-EAST ASIAN PULP PRODUCTION: PERCENTAGE OF WOOD AND 'OTHER' FIBRE SOURCES, 1965–91 (INDONESIA, MALAYSIA, PHILIPPINES, THAILAND AND VIETNAM)

Source: FAO 1997

dependent on those resources for sustenance, and on people throughout the region who have suffered severe smoke and haze from forest clearing. Serious questions have been raised regarding the environmental and social sustainability of such practices (see Carrere and Lohmann 1996; Marchak 1995; Mayer 1996).

What underlies the shift from waste and non-wood to wood-based pulp production in South-East Asia? What are its implications for theory and practice of industrial ecology? What are the prospects for revitalised non-wood pulp and paper manufacturing in the region? This chapter addresses such questions, drawing on field research in South-East Asia from 1993 to 1996, archival research in Australia and the USA and follow-up correspondence.[1]

1 The author visited wood- and non-wood-based pulp mills in Indonesia, Malaysia and Thailand; interviewed company and governmental officials, research scientists and representatives of non-governmental organisations; attended industry trade shows and conferences; and drew on archival materials available at the Australian National University, Canberra, and University of California, Berkeley. During the research period, the author was a member of the Technical Association of the Pulp and Paper Industry (TAPPI) and attended a TAPPI-sponsored short course on pulp and paper technology. As a young adult, he worked as a labourer for a wood-based pulp and paper firm in the Pacific Northwest, USA.

Company	Country	Bagasse	Bamboo	Straw	Kenaf	Other	Total
Aspex	Indonesia	40,000					40,000
Basuki R.	Indonesia		1,350				1,350
Bekasi T.	Indonesia	9,000					9,000
Blabak	Indonesia	5,400					5,400
Gowa	Indonesia		11,000				11,000
Leces	Indonesia	130,000†		20,000†			150,000†
Padalarang	Indonesia			2,720			2,720
Soear S.	Indonesia			4,500			4,500
Tjiwi K.	Indonesia	24,000‡					24,000‡
Canlubang	Philippines					8,000	8,000
Isarog	Philippines					5,000	5,000
Menzi	Philippines					1,070	1,070
United	Philippines	16,200					16,200
Bang Pa-in	Thailand			10,000			10,000
Phoenix	Thailand		76,000		6,000		84,000
Siam Cell.	Thailand		5,000†				5,000†
Siam P&P	Thailand	44,000					44,000
Vinh Phu	Vietnam		14,400				14,400

† estimate ‡ discontinued

Table 1: NON-WOOD PULP PRODUCTION IN SOUTH-EAST ASIA

Sources: Miller Freeman 1991; Thai Pulp and Paper Industries Association 1993

Use of non-woods

South-East Asian pulp and paper production was limited before the 1960s. As was the case in most developing countries and regions of the world, the mills were small (around 5,000 admt[2] of pulp per year) and utilised agricultural wastes, especially rice straw and bagasse;[3] waste paper;[4] and pulp imported from Canada, the US and Scandinavia (cf. Marchak 1995: 239). South-East Asia's forest resources were remote, inaccessible and costly to use for producing pulp and paper. Several larger-scale pulp mills utilising non-woods commenced operations in South-East Asia beginning in the late 1960s. These included Siam Kraft and Phoenix in Thailand, and PT Kertas Leces in Indonesia (see Table 1).

2 Air-dried metric tonnes. 1 metric tonne = 1,000 kg = 2,200 lbs = 1.1 English tons.
3 Bagasse is the pulp left over from the manufacture of cane sugar.
4 Surprisingly to many, the Thai pulp industry obtains approximately 70% of its raw materials from waste paper, both domestic and imported from overseas.

Siam Kraft

Siam Kraft, one of South-East Asia's earliest larger-scale[5] pulp and paper companies, commenced operations in Ratchaburi, Thailand, in the late 1960s. Initially, the company's Thai–USA management team[6] planned to use 'Thailand's extensive pine forests in the mountainous north'. They soon discovered 'transportation and harvesting costs [to be] prohibitive', however, and instead built their pulp mill to utilise bagasse from local sugar mills. 'Eucalyptus and native pine plantations' were seen as 'potential' resources for 'the foreseeable future' (Pollitzer 1968).

Three decades later, the mill, now owned by the Siam Pulp and Paper Co., a subsidiary of the Siam Cement Co., continues to make pulp from bagasse.[7] Today, the mill is unable to find enough bagasse to run year-round, however, as local sugar mills are burning the fibre in their power plants to generate electricity.[8] When bagasse is unavailable, Siam Pulp and Paper uses eucalyptus chips, even though the latter require 25% more chemicals for pulping and bleaching.[9]

When expanding virgin pulp production in the early 1990s, Siam Pulp and Paper designed its new mill[10] to use eucalyptus as primary raw material.[11] By then, eucalyptus had been planted throughout the region on public and company-owned and -leased lands. Even with substantial transportation costs, eucalyptus was cheaper than bagasse, given limited availability of the latter.

Phoenix Pulp and Paper

The Phoenix Pulp and Paper Company, in Khon Kaen, Thailand, is South-East Asia's second-largest producer of non-wood pulp (see Table 1). It started production in the late 1970s, using kenaf[12] as its raw material—one of the first production-scale pulp mills in the world to do so (Susangkarakarn 1971). The company was seen by government officials and its USA–Indian investors as an ideal rural development project—providing a new market for tens of thousands of small farmers.[13] It received the personal endorsement of Thailand's prime minister, General Chomanand (Kothandapani 1994).

---

5 Initial pulp production was approximately 25,000 tonnes/year (*PPI* 1970b).
6 Led by Parsons & Whittemore of New York, a one-third owner of the firm.
7 Interview with Mr Kaneung In-Dratanee, Siam Pulp and Paper Co., Ratchaburi, Thailand, 19 August 1994.
8 Ironically, the sugar mills have improved their industrial ecology through waste minimisation or use, at the expense of diminished availability of the same resource for pulp and paper firms.
9 Interview with Mr Kaneung In-Dratanee, 19 August 1994.
10 Operated as the Siam Cellulose Company Ltd.
11 When visited in 1994, the mill was using 90% eucalyptus and 10% bamboo (interview with Miss Orrawan Panichjarern, Siam Cellulose Co., Kanchanaburi, Thailand, 19 August 1994).
12 *Hibiscus sabdariffa var. altissima.*
13 (Interview with Mr S.K. Mittal, Phoenix Pulp and Paper Co., Khon Kaen, Thailand, 9 August 1994.) Kenaf had been planted widely in north-east Thailand and elsewhere in the 1950s and '60s under internationally agricultural development schemes. The world market for the plant collapsed in 1967, resulting in abundant crops and low prices (Subhadhira and Samart 1984 in Hurst 1990: 233-34; personal correspondence with Dr Suwit Laohasiriwong, Khon Kaen University, May 1995).

Soon after Phoenix commenced operations, however, local farmers switched to growing cassava, the latest boom cash crop.[14] Phoenix management was forced to search for new raw materials. They settled on bamboo, fast-growing and available in local forests; and eucalyptus, which would take several years to establish, but which could be used to produce a globally recognised market pulp.[15]

Kertas Leces

South-East Asia's largest non-wood pulp producer, PT Kertas Leces, in East Java, was one of Indonesia's earliest integrated pulp and paper mills. Established by the Dutch in 1939, the mill underwent major expansions in the late 1970s and early 1980s, with German–Austrian and French financing, respectively. In 1992, the government-owned company produced around 200,000 tonnes each of pulp and paper, all from bagasse and rice straw (APKI 1993: 68; Miller Freeman 1991; *PPI* 1981).[16]

These three firms, Siam Kraft, Phoenix and Kertas Leces, important early players in the modernisation of South-East Asia's pulp and paper industry, represent the 'high-water mark' of non-wood pulp production in the region. All major pulp mill development projects in South-East Asia since these firms' first efforts have been wood-based.

Wood-based pulp production

A new era in South-East Asian pulp and paper production began in the mid-1980s with construction of the first large-scale wood-based mills (see Table 2). Notable among these are Indah Kiat and Indorayon in Indonesia; Sabah Forest Industries in Malaysia; and three new mills in Thailand.

Indah Kiat

Operations at the Indah Kiat Pulp and Paper (IKPP) company's pulp mill in Perawang, Riau, Indonesia, on the island of Sumatra, began in 1984. The Sinar Mas Group, agro-business giant and Indah Kiat's majority owner, had gotten into paper-making just a few years before, through the purchase of a paper firm in West Java.[17] After making paper using pulp imported from its Taiwanese partners, Indah Kiat decided to

14 (Interview with Mr S.K. Mittal, 9 August 1994.) The price of cassava, used in animal feed, boomed along with the global livestock industry (Subhadhira and Samart 1984 in Hurst 1990: 234; personal correspondence with Professor R. Thomas Schotzko, Washington State University, February 1997).

15 Interview with Mr S.K. Mittal, 9 August 1994.

16 Today, the company uses hardly any rice straw, and *Albizzia falcatoria*, a fast-growing plantation species, is being used in partial replacement of bagasse in one of the newsprint lines. Marchak (1995: 240) describes *Albizzia* as 'possibly the fastest-growing [plantation] species in the world: from seedling to full size takes only four to five years'.

17 Interview with Mr Eddie E-Tak Shaw, Executive Vice-President Director, Indah Kiat Pulp and Paper Co., Jakarta, 11 July 1994.

Start date	Company	Country	Capacity	Fibre source
1984	Indah Kiat #1	Indonesia	100,000 (120,000)	MTH
1987	Sabah Forest Industries	Malaysia	100,000	MTH
1988	PT Inti Indorayon Utama	Indonesia	180,000 (240,000)	pine
1990	Indah Kiat #2	Indonesia	180,000 (380,000)	MTH
1992	Siam Cellulose	Thailand	50,000	eucalyptus, bamboo
1994	Phoenix II	Thailand	100,000	eucalyptus
1994	Indah Kiat #8	Indonesia	380,000	MTH
1994	Wira Karya Sakti	Indonesia	380,000	MTH
1995	Riau Andalan Pulp & Paper	Indonesia	750,000	MTH
1996	Advance Agro	Thailand	175,000	eucalyptus
1997	Kiani Kertas	Indonesia	472,000	MTH

Numbers in parentheses indicate total current capacity, including expansion projects.
MTH = mixed tropical hardwoods.

Table 2: NEW, WOOD-BASED, PULP MILLS IN SOUTH-EAST ASIA

Source: Sonnenfeld 1996a: 136

manufacture its own pulp. Its partners contributed Indah Kiat's first pulping equipment, floated from Taiwan on a barge.[18]

The government of Indonesia supported the pulp-making venture by granting IKPP exclusive use of an extensive timber concession. The company made pulp from native, mixed tropical hardwoods cleared from the concession, replanting fast-growing tree species. Although the company paid a nominal fee, use of timber from the native forest was, in essence, a government subsidy for the start-up operation. Villagers in the concession area without documented land claims were forced to abandon traditional areas and practices.

Sabah Forest Industries

In Sipitang, Malaysia, on the island of Borneo, Sabah Forest Industries (SFI) opened its new wood-based pulp mill in 1986, after more than a decade of planning (*PPI* 1970a, 1980). Developed by the Sabah state government and financed with commercial loans, SFI makes pulp and paper from mixed tropical hardwoods from a 300,000 ha timber

18 Interview with Mr Eddie E-Tak Shaw, 11 July 1994.

concession (Pappens 1993).[19] It took several years for SFI to make consistently high-quality paper from mixed tropical hardwoods (Pappens 1993). With assistance from international consultants, SFI's engineering staff ultimately succeeded. The Swedish International Development Agency (SIDA) trained SFI's engineers in Sweden. SIDA and the Japanese Overseas Development Agency helped SFI establish its plantation.

For years, SFI operated at a loss, utilising 'logging residue'. In late 1993, mill management was terminated by the Sabah state government, and the mill placed under the day-to-day supervision of international accounting and management consulting firm, Price Waterhouse.[20] Rumour had it that the former mill management, through ties to logging contractors, had profited handsomely on the logging, even while operating the mill in the red. Price Waterhouse investigated such claims and surveyed the concession in preparation for selling a majority stake in the firm.[21]

Like IKPP, SFI and its logging contractors cleared extensive portions of its forest concession, replanting fast-growing exotic trees. As in Indonesia, the forest concession was intended by the Sabah state government to help capitalise the pulp firm's start-up. At SFI, too, villagers in the concession area were forced to abandon traditional livelihoods. Once international development assistance funds ran out, SFI suspended replanting; logging continued unabated.[22]

Indorayon

In 1987, in North Sumatra, Indonesia, the Raja Garuda Mas (RGM) group commenced operations at the PT Inti Indorayon Utama pulp mill. RGM had been successful bidder for a Government of Indonesia project to use pine planted in the 1960s with Japanese assistance in the Lake Toba highlands region. RGM's prior experience had been in manufacturing plywood, rather than pulp. This was not was not a barrier to RGM's entry into pulp manufacturing, however, as the group was well connected to former President Suharto, Indonesia's head of state for three decades (*PPI* 1986, 1991, 1992; Abubakar and Sutton 1988; WIM n.d.).

Although the company was to use plantation pine, it had to construct logging roads to access it. In the rainy season, heavy rains turned those roads to mud, causing serious erosion and mud slides. In one case, a mud slide from a poorly constructed logging road buried a village. Local residents strongly protested the company's logging and road-building methods. Villagers protested again later, when the company attempted to establish new plantations in places used for growing crops and grazing animals.

The decision to build the mill in an area of traditional agricultural practices and lifestyles was made by central government authorities in conjunction with investors

19 Interview with Mr Wong Kong Min, Sabah Forest Industries, Sipitang, 14 December 1993. Under the terms of the concession, SFI operations were to be supported by revenue from logging of commercially valuable species, remaining trees were to be pulped and turned into paper, and forested areas were to be clear-felled and replanted with fast-growing pulp species.

20 Site visit, December 1993.

21 Site visit, December 1993. Subsequently, the sale did go through—to the Lion Group of peninsular Malaysia.

22 Site visit, December 1993.

and international agencies. Local residents were not consulted, yet suffered the consequences. The Indorayon mill has been involved in a continuing series of community and environmental conflicts since its conception.

New mills in Thailand

In Thailand, too, new pulp mill capacity has been based on fast-growing plantation hardwoods. Recently opened mills include the Siam Pulp and Paper Group's Siam Cellulose Mill, 1992; Phoenix Pulp and Paper Co.'s Pulp Mill #2, 1994, producing market pulp exclusively from eucalyptus; and Advance Agro's mill in Prachinburi, 1996, producing pulp and paper from eucalyptus (see Reuters 1994; *Nation* 1994; Advance Agro 1994).

All three mills are designed to use eucalyptus as primary raw material. The government of Thailand has embarked on large-scale 'reforestation', involving the establishment of eucalyptus plantations throughout the country. Such programmes have had the indirect effect of excluding small farmers from lands that have not had trees for decades, but are still classified as 'forest land'. The government, including the army, which has its own forest operations, has disputed those farmers' land claims. New, wood-based, pulp production fits neatly in this 'reforestation' strategy.

In barely a decade, then, South-East Asia's pulp manufacturing capacity increased exponentially, based largely on mixed tropical hardwoods and fast-growing tree plantations. Non-woods make up a diminishing proportion of South-East Asian pulp production (see Fig. 1). While lucrative for mill owners, at least in the initial stages of logging, wood-based pulping operations have had serious social and environmental costs. New wood-based pulp mills and fast-growing exotic tree plantations continue to be established in South-East Asia.

Why wood?

Pulp mills built in South-East Asia in the 1990s are markedly different from their predecessors (see Table 2). At capacities of up to three-quarters of a million admt per year, the mills are as much as 150 times larger. These mega-mills utilise advanced pulping and bleaching technologies from technology firms based in Sweden, Finland and Canada (Sonnenfeld 1999). All of the new mills use wood to make pulp—first mixed tropical hardwoods from native forests, then fast-growing plantation trees—following the path blazed by the Jari and Aracruz ventures in Brazil in the late 1970s and early '80s (see Marchak 1995: 276-84), IKPP in Indonesia, and SFI in Malaysia in the 1980s. Meanwhile, throughout South-East Asia, tons of agricultural waste are burned at the end of growing seasons, creating severe air pollution. Why are more non-wood mills not built?

Non-wood plant fibres have been used since paper was invented in China at the beginning of the second century CE.[23] Two centuries ago, rags were the predominant

23 The American Paper Institute locates the invention of paper in Lei-Yang, China, in 105 CE (API 1986).

raw material used to make paper in North America and Europe. Shortages of rags due to economic depression and war caused paper manufacturers on those continents to search for new sources of fibre. They experimented with straw, corn stalks and other agricultural wastes. The turning point came in the mid-1800s, with the invention of sulphite wood pulping (API 1987; Cohen 1983; see also Morrison 1982).[24]

Wood has been raw material of choice in temperate Northern countries ever since. It is of uniform quality, has greater strength and, given current technology, can be produced at a lower cost than most non-wood pulps. Also, trees are not subject to a restricted season like most non-wood plants. Trees can grow until needed. Once harvested, wood keeps well for long periods, under even relatively adverse conditions. These properties allow pulp mills to be supplied continuously with high-quality fibre.

Agriculturally derived raw materials for making paper such as kenaf are harvested during brief periods. Such materials deteriorate more quickly than wood and must be pulped within weeks of harvesting or stored carefully for maximum utilisation.[25] Also, non-wood raw materials have substantial impurities. Bamboo and some straws, for example, have a very high silica content, which, with current technology, limits chemical recovery, increases costs and produces more waste.[26]

In addition to storage and cleaning problems, agricultural wastes must often be transported long distances to 'feed' a pulp mill of any significant size. Raw material costs will give one manufacturer an edge over another: the greater the distance, the greater the cost of transportation, and the less profitable the manufacturing operation.

New South-East Asian mills have been built where they are, at the scale at which they are, with the technology that they have, because of the economics of raw materials costs combined with the availability of technologies and financing. The initial raw materials—mixed tropical hardwoods, i.e. native rainforest—are provided inexpensively, often as the government's or a prominent official's contribution to a joint venture. Politically easy—at least in the short run, in the context of authoritarian, military-dominated governments—such in-kind contributions have unfortunate long-term social and environmental consequences.

Nordic, Canadian, and US governments have given interest-free loans, trade credits and technical expertise to South-East Asian pulp and paper firms in conjunction with procurement of technology from national firms. In the Nordic case, governments are stakeholders in many of these firms. It is no coincidence that this technology is wood-based, nor that Northern governments and firms advise Southern governments and firms to adopt a wood-based strategy. Many Northern technologies are appropriate only for wood-based production.

---

24 Non-woods continue to be important raw materials for paper-making in regions that lack trees, e.g. China, India, Columbia, north-eastern Brazil. Small amounts of non-woods such as flax are used in speciality papers, e.g. filter papers, cigarette papers, for particular properties not found in wood.

25 Interview with Dr Subhash Maheshwari, Phoenix Pulp and Paper Co., Khon Kaen, 10 August 1994.

26 Interview with Dr Lars-Åke Lindstrom, Sunds Defibrator Co., Singapore, 22 April 1994.

A further factor affecting location of new pulp mills in South-East Asia is the population density of agricultural production centres. Older, smaller pulp mills in agricultural centres such as East Java operate with severe constraints. Land is expensive and situated in the midst of productive agriculture. There is no room for adequate waste-water treatment facilities. Every hectare is used to produce food. Costs of retrofitting smaller, older mills with environmental controls is prohibitive. As a result, these mills are significant polluters and were scheduled for closure (Hanafi 1994). Environmental officials would prefer production of wood-based pulp in large-scale, remote facilities, over multiple-source point pollution in heavily burdened local waterways.

A return to non-woods?

As protests continue against use of native forests and displacement of forest-dwelling communities for manufacturing pulp and paper (cf. Carrere and Lohmann 1996), renewed attention is being given by NGOs, policy analysts and governmental and intergovernmental agencies to using non-woods for producing pulp and paper (cf. Marchak 1995; Smith 1997). In the 1990s, international 'green' consumerism has created a significant demand for non-wood pulps and papers. Phoenix Pulp and Paper Co. in Thailand, for example, reports it is obtaining more than twice the price for kenaf pulp than for eucalyptus pulp; it is looking at expanding kenaf production once again.[27]

For decades, Indian and Chinese centres have led in research on non-wood pulping processes and technologies.[28] These institutions lack capital to develop and export commercially viable forms of these technologies. This knowledge has been disseminated through such vehicles as the United Nations Environment Programme's Network on Industrial Environmental Management.[29] But this support is largely communicative.

As interest in non-wood paper has grown, Northern technology firms finally may be paying more attention. Sunds Defibrator, of Sweden, for example, has increased non-wood research and development activities in response to increased interest among traditionally wood-based pulp manufacturers in North America and elsewhere.[30]

Not only technical, but also geographical, social and political challenges remain. As improvements are made in non-wood pulping, e.g. in removing silica and

27 (Interview with Dr Maheshwari, Phoenix Pulp and Paper Co., Khon Kaen, 27 December 1996.) As an indicator of such demand in the US, see the 144 'ecological paper retailers, printers and manufacturers' in 36 states plus the District of Columbia listed in an on-line guide produced by Earth Island Institute (ReThink Paper 1998). This number doubled in one year. In 1997, retail prices for kenaf paper provided by one supplier, PCW100, Inc., ranged from US$20/ream to US$22.80/M, depending on quantity.

28 Interview with Mr Mark Radka, Network for Industrial Environmental Management, United Nations Environment Programme, Bangkok, August 1994.

29 The NIEM has been financed by the Swedish International Development Agency (SIDA).

30 Interview with Dr Lars-Åke Lindstrom, 22 April 1994.

improving environmental performance, development agencies, manufacturing firms and financial institutions must confront issues of economy of scale, location and incentive. To co-exist in populous agricultural centres, pulping operations may need to be based on a different scale of operations than today's mega-wood-based mills, i.e. on mini-pulp mill technology. With mini-mills, pulp could be processed in areas of agricultural production, then shipped to paper-making centres. Although increasing utilisation of agricultural waste, improving air quality (through elimination of burning) and generating additional income for local producers, mini-mills may not be as profitable to timber concession holders, industrialists and technology firms as their mega-mill big sisters. A different calculation of benefits may be needed to justify mini-mills' economic viability.

Conclusion

Recent work in industrial ecology has used various units of analysis (cf. Socolow *et al.* 1994). Most typically, however, scholarship in the area has focused on the micro or firm level of analysis. Analysis at multiple levels, including national and international, political, economic and technological dynamics, is necessary to understand South-East Asian pulp industries' movement away from more 'industrial-ecological' patterns of resource utilisation, as well as those industries' prospects for dematerialisation and decarbonisation.

South-East Asian pulp and paper firms maintained complementary relationships with neighbouring firms and farms as long as pulp production was relatively small-scale, pollution was not identified as a problem, and there were surplus agricultural wastes. The industry shifted to large wood-based mills once technological advances allowed mixed tropical hardwoods to be turned into quality product, extensive forest resources were made available by authoritarian governments, and financing was provided by firms and countries anxious to develop new markets.

Certainly, much is involved in putting South-East Asian pulp and paper production on a more sustainable basis. As Marchak (1995) and Smith[31] point out, however, one part of that strategy may involve putting greater emphasis on pulp and paper produced from agricultural wastes and waste paper, rather than on wood from native forests or tree plantations. Growing international green consumption may help facilitate such a transition, through increased demand for paper derived from wastes and non-wood sources. South-East Asian pulp and paper producers have historical strengths and knowledge they are just beginning to use in meeting such demand. Together with government agencies, researchers and communities, these firms have considerable challenges ahead of them. Stronger backing by Northern governmental and intergovernmental agencies and technology firms will improve the likelihood of their success, while contributing to industrial-ecological goals of dematerialisation and decarbonisation.

31 Maureen Smith, personal correspondence, 1998.

5 ENVIRONMENTAL MANAGEMENT AND SUSTAINABLE DEVELOPMENT

18
Environmental Management and Organisational Change

The Impact of the World Bank

Ans Kolk

THE CASE OF ORGANISATIONAL CHANGE in the World Bank is relevant for other—profit and non-profit—organisations, for environmental management and for developing countries. It helps in understanding change in situations where societal attention to environmental issues ranks high and tends to harm economic performance. There is a clear parallel with other organisations that have also experienced both large societal pressure and internal problems, of which Shell is a case in point. Moreover, the adoption of more environmentally friendly practices affects other organisations: with its expertise, the World Bank usually sets standards, accumulating and disseminating knowledge. While this has a general impact, the effects on developing countries will be greatest, because the World Bank is still one of the largest lenders there and its approval serves to assure other lenders. Hence, a further integration of sustainable development concerns into policies and practices will have a positive effect on governments and other organisations in developing countries.

The impact of World Bank policies on environmental management in developing countries has been substantial. In the past decade, large changes have taken place within the World Bank: past mistakes are now candidly acknowledged and a restructuring is under way. Policy changes came about after fierce critique on both the negative environmental effects of lending and the declining effectiveness of development projects. Under pressure from non-governmental organisations (NGOs) and industrialised countries, the organisation adopted a more cautious attitude towards megaprojects, strengthened its environmental procedures and started to implement environmental projects. In some cases, such as the protection of Brazilian rainforests, the World Bank even co-operates with NGOs in the development and implementation of such environmental projects (Kolk 1998).

The landmark shift took place after James Wolfensohn became president of the World Bank in 1995. The organisation now openly admits mistakes, ineffectiveness, bureaucracy and arrogance, and seeks to improve its performance and the relationships with stakeholders. This implies a focus on development impact, on 'results on the ground', on 'putting quality ahead of quantity', as Wolfensohn put it in one of his numerous speeches (World Bank 1996b: 10). The new approach, exemplified by the statement 'We are anxious to find out what we can do better', has led to the request to NGOs to evaluate the World Bank's environmental and social record. Poverty alleviation and environmental protection, listed as central concerns, are to be realised with a more efficient and decentralised organisation. The restructuring was laid down in the 1997 'strategic compact' (World Bank 1997a, b).

Compared with the situation in the early and mid-1980s, these policy intentions and statements are almost revolutionary. At the time, the World Bank did its utmost to prove that NGOs were erroneous in campaigning against the negative environmental and social effects of projects. The organisation rejected the allegations, asserting that procedures had been followed, and pointed at its ultimate objective of fostering development. However, strong doubts were also expressed about these developmental achievements. The World Bank appeared unable to remove a large number of organisational impediments and to maintain good relationships with its stakeholders and shareholders.

In considering these two periods, what are the reasons for this seemingly momentous change, and which structural dilemmas does the World Bank face in realising the new policies? This chapter analyses these questions, focusing on the internal and external factors that incited change in the World Bank. It shows how the organisation moved from its traditional paradigm of 'frontier economics' to 'environmental management'. The feasibility of the reforms depends on the extent to which the organisation succeeds in reconciling the diverging demands. A stakeholder map of the World Bank will be given, identifying the character of the different dependency relationships.

The World Bank: development, purposes and influence

To understand the context of the issues raised later in this chapter, some attention will first be paid to relevant structural features of the World Bank: its origins, objectives, sources of funding, operations and power (Kolk 1996: 178-93). The International Bank for Reconstruction and Development (IBRD) was created in 1945. Its initial objective of financing the reconstruction of Europe became obsolete as a result of Marshall Aid. From the 1950s onwards, the World Bank concentrated on providing technical assistance and giving loans to developing countries for productive purposes and to encourage economic growth. In 1960, the smaller International Development Association (IDA) was established as an affiliate to lend to the poorest countries on more favourable terms than the IBRD could grant. Because IBRD and IDA share offices and staff, they are generally referred to as the 'World Bank'; this excludes the two other affiliates of the Bank Group, the International Finance Corporation and the Multilateral Investment Guarantee Agency.

IBRD and IDA are financed by the member states in different ways. IBRD capital is relatively stable: a minor percentage is paid in by the member states; the rest consists of callable capital (which is subject to call only when required to meet the obligations of the IBRD created by guaranteeing or borrowing loans). IDA's funds have to be replenished every three years; the agreed sum has to be paid by the member states according to the percentage of shares they have. This has given the member states a substantial leverage and the major industrialised countries—also the largest shareholders—led by the US, have increasingly used these occasions to put pressure on the World Bank.

Because of its ability to attach far-reaching conditions to loans, the large sums of money involved and the fact that its support is essential to mobilise other resources, the World Bank is the most powerful development agency. In addition, the organisation uses its know-how to produce many papers, documents and reports each year. It therefore serves as a think-tank which has the ability to introduce new concepts and interpretations, influence the terms of the development debate, and prove its crucial position in it. Finally, its technical expertise has increasingly been used to assist developing countries with the preparation and formulation of project proposals.

The World Bank requirements to lend for productive purposes and specific projects has traditionally resulted in support for large-scale infrastructural works. Agriculture and rural development, energy and transportation have been particularly important sectors. Shifting insights into the concept of development, in which ideas on a 'big push' and 'trickle-down' effects were called into question, along with continuing poverty and mounting evidence on the detrimental impact of projects brought about some changes.

Another change took place in the early 1980s, when the World Bank obtained an important position in the management of the debt crisis, together with the International Monetary Fund (IMF). As a result, it started to channel large amounts of money to developing countries. This drastic change in lending policy, in which sector adjustment and structural adjustment loans predominated, was accompanied by the introduction of a new kind of conditionality.[1] This meant that macroeconomic requirements applied instead of the traditional project criteria. The blame for the often severe social consequences of these measures was put on the World Bank and the IMF, and the popularity of these organisations further decreased. The opposition was especially large in Latin America, where the World Bank had supported authoritarian regimes in the preceding decades. Therefore, any type of protest against the World Bank, such as the environmental effects of project lending, could count on widespread support. For very different political reasons, in the US, where adjustment policies were greeted with enthusiasm, both Republicans and Democrats approved of the actions as well.

1 In the late 1990s, the World Bank has started to channel emergency structural adjustment loans to those countries that suffer from the (Asian) financial crisis.

In this same period, the economic position of the World Bank was also subject to change. Although the organisation channelled large amounts of money to developing countries as part of structural adjustment, this could not reverse the overall trend. The repayments of the loans disbursed in the preceding decades resulted in a large transfer of money from the developing countries to the World Bank in the 1980s. To correct this net negative flow and prove that the organisation was essential for development, the volume of lending had to be increased enormously. This further stimulated the so-called 'approval culture', which had a negative influence on quality requirements. The challenges to the political and economic legitimacy of the World Bank eventually led to organisational changes. Different kinds of pressures played a role, especially those from NGOs and donor states.

Reasons for change

Merging environmental and financial pressure

The dynamics of NGO influence on the World Bank can best be illustrated by a closer look at the 1980s. Co-ordinated opposition succeeded in forcing the organisation to make substantial concessions for the first time. This has had a lasting impact, because the World Bank experienced the power of NGOs, and their continuous 'Bank watch' has helped to put up the pressure.

The campaign against the Multilateral Development Banks (MDBs) was initiated in 1983 by US NGOs.[2] By showing the negative environmental and social effects of MDB project lending, public awareness and suspicion spiralled. NGOs focused on MDBs because of their importance for international development policies: if the evidence of their flaws led to changes, this could have a wide significance. The campaign fell in line with prevailing political sentiments against multilateralism and development aid, favourite objects of Republican hostility.

It was this political climate in the United States that led, almost paradoxically, to the strengthening of environmental NGOs, a wave of activities and an expansion of their membership and income. When Reagan assumed the presidency in 1980, the prospects for an active role of the state, advances in environmental policy and implementation of environmental legislation became dim. Environmentalists turned to the House of Representatives, where the Democrats still formed the majority, to reverse some of the measures taken by the Reagan administration. The political change also meant that Democratic politicians and civil servants had to leave their jobs and went back to universities, private enterprises and all kinds of NGOs, sometimes creating their own employment. The activities that had been carried out in the orbit of the state until then began to be undertaken outside government offices, which led to a strengthening of the opposition.

Other factors also played a role. In this period, international programme officers were appointed to the National Wildlife Federation, the Natural Resources Defence

2 For an overview of this campaign, see Kolk 1996: 245-54 and Wade 1997.

Council and the Environmental Policy Institute. They tried to find ways to deal with the international dimension of the environmental problem that would preferably be understandable to a wider public. Until then, US NGOs had generally restricted their activities to domestic issues. A campaign against the MDBs, which centred on the fate of the local population and their natural environment, was launched, and it turned out to be an excellent approach for attracting public attention to international issues. The programme officers selected the case studies on the basis of personal contacts with Southern NGOs or with US activists who knew about a particular project. This kind of coincidence also inspired the choice of Polonoroeste, a large colonisation and infrastructure project in the Brazilian Amazon, which assumed major significance in the course of the campaign. Evidence on the negative impact of the large-scale projects was provided by Southern NGOs, supplemented by information derived from informal contacts within the Bank and internal documents.

The MDB campaign made a difference because it posed a threat to the financial sources of the banks. In the US, the House and Senate Appropriations sub-committees on foreign operations decide on multilateral funding. In the case of the World Bank, the three-yearly replenishment of the International Development Association became the subject of Congressional discussion after NGOs had started to provide evidence on the destruction resulting from Bank projects. Both Republicans and Democrats had reasons for putting pressure on the World Bank. On the basis of ideological resentment to multilateral funding and development aid, the Republican Congress members considered it as an additional proof of their point, which could serve their objective to cut disbursements. Democrats, in favour of multilateralism, saw the importance of ensuring that the money was spent in a positive way, not only because of the desire to guarantee the adequate and effective use of federal budgets, but also to prevent political support for these causes from being further undermined.

In addition to the budget issue, NGOs influenced US voting behaviour in the World Bank. This successful lobbying was important because of the large US influence on both banks. Similar NGO pressure on the World Bank's executive directors was exercised in other Western countries, such as Germany, the Netherlands, the United Kingdom and the Scandinavian countries. These concerted activities produced considerable results: the World Bank was forced to propose changes in projects on which NGOs had been campaigning, introduced stricter environmental requirements, started to consult NGOs more frequently, and announced a new environmental policy in 1987.

The negative results of Polonoroeste and the protests it aroused were very important in bringing about this change. In a March 1987 speech, Bank president Conable alluded to Polonoroeste as 'a sobering example of an environmentally sound effort which went wrong' (quoted in Le Prestre 1989: 199). Although acknowledging the destruction, he still adhered to the original correctness of the project. The Bank's 1992 *World Development Report* put it much more bluntly, by characterising Polonoroeste (and an irrigation project in Sri Lanka) as 'vivid illustrations of the environmental damage from ill-conceived and badly implemented development projects' (World Bank 1992a: 80).

In the World Bank's environmental policy, laid down in the annual environmental reports published from 1990 onwards, the following strands have developed:

minimising adverse impacts of Bank-financed investments; assisting countries in the environmental area; building on the positive synergies between development and environment; and addressing regional and global environmental challenges. Pressure from donor countries and NGOs has in fact strengthened the Bank to move from the traditional paradigm of 'frontier economics' to 'environmental protection' and, since the early 1990s, to 'environmental management'.

However, over the years, the World Bank repeatedly announced changes, accompanied by increased budgets and staff for specific purposes, which did not really affect the overall direction of actual practice. Like environmental management in general, the extent of overall organisational change determines the feasibility rather than the mere announcement of attention to environmental issues or the allocation of budgets. The environmental consequences of World Bank projects resulted from entrenched practices. This broader organisational context and its contradictions will be examined next.

Internal contradictions

Continuous NGO scrutiny and internal evaluations revealed much about the weaknesses of the Bank. Similar results had been produced by the Portfolio Management Task Force (PMTF, also known as the Wapenhans Commission), which was installed by World Bank president Preston following mounting concern over the quality of projects and persisting criticism. The commission showed the declining performance of the project portfolio, and convincingly underlined many of the shortcomings that had already been suggested in preceding years. Although the success of projects is determined by many factors, which can only be partly influenced by the World Bank,[3] the most salient findings concerned the Bank's culture and the organisational features that incited a 'pressure to lend'.

The Bank already suffered from a lack of fundable projects in the 1950s and 1960s, a tendency that was aggravated as a result of the continued expansion of funds. In the 1980s, the large amount of funds lent to developing countries engendered a reverse flow of money, which further increased the pressure to lend. Ambitious lending targets pressured the staff to come up with enough projects in time. To achieve this, the Bank showed a clear preference for large-scale projects that involved large amounts of funds at once. The number of approved proposals and the amounts involved started to play an important role in the judgement of the staff's career perspectives, while efficiency was measured by the number of hours spent to get a project through the cycle. The Bank's institutional interest in expanding operations merged with loan requests of developing countries.

The emphasis on loan approval also implied that interest diminished after project proposals had been finally accepted. Staff members that were interviewed mentioned

3 The interplay of international, country and project factors, and the Bank's limits and possibilities in influencing performance and social and environmental impact, is clearly shown by two projects in the Brazilian Amazon (for an examination, see Kolk 1996: 203-13). Another well-known example is the Indian Sardar Sarovar project (see the highly critical, internal evaluation by Morse and Berger 1992).

that conceptual and planning activities were valued much more highly than implementation and practical management, and that, when striving for promotion, work on lending (especially on adjustment programmes) offered the best opportunities. As noted by the Wapenhans report, 'Signals from senior management are consistently seen by staff to focus on lending targets rather than results on the ground' (PMTF 1992: 23). A practical orientation was also hampered by the centralisation of the World Bank. Traditionally, it was not considered effective to have sizeable regional or national agencies in view of the distribution of loans over many countries. The centralist origin led to concentrated decision-making and an inability to decentralise functions as a result of vested interests.

Finally, the World Bank has also frequently been charged of reacting in an arrogant way, by relying on its supposedly superior knowledge and insights. This arrogance has been explained by the stringent selection procedures; as a result, only a small number of highly motivated people with specific qualifications, who have been through a demanding and very competitive process, are allowed to join the Bank. The highly privileged status of its staff has encouraged strategies of job retention, contributing to a strong internal culture (Naim 1994). To ensure their survival within the organisation, the creation of personal networks and connections with influential staff members is crucial for Bank employees; risk aversion, a good internal reputation and resistance to change are part of this strategy.

Comparable with the environmental critique, the explicit analysis of organisational problems also induced considerable change. A whole range of measures has been taken, culminating in the 1997 restructuring plan. According to this strategic compact, 'the past pattern of incremental change, punctuated by disruptive reorganisations, has failed to reverse the slide in relevance and performance' (World Bank 1997a: iii). Indicators of this crisis in effectiveness included negative project evaluations, the increasing number of complaints by borrowing countries, and an actual volume of lending which was lower than possible. The compact differs from previous plans in that the World Bank itself officially recognises the problematic situation, describing the internal and especially the external reasons for change. The measures encompass decentralisation, downsizing, diversification of the Bank's product range, customisation of assistance strategies, a focus on results, and a 'multilayer partnership programme' to improve relationships with the different stakeholders.

The feasibility of change: the role of stakeholders

Compared with the early 1980s, the situation has become more complicated for the World Bank as pressure comes from many different sides. In reaction to these demands over the years, the Bank has continued to add new, often contradictory objectives, ranging from more efficiency, decentralisation and downsizing to higher effectiveness, more intensive supervision, and stricter conditions with regard to the environment and governance. Although it seems difficult to meet all these conflicting demands and improve relationships with all parties, mutual dependencies can be recognised as well.

The feasibility of the organisational reforms will, therefore, depend on the extent to which the World Bank succeeds in managing these relationships. The political support, the budgets available and the request for loans are crucial aspects for the World Bank which are shaped by member states in particular, but also by NGOs and private lenders. This section examines the different stakeholders and the opportunities for forging a coalition.

Traditionally, a stakeholder map has included all parties with a potential impact on an organisation without specifying their relative importance (Freeman 1984). Gradually, this has evolved into a more differentiated picture, in which primary and secondary stakeholders are identified (see also Kolk 2000). A primary stakeholder group is 'one without whose continuing participation an organisation cannot survive as a going concern', whereas secondary stakeholders are 'those who influence or affect, or are influenced or affected by the organisation, but they are not engaged in transactions with the organisation and are not essential for its survival' (slightly adapted from Clarkson 1995: 106-107). According to such a classification, primary stakeholders are shareholders, investors, employees, customers, suppliers, governments and communities (the last two compose the so-called public stakeholder group). Secondary shareholders include the media, NGOs and competitors.

Applied to the World Bank, this distinction can be further specified on the basis of the preceding information and considering its peculiarities as an international non-profit organisation. Primary stakeholders are *donor countries* (financiers and usually also suppliers), *borrowing countries* (customers and communities) and *employees*. The main secondary stakeholders include *private lenders* and *international organisations*, especially the IMF (the World Bank's 'competitors') and *NGOs*, which provide an additional linkage with communities and have the ability to influence the media. They all affect, to varying degrees, the feasibility of overall organisational change within the World Bank and, hence, the room for environmental management.

Bank staff

The strategic compact recognises the need to change the organisation and move from an 'approval' to a 'results' culture. It underlines that no lending targets will be imposed, as 'the primary measure of success will remain development impact' (World Bank 1997a: 30). Similarly, the re-organisation aims to improve quality and effectiveness. After one-and-a-half years, the first results indeed indicate a declining share of so-called 'problem projects' and a decrease in preparation time of projects, accompanied by rising volumes of lending (World Bank 1998: 2).

Ultimately it is the Bank staff, at all levels of the organisation, that has to adapt to changing objectives and working methods. These include steps towards further decentralisation, which also serve to improve the relationships with borrowing countries. In the compact, the Bank notes a 'boosted field presence', reflecting a process which has started since the 1992 Wapenhans report. However, when analysed in more detail, these figures are less impressive (see Table 1). The change involves a minor percentage as far as headquarters staff in Washington are concerned and an actual decrease with regard to headquarter staff based in the field. Local field office staff has

	1990	1995	1997
Headquarter staff, based in Washington	**6,210**	**7,147**	**6,577**
▶ Long-term consultants	558	1,106	1,181
▶ Regular staff	5,652	6,041	5,396
(of which higher level)	3,625	3,954	3,611
Headquarter staff, based in field	**195**	**246**	**232**
▶ Long-term consultants	6	22	15
▶ Regular staff	189	224	217
(of which higher level)	178	206	199
Local field office staff	**639**	**1,050**	**1,254**
▶ Local consultants	2	54	107
▶ Regular staff	637	996	1,147
(of which higher level)	116	211	286
Total	**7,044**	**8,443**	**8,063**
Volume of lending (commitments in US$ million)	**20,702**	**22,252**	**19,147**

Table 1: WORLD BANK HEADQUARTER AND FIELD OFFICE STAFF, AND LENDING VOLUMES

Source: World Bank 1997a: Annex 2, 2; 1996: 17; 1998: 8

increased considerably, but is still only one-fifth of the Washington staff, and a relatively low percentage is higher-level staff.

In the attempts to transform the World Bank, vested interests have to be confronted, particularly those represented by senior management. One year after Wolfensohn assumed office, he had already accused this management layer of obstructing the reforms he advocated (*Financial Times* 1996). While this may continue to be a problem, it should be noted that considerable changes have taken place at the project level in the meantime (see below for the interesting example of the Brazilian Amazon). A 'sandwich model' has emerged, in which the top and bottom layers of the World Bank show more willingness to adapt to new circumstances than the middle. Whether the difficulties involved in transforming the organisation can be surmounted depends not only on internal change; external stakeholders, perhaps, play an even larger role.

Donor countries

The general tendency in Western countries to weigh the costs and benefits of foreign aid falls in line with the movement towards a reconsideration of the contribution to the World Bank. The three-yearly replenishment of the International Development Association (IDA) has become increasingly difficult, with donor countries hesitating to commit the requested amounts. Although more countries reduced their contributions, the budget cuts by the US, the largest donor, have posed the major threat to the Bank. Over the years, US NGOs have used the financial instrument against the

Bank, requesting Congress to withhold IDA funds or to appropriate them only on strict conditions. From 1995 onwards, existing reservations in the US about foreign aid have been strongly fuelled by the Republican majority. In an unusual response, the Bank even started an advertising campaign in major US newspapers in 1995 to convince taxpayers of the value of its work and the benefits accruing to the US economy in terms of jobs and contracts. The stakes are considerable: the largest part of World Bank foreign disbursements has traditionally flowed back to the industrialised countries through the supply of goods and services. Until July 1998, the main supplying countries, which received the largest share of IBRD and IDA payments, were the US ($27 billion), Japan ($19 billion), Germany ($17 billion), the United Kingdom ($14 billion), France ($13 billion) and Italy ($9 billion) (calculated from World Bank 1998: 158-59).

In Bank circles, concern has also repeatedly been expressed about the high degree of politicisation surrounding IDA replenishments. Wapenhans, for example, stated that donor countries must choose between the realisation of political objectives (in which case bilateral aid would be more appropriate) and the allocation of concessional resources in a way that is acceptable to all member states. He warned that the Bank's efficiency and effectiveness could suffer from the recurring problems on IDA replenishments and the fulfilment of donor 'biases and wishes'; 'without risking loss of credibility in its borrowing membership, the Bank cannot, in perpetuity, submit to the whims of special interest groups that member governments fail to address' (Wapenhans 1994: 295-96).

Other interest groups, however, including companies which carry out the majority of World Bank projects, provide a pressure for continuation of funding. Moreover, donor countries do not have many good alternatives to the World Bank with regard to channelling development assistance to the poorest countries and ensuring policy discipline. Recently, they have even assigned the World Bank the new task of providing emergency loans to help solve the financial crisis emanating from Asia. This type of lending to a limited number of middle-income countries involves high risks and will imply a new direction for the World Bank if it has to be carried out on a large scale. It will also change the relationship with borrowing countries.

Borrowing countries

With regard to lending, the situation is partly different for IDA and IBRD: whereas IDA suffers from funding problems, the IBRD faces increasing competition from other capital suppliers. For the IBRD, lending on international capital markets poses no problems in view of its high credit rating and reliable image. Whereas IDA's problems are related to 'supply', IBRD has difficulty with the demand for lending. The idea of lending to countries that could not obtain money elsewhere, the original objective of the World Bank, has become outdated for a group of countries. Middle-income countries in Asia and Latin America increasingly rely on capital markets and, in many cases, do not need IBRD loans: especially if charges will rise further. As a result, the organisation competes to some extent with private financiers. With regard to the emergency loans, an overlap exists with the IMF, which has to be sorted out. Traditionally, the IMF has had a short-term macroeconomic focus and the World Bank a more structural one. Structural adjustment lending in the 1980s and current emergency lending blurs this distinction.

An increasing reliance on private sources means that the borrowing countries in question can choose more flexible lending instruments than those offered by the Bank and do not have to meet its requirements. To borrowing countries, private lending has the advantage that no additional conditions apply. This undermines the effectiveness of new policies adopted by the World Bank, often at the instigation of Western donor countries, with borrowing countries expressing their objections. For NGOs, this tendency is disturbing and contradictory: having campaigned for better environmental procedures in Bank-funded projects, they might end up empty-handed since private financiers will not apply environmental conditions to lending for, for example, energy and infrastructure. Even other international organisations may attach less stringent conditions to loans and, therefore, be more interesting to borrowing countries.

To put things into perspective, however, large borrowing countries (such as Brazil and India) have already used the possibility of shifting funds: if considerable amounts of capital were available, they sought Bank loans for non-controversial projects and financed contested elements in other ways. For highly indebted, low-income countries, which are eligible for IDA and do not attract much private investment, the situation is different. They usually have difficulty servicing their debts and cannot afford to attract substantial new flows of funds; they are looking for debt reduction instead.

The increasing differentiation between borrowing countries is accompanied by rising tensions in general in their relationship with the World Bank. The emphasis on governance, accountability and, most recently, on the elimination of corruption has evoked strong reactions on the part of developing countries. They regard the recent Bank fight against 'the cancer of corruption' as hypocritical because corrupt regimes have not only been tolerated but also received substantial loans. Besides, developing countries fear intervention into domestic matters, a recurrent argument with regard to World Bank conditionality.

NGOs

NGOs have played a crucial intermediary role in exposing the negative environmental consequences of lending, and in forging alliances against the Bank. The international coalition sought to improve the environmental situation in developing countries by lobbying the World Bank directly and indirectly, through the most powerful member states. At times, vital information about projects was provided by sources from within the Bank, particularly the environmental and evaluation departments. Evidence about the negative social and environmental effects of IBRD lending made IDA controversial.

Requirements to reckon with the environment and to involve local organisations in the preparation and implementation of projects have enlarged the Bank's influence on borrowing countries' policies. This is a paradoxical effect of NGO actions: although they opposed conditionality in general, their campaigns in fact strengthened conditionality, albeit on different grounds. Another dilemma for NGOs consists of the course to follow: should they co-operate, or should they press for more radical change, with the risk that donors will further cut back their funding.

While very powerful in pressuring the World Bank in the 1980s, NGO influence has diminished somewhat for two reasons. First, the Bank has built up substantial environmental expertise and underlines the importance of good environmental planning in its projects. The campaign against the Bank thus in fact strengthened the organisation as far as environmental 'stewardship' is concerned. It has also enlarged the Bank's influence on borrowing countries' policies. Second, in the NGO–Bank relationship the importance of local organisations has increased compared with the period of intensive lobbying in the 1980s. International NGOs are frequently consulted and play a role in project implementation, and also the Bank attaches much importance to involving local NGOs.

The differentiation among NGOs and the installation of co-ordination mechanisms means that the World Bank can count on considerable support as long as poverty reduction and environmental protection are central objectives. Concurrently, NGOs remain critical and alert to signal potential wrongs.

Peculiar to environmental concerns is that their promotion within the World Bank's operations is not wholly dependent on the success of overall organisational change. As long as a certain commitment to the environment exists within the organisation, which allows staff to devote time to project preparation, considerable progress can be made. Environmental projects usually do not require large amounts of money; instead, supervision and co-ordination costs are higher. Small-scale projects can have significant, positive environmental effects, help to increase local involvement and promotion of local, more environmentally friendly techniques (Kolk and Van der Weij 1998). The past few years have seen some remarkable changes in World Bank practices, in which previously unthinkable coalitions and co-operation patterns emerged. An example will be given in the next section.

The impact of change: the example of the Brazilian Amazon[4]

The Brazilian Amazon is an interesting case for various reasons. First, it played an important role in exposing the negative environmental and social effects of World Bank loans. Second, deforestation in Brazil has caused great international concern since the late 1980s. Alarming pictures of burning forests focused attention on the destruction of a unique ecosystem, the fate of the local population and the potential consequences for global warming. This took place in a period of great interest in environmental issues, culminating in the 1992 United Nations Conference on Environment and Development, held in Brazil.

Third, Brazilian nationalist forces showed a strong sensitivity with regard to the Amazon, rejecting every proposal for the supposed 'internationalisation' of the region.

4 This section is based on Kolk 1996 and 1998.

It was seen as a threat to Brazilian sovereignty and the country's legitimate right to use and manage the Amazon. Western countries and their 'agents' (such as multinational corporations, international organisations and NGOs) were accused of hypocrisy since they neglected the enormous environmental problems caused by their own industrial development. Although it remained a delicate issue, conflict gradually gave way to a more co-operative attitude on the part of the Brazilian government.

At the same time, Brazilian renunciations of foreign interference and international hypocrisy had contributed to the creation of a climate for positive steps to address deforestation. It paved the way for the largest international environmental project for a single country, the Pilot Programme for the Brazilian rainforest. Launched by the group of the seven most industrialised countries (G7) in 1990, the programme has been co-ordinated by the World Bank and the European Commission. In the preparations and the implementation, the co-ordinators and donors have adopted a cautious approach in order to prevent particular sectors within Brazilian society and the government from being offended. Because of their intention to set the programme in motion, the World Bank and the European Commission almost automatically entered into a coalition with the Brazilian proponents, both within the government and NGOs.

It is this set of factors that makes the Brazilian Amazon a salient example, especially for the World Bank. The Pilot Programme represents a new tendency in a region where the World Bank has negative experiences. Once the target of international action for its activities in Brazil, the organisation's current role in the Pilot Programme receives much more support. Some NGOs remain fairly critical, if only because they basically distrust the World Bank. They point at the Planafloro project, also in the Brazilian Amazon, which showed that the new approach does not always proceed smoothly. Designed to diminish the negative effects of Polonoroeste, Planafloro became the subject of NGO criticism because the conditions and local participation were considered insufficient. These charges have been confirmed by the World Bank's own inspection panel.

Nevertheless, the coalition between the World Bank, donor countries and Brazilian government and NGO proponents produced remarkable results, especially in the period when Brazilian political interest in the Amazon waned. Nationalist forces organised a strong opposition to particular projects within the overall Pilot Programme: the demarcation of Indian lands, the funding of extractive reserves for rubber tappers and the support for Brazilian NGOs. Donor countries have pledged approximately $300 million, consisting of grants instead of the usual loans. By now, the Pilot Programme is recommended as a promising example of international environmental co-operation by the participants, in spite of its difficult and protracted negotiations.

The strength of the programme is that it actively seeks the participation and support of the local authorities and the population. Previous Bank-funded projects in the Brazilian Amazon did not sufficiently reckon with the political situation to ensure that they were profitable for the most important stakeholders. By analysing the potential winners and losers beforehand and, if necessary, adjusting conditions and increasing involvement, the group of actors that may benefit from the project one way or another, has been enlarged. The recognition that such an approach is particularly useful in a large and complex country such as Brazil is one of the main differences with past World Bank practices.

Conclusions

This chapter has analysed the evolution of the World Bank in the past two decades. It has paid specific attention to two instances that highlighted existing intra-organisational conflicts and contradictions, and forced measures on the part of the Bank. In the 1980s, NGO actions exhibited the 'by-products' of projects and gave Republican critics in the United States the opportunity to increase financial pressure on the World Bank. This eventually resulted in the adoption of a new environmental policy in 1987. Five years later, an internal evaluation provided evidence on the declining economic performance of projects, which incited donor countries to require substantial reforms.

Over the years, a differentiation of the relevant stakeholders has taken place. Whereas the influence of NGOs has diminished somewhat, donor countries (shareholders, financiers and important suppliers of goods and services) and borrowing countries (shareholders and customers) continue to be crucial for the World Bank. In addition, the success of the transformation hinges in part on the staff's capacity to change, especially on senior managers who seem more reluctant than those below and above them.

The broader lessons of this case study are twofold. First, it shows how environmental practices can change as a result of external pressure and as part of overall organisational transformation. This experience has been shared by other organisations, both profit and non-profit. Second, changes in the World Bank have affected environmental management in developing countries. The Brazilian Amazon is a case in point, and shows the tendency to form coalitions across stakeholders. As an important lender, think-tank, provider of expertise and standard-setting agency, such new developments in the World Bank are likely to have a much broader impact.

19

Sustainable Development and the Environment

Lessons from the Development Experience of Kerala State in India

Govindan Parayil

SUSTAINABLE DEVELOPMENT or SD has been hailed as a potentially new developmental paradigm that can alleviate the immense environment and development problems facing the developing world. However, a closer examination of the SD thesis reveals that there has been no change in the development practice of growth economics. The SD thesis, as it is being promoted now, is based on the premise that environmental problems and poverty in the developing world can be eventually solved by treating them as technical fixes such that they can be dealt with as a global environmental management problem. It is being argued that instead of relying on a vague and untested notion of SD, one needs to follow a radically new approach of looking for cases where the ideals of sustainable development may have been in practice already. In this regard, we argue that the Indian state of Kerala, with a population of 30 million (more than the population of Canada), can show us how, during its remarkable development experience of the past three to four decades, it has been putting in practice some of the ideals of SD. We will argue that, despite its limitations, what has come to be known as the 'Kerala model' of development should be examined as a possible case of SD in practice that other nations and states in the developing world may find useful to learn from and possibly replicate.

The evolution of sustainable development

Immediately after the Second World War when the nations of what we now call the 'developing' or 'third world' began to gain independence from their erstwhile colonisers, the unchallenged inductive thinking among development experts (who were mostly from the 'developed' world) who were ostensibly engaged in alleviating the poverty and deprivation that afflicted these decolonised nations, was to induce economic development. Economic development was to be achieved by attaining rapid economic growth through an infusion of capital and modern technology, whether the particular development model was based on the neoclassical growth theory or planned state capitalist growth theory. The goal-directed activity of modernisation of the developing nations was initiated, mostly, by transferring capital and technology to these countries by bilateral and multilateral aid agencies and multinational corporations. The outcome of economic development was measured by the increase in per capita income and the growth of gross national product. While many nations have achieved growth and many people have benefited from it, there still exist acute poverty, deprivation and severe environmental problems in the developing world. As will be argued later, achieving economic growth without a clear framework of distributive justice will be counter-productive, not only in terms of reducing poverty and disparity but for ameliorating environmental problems as well.

While economic growth programmes were being vigorously promoted the world over, the global agenda for development began to shift from its emphasis on economic development alone to environment *and* development in the 1960s and 1970s with the recognition of serious environmental problems and concerns about the depletion of terrestrial resources.[1] The 1972 UN Conference on Human Environment held in Stockholm 'brought the industrialised and developing nations together to delineate the 'rights' of the human family to a healthy and productive environment' (WCED 1987: 11). After Stockholm, a strategic merging of environmental concerns with population growth and economic development began to take shape as a global agenda. In 1982, the UN celebrated the 'Decade After Stockholm' and in 1983, the UN General Assembly passed a resolution to form an independent World Commission on Environment and Development (WCED) in order to propose 'long term environmental strategies for achieving sustainable development by the year 2000' (WCED 1987: 9). Thus the official and widely accepted concept of 'sustainable development' appeared in the WCED report known as *Our Common Future*. Sustainable development received official blessing from the heads of all the nations of the world who gathered at the 1992 'Earth Summit' in Rio de Janeiro.[2]

Sustainable development has become the latest growth industry in the environment and development field. Because of the apparent unwillingness or even inability of

1 An important event that attracted the attention of the US, the leading light of the industrialisation model for the developing world, was the publication of Rachel Carson's *Silent Spring* (1962). Carson set off a chain reaction in public awareness to the horrors of environmental destruction from industrialisation (in her particular case the horrors of ecocide from pesticide pollution). It must be noted that serious concerns about the state of the environment occurred in the developing world as well, focusing on such problems as desertification, deforestation and soil erosion brought on by unsound development practices.

2 It may be recalled that the 'Earth Summit' or the United Nations Conference on Environment and Development (UNCED) was convened to commemorate the 20th anniversary of the Stockholm conference. How SD can be and should be practised is amply illustrated in the UNCED report, popularly known as *Agenda 21*. See United Nations 1993.

concerned international development bodies to address the ideological content of the economic principles of development, and the nebulous nature of the definition given to sustainable development, everyone interested in development has his or her own interpretations of SD. Although the WCED urges the world to follow a 'new development path', unfortunately, no new development trail has blazed. The Commission still urges the world to follow the beaten path of the economic growth paradigm that was in vogue for the past several decades. The ideology of growth economics is retained without looking into the normative and ethical concerns embedded in modern economic discourses that brought about these problems in the first place. Although WCED urges the developing world to 'revive growth' to alleviate poverty and deprivation, to be fair to this well-intentioned UN Commission, one should concede that the Commission does emphasise the importance of bringing about qualitative changes in the nature of growth to attain sustainable development (WCED 1987: 49). However, the WCED report does not make explicit how to operationalise its normative prescriptions for sustainable development into concrete economic practice. The WCED report does not challenge the neoclassical economic growth theory that pervades the development paradigm the world over. According to Drummond and Marsden, research work and discourse on SD

> has tended to highlight the problems inherent in articulating a capacious, ambiguous and inherently contradictory concept and little consensus has emerged regarding either the substance of the idea itself or in respect of the most appropriate methodologies for its articulation and operationalisation (Drummond and Marsden 1995).

As Redclift has argued, sustainable development is the latest incarnation of the discourse of modernisation in the name of 'development as progress' made more palatable by linking 'natural limits' expressed through the concept of 'sustainability' (Redclift 1994). What has transpired lately is that the official development agencies in both the developed and the developing countries and the business community take it on faith that sustainable development and GNP growth go hand-in-hand and are not in conflict with each other (Ekins 1993).[3]

Ideological contradictions in the sustainability thesis

There is an environmental crisis in the world, and it may not be too late to reverse it if prudent policies and practices are put in place. The important issue is to identify the exact sources of this crisis and make the parties responsible for the problems pay their due share in dealing with it. Potential environmental problems such as global warming, depletion of the ozone layer, proliferation of industrial and nuclear

3 It may be remembered that much of the organising of the official part of the 1992 'Earth Summit' was undertaken and underwritten by the Geneva-based Business Council for Sustainable Development or BCSD.

wastes, and tropical deforestation, among others, threaten the stability of the biosphere and global climate. Significant amounts of the greenhouse gases are produced by the industrialised nations. The energy intensity of economic production per capita in the US is 370 times that of Sri Lanka (Redclift 1994: 17).

The tropical deforestation under way in the Philippines, Indonesia, Malaysia, the Brazilian Amazon and elsewhere in the developing world is a direct consequence of the high demand for tropical timber, beef and minerals in the industrialised world. The major cause for the disappearance of tropical forests of the Amazon can be traced to the formation of large cattle ranches (for producing hamburger beef for exports) which were subsidised by the several erstwhile military governments of Brazil and through loans obtained from international development banks. Recently, deforestation has been triggered by logging companies that export their products to Japan, the US and Western Europe. The direct actions of the poor and the underprivileged of the developing world, which are typically blamed for deforestation, cause only peripheral environmental problems. Deforestation in the Brazilian Amazon was not due to 'population explosion' or landlessness, as is usually alleged by neo-Malthusian environmentalists. The indigent migrants from outside the Amazon region and the rooted forest people often become hapless victims of deforestation initiated by pasture builders and logging companies by becoming hired hands for burning the deforested land (Parayil and Tong 1998). The devastating smoke haze that hung over South-East Asia for many months in 1997 was caused by the logging companies, which burned forest land after felling the trees to make way for land for development. The rooted people of Borneo who practised swidden agriculture were only a minor party to this large-scale environmental conflagration. As Shaw correctly points out, the actions of the world's poor may be responsible for some of the 'proximate causes' of environmental degradation while the 'ultimate' or 'deeper' causes of global environmental problems rest with the industrialised affluent nations and their agents in the developing world (Shaw 1989). As we argue below, in order to save us from ecological crisis and render economic justice to the majority of the people in the world, we need to expose the ideological bankruptcy of modern economic development practice in the developed world which is now vigorously copied by the developing world.

One of the major fallacies of the growth expectation imbued in the pronouncements of global development agency reports on sustainable development is the belief that, by maximising economic growth, poverty can be eliminated in a trickle-down process. Despite the phenomenal economic growth enjoyed by the industrialised countries, millions of people still live in poverty in these affluent nations. The poor in the developing world should not think that copying the growth models of the developed countries would regenerate their environment and lift them from acute poverty and deprivation. In fact, because of the worse social relations existing in countries such as Brazil, India, Indonesia and the Philippines, any economic development model that emphasises only growth will exacerbate the existing inequalities in income and wealth distribution and resource consumption. The recent collapse of the East Asian 'tiger' economies best shows the meaninglessness of pursuing economic growth at any cost. While these Asian countries grew phenomenally until recently, no one asked at what cost to the environment and the workers and who benefited from the expansion of the economic pie. In the name of political stability and improving the living standard of the poor, corrupt and autocratic governments were propped up in Indonesia, South Korea, Thailand and elsewhere by the IMF, World Bank and the industrialised nations. Transparency in politics and governance, and freedom of expression and democratic aspirations of the people were muffled in the name of preserving 'Asian values'. These countries were to be the shining examples to demonstrate the universal validity of neoclassical economics, the ideological basis for sustainable development.

The sustainable development thesis as it is being promoted now is based on the premise that global and regional environmental problems can be attenuated and eventually ended if they are recognised as technical problems of global management. Although critical of existing forms of development as deficient and needing a reformulation, SD does not recognise the inherent contradictions in the economic doctrine that still lies at the core of the development strategy. Promoting economic growth and environmental prudence alone without prioritising distributive justice is antithetical to a healthy environment and a free society of unexploited citizens. In view of the realities of human social relations and deteriorating ecological conditions, no satisfactory economic system can be distilled and made to look value-free as neoclassical economics claims to be. Instead of looking at outmoded economic theories to determine the distribution of the benefits and cost of development in the supposedly value-neutral market sphere under the 'naturalised' constraint of 'scarcity', we should look at economics as a 'social movement' to make it a meaningful concept for practising SD.

The task of economics as a social movement is to address the political economy of exploitation founded on class, race, gender and other modes of exploitation based on constructed social categories. Economics as a social movement must address the subordination of humans and nature in the name of value-free economics. Egalitarianism and social justice must be the central concerns of such economics. In order to analyse and solve environmental problems properly, economics as a social movement should strive to end what Samir Amin (1993) calls the 'totalitarianism of economics'. Economics as a social movement should understand the essential unity of politics, economics and ecology (Singh 1976). It is from this vantage point that governments, aid agencies, NGOs and social movements should approach economics as a unitary force of theory and practice for implementing SD. Sustainable development must pay attention to economic justice and equity before economic growth. It is in this context that the development experience of the state of Kerala in India is examined here to provide an alternative interpretation of SD.

A 'Kerala model' of sustainable development?

If the achievement of very low infant mortality and population growth rates and elimination of acute poverty and deprivation (which afflicted the majority of the people) without significantly eroding the environmental base are corroborating

Features	Kerala	India	USA
Area in 1,000 km^2	39	3,288	9,364
Population in millions	30	935	263
Per capita availability of land (ha)	0.13	0.32	3.6
Per capita income (US$)	300*	340	26,980
Per capita energy consumption (kg OE)	<300	248	7,819
Life expectancy at birth (years)	72	60.4	76
Crude death rate per 1,000 population	6	10	8.8
Infant mortality rate per 1,000 live births	12	82	9
Birth rate per 1,000 population	15	29.1	15.9
Total fertility rate	1.8	3.2	2.1
Adult literacy rate (%)	93	48	96

* M.P. Parameswaran (2000) claims that the per capita income of Kerala should be augmented by $120 for foreign remittance because of the large number of Keralans who work outside Kerala, mostly in the Arabian Gulf countries.

kg OE = kilogram oil equivalent

Table 1: SELECTED INDICATORS OF DEVELOPMENT OF KERALA, INDIA AND THE USA FOR 1995

Source: World Bank 1997c; World Resources Institute *et al.* 1997; Government of Kerala 1997

evidence for practising 'sustainable development', then the Indian state of Kerala should be counted as an early example of a state/society that practises some form of SD. The Indian state of Kerala, with a population of 30 million people, has become an 'enigma' to economists and international development experts.[4] Kerala is one of the smaller states in the Indian union situated on the south-western corner of the sub-continent. It occupies only 1.18% of the total land area of India, but carries 3.43% of the total population of India at the 1991 census. However, this was 0.5% lower than the 1971 census figure (Prakash 1994).

In less than 40 years, Kerala has made a transition from a state with high infant mortality rate, high total fertility and population growth rates, and high crude death rates to a state where its indicators of social development are comparable with those of many developed countries. Its indicators of development consistently surpass all the states in India. Table 1 gives a comparative account of Kerala's development indicators with those of India and the USA, the world's richest country.

One of the most notable features by which Kerala was known, before its 'model' of development became a fascinating topic for international development experts, was its demographic transition and the dramatic decline in its population growth rate. Kerala's total fertility rate of 1.8 shows that the state has not only achieved the

4 See, for example, Wallich 1995. Writing under the column, 'The Analytical Economist', Wallich claims that 'the Indian state of Kerala has been one of economists' favorite anomalies' (p. 37).

Feature	Kerala's rank	Percentage of villages covered *in Kerala*	*in all India*
Within two kilometres			
All-weather roads	1	98	46
Bus stops	1	98	40
Post offices	1	100	53
Primary schools	1	100	90
Secondary schools	1	99	44
Fair-price shops	1	99	35
Health dispensaries	1	91	25
Health centres	1	47	12
Within five kilometres			
Higher education facilities	1	97	21
Hospitals	1	78	35
Fertiliser depots	1	93	44
Agricultural pump repair shops	1	65	19
Veterinary dispensaries	1	82	45
Credit co-operative banks	1	96	61
Commercial banks	1	96	40
Seed stores	2	63	40
Railway stations	8	23	18
In the village			
Drinking water	5	96	93
Electricity	3	97	33

Table 2: PROVISION OF SELECTED BASIC SERVICES AMONG ALL INDIAN STATES, BY LATE 1970S

Source: Franke and Chasin 1994

demographic transition, but the population growth has declined below the demographic replacement level net reproduction rate (NRR) of 1 (Kannan *et al*. 1991). Unlike in the industrialised (developed) nations, the fertility decline has not occurred because of high economic growth and a transition from agrarian to modern industrial modes of production, or due to a rural-to-urban transition. The fertility decline was due to high age at marriage, low infant mortality rate, access to healthcare, high levels of literacy, widespread adoption of family planning and emancipation of women (UNICEF 1995). Interestingly enough, the crude death rate is lower in rural areas than in the urban areas. Kerala also stands unique in India for its sex ratio which favours women at 1.04 to 1 as opposed to the Indian ratio of 0.93 to 1 and the Chinese ratio of 0.94 to 1 (Sen 1993). While Kerala has achieved almost full literacy (all persons below 25 years in Kerala are literate), the all-India average is only half of Kerala's.

According to Franke and Chasin 1994 (see Table 2), by the late 1970s, Kerala ranked number 1 in 15 out of 21 selected infrastructural and basic services among all the states in India. A significant facet of Kerala's high social development is that it came about despite very low per capita income and energy consumption as is evident by comparing

State	PQLI	HDI	SDP (rupees)
Andra Paradesh	42.70	0.3397	5,570
Assam	44.03	0.2542	4,230
Bihar	18.17	0.1334	2,904
Gujarat	58.38	0.5453	6,425
Haryana	55.68	0.5995	8,690
Karnataka	39.55	0.4772	5,555
Kerala	89.11	0.7749	4,618
Madhya Pradesh	16.08	0.1863	4,077
Maharashtra	53.27	0.6430	8,180
Orissa	6.70	0.2132	4,068
Punjab	66.28	0.7115	9,643
Rajastan	28.41	0.2294	4,361
Tamil Nadu	48.09	0.4873	5,078
Uttar Pradesh	15.39	0.1095	4,012
West Bengal	48.31	0.4176	5,383
All India	36.14	0.3974	5,424

Table 3: PQLI, HDI AND PER CAPITA STATE DOMESTIC PRODUCT (SDP) FOR 15 MAJOR INDIAN STATES FOR 1991

Source: EPW Research Foundation 1994

with the United States (Table 2). The meaninglessness of income and GDP per capita as measures of socioeconomic development becomes obvious when we compare these data with other states within India. In 1991–92, the state of Punjab, India's richest state with more than twice the per capita income of Kerala, had 33 PQLI points less than that of Kerala (see Table 3 for a comparison of Kerala with other major Indian states).[5] According to Richard Franke (1993), while Kerala had a PQLI of 82 in 1981, the USA index stood at 96. While the human development index was 0.925 for the USA in 1994, Kerala stood at 0.775, with a per capita income of about one-eightieth of the former (EPW Research Foundation 1994; UNDP 1994).

As argued earlier, one of the fallacies of development economics that the SD thesis still retains is the belief that, by maximising economic growth, poverty can be eliminated. And, doing that in an 'environmentally prudent' way would supposedly give us SD. As Herman Daly (1990) persuasively argues, 'it is precisely the non-sustainability of growth that gives urgency to the concept of sustainable development'. Kerala's development experience is a telling story in this context that achieving growth should not be deemed as an end in itself. At most, achieving growth ought to be taken

5 PQLI or physical quality of life index is a composite measure of three indicators of development: infant mortality, life expectancy and literacy. HDI or human development index is a deprivation measure developed by the United Nations Development Programme (UNDP 1994) which, unlike PQLI , includes per capita GDP as well. The HDI composite is constructed with three indicators: life expectancy at birth (longevity), adult literacy rate (knowledge), and the log of GDP per capita (standard of living) adjusted for purchasing power parity (PPP).

as a means to a social goal of increasing (or providing equal opportunity to the means of) the wealth of every citizen in society. Paying attention to the means is more important than aiming for the end (growth) in itself in achieving development.

It should be reiterated that reducing social and economic inequalities through democratic means, as is the case with Kerala, is the best way to practise SD. And, to a large extent, Kerala has shown that, despite tremendous odds, it was able to eliminate acute poverty and deprivation without attaining rapid growth in per capita GNP as is 'expected' of all economic development models/theories. Kerala is a paradigmatic case because conventional development models legitimised through quantitative growth measures such as GNP, energy consumption and per capita income failed to account for the indicators of social progress in the state. It is thus important to look for sustainability indicators not in quantitative measures alone, but in qualitative indices as well.

The factors that contributed to Kerala's achievements are:

- Meaningful land reforms
- 'Food for all' schemes through fair-price shops and feeding programmes for schoolchildren, infants and mothers
- Provision of easy access to primary and preventative healthcare
- Promotion of high levels of literacy, particularly among women, through free and universal primary and secondary education
- High mandated agricultural (primary) and industrial (secondary) sector wages
- Cost-effective transportation facilities
- Rural electrification
- Public action and mobilisation, especially engaging peasant farmers and the working poor in the democratic and electoral process
- Encouragement of public dialogue on environmental issues through the mobilisation of social movements and civil society

Various analysts attribute Kerala's success to either one or a combination of the following factors:

- Kerala's ability to undertake public action through the mobilisation of peasant farmers, agricultural workers, industrial workers and other working people by mostly leftist parties (Franke and Chasin 1995; Ramachandran 1995; Heller 1995, 1996)
- The spread of literacy and maintenance of women's rights (Sen 1992, 1993, 1994; Jeffrey 1992)
- Reducing social inequality and decreasing inequalities in income and consumption (Ratcliffe 1978; Alexander 1994)
- Public action and poverty alleviation (Kannan 1995)

- Indigenous evolution and popularisation of social movements concerned with environment and development issues (Isaac *et al.* 1997)

According to Franke and Chasin (1995), the best description that can be ascribed to Kerala's experience is a 'social justice model' of development.

It is being argued that the 'Kerala model' of development may be taken as an early prototype of SD because of the following factors: (i) improvements in the quality of life indicated by sustained and progressive improvements in the standard of living evidenced by the reductions in infant mortality and birth rates, substantial increases in life expectancy at birth and overall improvements in the welfare of women; (ii) improvements in environmental stability indicated by the disappearance of irreversible ecological changes and frugal and efficient use of energy and natural resources; (iii) reductions in relative social and economic inequality and the importance accorded to social justice as a prerequisite for development; and (iv) relative decline in political and social strife orchestrated by the establishment of democratic institutions, and better communal relationships maintained between the major religious groups.[6]

It has been observed that, since the inception of the redistributive development programmes, the environmental conditions in Kerala have improved. Although the acreage of rainforests has declined from pre-independence figures, popular campaigns to preserve the existing forests seem to be successful. If we look at the state of India's environmental conditions in general, Kerala suffers fewer environmental problems than the rest of the country. Kerala suffers less deforestation, industrial pollution, soil erosion, loss of soil nutrients, groundwater depletion, salination and waterlogging due to canal irrigation (Centre for Science and Environment 1985). Although Kerala has its share of localised environmental problems, it does not face severe ecological crisis and the 'low population growth rate and relatively equal land distribution may reduce the risk of environmental degradation' (Veron 1998). But the greatest hope for Kerala to improve its environmental conditions and achieve self-sustaining SD may come about as a result of the inception of community-based and decentralised development planning and democratisation that began in the 1990s (Kerala State Planning Board 1996; Franke and Chasin 1997; Bandyopadhyay 1997).

The 'Kerala model' delineated by the above changes is undergoing a major structural change in the 1990s as a result of a massive experiment unleashed by the state government in tandem with the major grassroots-oriented campaign orchestrated by the largest NGO in Kerala known as the *Kerala Sastra Sahitya Parishad* or KSSP. The essence of the new initiative is to decentralise democracy and bring people's participation into planning starting at the neighbourhood and village levels and then moving up to the *Pachayat* (village council), sub-district, district and state levels. In 1996, the newly elected left-front government of Kerala took a bold decision to invert

6 Critics and some analysts argue that the recent changes in Indian polity and economy, the drive to accelerate economic liberalisation, globalisation and reduce welfare spending is cutting into Kerala's gains. Being only a sub-national entity, Kerala is not immune to national policy strictures, market convulsions and political realignments. However, my basic arguments stand. These new changes are not a result of the earlier policies that created the near sustainable development indicators that Kerala achieved.

the planning process for development by introducing decentralised planning, and directed the state planning board to draw up a major campaign to plan from below as the cornerstone of its ninth five-year plan, which began in that year.

The impetus and intellectual basis for the People's Campaign for the Ninth Plan was laid in 1990–91 when the Integrated Rural Technology Centre (IRTC, established in 1987 by the KSSP) and the Centre for Earth Sciences Studies (CESS—a state government-funded research institution) together initiated the 'Panchayat Resource Mapping Programme' (Centre for Earth Science Studies 1992). The Resource Mapping Programme mobilises villagers and village-level institutions (*Panchayats* and neighbourhoods or wards) to develop detailed maps of their natural and human resources. These resource maps and information, combined with technical data, form the knowledge basis for conducting micro-level planning for development. The KSSP with technical assistance from CESS and the Centre for Development Studies (CDS—a Thiruvananthapuram-based independent state- and central government-funded development research body that offers postgraduate degrees in development studies) initiated a comprehensive micro-planning experiment in 1991–92 in Kalliasseri Panchayat in northern Kerala. The success of micro-level planning conducted in Kalliasseri became the impetus for the state-level campaign for people's planning for the Ninth Plan.

Kerala's decentralisation programme in development since the Ninth Plan's inception in 1996 is probably the largest of its kind in the world, bringing in nearly 3 million people (10% of the state's population) to air their concerns and put forward their visions of development at the village and neighbourhood meetings for drawing up development plans and solving problems at the local level.[7] For mobilising ordinary citizens at the grass-roots levels to take part in micro-level planning, more than 125,000 resource persons are deployed at the local, district and state levels. The total financial outlay for the 1997–98 and 1998–99 revenue years are 10 and 12 billion rupees, respectively. It is anticipated that the People's Campaign for Planning unleashed in Kerala, if successful, would make it a lasting exemplar of sustainable development.

Conclusion

Criteria for sustainability should include not only indicators of social development and social, political and economic justice for the vulnerable sections of society, but also environmental stability and improvement. Although Kerala has a low throughput, the indicators of social progress have not suffered because of sustained efforts to limit population growth rate and social inequality, and to conserve resources and use them frugally on a shared basis. Environmental analysts such as Hazel Henderson (1990) and Herman Daly (1991) argue that managing with low throughput itself is an indication of sustainability within a steady-state economic framework. William

7 Franke and Chasin (1997), 'Power to the Malayalee People'. The people of Kerala are also referred to as *Malayalees*, speakers of the local language, Malayalam.

Alexander (1994) claims that Kerala may already be a prototype of sustainable society because of its low throughput and the high rate of sharing of resources among the people. Bill McKibben (1995) hopes that, in a hopeless world, Kerala is a shining example of prudence and sapience for those looking for a sane way of living.

The test for practising SD should be based on a society's ability to maintain and further improve on the quality of life of its citizens by living within its own resource means. The development policies pursued by the state of Kerala so far show that there are hopeful signs for the state to enter into a self-sustaining developmental trajectory. The initiation of a people's campaign to manage their community-based resources and work out a bottom-up planning process of development bodes well. However, Kerala must still go a long way before becoming an 'exemplar' of sustainable development. Nevertheless, there are many lessons that we can learn from the development experience of Kerala in order to challenge the meaninglessness of economic development in which economic equity and social justice are not made the central concerns of economics and development models.

The reason why Kerala succeeded while other states failed in bringing about development is the radical nature of the development path that Kerala has followed. The nature of development that Kerala followed from the beginning was driven by popular mobilisation which in turn was delivered through proper public actions undertaken by the state government. Kerala's development path emphasised economic equity and distributive justice above economic growth. The redistributive development practice followed by the state through meaningful land reform and other such activities rendered justice to millions of former tenant farmers and landless people. Empowerment of the underprivileged through a genuinely democratic process is what sets Kerala apart from other developmental states. The greatest lesson other developing states can learn from Kerala is that improvements in the standard of living of ordinary people are possible without waiting for the panacea of economic growth to arrive.

Sustainable development, in order to be a meaningful alternative environment and development paradigm, needs to internalise the limitations of the existing development practice in the developing world, and the limits of markets as the primary agent of economic organisation to resolve and manage local and global environmental problems. As Redclift correctly observes, '[T]he constant reference to "sustainability" as a desirable objective has served to obscure the contradictions that "development" implies for the environment' (Redclift 1994: 2). Instead of following a metaphysical approach of postulating *a priori* how SD ought to be practised, it may be desirable to follow a practical reflexive approach of tracing a paradigmatic case of a state or society with some characteristic features of what might appear to be sustainable development. The development experience of Kerala might be looked at for analysis and reflection in this regard. However, there is no non-circular way of affirming that a metatheoretical claim that the 'Kerala model' of development has paradigmatic features of SD based on the empirical observations enumerated above, given the radical contingency of observations, theories and knowledge claims. As is well known, theories or hypotheses cannot be proved true or false, they can only be corroborated as probable states of reality by further studies and observations (Popper 1992). But we can make the normative claim that the developmental trajectory charted by Kerala state shows a resemblance to a possible SD model is very much in solidarity with the above reflection on the validity claims of models and theories.

20

Searching for Sustainability in the Marshall Islands

Development Dreams Clash with Ecological Reality

Barbara A. Ribbens and Eric Ribbens

THE CONCEPT of sustainable development has gained the attention of researchers, the media and the international community as the effects of human actions on our planet become more obvious. The World Conservation Union (IUCN) was begun 50 years ago as the 'United Nations for Nature' (Holdgate 1996). As the work of this organisation has grown, much of its attention has focused on defining sustainable development and making it a concept that is useful to governments and non-governmental agencies.

While many have struggled with the concept of sustainable development, there is still conflict over what it means, and even more conflict about how it can or should be applied. Not everyone even agrees that sustainable development is possible or important. The intensity of the disputes about the nature and applicability of sustainable development illuminates the importance of resolving human disharmony with our environment, and indicates that there are still likely to be problems with sustainable development as it is currently defined.

We apply the sustainable development concept to a specific situation in which we believe the standard process of sustainable development will not work. This situation is the Republic of the Marshall Islands (RMI). RMI is a small country with a small economy that is easily analysed. Thus, it is an ideal test site to examine the feasibility of sustainable development. Its plans for development confront a high population growth rate, a limited resource base and a history of abuse of natural ecosystems. After examining this challenge to sustainable development, we define boundary conditions for the application of sustainable development and propose modifications to the sustainable development concept.

Sustainable development

One widely used definition of sustainable development is 'meeting the needs of the present without compromising the ability of future generations to meet their own needs' (WCED 1987). Farrell and Hart (1998) described two different interpretations of sustainable development. First, some interpret sustainable development to mean that there are critical limits on natural resources which people cannot exceed. Thus, society needs to restrain resource consumption or critical elements upon which our society depends will be depleted. Second, others interpret sustainable development to mean that society needs to learn to balance competing economic, social and ecological goals. While there are conflicts between specific applications of these two alternatives, both support maintaining the quality of human life without destroying or irreparably damaging the underlying ecological systems.

Gladwin *et al.* (1995) specified how organisations should act in the process of reaching the goals of sustainable development. They defined sustainable development as 'the process of achieving human development in an inclusive, connected, equitable, prudent and secure manner'. This definition shifts the focus of sustainable development from outcome to process, and emphasises that by improving the process society can move the outcomes closer to achieving the goal of sustainability. Such movement in itself is a worthy goal.

The Republic of the Marshall Islands

The Republic of the Marshall Islands (RMI) consists of approximately 29 coral atolls roughly organised into two chains in the western Pacific Ocean north of the equator between 4° and 14° North, and 160° and 173° East (Levy 1996). The total land area of RMI is 180 km^2 (World Bank 1997c). The official 1995 population estimate was 55,575 people, with 49.2% of the population in that year under age 15 (RMI Online 1998).

The estimated annual population growth rate in 1988 was very high (4.3%) and by 2010 the population was predicted to be 91,411 people. However, by 1993, the growth rate had dropped to 3.6% after the government increased its health education and family planning resources (Cappelle 1996). The Philippines, Papua New Guinea and Jamaica, all island countries with a similar economy, have a much lower rate of population growth (Table 1). The Netherlands, often referred to as a country that has succeeded economically despite a population density even higher than that of RMI, only has one-sixth of RMI's population growth rate.

The present explosive rate of population growth contrasts sharply with its pre-Western history. Only a few islets in each atoll had adequate groundwater and soil quality to support cultivation and permanent settlement. While the ocean provided abundant protein, carbohydrate supplies were limited by low soil fertility. Many islands have saline soils due to salt spray, which restrict the variety and quantity of crops that can be grown (Connell and Maata 1992). These conditions, along with the difficulties of storing food in the tropical climate, forced the inhabitants to limit their

	Average population growth rate per year	Average population density per km	GNP per capita in US$
RMI	**3.6**	**311.11**	**1,487**
Netherlands	0.7	418.92	24,000
Philippines	2.2	228.67	1,050
Papua New Guinea	2.3	9.29	1,160
Jamaica	1.0	227.27	1,510
Average East Asia and Pacific	1.3	10.50	800

Table 1: COMPARISON OF RMI POPULATION CHARACTERISTICS WITH OTHER SELECTED COUNTRIES

Source: RMI Online (1998) and World Bank (1997c)

population growth via infanticide, geronticide and genocide (Spennemann 1992). Abortion was common when unmarried girls became pregnant. More recently, the acceptance of Christianity introduced a new value system, and the introduction of money resulted in a storable commodity that could be used to purchase food. As a result, the people stopped practising population limitation methods (Spennemann 1992), and about 90% of the food consumed in RMI is imported (Connell and Maata 1992).

RMI is classified as a lower-middle income economy by the World Bank (1997c), with a per capita GDP of $1,487 in 1990 (all currency values are in US dollars). The largest sector of the GDP in RMI is community, social and personal services, which composed 33.8% of the economy in 1993. The other major sectors of the economy are business services (16.3%), wholesale and retail (14.0%) and agriculture/fisheries (13.2%). Thus, over half of the economy is service-based.

In 1994, 68.1% of total RMI exports comprised chilled fish and frozen fish, which together accounted for $15.1 million, and the major import by RMI was food and live animals, which constituted 28.2% of imports and was valued at $19.9 million. The next largest import was mineral fuels and lubricants, $15.3 million and 21.8%. Thus, the two biggest categories of imports were consumable goods. Overall, in 1994 RMI imported $70.4 million in goods but only exported $22.2 million, resulting in a negative balance of trade of $48.2 million, which is a per capita annual deficit of $867. The largest trading partner was the United States, with 61% of the trade; Guam was second, with 24% (RMI Online 1998).

When the economy of RMI is compared with a variety of other small countries (Table 2), it becomes evident that RMI has a very small economy with an extremely large deficit. The ratio of imports to exports is 3.18, more than three times higher than the regional average. The Philippines, Papua New Guinea and Jamaica, all island countries classified by the World Bank as having a lower-middle income economy, have an import:export ratio less than half the size of that of RMI.

	Exports (million US$)	Imports (million US$)	Ratio of imports: exports
RMI	**22**	**70**	**3.18**
Philippines	5,740	8,300	1.45
Papua New Guinea	1,030	1,180	1.15
Jamaica	963	1,100	1.14
Average East Asia and Pacific	69,623	65,139	0.94

Table 2: COMPARISON OF RMI TRADE WITH OTHER SELECTED COUNTRIES

Source: RMI Online (1998) and World Bank (1997c)

Prior to the introduction of Western cultural traditions, the RMI atolls were sparsely populated by a subsistence-level economy, with the largest atoll having fewer than 1,000 inhabitants. The islands have a rich cultural tradition centred around their oceanic surroundings (e.g. Hart 1998). Since discovery by Western civilisation, RMI has been a Germanic territory (1885–1914), controlled by Japan (1914–44), and finally a territory of the United States (1945–79). Since 1979 the country has gradually moved towards independence, which occurred officially in 1986.

Its history includes repeated international indignities, including occupation by both Japanese and American troops during the Second World War, the construction and destruction of numerous military bases, the detonation of nuclear test warheads in Bikini Atoll, and most recently overfishing of RMI-controlled oceans by Japanese fishing vessels. In 1988, the Japanese paid fishing lease payments of $1.2 million to catch 19,167 metric tonnes of fish in RMI waters, mainly skipjack tuna (Connell and Maata 1992). Marine resources in RMI are not fully protected and the focus remains on exploitation, not conservation (Harding 1992). Three of the atolls are still controlled by the United States, which uses them as military satellite launch and weapon testing sites.

One impact of the infusion of United States personnel and technology has been the concentration of Marshallese people on Majuro and Ebeye atolls, so that today only 35% of the population live on the remaining 24 atolls. Salaries from the United States Army or from the Marshallese government have enticed 65% of the population to move to Majuro or Ebeye (Roylance 1997). When one family member successfully finds employment, the immediate and then extended family come to share the income. About 50% of all jobs in RMI are in the public sector (Connell and Maata 1992).

Current environmental status of RMI

The current environmental status of RMI is bleak. Although these islands should be the epitome of a Polynesian paradise, in reality there are too many people living on two crowded islands, in a country with too few exploitable natural resources and a severely negative balance of trade. The main exploitable natural resources, in addition to the currently heavily used fishery resources, include some phosphorus deposits and the intriguing but technologically complicated possibility of deep-sea mineral extraction. Past military activities by occupying forces have left a trail of debris and environmental contamination, ranging from stacks of vehicles dumped in lagoons to radioactive contamination of several atolls.

The cultural norms of the inhabitants are shifting as well. The population growth rate is extremely high, and the inhabitants of the two most heavily populated islands in particular have a growing expectation of Western-style consumerism, fed by exposure to US military personnel and Western lifestyles (Roylance 1997). The government is young with little tradition of setting or managing environmental policy. The national environmental protection authority (RMIEPA) was created in 1984. 'A great deal of legal and administrative work remains to be done within RMIEPA and government Ministries before a strong national assessment program is put into place' (Harding 1992: 18). As of 1992, its 12 employees focused on solid waste, earth-moving, water quality and pesticide use (Harding 1992), leaving scant resources for larger strategic issues or education. Marshallese individuals focus on jobs and economic issues, and the RMI government is preoccupied with overall economic difficulties, which are exacerbated by the fact that it has little or no power to influence its global partners.

Furthermore, the low atolls that comprise RMI are highly susceptible to damage if the global warming scenario produces any significant increase in sea level. The average height above sea level on most islands is 2 m, so an increase of the sea level of just 30 cm would significantly encroach on the already limited land mass. The recent El Niño event of 1997–98 created a temporary sea level rise of 2 cm (Environmental News Network 1998), and a 2.5°C warming is estimated to create a net rise in sea level between 0.5 and 1.5 m (Bush 1997). Thus, while sea levels will not change dramatically over short time-frames, the potential for catastrophic conditions in the RMI from sea level changes is very real. Additionally, changes in climate patterns could substantially lengthen the drought season and increase the severity of typhoons (Connell and Maata 1992).

Because it will be one of the first places on the globe where global warming will have catastrophic effects, RMI is referred to as a 'front-line state' regarding climate change issues (RMI Online 1998). It is important to note that, once RMI has been affected by climate change, it will be too late to reverse the effects before other coastal regions elsewhere on this planet will also be affected. Amata Kabua, the first president of RMI, told the United Nations that, while global warming is the most formidable challenge RMI faced, there is nothing they can do about it except continue to air this concern in international arenas (Connell and Maata 1992).

While the high population density (Table 1) alone may not be a challenge to sustainable development, when there is an imbalance between consumption and supply any increase in population size will only exacerbate this tension. The Netherlands is frequently cited as an example of a country with a high population density and a relatively sustainable economic system; however, the success of the

Netherlands is due in part to a much more fertile soil, an ideal geographic location for serving trade requirements, and a long history of economic development at the expense of its colonies. Furthermore, while the Netherlands is very dense, its per capita growth rate is very small compared with that of RMI; therefore, even if it were not a much more wealthy economy, it would still be better able to absorb and accommodate projected growth due to the slower pace of population growth.

In summary, RMI suffers from an unpleasant mix of environmental dilemmas. In the short term, they need to control environmental degradation while satisfying the increasing demands for development and growth. Additionally, the trade imbalance will continue to demand additional financial resources and attention. In the medium term, the current rate of population growth is not sustainable, and will exacerbate the short-term problems. Finally, global climate changes are a serious long-term threat to the country's existence.

Traditional sources of capital to drive development are not available.

Can the sustainable development paradigm be successfully applied to RMI? At this point in time, RMI must resolve its trade deficit and identify additional sources of revenue if development dreams can be realised. Specifically, what do undeveloped countries have to trade to build the capital necessary to become sustainable? One commonly employed method is natural resource extraction. However, this is not available to RMI as a revenue source because of the extremely limited natural resource base. Phosphorus mining can be accomplished only with the side-effect of removing the atoll; this can hardly be considered sustainable. Deep-sea mineral extraction is not a mature revenue-generating industry, and will require enormous amounts of initial capital and a base of highly skilled workers. Increasing the export of chilled fish and frozen fish is not feasible, because the fishery is already over-exploited by Japanese competitors. Mariculture, particularly the cultivation of giant clams, is one possibility which is being explored, but so far no mariculture ventures in Oceania have become commercially viable (Connell and Maata 1992).

A second widely utilised method for bootstrapping a developing economy is to be strategically located in an international commerce nexus, from which shipping, processing, redistributing and value-added services can be easily sold. Because there are few locations on this planet that are more isolated from key international commerce pathways than RMI, this option is also unavailable.

The third possibility is to provide a unique human resource service. However, while literacy rates in RMI are quite high, the social, governmental and technology-training support systems are fairly basic, and the difficulties of implementing a long-distance service will probably outweigh the possible benefits that might accrue to interested outside sources. In the 1990/91 school year, while 85% of the children completed the compulsory 8th grade education, only 46% attended high school and fewer than 10% attended post-secondary schools. Of the 427 students who attended post-secondary school in 1990/91, 41% left RMI to attend schools in other countries (RMI Online 1998). The other 59% attended the local College of Marshall Islands, a two-year community college which emphasises vocational training in health and education, and also offers a limited liberal arts programme.

Thus, the average education of the population is fairly limited, which restricts the ability of RMI to implement technological advances without extensive additional investment in education. Currently, the RMI government spends no more than $900 per pupil to cover all education expenses, including teacher salaries, building maintenance and teaching materials. Given other issues facing the government, such as the negative balance of trade, an education allocation large enough to raise the educational level of the population enough to enable high-tech ventures is unlikely.

Probably the most attractive form of capital generation for RMI is to capitalise on its isolated geographical position. There are two forms that such capital generation could take, both of which already exist to some extent. First, the RMI atolls can be used as sites for technologically intensive operations which are too dangerous to be implemented in more populated regions. The Kwajalein military satellite test launch base is a good example, as is the use of Bikini Atoll as a nuclear test site. Space launches, extremely dangerous chemical manipulations, nuclear waste storage and test releases of genetically engineered organisms are all possibilities. The advantage of this form of capital generation is that, because of the high risks involved, a high user fee can be commanded. The disadvantage is the high likelihood of damage or destruction of an atoll, and that the extent of risks may be difficult to assess prior to implementation of the use. Bikini Atoll is the seminal high-risk use event for RMI; while the information generated was immensely valuable to the United States, RMI was not adequately compensated. In fact, more than 50 years after the test, the residents of Bikini Atoll are still displaced to Majuro Atoll.

Second, RMI can exploit its remote location as an attractive tourist destination to increase revenue. Deep-sea fishing, coral reef scuba diving and lounging on a tropical island under coconut palms while watching the waves wash up a sandy beach collectively describe an extremely desirable vacation destination. In fact, RMI already is a tourist destination. Tourism is still very small, providing only 4.6% of the GDP in 1994 (RMI Online 1998). Only 12.6% of the 5,500 visitors to RMI in 1995 came for the purpose of tourism and they stayed an average of 5.5 days (RMI Online 1998). Increases in tourism could have enormous economic benefits, and employment at tourism service industries is highly desirable. However, tourism can easily be oversold, which degrades its commercial value. Furthermore, a large portion of the revenues do not accrue to the destination country if the tourism infrastructure is financed by outside interests, and tourism usually increases natural resource demands. Finally, tourism and dangerous technologically intensive operations are inherently mutually exclusive.

In summary, the conversion from undeveloped to developed country is usually accomplished by exploiting an existing natural resource base using non-capital-intensive extractive techniques. This option simply is not available to RMI unless more atolls are destroyed. The most viable alternative is to attempt to increase tourism revenues by carefully constructing eco-tourism packages designed to promote the atoll environment as a desirable destination without establishing extensive physical infrastructures. For example, the recent development of an Outrigger Resort on Majuro has provided a tourism venue designed within the environmentally conscious philosophy of the Outrigger Corporation.

What alternatives exist?

If RMI cannot attain sustainable development in any traditionally employed way, what then? One good possible solution would be to form partnerships with other countries. Such partnerships could be developed out of altruism by the external partner, but would be most feasible if RMI had some leverage as well. One option would be for RMI to emphasise the history of aggression and abuse by other countries, especially Japan and the United States. For example, RMI could substantially increase the lease it charges to the United States to maintain its satellite launch base or increase Japanese fishing lease fees. It could also request that the United Nations investigate the lack of compensation or implementation of a clean-up of radioactive sites by the United States for the 67 nuclear test detonations that it conducted within the Marshall Islands archipelago, leaving four atolls uninhabitable (Cappelle 1996). However, changes in the world political situation have rendered RMI less strategically important for the United States (Roylance 1997), both in terms of any Pacific threats and a reduced commitment to weapons development and testing.

Finally, RMI could form economic partnerships in which RMI attributes can be exchanged if economically advantageous attributes can be identified. One good option could occur as a result of the Kyoto accord to reduce global carbon dioxide emissions; if countries begin trading carbon dioxide emission allotments, RMI should be able to sell its emission credits (Panayotou 1993). Ultimately, RMI will be most sustainable if its economic goal is to move from dependency to global interdependence with trading partners.

Assessing sustainable development in RMI

We have stated that the concept of sustainable development is multifaceted. Clearly, RMI is currently compromising its economic and ecological future. Furthermore, its high rate of population growth is a very serious obstacle to ever achieving sustainable development under any of the set of concepts included in the definition of sustainable development.

First, consider the concept that sustainable development is meeting the needs of the present without compromising the future. RMI is not adequately meeting the needs of its inhabitants, and the demand for material goods is expected to increase at least as rapidly as the population increases. Increasing exposure to outside media via Majuro's satellite dish and local television distribution system will also continue to increase the appetite of the population for consumable goods. The trade deficit already represents a very serious economic problem that must be solved if RMI is to be sustainable.

Second, there are stringent limits on the natural resources of RMI that should not be exceeded. The capability of RMI's environment to detoxify sewage and break down organic waste is quite small, and there is very limited space for landfilling unwanted refuse. Furthermore, the likelihood of contamination from these landfills is extremely high due to the lack of clay caps, the proximity of saltwater and the frequency of destructive typhoons striking the islands. Additionally, physical space, water and food resources are shrinking due to higher ocean levels and droughts. Indeed, the marine environment is also at risk. Coral reef heads within some lagoons are dying, some atolls are overfished, and the RMI fishery must be carefully managed to avoid overharvesting marine protein resources (Connell and Maata 1992). The ability of RMI to generate food, energy and building materials is very small, and development will only be sustainable if viewed within a context of interdependence with other countries.

Third, RMI must balance competing objectives before it can achieve sustainability. The current economic goals of RMI are to develop more income production for their citizens, increase job availability for those who want to work (the 1988 unemployment level was 12.5% [Connell and Maata 1992]), and decrease their negative balance of trade. The current social goals of RMI are to preserve their culture and improve the quality of life of the poorer segments of their society. Attempts to reach the economic and social goals through education, privatisation of government services and slowing of population growth were described by Rhea Moss, an adviser to the RMI government, to the United Nations General Assembly on 26 October 1995 (RMI Online 1998). The current ecological goals—as described in 1996 by Phillip Muller, the RMI Minister of Foreign Affairs, to the United Nations General Assembly—are to preserve their marine and terrestrial ecosystems, or at least maintain them at or above the present conditions (RMI Online 1998). These goals cannot be mutually accomplished without compromising or refocusing some of them. For example, development to improve employment and increase income is likely to cause ecological degradation. Development is also likely to introduce new ideas, values and desires which may erode the strong cultural traditions.

Fourth, the philosophy of sustainable development is not only an outcome but also a process or an attitude. In Majuro, we have seen broken glass on the beaches, rubbish in the streets, and poorly designed landfills, and found that generally the residents are not aware that their actions affected the ecosystems supporting their existence. The citizens of RMI told us that they were much more worried about government priorities of enhancing employment and continuing education support than about whether the government is preserving the ecosystem. Environmental protection is an intermediate function of the state which should begin occurring once the basic public goods of safety, public health and civic order are secured (World Bank 1997c). RMI has these basic issues quite securely in hand: crime is low, a public sewer system is established and roads are being improved. However, the citizens do not seem to be secure enough yet in their young life as an independent country to tackle these broader issues. The government of RMI has taken an outspoken role in the United Nations discussions of environmental issues, especially climate change (Cappelle 1996).

Unfortunately other segments of society are not yet involved in sustainable types of decision-making, in which the process incorporates inclusive, connected, equitable, prudent and secure choices at every level (Gladwin *et al.* 1995).

Finally, sustainable development is a concept that is not intrinsically scale-dependent. RMI is a relatively isolated country; however, it does not and can no longer exist in isolation. Relationships with other economic entities can be both bane and boon, but to the extent that an economic entity is interacting with other entities, sustainable development is a goal that should be applied not to the individual entity but to the entire network of partners. Furthermore, too many of our developing countries have been parasitised by their more developed economic partners; effective sustainable development must include a shift from parasitism to mutualism, in which each partner provides the other with a resource which it cannot easily acquire elsewhere.

In summary, there are serious and substantial obstacles that are unlikely to be successfully overcome if the traditional concept of sustainable development is ever to become a reality in RMI. The high rate of population growth, increasing demand for consumable goods, severely limited ecological resilience and the need to transform decision-making are all serious challenges to any successful implementation of sustainable development.

Solving the sustainable development dilemma

Is the concept of sustainable development a dream that can never be fulfilled in RMI? We believe this is true, at least for the current paradigm. We propose that solutions to enable the application of sustainable development to all countries, not just those with a large natural resource base, can only be found if the framework of the sustainable development concept is redefined. Development is defined as the process of becoming a country with a relatively high level of industrialisation and standard of living, but sustainable is defined as consumption without depletion or damage of the resource being consumed (Merriam-Webster 1998). Development, which requires depletion or damage of resources utilised in industry, is therefore intrinsically not sustainable. Thus, because the concepts 'sustainable' and 'development' as normally visualised are opposing values which may be inherently oxymoronic and in need of modification, we propose that two paradigm shifts are required.

First, is the definition of sustainability realistic if it requires that society never compromises the needs of all future generations? It is impossible to find or create substitutes to maintain a Western-style concept of development, nor can success ever be determined. Perhaps a better definition would be to avoid compromising the needs of the next generation. Even this reduced concept of sustainability will still be difficult for many countries to achieve. The only way to determine that sustainability has been achieved is to measure the impact of our current actions on future generations.

The time-lag inherent here has three important implications. First, it is impossible to redo developmental impacts if sustainability was not achieved after all. Second, vaguely defining impacts as applicable to 'all future generations' ensures that sustainability can never be measured. Finally, one of the best ways to determine the impact of present events on the future is to evaluate the impact of past events on the present. Thus, sustainable development should not only include the design of protocols with future evaluations, but also the conducting of evaluations now of past mistakes and past attempts at a more sustainable mode of development.

Second, development is too narrowly defined. Society needs to reassess what constitutes wealth and the quality of life. Consider these words from Holdgate (1996):

> A community can be wealthy in terms of true quality of life without being affluent. Many island people know this, treasuring the freedom that their isolation brings, their right to use the products of land and sea, and the enrichment that comes from being part of a tightly knit community.

Development should not necessarily mean economic growth or the introduction of an individualistic, materialistic culture in which resources are applied to generate goods which quickly become obsolete and are discarded.

Of course, this is not a new argument. While Western civilisation is still experiencing a paradigm shift in attitudes to the environment, and has not yet constructed a well-designed environmental ethic, America has a rich tradition of naturalist philosophers espousing a more comprehensive definition of development, beginning with Thoreau and John Muir. Aldo Leopold's 'Land Ethic' eloquently delineates a restructuring of attitudes to development from natural resource exploitation to natural resource harmonisation (Leopold 1987), and Wendell Berry has more recently explored this issue in many of his writings (e.g. Berry 1986).

A lack of consideration for the environment is not unique to a capitalist economy; when King Juda of Bikini Atoll consented to nuclear warhead testing in his atoll, he placed global technological goals over ecosystem integrity (Roylance 1997). However, the rush to merge sustainability with development to produce the concept of sustainable development seems to have overlooked the fundamental question of the intrinsic value of the environment, reducing it merely to avoiding compromising the needs of future generations, which is a very human-centred viewpoint.

In summary, Western consumerism is experiencing a paradigm shift in attitudes to the environment as it shifts from valuing a good only in terms of its perceived ability to enhance the consumer's quality of life to also valuing the environmental base that is affected by the production of the good (Holdgate 1996). Society has generally accepted the concept that goods should not be purchased which also directly reduce the human ecological environment, and are increasingly willing to create legislation designed to reduce pollutants. These societal changes are evidence of tentative movement towards sustainable development, at least in terms of the process components defined by Gladwin *et al.* (1995), such as inclusiveness, connectedness and equitability.

In particular, society is gradually becoming more inclusive. Our point is that society must also visualise sustainable development as a connected process, because at least some regions, including RMI, cannot achieve sustainable development in isolation. While of course the planet must be divided into political regions in order to develop realistic plans for sustainable development, this approach cannot work when it artificially separates units intimately connected by resource flows. The shifting restless movements of humans further confound our ability to divide the world into discrete units; migration is an increasing consequence of our mobile society. In fact, RMI negotiated unrestricted migration into the United States for its citizens as a safety valve for expected overpopulation pressures (Connell and Maata 1992). Planners cannot assume unchanging conditions, but must anticipate new interdependencies being created in order to satisfy future lifestyle expectations. Further, due to human impacts on the planet, some resource banks have already been diminished; other resource banks are truly global, such as climate. Thus, one fundamental mistake sustainable development planners can make is to think of regions in isolation.

Conclusions

We have delineated a serious challenge to the implementation and promulgation of the concept of sustainable development. However, how does examining a country that is an exception to the goal of sustainable development clarify the concept of sustainable development? First, it clearly illuminates the boundaries of this concept and the underlying assumptions that are built into it. Inherent in the idea of an undeveloped country developing is the concept that development means economic growth within the context of our capitalistic global economy. Thus, development can only be attained if a wealthier country diverts some of its revenue stream into the local economy or if the undeveloped country has an exploitable resource base. Second, it is assumed that it is possible to balance economic, social and ecological goals, but too frequently this is simply impossible without significant redefinition of these goals. Third, as long as a developing or developed economy is consuming non-renewable resources, it is impossible to claim that the development is not compromising the needs of any of all future generations.

If RMI was the only location on this planet that was not able to ever attain sustainable development, then the argument we have constructed is largely a curious footnote; a few small atolls are not that important in comparison with the rest of the planet. However, most of our undeveloped countries are in the same situation as RMI, struggling to satisfy the needs of too many people from an inadequate resource base. While the environmental conditions and abuses of RMI are unique to RMI, the result can be generalised to many countries; limited resources and environmental degradation, combined with rapid population growth produce an intrinsically non-sustainable condition. It is one thing to discuss how a large economic entity such as the United States could attain sustainability if it exerted the political will to become sustainable, but it is entirely different to expect every country to be able to do so. In fact, this problem can only be expected to increase in this era of countries fracturing into smaller entities. Canada may be able to achieve sustainable development, but Québec is less likely to be able to do so, and the Gaspé Peninsula is even less able to be self-sustainable.

So, what research and assistance is needed to help small countries find the best route toward a sustainable future? Perhaps the most important point that small countries such as RMI bring to sustainable development is the importance of economic interdependence. It has been said that no man is an island, but no country can be an island of sustainability either. The problems of RMI are severely exacerbated by its inability to change the behaviour of other players influencing its development. In addition, it is essential that any government, especially a government of a small country that attempts to implement sustainable development, must carefully consider what those terms imply. Second, sustainable development is a cultural and a process-oriented concept. Failing to recognise this will ensure a failure to achieve sustainable development. Alternative models of development should be identified, and the most appropriate one chosen.

21 The Role of Stakeholder Participation

Linkages to Stakeholder Impact Assessment and Social Capital in Camisea, Peru

Murray Jones

THE CAMISEA AREA lies some 500 km east of the Peruvian capital of Lima, on the eastern side of the Andes in Region Inca. It lies in the Lower Urubamba Valley, one of the world's foremost areas of natural biodiversity and home to a number of indigenous peoples, primarily Machiguenga.

The Camisea area is also home to world-class hydrocarbon reserves. Containing some 11 trillion ft^3 of natural gas and 600 million barrels of natural gas liquids, the fields contain enough to serve Peru's energy needs for over a century. These reserves are seen to be of great importance to the people of Peru.

The bulk of the reserves were discovered in the mid-1980s and can be found in two fields known as Cashiriari and San Martin, which sit on either side of the Camisea River in a licence block now called 88B. Discussions with the Peruvian authorities in the 1980s about developing the reserves did not lead to an agreement.

In 1994 Shell and Perupetro, a state agency, agreed to re-examine the commercial potential. At the same time, environmental and social studies together with consultation with third parties began. In May 1995, a feasibility study was submitted to the authorities and negotiations commenced shortly afterwards.

On 17 May 1996, Shell Prospecting & Development (Peru) (SPDP), a new company, and its minority partner, Mobil Exploration & Producing, Peru, Inc., signed a licence agreement with Perupetro to undertake appraisal of drilling activities and to study options for the future development of the reserves. The 40-year agreement includes terms for various options of full production development of the fields. With a 57.5% interest, SPDP is responsible for operating the venture.

The licence agreement provides for a period of two years to study options for the possible future development of the reserves. During this period, SPDP will drill three appraisal wells. The data obtained will be used to improve the definition of the fields and to supply technical information for the design of the possible future production facilities.

The appraisal phase 'Environmental Impact Assessment' was approved on 26 August 1997 following a public hearing in Lima. Construction activities commenced at the operations base soon after, following an agreement with its host, the neighbouring community. Appraisal drilling commenced at the Cashiriari field on 11 May 1997, some ten months after the Camisea licence agreement was signed and almost exactly ten years since the field's initial discovery

In May 1997, SPDP was also awarded a licence agreement for Block 75 which lies adjacent to the Camisea fields. An Environmental Impact Assessment for the drilling of an exploration well was approved in September 1997. Site preparation commenced soon after and drilling was planned for early 1998. SPDP and its partner Mobil were obliged to inform the Peruvian authorities about whether they wished to enter the main development phase of the Camisea project by mid-May 1998.

The full Camisea development would consist of clustered wells that feed natural gas and liquids to a local plant in which they will be separated. The plant would feed two parallel pipelines of some 600 km which cross the Andes to markets on the Pacific coast. The preferred pipeline route leaves Camisea in a southerly arc following the Rio Urubamba. Once south of the Pongo Manique (a canyon), it turns westward through the cloud forest to the *altiplano*, and then on to the coast south of Lima. The liquid line would cease at a coastal port facility where tankers could be loaded. A natural gas line would extend to Lima to serve industrial and possibly domestic markets. A natural gas line may also extend to the Ilo area in southern Peru to serve the growing energy needs of the mining sector. The exact definition of the pipeline routing will be determined once a final investment decision has been taken and in light of studies and consultation.

The Camisea natural gas and condensate reserves are regarded as one of Peru's most important natural assets, capable of generating the income to pay for improved living standards for its people. The development also offers environmental benefits through the replacement of imported liquid fuels with natural gas. There will also be impacts for people and the environment at or near operations. SPDP aims to avoid and minimise these wherever possible.

Objectives

It is the policy of SPDP to take foremost account of the environment (which includes the social component) in all activities. Identified in particular was the need to promote initiatives that will benefit the local peoples. The company's policy (see Box 1 and Box 2) states that it will respect the needs of the local indigenous communities. A consultation process is mandated through policy and through management commitment, as stated in the company's business objectives.

Shell Prospecting & Development (Peru): Health, Safety and Environment Policy

Shell Prospecting & Development (Peru) will conduct its activities to take foremost account of the health and safety of employees and of other persons who may be affected by our activities and to give proper regard to the conservation of the natural environment. In implementing this policy, Shell Prospecting & Development (Peru)—SPDP—our alliance partners and our principal contractors will not only comply with the requirements of all relevant Peruvian legislation and international agreements, but will also promote initiatives that lead to continuous performance improvement to protect and benefit the health, safety and the environment of all who may be affected directly or indirectly by our activities with particular attention to indigenous persons.

Principles

In adhering to this policy SPDP will maintain a Health, Safety and Environmental Management System that will allow it to meet the following principles:

Health

- We will conduct our activities in a way that avoids harm to the health of our employees and neighbours.
- We will actively promote the health of our employees and neighbours.

Safety

- We believe that all injuries can be prevented.
- We will actively promote high standards of safety-consciousness and discipline.
- We will design all our activities and operations to minimise risk to employees, contractors and third parties.

Environment

- We will maintain a consultation process with our neighbours and other stakeholders.
- We will design operations to avoid impact where possible and minimise impact where inevitable.
- We will rehabilitate land after the completion of operations.
- We will control our use of natural resources.
- We will limit our access and intrusion into sensitive environments.
- We will pursue in our operations progressive reductions of those emissions, effluents and discharges of waste materials that are known to have a negative impact to the natural environment.
- We will promote protection of the natural, physical and social environment which may be affected by SPDP activities, and seek continuous improvement in efficiency of the use of natural resources and energy.
- We will actively contribute to sustainable development.

Alan Hunt
General Manager
1 September 1997

Box 1: SPDP: HEALTH, SAFETY AND ENVIRONMENT POLICY

The HSE policy will be implemented in SPDP, alliance partners and principal contractors through Health, Safety and Environmental Management Systems.

In executing this policy, we will;

- Reduce the HSE risk to a level as low as reasonably practical (ALARP)
- Establish HSE practices and procedures in all operations and strive for an incident-free operation
- Recognise the importance of HSE objectives in relation to other main business objectives
- Recognise the unique social and societal structure surrounding SPDP activities and the importance of community health
- Undertake sustainable development through implementation of Social Capital, partnerships with government and NGOs, and openness and transparency in a consultation programme
- Carry out assessments (EIAs) before commencing new activities or changes to existing facilities
- Listen and respond to the concerns expressed by any company shareholders, employees and society on HSE matters and to provide to them relevant information on company policies and procedures
- Report our HSE performance annually to the public, establishing targets and plans and including external verification
- Provide HSE training to all staff
- Undertake HSE awareness and education campaigns
- Include HSE performance in the appraisal of all staff
- Conduct or support research that can improve HSE practices in the upper Amazon area of Peru
- Facilitate the transfer of experience and technology in HSE areas to Peruvians
- Require joint ventures under SPDP operational control to apply the SPDP policy and SPDP will promote this policy in its other ventures
- Develop and maintain contingency procedures and measures to minimise the consequence of any accident
- Promote among all those associated with its activities a high standard of HSE awareness, motivation and discipline and provide the necessary education and training to achieve this standard
- Achieve those standards that denote international leadership including but not limited to E&P Forum, EP 9500, ISO 14001, World Bank and IFC

Box 2: IMPLEMENTING THE HSE POLICY

SPDP has set as its goal the achievement of the highest standards: standards that are derived from a number of international and national sources. Shell International has guidelines both for Environmental Impact Assessment (EIA) and Social Impact Assessment; the World Bank has EIA and consultation guidelines, the Exploration and Production Forum (E&P Forum), London, has waste management and decommissioning guidelines for facilities, and numerical standards are available from UNEP, the International Finance Corporation (IFC) and a number of leading countries.

In keeping with the guidelines found in these references, the objectives for SPDP's participation programme are as follows:

- To ensure the identification of stakeholders
- To ensure the availability of timely information

- To make publicly available all environmental and social studies
- To ensure that means of communication allow for a two-way flow of information
- To ensure that SPDP staff listen to external messages
- To ensure that the information, messages and concerns received are communicated within the system to determine what changes in the project will assist in alleviating or minimising the concerns
- To feed back to the stakeholders the results of how their concerns have been addressed

Stakeholders

Stakeholders have been identified as those on whom the project will impact (primarily the local native communities that have land tenure and land rights) and those groups or agencies who can impact the project. The primary stakeholders include the representative federations. This definition is extended to those parties who are already active in the region through special interest, responsibility or long-term presence. Examples would include the Catholic Mission, the Ministry of Health, and the Proyecto Integral de Salud en la Amazonia Peruana (PISAP), part of the Vicariato Apostolico de Puerto Maldonado and an NGO active in healthcare delivery.

The indirect (or secondary) stakeholders include those with specific interest in the region (but who may not be directly active) or those who have planned programmes that relate to regional improvement or regional study. It is the objective of SPDP not to interfere with such programmes but to look for synergy with the company's own activities. Indirect stakeholders also include those with an interest and/or concerns in the issues at hand—rainforest protection, indigenous communities, biodiversity, and oil and gas operations. Many of the international stakeholders fall into this category.

Combining direct and indirect stakeholders provides a lengthy list of consultees. It has been learned through consultation that many groups simply want to be kept informed and aware. Others are more directly involved to the point of weekly and sometimes daily contact.

Delivering the goods

In the early days of the project, SPDP established a number of key steps to initiate consultation with the identified stakeholders. These steps were listed in *Briefing Paper 3*, distributed in June 1996 just after the signing of the licence agreement with Perupetro. As originally stated these steps were:

1. Stakeholder identification and prioritisation
2. Initial meetings with all key stakeholders (to confirm interests, provide information and seek involvement)
3. Provide information; for example, through such means as 'briefing papers' (two papers had been released at this point; this was the third), together with an EIA Scope document, maps and plans of activities
4. Repeat meetings with key stakeholders who confirmed their interest in the project (based on mutual understanding with the stakeholders)
5. Recognition of stakeholders' information, comments and concerns in feedback letters and in environmental and social studies
6. Integration of consultation results into formal EIA documents
7. Feedback on issues and actions to SPDP management
8. Establishing key external groups for collective discussions (e.g. community meetings, topic-specific workshops)
9. Commissioning specific research or studies to assist in understanding (Environmental Profiles, EIAs)
10. Broadening relations to create partnerships within communities and key stakeholders, to find solutions to problems and to provide delivery of benefits
11. Establishing long-term management relationships for the delivery of social capital[1]
12. Releasing EIA documents to the public. The appraisal well programme EIA will be used further to understand concerns and to form the basis for discussion of the terms of reference for subsequent EIAs.

These steps have proved a good model. Participation means that SPDP must provide information in a timely and efficient manner so that stakeholders can contribute. All reports are considered public. SPDP in turn must indicate how the information received is used and how the project has changed as a result of input. All information is bilingual and some is translated into Machiguenga.

A variety of techniques to deliver and receive information and comment are required due to the geographic location of the project and its limited infrastructure. In addition, the native communities require a certain formality within which information is received and decisions are reached. Formal notice of visitation is required. Community meetings are held and joint decision-making is the social etiquette. Agreements must be formalised and are often signed by the full community. This process is repeated for each community visited. Currently SPDP is visiting about ten communities, but

1 Social capital is the term used to describe the mechanisms and attributes by which a community interacts within itself to utilise its social assets to the wellbeing (i.e. development enhancement and benefit) of the community as a whole.

A COMBINED EFFORT by the Smithsonian Institution 'Man and Biodiversity' programme and experts from the University of San Marcos, University of Cusco-San Antonio Abad, University of Ricardo Palma and the University of Trujillo is monitoring effects on biodiversity and conducting biodiversity studies at test plots near well sites. Flora and fauna have been extensively sampled and analysed by botanists, biologists, avian specialists and experts on amphibians and reptiles. The plots are Global Positioning System (GPS)-located, so that return visits may be made to the same locations in future years. The results will be used both to understand biodiversity and to assist in the development of a long-term indicator species monitoring programme that will indicate the impact of the drilling activities. Additional testing and sampling will be undertaken between the well sites and the Urubamba River along the Camisea River.

The programme is expected to complete this phase by the end of 1997. A report will be made available. Species that are taken for analysis and preservation are shared equally with the Peruvian National Museum and with the Smithsonian in Washington, DC, under permit requirements of the Peruvian national parks institute. Cross-training is occurring between Smithsonian and Peruvian scientists. Of particular interest is the inclusion of Yaminahua and Machiguenga people who have been trained as technical assistants.

Box 3: BIODIVERSITY STUDIES ALONGSIDE APPRAISAL DRILLING

this number will expand to reflect all communities within the exploration licence block and an additional number outside—approaching 30 in all.

For other stakeholders, techniques such as one-on-one meetings and workshops are widely used to generate direct responses. Written information is provided in advance. This has included the series of briefing papers already mentioned (nine to date) that provide approximately bi-monthly updates in which SPDP tries to indicate both positive progress but also any mistakes or areas requiring particular attention. SPDP has received suggestions that the briefing papers should be issued monthly; the company also been advised that specific papers should be directed at the communities themselves to enhance appreciation of the technology terminology and general understanding of what is coming in the form of development. This suggestion has been acted on through 'letters to communities': two such letters have been issued so far in both Spanish and Machiguenga.

Scoping reports have been published ahead of the company's first two Environmental Impact Assessments. In distributing scoping reports to all identified stakeholders, a request is made for written comments and an offer is made for direct meetings; EIAs are publicly distributed. Outside the EIA process, other studies are undertaken such as a Health Baseline Assessment, Biodiversity Study (see Box 3) and (currently under way) a Regional Social Baseline Diagnostic. Two health workshops were held in December to discuss the findings of the Health Baseline Assessment of the Lower Urubamba area which was conducted by the Royal Tropical Institute of Amsterdam in co-operation with Peruvian health experts (Ministry of Health, Universidad Cayetano Heredia and PISAP). The study aimed to provide the foundation for long-term improvements including positive and sustainable development by recording the existing health situation in the region, the availability of healthcare and to provide recommendations for the future. These programmes are always completed with regional workshops and with report distribution. The regional workshops provide an opportunity for the native communities to take part in information review and, more importantly, they help in prioritising the recommendations. SPDP was alerted early on, by the communities themselves, that in the past they had been studied too many times by many different groups and rarely, if ever, did they receive the results of the studies. Expectations of the native communities range from the need for benefits, a desire to preserve their environment, recognition and awareness that oil companies in general do not have a good reputation, and the desire for continuous participation. However, the overall tone of discussion is largely positive, recognising the desire for improvements in lifestyle and the high expectations for the future. Recently the leaders of the three federations that represent all the communities of the region participated in a joint workshop with SPDP in Lima. This meeting resulted in commitments to proceed on both sides toward joint collaboration. The federation leaders indicated their intention to use the meeting as a springboard for capacity-building in the communities and for the founding of their own mechanisms for review and co-operation. They also immediately committed to a follow-up meeting which they would host in their own region.

Expectations of groups outside the region vary, including: demands for outright preservation; some wanting to speak for and on behalf of the local peoples; the desire to participate and inform; the wish to monitor; and even the desire to support and partner.

To help capture the range of views concerning the full field development—the main phase of the project—SPDP will have hosted, by mid-December 1997, three important workshops for stakeholders, held in Lima, Washington, DC, and London. The aims are to:

- Provide stakeholders with an overview of the full field development and to give them an opportunity to discuss uncertainties and sensitivities
- Present SPDP's decision methodology for key project decisions such as plant location, pipeline route, etc.; to invite comments and suggestions on the criteria used, methodology employed, SPDP-preferred options and stakeholder participation in the process, including the design of the EIA

These workshops will also provide a forum for design engineers to present key health, safety and environment issues or challenges, and for stakeholders to enter into dialogue. This will provide stakeholder participation via direct contact with engineers. 'Ambassadors'—the leaders of the three regional native federations—will attend all workshops. The aim is to ensure local views are heard internationally and vice versa.

The broad range of stakeholders provides a challenging spectrum within which the company must determine its operations. Opinions for outright preservation have to be considered in light of both national interests and the will of the local people themselves. Of particular concern is the fact that part of the area needed and approved by government for development lies within an area titled the Reserve for the Nahua and Kugapakori. This reserve was created in 1990 by the Peruvian government as a holding designation for an area where there were still suspected to be isolated peoples. Nucleated communities were only just forming and the government wanted to ensure protection until such communities could seek and be granted their own land rights. This issue has become perhaps the most discussed among international NGOs, and some have indicated to SPDP that operations should cease in the reserve. Due to the location of the gas reserves extending under this area, such a decision would effectively curtail the whole project. SPDP has made contact with the newly created communities inside the reserve to gain advice. These communities have indicated that the isolated peoples have long been located further to the east and south of the gas fields and that there should not be a conflict. The company has listened to these messages of concern and special provisions have been placed on workers in this area, including an 'offshore' policy to keep workers on-site, full vaccinations for all workers, a contingency plan in place in the unlikely event that a native person approaches one of the sites and the presence of native workers on-site at all times to act as translators should it be necessary

Linking to Stakeholder Impact Assessment (SIA)

Stakeholder participation is seen as a continuum within the project. This means that it continues despite the current stage of development, the current EIA or whether or not a significant event is about to take place. There are, however, identifiable stages where consultation is directly connected to required studies. The most obvious is the need to gather social baseline information. Stakeholder Impact Assessment (SIA) is inherent within the EIA process. Using Shell International Exploration and Production (SIEP) EIA and SIA Guidelines as the base, the scope for all EIAs includes the social dimension and, as field studies are undertaken on the natural environment, so too are anthropologists and sociologists involved with the people. For appraisal drilling and exploration, the EIAs have tended to focus on the communities in the immediate area. In addition, more wide-ranging regional social studies are undertaken. Prior to operations, a health baseline study was initiated, aimed at the implementation of recommendations for improved healthcare.

In June 1997, a regional diagnostic was started. This was undertaken by parties from regional governments and NGOs independent of SPDP recognising the need to involve those that are key to the delivery of long-term benefits. This diagnostic involves an interactive process of information-gathering as recommended in the SIEP Guidelines. Techniques such as 'rapid rural appraisal' (involving workshop-style discussions with communities) are used in interviews held in a community over a two- to three-day period in order for local people to contribute information in a comfortable setting and to encourage them to participate further in the recommendation and design of solutions. These are repeated in a number of communities representing the region, including local as well as more distant communities. Issues covered include education, agricultural practices, hunting territories, women's issues, training, state of planning and economics.

Regional studies are the base for the long-term overall improvement of the region, not just the communities within which the gas fields are located. The commitment of net benefit by SPDP addresses the desire expressed by the communities that they will be better off over time with SPDP presence. Net benefit is discussed in consultation. It can vary from one community to another (some want the focus to be on health, others education). This does not mean that SPDP becomes the government or a hand-out agency, but instead the catalyst for improvement, working with the skills, responsibilities and abilities of others, be they government, NGOs, the Catholic Church, aid agencies or multilateral agencies (such as international banks). Social capital is the core of improvement. Essentially, this means providing the means for communities and individuals to manage and control their own futures.

Initial activities to improve social capital have been based on the Health Baseline Study. Future efforts will arise from the Regional Diagnostic. These initiatives will cover, among others, healthcare, drinking water, training, education and understanding of small business economics. In the shorter term, SPDP is still obligated to compensate communities for the use of their lands and for nuisance impacts (such as helicopter noise). The compensation packages are designed with sustainability in mind. Agreements are written in consultation with communities and with the aim of enhancing health and educational facilities, building and equipping mothers' clubs, providing communication through solar radios, providing medicinal cold chain through solar refrigerators that ensure medicines are kept cool and thereby effective, providing clean water through water wells and beginning the training process through specific courses such as animal husbandry

Conclusions

The stakeholder participation process is key to the success of the Camisea gas and condensate development project. The unique and wide-ranging focus on local, national and international stakeholders will allow for maximum input. As the project grows from the current appraisal and exploration wells to gas development, production and shipment to Lima, the challenges will grow. Thus, SPDP is continuing to learn from experiences and is continuing to solicit advice on the way forward. There is no single means or method that will meet all needs. Participation is seen as a combined effort extending inside the company to the planners, designers and operators and outside to a wide hierarchy of individuals and organisations. The key to success will be the continued commitment to openness and transparency

Appendix 1: independent monitoring of the Camisea project

In April 1997 a Peruvian social and environmental network comprising 35 NGOs, called Red Ambiental Peruana (RAP), agreed to monitor independently the social and environmental performance of the Camisea project.

RAP members and representatives from native communities perform the work. RAP chooses the composition of the teams that visit on a quarterly basis.

Eric Cardich, President of RAP said:

> Given the responsibility this agreement accords Red Ambiental Peruana, it was only entered into after discussion and agreement among the nine co-ordinating members of the organisation. The Camisea area is rich in biodiversity and home to many indigenous communities. We will ensure that the social and environmental integrity of the zone is maintained.
>
> We want to see the Camisea Project, an important part of the country's future economic progress, conducted to the highest standards of environmental care and with respect for the rights of the indigenous population. While we have made an agreement, we maintain full independence and freedom to act as we see fit. The terms of the agreement are available to anyone. We have no restrictions on our reporting and are prepared to be critical as well as constructive.

Shell Prospecting & Development (Peru) provides RAP study teams with transportation into the area.

The first visit was carried out in April 1997. During this visit, the RAP team reviewed well sites and the logistic base at Nuevo Mundo and visited a number of native communities for specific interviews. The report produced recognised the efforts of SPDP to meet highest environmental standards and maintain a fair approach to the native communities through openness and transparency. No major complaints were raised during the interviews. However, it is recognised in the report that noise caused by logistic transport (helicopter, hovercraft) is one of the main concerns. As a consequence, flight paths were adjusted to help minimise the effect of noise.

The second visit took place at the end of July 1997. Issues identified focused on the operation of the sewage treatment plant at the Nuevo Mundo base and continued implementation of revegetation programmes. At the time this chapter was first published (August 1997), the sewage treatment plant was about to be upgraded.

Appendix 2: update[2]

Since the completion of the original paper in August 1997, a number of key events have taken place. Regrettably, when it came to the final investment decision in mid-July 1998, SPDP was not able to reach an agreement with the Peruvian authorities for commercial reasons. Thus the project could not continue. Peru has since moved to a new bidding process to determine the new operator by late 1999.

However, within the process of stakeholder participation and the move to increasing regional social capital, a number of important actions were completed. First was the design of a series of six consultation rounds with the local communities. Over 40 communities became involved. Through a progressive series of meetings, project

2 19 March 1999.

information was discussed from general principles to particular details. Recognising that communities would not grasp all of the complex details, materials and presentations were designed around the key issues that the communities themselves had raised: pollution, impact on resources, protection of villages, hunting, culture, etc. This consultation phase resulted in a clearer understanding for the design engineers of acceptable means of resolving issues. For instance, the route for the flow lines from the well sites was chosen to meet community recommendations (i.e. stay out of the river valley); the gas plant site was located on *campesino* land remote from native villages and a logistics procedure for barge and hovercraft movement was developed. This resulted in publication and distribution of the final guide along with the placement of solar radios to facilitate reporting of incidents or concerns.

The Health Baseline Study and feedback process grew into combined effort between regional and national governments and the local people themselves. An Inter-regional Health Committee was started—the first in Peru—and the recommendations were turned into a three-year health plan. The first phase (one year) addressed the need to increase the capacities of the healthcare providers and others identified by the communities to provide better care and to train others. SPDP agreed to continue funding to complete this phase.

The socioeconomic diagnostic undertaken in the dry season of 1997 by a team from government and NGOs in the Region Cusco resulted in a documented study and a series of recommendations for future actions. These results were taken back to the communities and, by April 1999, three workshops had been held to both prioritise the actions and to establish the framework for a Regional Sustainable Development Plan. This plan is to be owned locally and will be led by a selected steering committee. It has strong support from the regional government.

In 1998 SPDP agreed with the Energy and Resources Group at the University of California, Berkeley, to undertake case study of the Camisea community relations process, assess the extent to which the consultation was constructive in project design and to develop lessons learned to guide other developments in the Amazon. The resulting report has been made public.[3] For about four months, staff of the ERG worked in SPDP offices, field locations and communities. Some of the key lessons included:

- Companies must build sensitivity through consultation.
- Management must internalise the issues identified.
- Companies must make early commitments at the highest level.
- Companies must plan for staff continuity for corporate memory and commitment.
- Companies must set creative and modest targets.

In closing its operations, SPDP made and completed the following commitments:

- Finalise delivery of all legal contracts

3 *http://socrates.berkeley.edu/erg*

- Meet all commitments linked to community impacts (i.e. provide compensation to communities even where direct land use is not involved)
- Continue to fund the first-phase health programme through to late 1999
- Continue to fund all scholarships through to completion
- Continue to build local capacity with facilitation of community/government workshops as long as SPDP has a logistical presence
- Undertake a close-out due-diligence audit to ensure both site restoration completion and community satisfaction on commitments

22

Indonesia in the 21st Century

Environment at the Crossroads

Peter Koffel

Put a frog in hot water and it will try to escape.
Put a frog in cold water and boil it and the frog will not try to escape (proverb).

All things are toxins, and there is nothing which would not be toxic; it is only the dosage which makes a thing toxic
(Paracelsus, AD 1574; cited in Claus and Bolander 1982).

THROUGHOUT THE FIRST HALF of the 1990s Indonesia was increasingly being looked upon with ambivalence. One the one hand, international development institutions saw Indonesia as an exemplar among the ASEAN and the Pacific Rim nations as one 'doing development right'. The business and financial world believed that the decade-long pattern of 6% growth would continue as if inevitable, that industrial production would substitute for raw resource extraction, and finally that the environmental health of cities and the ecological integrity of other environments such as forests, water and land would keep pace with the economic prosperity that development promised. On the other hand, and at the same time, these same international institutions were expressing some doubt about the unevenness of Indonesia's development initiative, the inequity of its outcomes and the inevitable assault on ecology that resulted. The unleashing of capitalist desire led to a criminalisation of the polity and its economy, what Indonesians now openly call *'kkn'—kolusi, korupsi, nepotisme* (collusion, corruption, nepotism). No one could ever have predicted Indonesia's fall. Yet during the 1990s there were clear signs that Indonesia was hovering over a threshold of unsustainable growth—ecologically, economically and socially. The words *kolusi*, *korupsi* and *nepotisme* are relatively recent borrowings that Indonesians have adopted to help to define their current fate. If environmental management *and* the environment were neglected in Indonesia when there was economic boom, what will be their fate in the face of sociopolitical upheaval and economic stagnation?

This chapter aims to look at Indonesia's environmental conditions leading up to the meltdown and how they may transpire over the next generation, that is, over Indonesia's official second 25-year Long Term Plan (*Pembangunan Jangka Panjang Kedua*, PJPT II). It aims also to signal a plea for Indonesia to avoid practising 'business as usual'. This plea stems from the theory of the precautionary principle which focuses on two issues: the need to halt pollution in advance of concrete knowledge about its impacts, and the need to take responsibility for pollution that is occurring. By definition, the principle also focuses on the 'worst edge' of ecological impacts that may occur if action is not taken to change the nature of development (Costanza *et al.* 1992: 16). The principle also appeals to the idea that 'common sense' must prevail if development is to be sustainable.

The precautionary principle had from the beginning a global or transnational perspective gaining prominence in the 1980s through efforts to tackle the pollution of the North Sea. Throughout the 1960s and 1970s a number of industrialised European countries were deliberately dumping toxic waste into the North Sea while for many decades longer it had been a natural sink for other industrial waste and sewage discharged into rivers flowing to the sea. Large fish kills were occurring in the 1980s and fisherman were catching fish with deformities and cancers. However, it was impossible to allocate blame on any one country's industrial contribution because the complexity of the chemical combinations made it impossible to clearly define the exact causes of the diseases in the fish and made it impossible to define the exact sources of the pollution (Lutter 1991: 12). Therefore the precautionary principle also facilitated a local perspective because each country had to take responsibility for its pollution in order to achieve a positive outcome. Science could not determine the problem with any precision but knew it had to act on what it knew, i.e. that each country had to stop dumping waste.

This issue has strong relevance to Java, Indonesia. Take, for example, the pollution loads in the Surabaya River between the cities of Mojokerto inland and Surabaya on the coast. Within this 60 km stretch there are more than 40 large factories, hundreds of small cottage industries, scores of hospitals, and riparian communities without sanitation provisions, all discharging their waste-water into the river. It is difficult to lay blame on any one particular industry, hospital or community for the pollution loads in the river. If an affected community seeks compensation for their losses due to a factory's pollution upstream they have no standing because the factory can claim that the pollution comes from other sources further upstream or from the affected community itself. Blame cannot be attributed to any one polluter. Like the North Sea example, each polluter must take responsibility for the waste being dumped. Hence there is a common-sense status to the precautionary principle. As O'Riordan and Cameron (1994: 17) state, 'preventative anticipation', a fundamental concept of the principle, is:

> a willingness to take action *in advance* of scientific proof of evidence of the need to take action on the grounds that further delay will prove ultimately most costly to society and nature, and, in the longer term, selfish and unfair to future generations [emphasis added].

That O'Riordan points to societal costs is poignant when considering Indonesia; no doubt human inhabitants and social realms will shape the breadth and depth of environmental action or inaction. Indeed, the precautionary principle has a determinate social arena. Thus a sense of uncertainty seems to underpin the willingness to take action, especially where incentives to do so are few and far between. Unfortunately, human frailty in the face of uncertainty does not evoke a public vision of political will and determinative action. Rather, a picture comes to mind of a hedgehog myopically muddling through change.

Anticipating change

The first official 25-year plan (PJPT I, 1968–93) revolved around three basic factors: the exploitation of oil and forest resources, the development of rice production, and the reduction of poverty in order to bring Indonesia to a point of economic and social security. In 1994, Indonesia entered its second PJPT and the central government élite was excited about the economic change it would pilot. Élite authority was aware that the second PJPT revolved around industrial deepening and urbanisation, particularly in Java. But it was also clearly informed of the environmental changes that could result from an ill-planned and ill-managed take-off. In 1994 an important World Bank report entitled *Indonesia Environment and Development: Challenges for the Future* was circulated among government's key officials. The Executive Summary of the report spelt out quite clearly the impact of Indonesia's trends in development upon the environment:

> The analysis of current environmental conditions and trends, and the likely impact of future growth and development under existing policies and practices . . . call into question the sustainability of even current levels of economic activity in a number of key sectors (World Bank 1994c).

The analysis came to three main conclusions. First, current inefficiencies in the allocation and use of natural resources, and the prospects for continued degradation of critical ecosystems (including urban areas), make future growth and development unsustainable. Second, industrial development predominantly located in the urban areas of Java will 'pose an immediate threat' to community health, erode investment and strengthen community resistance to contamination. Third, conflicts over land use combined with environmental threats, resultant health risks and the inevitable increase in demand by affected communities for environmental quality will increase (World Bank 1994c: Executive Summary). The report stated that 'to deal with these issues will not be easy'. Near impossible, perhaps—these scenarios were manifesting themselves at a pace far beyond any capacity to deal with them.

Before Indonesia's fall, infrastructural public works to meet the demands for urban air quality, urban water supply, sewerage, solid waste management and industrial pollution control were claimed by government to be its highest priority. However, meeting those demands was always going to require a definitive shift from the 'ceremony of word' government practised to embalm those priorities, to authentic engagement in both intervention and public spending, and their accountability. That shift never happened, but the role that oil and forest exploitation played in the economy shifted sharply. Once Indonesia's best revenue earner, oil succumbed to global price collapse. Now oil not only runs cheap but it may also begin to run low as major wells are subject to issues of regional autonomy. Indonesia's second-best earner, forests, have been exploited with no positive outcome for internal revenue. This revenue was rendered all but bankrupt and the fruits of the first long-term plan squandered. In Indonesia, control over codes of practice in public expenditure and control over implementation of regulations are far from transparent and, if not arbitrary, then definitely interest-focused. Now more than ever, Indonesia is poised at the crossroads. Can the machinations of the post-meltdown governments, resource extractors and resource processors shift away from these practices and provide the dead investment required to provide essential environmental services, particularly when capital has stagnated and there seems no easy incentive to entice it back on track. Can Indonesia afford the costs of effective environmental management?

The costs of clean-up: corruption and disappearing aid

Normatively, the burden of industrial pollution control lay with those who own the industries. Proven abatement technology and cleaner production methods were readily available and no doubt big polluters could afford the investment, or could have. However, industry leaders ignored appeals to view these measures not as an added cost, but as an internal extension and integral part of production processes, and as an investment in Indonesia's future. So did government—its role to monitor industrial compliance was thwarted by the expanse of its own industrial involvement and its historically co-dependent relations with the private-sector big polluters. On par, the circumstance-driven poor have had the least choice.

Government in Indonesia acknowledges that sustainable levels of pollution control will be a costly exercise. Over a wider commitment, current expenditure on water supply and sewerage would need to double to facilitate establishing a threshold between the backlog of provisional absence and meeting the needs of regulating future development. This will require, above all, basic urban infrastructures to sustain public health. Yet urban water infrastructure investment declined by almost half in per capita terms by the beginning of the 1990s when less than 40% of urban populations had piped water (World Bank 1994c). In a keynote address, the Director General of Water Resources Development, Ministry of Public Works, admitted that the transfer of water technology 'had not produced the results that we had anticipated' (BAPPENAS 1992: xxxi). Though treatment of sewerage has thus far only entered into the equation to a small degree, a strong reliance on already stressed groundwater into the next generation may hopefully redress the balance.

However, adequate public works expenditure on 'brown' environmental projects for urban sustainability may remain difficult to propagate for a number of reasons. First is the problem of deeply entrenched corruption and it is undoubtedly a significant threat to development. Indonesia is one of the largest recipients of foreign financial aid, administered through the Consultative Group on Indonesia (CGI) which includes the World Bank Group. The Ministry of Public Works is traditionally the largest recipient of that aid and it has become widely acknowledged that a third of infrastructure funds leach into the private pockets of closely knit government networks. Instances of embezzlement were exposed throughout the first half of the 1990s with only minor money retrieval. While exposed cases are acknowledged to be the 'tip of the iceberg', these cases alone reached US$640 million annually throughout the early 1990s, or about 1% of pre-meltdown GDP.[1] The bulk of the leakage from large-scale infrastructural projects and programmes was ignored (Server 1996: 37). Preventing spills as large as these would by themselves contribute towards funding the sustainability of Indonesia's future. In June 1996, the second stage of East Java's Indonesian Urban Infrastructure Development Programme (IUIDP) funding from the Asian Development Bank was approved for US$150 million. If the normative 'third' leaks out of the programme, the loss to urban quality of life can be quantified conservatively at US$50 million (the real loss through such projects has always been much more). Within the same year the World Bank itself fanned a warning that it would 'restructure' its lending policy, threatening to pull out of projects shaded with corruption. When the Bank came under pressure from industrialised donors who recognised that their public taxes were ending up in the hands of corrupt officials in recipient countries, Bank President, Wolfensohn, said it would try to 'create a climate in which people fight corruption' (*Jakarta Post* 1996a, b, c, d).[2] Post-fall conditions would suggest template Bank policy interventions have indeed facilitated a climate of fight.

Second is the significant problem of food. To buffer Indonesia's rapid shift towards becoming a net importer of food, agriculture's allocation of foreign aid increased from one-third to a half of the total agricultural expenditure throughout the 1980s and early 1990s. In post-fall Indonesia, agriculture and irrigation will remain a major recipient of aid as poverty strikes the nation (and more so if the poor soils of the outer islands are brought into the equation) thus placing further pressure on allocating critical funds to urban brown infrastructure development. Finance

1 In 1994, within the Ministry of Mines and Energy, funds totalling US$150 million collected from state-owned mines never reached the state treasury. Out of those funds, $23 million were transferred into the private bank account of the Mines and Energy Minister—with President Suharto's approval (*Jakarta Post* 1996a, b, c, d). In such down-line hierarchical agencies a few others siphon their lot. The fiscal year of 1995/96 saw over US$5 billion lost in bad bank loans, mostly through corruption and mostly through the government's Bank of Indonesia.

2 In 1996, JETRO filed a survey on the most favoured ASEAN nations as recipients of Japanese investment. The survey showed that Japanese firms in Malaysia and Thailand (with higher wage rates than Indonesia) made better profits than firms in Indonesia. In all, 22% of Japanese firms planned to relocate out of Indonesia preferably to Singapore, Malaysia or Thailand. The report stated that bureaucracy was the main deterrent to staying in Indonesia (*Jakarta Post* 1996a, b, c, d).

Ministry officials were aware that aid was not going to last indefinitely. Indonesia's rapid growth meant that GDP was approaching the cut-off point designated by some donor countries. Swiss aid, for example was to start winding down in 1997/98. Third, and related to the above, continuing downward economic conditions in the donor countries had forced Japan, by far the largest donor, to cut its overall aid to Indonesia by almost 60%, and the UK to plan a cut of 16%. Both the US and Japan began to shy away from large infrastructure development funding. Approximately 17% of Indonesia's yearly budget expenditures are derived from aid. With a total foreign debt of US$100 billion (around 72% of GNP) and a debt service ratio of around 32%, the Indonesian government may find itself falling short of infrastructure development funds within the next decade. These 'pressures' may be accompanied by opportunistic struggle among an élite more focused on keeping their dwindling interests alive than providing environmental investment for the future.

Learning from the first world? Institutions, policies and the rule of law

There is no doubt that Indonesia is on a steep learning curve *vis-à-vis* environmental management. One lesson it has faced over the last decade is building up the institutions in charge of controlling pollution, in particular the central government's chief environmental regulatory arm, BAPEDAL (Environmental Impact Management Agency). One prominent NGO, the Centre for Environmental Law (ICEL), noted the need for the government to clarify the mandate of BAPEDAL: how it will develop in the provinces and how its functions and responsibilities will be allowed to adapt to the pace of change (ICEL 1994). However, it seems improbable to wait for the event of 'institutional building' to assist in securing a sustainable future. Analogous would be to wait for the training of the doctor tomorrow for a patient requiring surgery yesterday.

Institutional development is a lengthy process. The BAPEDAL mandate is still not fully resolved with only three provincial offices open after years of central government indecision and bureaucratic infighting. It remains an inoperable agent. In 1994, after four years of operation, BAPEDAL employed 100 professional staff members. However, it is severely restricted from increasing staff numbers because of policies held by the Ministry of Manpower to keep staff numbers in Indonesia's bureaucracy down. While BAPEDAL relies heavily on collaboration with NGOs such as the Indonesian Environmental Forum (WALHI), the Legal Aid Foundation (LBH) and ICEL, these NGOs are themselves severely under-staffed, under-funded and under pressure from the government because their stance on environmental issues is often labelled as 'anti-development'.

ICEL recognises the constraints inherently involved—weak institutions, conflicts of sectoral interests and a lack of transparent legal infrastructure—which ICEL maintains will require ten years to subdue. However, lessons from America and Japan indicate that this time-frame is rather optimistic. The USA EPA needed 22 years to reach staffing levels of 22,000 with most (70%) of its policing activities occurring only in the last six years. In Japan, where municipal governments factor heavily in pollution control, within 20 years (1971–91), some 12,000 were employed in pollution control by local prefectures, and some 39,000 registered pollution control managers were employed at the factory level. When these numbers are translated into staff per capita figures both the USA and Japan ration one employee per 10,500 citizens. Indonesia's current ratio stands at one employee per two million. It is doubtful whether Indonesia has the same time-frames as the USA and Japan in order to develop comparable staffing levels, not to mention comparable levels of expertise.

However, an over-reliance on well-groomed environmental institutions in the first world has in no manner been a panacea for developing more sustainable practices. If Indonesian legal experts such as ICEL voice concerns over a legal infrastructure that is under-developed, the USA provides examples of a legal system that is over-developed, and the concomitant inadequacies exposed in negotiating the cost of the backlog of clean-ups. In the USA the $16.3 billion Superfund allocated by the government in 1980 to register and clean up toxic sites has mainly been used in highly technical and protracted court cases. It was calculated in 1994 that 75% of the $10 billion in funds spent had gone to outside consultants, administration and, in particular, to lawyers battling out litigation cases, leaving only 25% for the actual clean-ups. Perhaps only in the US, interpretation of ambiguous terms such as best available technology (BAT), best practicable technology currently available (BPT), and best available technology not entailing excessive cost (BATNEEC) have tied up the courts, the regulators and the regulated (O'Connor 1994: 87). In 1992, 12 years after the Superfund was legislated, the EPA could declare a mere 64 out of the registered 34,000 toxic sites as cleaned up (Tyler Miller Jr 1994: 563). The principle of 'polluter pays' has become a weak and trivialised foundation on which to launch allegations of liability. US consumers can be liable for hazardous chemical pollution caused by the glue used to stick labels on jars and tin cans that they dispose of after use. First-world environmental NGOs would agree that environmental policy at home is a downward-spiralling compromise that neglects fundamental principles of ecological rule of law.

Although policies which are, in part, successful in industrialised countries may not be suitable in Indonesia, even local solutions sought will need to adhere to the rule of law. The issue of public monies ending up in private bank accounts has definitive consequences for the policies that Indonesia chooses to control industrial pollution. According to Castles (SPES 1992: 265), the main constraint on seeding sustainable development (in this case pollution control and prevention) in Indonesia lies with an entrenched lack of 'rule of law'. Its political culture is 'allergic' to it (SPES 1992: 265). This allergy undoubtedly affects efforts in establishing and implementing environmental policy regulations. Eskeland and Jiminez (1991) analysed the prospect of Indonesia following interventionist policy instruments derived from public finance, such as pollution levies, taxes and subsidies (market-based instruments [MBI]), to persuade industries to adopt abatement practices. Their study compared MBI that regulate ambient quality of a receiving body (e.g. river water or air) with the other widely used policy of command and control (CAC), which regulates pollution at the 'end-of-pipe' source. Although favouring MBI, they expressed dismay at the prospect of Indonesia adopting such instruments because of 'public revenue constraint . . . [an] inability to monitor emissions and damages . . . uncertainty . . . and [a] non-competitive market structure'.

O'Connor (1994) also cited MBI as a solution to Indonesia's industrial pollution control—its soft-touch approach seemingly suited to a scenario of latent volatility. However, there is no guarantee that these instruments will produce the desired incentive of reducing pollution. In East Java, for example, industry's current practice of avoiding complicity by 'buying out' officials in order to stall the inevitable abatement costs has created a rent-seeking opportunity for those in charge of pollution surveillance at the regional and local level. Not only may MBI legitimise such rent-seeking opportunities, there would also be no guarantee that levies collected would be transferred to consolidated revenue which in return can be recycled back into an urban sustainability initiative. Put simply, without rule of law, pollution tax systems have little hope of efficacy because it is relatively easy to manipulate the collection agency whose officials are vulnerable to manipulation because of wage constraints. The Indonesian taxation system operates through a bargaining process in which the business person, the tax official and the relevant sector official from government prosper at the expense of an impoverished public revenue. Collusion provides no safe ground on which to build a tax-based regime to curb current polluters and prevent future ones.

Indonesia's official environmental efforts have had a wealth of donor funding, which in turn has fostered considerable consultancy exchange. International environmental projects have grafted themselves on to the upper levels of bureaucracy with élite backing. However, environmental institutions, rights and preservation are increasingly being seen as coming from abroad and, hence, as foreign Western liberalism propagated by what even the current champion of *reformasi* (reformation), Amien Rais, called in a national daily press article, 'blond-haired, blue-eyed experts' who do not understand the 'Indonesian way of doing things' (*Republika* 1993). While many of these 'experts' have indeed been ill-equipped to face particular Indonesian nuances, they themselves believed that doing things the Indonesian way meant doing little at all.

Uncertainty

The least these 'lessons' suggest is that no matter how sophisticated or autonomous institutions are, nor how transparent or 'democratic' government is, efforts to clean up contaminated sites, prevent future pollution or, for that matter (closer to home), protect remaining forests, definitive action needs to be taken. No matter which country, 'doing sustainable development' requires consensual and consistent political will as a fundamental prerequisite. But in which country, if any, is there consensus on the issue of sustainable development and where at all has there been consistent political will? If first-world states with their advanced political and capital formations have not managed to establish a sustainable future, then how can intervention on behalf of ecological integrity be effectively implemented within the current political and economic culture of the Indonesian state. The need to act to prevent transgression has struck upon the country far in advance of any capacity to do so. Though the emergent needs are clear, inertia preventing positive change is entrenched. Not only is the Indonesian regime allergic to the rule of law, it is also showing degenerative symptoms of regime responsibility neglect. It is these issues that most Indonesians are currently alarmed by, rather than the depleted environments that result.

So where do environmental issues in the ecological sense lie in a rapidly changing and quite unpredictable political economic landscape? How does the collapse of large-scale capital and its political disgrace affect the continued propensity to wreak havoc on nature. On the one hand, greater freedom of grass-roots expression and activism places increased pressure on polluters by those most immediately polluted. On the other hand, the financial imperatives of private- and public-sector corporations may place pressure on the costs of their operations and opportunities for windfalls in ways that result in instrumentally justifiable environmental damage and unsustainability. Indeed, how will the chiefs of *reformasi* reposition public attention onto the environment?

The Indonesian regime abhorred uncertainty—ideologically, psychologically and politically—and, as Przeworski (1986) states, in such a regime to seek or explore an alternative and to cultivate a belief in that alternative is full of risk and uncertainty. Before the fall there was an excess of certainty and absence of alternatives. Today in Indonesia it is the reverse—and neither the status quo nor the alternatives are safe propositions. But at some point a threshold was reached: that which was not yet, and therefore uncertain, became more attractive than that which was imminent but no longer attractive. Uncertainty, according to Przeworski, is the 'original ground' freed from historical condition, bearing new relations to older practices as emergent needs put pressure on existing social formations. It is uncertain whether the emergent volume of uncertainty can be poured back into the old bottle of authoritarian values.

Conclusion: thresholds, 'development' and regime dilemma

For any effective environmental policy intervention, a determination of environmental thresholds needs to be established, i.e. how and where the point of irreversibility of environmental damage should be set, and how the cost of regulatory inaction should be assessed in the face of future uncertainty (Cameron 1993). These 'ultimate environmental thresholds' (UETs), as Koslowski calls them, are not only the limits that humanity imposes on the environment. Rather, by definition of final limits, they are also the limits that the natural environment may impose on various types of development (Koslowski and Hill 1993: 5). The gestalt in this view is the image of humanity and development nibbling at the edges of ecological integrity, and also the image of a rapidly deteriorating environment nibbling at the edges of development and human integrity. A systems theory notion comes to mind of an ecological immune system rejecting foreign elements, that is, development done badly. The environment itself rather than human agency upon it is the subject making the moves. But if ecological uncertainty is at stake here then how indeed can such intervention be nurtured in the face of economic collapse and political uncertainty and possible national disintegration?

Two related questions emerge. First, can Indonesia recognise the importance of creating a threshold between the backlog of clean-up required in order to address a plethora of negative impacts brought on by a generation of haphazard development, and future development nurtured out of common good sense. Second, can it muster the consensus to act on that recognition? As for anywhere, establishing the threshold will require all development stakeholders to understand that: (i) existing sources of pollution must be cleaned up and future sources prevented; (ii) pollution or waste control is an inherent part of any production process; (iii) urban infrastructure is an inherent part of good development; and (iv) when there is consensus on the need for rule of law, then strict adherence to funding and planning regulations can take place to ensure the uptake of clean technologies, waste treatment facilities and operation, the transparent fulfilment of Environmental Impact Assessment requirements, proper practice in project design, site location, etc. Public health and civil stability are crucial substrata of future development in Indonesia.

Over the next generation, Indonesia's priorities for ecological sustainability lie in the development of infrastructure: water supply, sewerage and solid waste management, industrial pollution control and air pollution. These priorities involve the quality of urban habitats which in themselves will increasingly become the barometers of success or failure. National Development (*Pembangunan*) is a primordial concept on which the Suharto government has based its legitimacy, and 'doing development right' is what that legitimacy has depended on. One of the foundations on which Indonesia pursued *Pembangunan* is the 'trilogy' of *growth* with *stability* and *equity*. However, growth is undermined by the deterioration of the environment and stability is undermined by the consequences of that deterioration. Equity, unfortunately, never had a chance.

All Indonesian citizens want development, but none wants the negative impacts of ill-managed development. Just as UETs are defined as final limits that the natural environment may pose on development, so too there may be final limits that the civil environment may pose on development, especially in Indonesia where the word 'environment' (*lingkungan*) has historically had an inextricable link to social context. In the manic practice of management in Indonesia over the last generation, the term *tidak bersih lingkungan*, officially meaning 'environmentally unclean', was a extremely powerful term in the Suharto regime. It described a condition of kin and/or organisational contamination by left-wing ideology and affiliations most despised from the mid-1960s onwards. The claim to a 'clean environment' is a declaration that civil servants still have to make that no one in their immediate and extended family dating back unlimited generations has ever been a member of the Indonesian Communist Party, which was ruthlessly outlawed in 1966. 'Development' has been one of the most used words in the last 25 years of Indonesia's history and all land, sea, forest and people are judged by their actual or potential contribution to the nation's economic growth (Reeve 1996: 131). It was believed that development would take away uncertainty because development meant liberation. In turn, political life was driven to the same end; political, social and environmental dialogue seeking alternatives was seen as 'anti-development' creating uncertainty. Interestingly, with growing calls for clean government, a more recent gloss for environmental contamination of holders of public office has contracted to the immediate milieu of *tidak bersih diri*, that is, *personally unclean*.

If ultimate environmental thresholds are a probable location of ultimate civil thresholds, transgression of the former may bring transgression of the latter. If Indonesia continues a 'business-as-usual' approach to development, the government legitimacy will be stretched and citizen reaction may be inevitable. It would be more constructive to invest political capital (legitimacy) in order to retrieve the public capital (consent) that leaks out of the system. The cost of clean-up is far more expensive than orderly prevention. Indeed, it would be far more cost-effective for the government to use its remaining legitimacy to put both industry and urban infrastructure right than it would be to lose the consensus of the citizens. Unfortunately, environmental agendas can become overshadowed by preoccupations with ideological, administrative and moral hygiene.

The centrist government cannot unravel the mess and tangle of its own central conurbation of Jakarta let alone unravel regional environmental needs. It is imperative to ask, therefore, whether in Indonesia the quest for a sustainable future providing quality urban life is too complex for a centralised management approach. Environmental protection is embedded in political choice and requires negotiation of vested interest at all levels of society. It also requires considerable public and private investment and a definite shift in the arrangements of power at the political level. Outmoded economic, social and legal priorities based on dominance over and exploitation of nature are a worldwide problem. But this assemblage coupled with a dominance over and exploitation of civil society dictated by a highly centralist regime is a problem particularly acute in Indonesia. Here nature has been used as a means of social control while environmental management has been used as a means of generating the continuity of a centrist regime shadily funded by an entrenched trilogy of rent seeking, graft and embezzlement. Unlike the trilogy of Indonesia's official development ethos, here all three pillars have prospered well.

As a foreign element or import, environmental management could only be grafted on to an already existing polity. It was hounded to propagate the status quo. In Indonesia thus far, it has been a mask used by bureaucracy to siphon off the profits from resource exploitation, and to extract from an excessive spill towards urbanisation and industrialisation. When the dominant hierarchy imposes its will-to-power in the name of environmental management, entities of water, land, forest and place are used as tools of regime control. This is significant: the drive to maintain the status quo of a civil society historically engineered to befit the established hierarchy, may expose, through another window, a deep dissatisfaction among those left out or negatively impacted upon by the fickle nature of the development path.

The current situation in Indonesia is moving so quickly, it is impossible to make predictions about policy directions and accountability. The sheer urgency of economic crisis, watershed regime change, the uncertainty of political contestation and national disintegration has shunted the environment into the background. This could result in a number of scenarios. The economic crisis could put further pressure on nature (forests, swamps, etc.) for extractive purposes while the collapse of industry could provide a 'fallow' for the rivers, canals and other sinks of industry wastes and allow some respite. Another scenario could see increasingly militant villagers downstream ready to put pressure on the upstream factory because of a perception that the factory owner belongs to an élite group that has failed them. And, if bureaucracy, itself discredited, has abandoned its traditional favour of this élite, then the villagers would be all the more inclined to confront polluters. Local people are now in a stronger position to demonstrate because the big polluters are on the back foot for their *kolusi, korupsi, nepotisme* habits and for their contribution to the current failure of the nation. However, one point is worth noting: Bob Hasan, the timber baron and Suharto's close business ally, was not discredited because he had destroyed the forests and forest communities. He was exposed because the ethical and political principles he openly professed to adhere to did not match the economic outcome that his development practice so openly promoted. There are sentiments of 'moral legitimacy' and 'moral economy' at play here. Pre-meltdown Indonesia collectively had the required funds to put development right but did not. Now Indonesia can claim it does not have the funds because it is too poor to exercise environmental concerns (and therefore still will not).

There is no doubt that, in Indonesia's near future, environmentally responsible behaviour will be a site for a predatorial hierarchy of priorities with multiple layers of contention. Development is diverse arena of struggle between urban and rural needs, between forestry and agricultural needs, between industrial growth and pollution control and between the current centrist management practices and the demand for further participation—all within a climate of economic uncertainty. With a current situation of weak institutions, conflicts of sectoral interests and a lack of transparent legal infrastructure, much will depend on putting politically responsible behaviour right. Indeed, the government may have put itself in a 'Catch 22' situation: that is, there are attendant risks of social and political instability if wider participation is allowed in the development process, but there may well be the same risks of instability if wider participation is not allowed. The current paternalistic approach of 'doing development' *for* communities may bite back at the regime because the outcomes of this approach in the past have favoured the interests of government, bureaucracy and the élite at the expense of civil society. A civil-based approach of doing development *with* communities may also bite back because the aspirations of the bulk of civil society will undoubtedly be in opposition to the interests currently being served. There is no guarantee concerning the degree of ferocity of either bite, but the captive hound is baring its teeth. Indonesia is fast heading towards perhaps catastrophic environmental thresholds in its pursuit of development. In parallel, the Indonesian regime has also been heading towards an ultimate civil threshold, an irreversible crack in the regime wall. Over the last 25 years Indonesia has relied on both a strong environmental base and a weak civil society. Over the next generation the bankrupt nation faces an abyss between a rapidly diminishing environmental base and a civil society of rapidly diminishing tolerance on the threshold of arbitrary revenge in its demand for quality of life and equity. But some in deeper moods may ask whether this is different to the fate anywhere else.

Under such circumstances one can offer merely pleas; recommendations would only be viewed as paternalistic. First, Indonesia cannot afford to repeat the squander and the squalor, even though instrumentalist justification to continue past practices remains a sticking point. Second, even though public attention is distracted, capital has taken flight and development has stalled; in some ways Indonesia stands at an advantageous position from which to kick-start a possible future that pays service to environmental integrity and public health rather than succumb to a probable future overwhelmed by civil and ecological dysfunction. Those with the most power to act are also the most informed. To act on preventative principles of a shared environmental responsibility and a common good sense would be a step in the better direction. If they cannot act so, then all we are left with are pleas for compassion.

23

Competing Discourses of Environmental and Water Management in Post-Apartheid South Africa

Patrick Bond and Robyn Stein

OVER THE PAST COUPLE OF DECADES, at least three distinctive discourses associated with environmental management have emerged that seem to apply equally well—though with different implications—in developed and developing countries (Harvey 1996: ch. 13). South Africa is a semi-industrialised nation largely reliant on minerals, energy and associated manufacturing (Fine and Rustomjee 1996) but also suffering high levels of poverty. It is, therefore, appropriate to consider the three discourses as having features that stand out particularly well against the very stark inequalities and socioeconomic challenges facing this middle-income country today.

The first discourse is an 'orthodox economic' concern with maximising gross domestic product, showing only passing attention to associated environmental problems. The orthodox economic approach was expressed, if in a caricatured manner, in a 1991 memo signed by the World Bank's then chief economist, Lawrence Summers: 'I think the economic logic behind dumping a load of toxic waste in the lowest-wage country is impeccable and we should face up to that' (*Economist* 1992). Rather than 'internalise the externalities' associated with pollution or ecological damage, the ready solution is to try to simply displace these to a country where political power is negligible and the immediate environmental implications are less visible, in the name of overall economic growth. Versions of this discourse include the Wise Use movement and other arguments that place private property relations first and foremost in the ordering of society.

A second discourse offers a longer-term, more comprehensive accounting of environmental processes within society, namely the argument on behalf of 'sustainable development' which, drawing from the Brundtland Commission, has been termed 'ecological modernisation'. Externalities such as pollution should, in the classical example, be brought into the marketplace in such a manner as to assure that these costs are adequately accounted for in 'polluter-pays' profit–loss calculations. However, prevention is preferable. State regulation and even outright controls on environmentally damaging activity are willingly recognised as potentially beneficial within this school of thought, and the rights of future generations are also factored in.

The third discourse we can label 'environmental justice', for it sites ecological issues within a sociopolitical context first and foremost, and poses firm moral and distributional questions about that context (sometimes resorting to cultural defences and symbolic critique). At one level this rights-based discourse is grounded in values so well recognised that they were included in the South African Constitution's Bill of Rights in 1996:

> everyone has the right to an environment that is not harmful to their health or well-being . . . everyone has the right to have access to healthcare services, including reproductive health care; sufficient food and water; and social security . . . (RSA 1996: s.24.a, s.27.1).

Tellingly, however, that constitution also provided a caveat in mandating 'reasonable legislative and other measures that prevent pollution and ecological degradation, promote conservation, and secure ecologically sustainable development and use of natural resources *while promoting justifiable economic and social development*' (RSA 1996: s.24.b, emphasis added), quite consistent with ecological modernisation. And, underlining the central orthodox economic precept, it went on immediately to specify that 'No one may be deprived of property except in terms of law of general application, and no law may permit arbitrary deprivation of property' (RSA 1996: s.25.1). Hence democratic South Africa is, even in its founding document, beset by conflicting discourses, the ramifications of which will be tested in the Constitutional Court for decades to come.

This is no mere academic exercise in discourse analysis, however, for we seek here to establish some of the ways in which these divergent arguments have competed to win public policy favour within the first democratic government, led by the African National Congress (ANC), which won the 1994 election with 63% of the vote. The case of water management is most useful in this respect, for it combines South Africa's extraordinarily damaging historical use of water from an ecological perspective with policies aimed at addressing the maldistribution of water, together with a legislative approach that requires a rigorous reading to get beyond the government's superficial discursive strategy.

The legacy of apartheid water

Water management offers South African government and society possibly the most serious contemporary challenges (Hallowes 1997). Among the main problems for environmental management are: water scarcity; the maldistribution of water; pollution of water sources; other forms of structural damage to water ecosystems; and substandard or non-existent sanitation.

First, 42 million South Africans have access each year to, on average, only 1,200 kl of available water, of which half is already dammed. Ineffective and destructive uses of water are prevalent, as described below. Water scarcity is exacerbated by South Africa's erratic rainfall patterns, and the effect of periodic droughts on low-income people is particularly devastating (whereas wealthy white farmers have traditionally gained access to state compensation during droughts). There exists a worrying potential for both domestic and regional geopolitical conflict over access to water, with South Africa already draining Lesotho's water and with controversial plans under way to tap other regional sources, as well as border rivers (such as the Orange River bordering Namibia, via the Lesotho Highlands Water Project).

Second, the distribution of South Africa's water across the population is even more unequal, measured in class, race and gender terms, than the distribution of income. More than half of the country's raw water is used for white-dominated commercial agriculture, of which half is considered to be wasted due to poor irrigation techniques and inappropriate crop choice. Another quarter is used in mining and industry. Around 12% of South Africa's water is consumed by households, but, of that amount, more than half goes into (white people's) gardens and swimming pools, and less than a tenth is consumed by all-black South African households. Minimal water access is one reason why black South Africans suffer by far the highest infant mortality and water-related disease rates in all of Africa in relation to per capita GDP. Access by the majority is improving only marginally, notwithstanding massive cross-watershed pumping of water, for example, from Lesotho, undertaken inexplicably in the name of development (Letsie and Bond 1999). In rural areas, the Departments of Agriculture and of Water Affairs and Forestry are making only minimal efforts to improve water access to black farmers and, indeed, due to impending water shortages the government will only expand existing water supply systems (which irrigate white farmland)—the Lesotho Highlands, the Tugela, Mkzomazi and Mzimvubu basins, the Orange River and Western Cape sources—with only a tiny fraction of resources spent on new irrigation schemes for emergent farmers.

Third, pollution of water ultimately destined for human consumption arises from largely unregulated discharges from industry, from waste dump run-off, and from agricultural chemicals and mine tailings/slimes dams. Faecal pollution is a problem in many urban areas due to the inadequate sanitation in most low-income households. Acid rain is considered to be extremely prevalent in coal-burning regions of the country. All these features of pollution increase water treatment costs and raise public health risks to many low-income households dependent on direct access to unpurified water.

Fourth, water ecosystems suffer enormous soil loss and siltation through commercial agriculture, erosion caused by overcrowded rural areas, polluted aquifers from mining waste, the exhaustion of aquifers from excessive irrigation, and drainage of wetlands and regions with high levels of forestry (especially invasive-alien eucalyptus and pine plantations). There are also problems in declining natural flow rates of rivers due to cross-watershed pumping (resulting, too, in increased urbanisation pressure), siltation of dam storage capacity (costing up to $30 million per year), and salination and waterlogging of land due to intensive irrigation.

Fifth, water-borne sanitation is available to only around one-third of black South Africans, and excessive amounts of water (typically 13 l per flush) are used in virtually all middle- and upper-class areas. Although a solid-waste sanitation system is desirable, so too is universal installation of low-flush and dual-flush toilets (as well as low-flow showerheads) which save water and cut sewage treatment costs, while sanitation services could be extended to all households. (That this would contradict current policy on household affordability grounds, regardless of the social and ecological consequences, is shown below.) Dumping of untreated sewage into the sea remains an issue. As discussed below, mass pit latrines in urban and peri-urban areas remain factors in the spread of faecal bacteria.

Basic water services policy

Decisions about municipal water services provision to low-income urban and rural South Africans—what kind, how much and at what price—offer an opportunity to reflect on the policy approach the South African government adopted amid competing socio-ecological discourses (for more details, see Bond 1999; Bond *et al.* 1999). The *Municipal Infrastructure Investment Framework* (MIIF) describes the main infrastructure and services options planned by central government for local government's implementation. This framework, according to the Department of Constitutional Development's (DCD 1997: 2) 'User-Friendly Guide' to MIIF, entailed 'an economic modelling exercise to estimate services backlogs, assess the capital costs that are involved in removing these backlogs, and calculate the recurrent costs of operating and maintaining the services'. The model thus simply compared the capital investment associated with various options against available fiscal resources (with some 'public–private partnership' augmentation through privatisation of some municipal functions). In the process, it correlated the amounts of services to be provided—whether a house/yard tap or communal tap; whether a flush toilet or pit latrine; whether a 60 amp electrical connection or none at all—to households' ability to pay. And it established prepaid metering systems or assured recourse to services cut-offs so as to diminish the incentive of consumers not to pay for what they received.

Such an orthodox economic perspective—with no consideration for ecological values, for the need to mitigate public health hazards, for potential economic spin-offs from municipal services, for the importance of relatively high-standard service levels to geographical desegregation, or for the gender equalisation potential of better municipal services—was the core discourse adopted in the initial (1994–95) *Urban Infrastructure Investment Framework* (UIIF), based mainly on World Bank policy advice. The key constraints in the UIIF reasoning included the overall fiscal resources available to South Africa for the purposes of subsidising recurrent (not even capital) expenditure on municipal services, a cost-recovery approach so that 'operating and maintenance' (marginal) expenses would be covered in full by recipients, and low-income households' quite limited ability to pay (given South Africa's vast impoverished population). By late 1995, a draft *Urban Development Strategy* (UDS) reflected government thinking on service provision. The UDS summary demonstrated the low level of standards then contemplated for *urban* areas (rural infrastructure plans had not been developed at that stage) (Ministry of Reconstruction and Development 1995: 24-25):

> communal standpipes (water), on site sanitation, graded roads with gravel and open stormwater drains and streetlights (electricity). These services will be targeted at households with an income of less than US$200 per month and charged for at between US$9 and US$12 per month.

While the rationale for such low standards and such careful correlation of ability to pay appeared economically reasonable, it did not account for either the multiple positive externalities associated with provision of higher levels of services or the political mandate with which the ANC had won the election, namely the *Reconstruction and Development Programme* (RDP). By way of illustration, the UIIF claimed, notwithstanding great evidence to the contrary, that 'There are no major environmental problems anticipated for this project' (World Bank 1994–95: 54). In contrast, the RDP (ANC 1994: s.2.6.10, 2.7.8) recognised the funding gap and specified the need for tariff restructuring and cross-subsidies with respect to both water (including sanitation) and electricity. Moreover, according to the RDP, in the case of water 'the national tariff structure must include . . . a lifeline tariff to ensure that all South Africans are able to afford water services sufficient for health and hygiene requirements'.

Yet the possibility of charging large-volume users of water higher than their marginal cost—not least so as to promote conservation, given the enormous wastage mentioned earlier—was ruled out (the World Bank did not even include it within the four funding options under consideration), apparently for two orthodox economic reasons. First, as expressed by a leading DCD official, such cross-subsidisation would make the products—typically agricultural and mineral exports—less competitive, 'and that would affect our balance of payments' (*Mail and Guardian* 1996). In other words, the growth imperative outweighed equity and the externalities associated with lifeline infrastructure access to the poor. Second, cross-subsidisation was intrinsically a market-distorting device, in the view of World Bank resource economists. Thus Roome (1995: 50-51) firmly advised the Minister of Water Affairs that cross-subsidies 'may limit options with respect to tertiary providers' and that 'in particular private concessions [would be] much harder to establish'. The orthodox economic argument here was that a declining marginal cost curve associated with bulk supply to large users would, through cross-subsidisation of low-income, small-scale consumers, be translated into a rising marginal revenue curve (and vice versa), which would distort the profit maximisation calculus (by which marginal costs and marginal revenues run in parallel). Forcing service providers to cross-subsidise low-consumption blocks by raising the marginal price for high levels of consumption would, hence, serve as a formidable disincentive to water privatisation.

However, there was increased public criticism that the low UIIF/UDS services standards and government's failure to provide for recurrent subsidies were incompatible with ANC election promises. After the UIIF, draft UDS and early drafts of the MIIF (which added even lower rural standards) were published, the controversy intensified and in 1997, facing political pressure, DCD made some modifications to urban infrastructure standards. Instead of no electricity, there was the potential for urban households to receive an 8 amp supply (not strong enough, however, for heating or cooking), and instead of paying US$9–12 per month for these services, a subsidy of approximately US$12 per low-income household was planned. (Whether this was enough to cover basic operating costs was questionable, and indeed whether the grant was sustainable given budget constraints remained to be seen, but there were in any case substantial doubts about this method of subsidy given the administrative costs of means-testing and the stigmatisation with which means-testing is associated.) Rural households would still have much lower standards, and, for urban households with less than US$200 income per month (i.e. between a quarter and a third of urban households within a decade), the new MIIF continued to recommend a ventilated improved pit-latrine given that poor households would not be able to afford to flush, as well as communal (not house or yard) standpipes, a weak electricity supply, gravel roads, open storm-water drains, and communal waste dumps (not kerbside removal) under the (in retrospect, optimistic) 'low-growth' late-1990s macroeconomic scenario.

Part of the rationale for the marginal improvement in MIIF's service standards and the new recurrent subsidy was the recognition, compatible with the ecological modernisation perspective, that indeed there were some important public health and economic benefits associated with infrastructure and services. But this calculation was notional and, for example, the ecological harm associated with the still-low standards was not considered seriously. It must be acknowledged, of course, that the environmental impact of increased infrastructure and services is complex, for both benefits and costs are associated with higher levels of services and consumption. It is generally accepted that large-scale bulk infrastructure projects (such as major dams or roads through ecologically sensitive areas) are to be avoided. But incorporating the benefits of infrastructure remains crucial. It is clear from South African research that, for example, when simply comparing pit-latrines with water-borne sewage, if installed properly, the latter is potentially a far more environmentally friendly approach (particularly in the many areas affected by inopportune geological conditions). Similarly, there is likely to be environmental damage that may arise from increased utilisation of water by those who presently do not have access. And the replacement of electricity for coal or wood when cooking and heating would have important household and urban environmental benefits.

None of these arguments was terribly controversial within the ecological modernisation discourse, as the World Bank's (1994d: 20) *World Development Report* on infrastructure confirmed:

> Environment-friendly infrastructure services are essential for improving living standards and offering public health protection. With sufficient care, providing the infrastructure necessary for growth and poverty reduction can be consistent with concern for natural resources and the global environment (the 'green' agenda). At the same time, well-designed and well-managed infrastructure can promote the environmental sustainability of human settlements (the 'brown' agenda).

(That 1994 report even endorsed cross-subsidies and lifeline tariffs, but was ignored by the Bank's South Africa staff later the same year.) But, while the final MIIF recognised the environmental issues more explicitly, it often did so by way of denying that low standards would have an adverse impact. DCD thus considered it reasonable to incorporate ecological modernisation discourse yet remain within a framework ultimately defined by orthodox economic cost-recovery principles (a common danger, internationally). Indeed, as we see below, the very term 'lifeline' was redefined by the Department of Water Affairs and Forestry to mean 'operating and maintenance charges' (i.e. 'marginal cost pricing' fully in tune with an orthodox economic approach).

The response of social change activists and community organisations

The alternative proposal advocated by social change activists from community organisations and associated NGOs, compatible with an environmental justice perspective (and with the constitution and RDP), was a universal *free* lifeline to all South African consumers for the first block of water (50 l of water per person each day) and electricity with steeply rising prices for subsequent consumption blocks. There would be no need, in this policy framework, for means-testing or a complex administrative apparatus. Thus recurrent consumption expenses would be paid for entirely from within each sector, although an additional 10% expenditure would be needed, beyond the MIIF budget, to finance the added capital costs (totalling US$28 billion—to be invested over ten years—which was reasonable in relation to mid-1990s GDP of US$110 billion and an annual state budget of close to US$40 billion). The social change option was thus radical yet eminently realistic. More than the final MIIF, it took seriously the environmental and other externalities associated with infrastructure and services.

Where the social change advocates came up short, however, was in turning an extensive series of urban popular riots over municipal services—which, tragically, included the assassination of an ANC mayor known for willingness to cut power and water, as well as the burning of several ANC councillors' houses—into more sustained, constructive political pressure (this partly reflected the demobilisation of the national 'civic association' movement during the late 1990s). In contrast to an alliance between DCD and the big business lobby within the National Economic Development and Labour Council (the stakeholder forum at which state policies were often debated), the progressive forces failed, in 1996–97, to successfully contest the intensification of services commodification and, notwithstanding firm opposition by a progressive municipal workers' union (which campaigned for 50 free litres of water per day), to challenge central government's inclination to see large parts of municipalities privatised (to the latter end, the DCD leaders attempted to pit services-starved residents against allegedly labour-aristocrat municipal workers). Also at stake in this class struggle was, as ever, the degree to which a modern state that aimed at establishing a good business environment could construct a 'social wage' policy framework that had, as a central objective, maintaining relatively low upward pressure on the private-sector wage floor; in other words, by keeping monthly operating costs of services low through denying workers access to flush toilets, hot plates and the like, the MIIF also reduced the pressures that workers would otherwise have to impose on their employers for wages sufficient for the reproduction of labour power.

The oppositional discourse alone—based on ecological modernisation arguments (public health savings of giving people free services, etc.) and abstract rights principles—may not have been at fault in all of this, for in very practical ways the social and labour movements were too weak to successfully contest the broader trajectory, and not even the strongest eco-socialist rhetorical critique could have made up for lack of political clout. What loomed ahead, as more than half of South Africa's 878 municipalities prepared to face formal bankruptcy at the turn of the 21st century—due to inadequate central-local grants and low levels of service payments by residents—was a (neoliberal) version of municipal environmental management that would, in future, have to grapple with a variety of urban pollution problems associated with the low levels of basic-needs infrastructure and the inadequate consumption subsidies. This will transpire, in part, when municipal officials blame the victims for non-payment and engage in widespread cut-offs of municipal services, hence generating future environmental crises of both a green and a brown character.

Although at the national scale, official water-related rhetoric—in white papers, ministerial pronouncements, a 1998 water pricing policy and legislation—was more in keeping with sustainable development and environmental justice discourse, a brief examination of two key laws uncovers a variety of orthodox economic loopholes.

Environmental management and water legislation

Of foremost interest in post-apartheid environmental legislation is the introduction of environmental rights into formal jurisprudence (Stein and Tucker 1997: 22). Both the interim (1993) and final (1996) versions of the constitution guaranteed every person the right to an environment that is not 'detrimental' (1993) or 'harmful' (1996) to their health or wellbeing, with the final constitution adding further socioeconomic rights with environmental implications. Coupled with the enjoinder to parliament to ensure public participation in law making, the final constitution required legislation that would give effect to the rights enshrined in the bill of rights and to the founding values of the constitution, including the achievement of equality and the advancement of human rights and freedom (RSA 1996: s.1).

It is useful to consider the two most significant pieces of environmental legislation in the ANC's first term of government: the National Environmental Management Act 107 of 1998 and the National Water Act 36 of 1998. Both give a degree of legislative effect to the concept of 'sustainable development', in keeping with the discourse of ecological modernisation. Both rely heavily on a highly regulatory 'command-and-control' approach, and incorporate environmental and social justice values. However, both are also ultimately designed for federalist enforcement at the 'lowest most appropriate level'. And, as with the constitution, the enforcement of these laws' environmental rights are, in the end, dependent on the South African legal system's ability to deliver on the constitutionally guaranteed right of access to courts or any other independent or impartial tribunal or forum (RSA 1996: s.32).

Some of the more important contradictions contained in the two statutes must also be identified in the process, for it is evident that they arise from the sociopolitical context and the need for compromise in what was still, in 1998, a tentative first term of democratic government. What is ultimately most obvious is that, notwithstanding rhetoric to the contrary, the apartheid-era state support for industrial development and capital accumulation at all costs (see, for example, Fine and Rustomjee 1996) was not significantly tampered with in the new laws.

The National Environmental Management Act (NEMA) came into effect in January 1998. It called for 'co-operative environmental governance'—a phrase derived from the constitutional mandate (RSA 1996: ch. 3) that all spheres and organs of government are obliged to co-ordinate their actions—by establishing principles to be taken into account in all decision-making processes affecting the environment. Apartheid-era South African environmental law, in contrast, was fragmented and disbursed among a wide variety of statutes and subordinate legislation and was administered by a multitude of regulatory authorities (Fuggle and Rabie 1992). NEMA represents law-making in the ecological modernisation mode, for, while insisting that 'environmental management must place people and their needs at the forefront of its concern, and serve their physical, psychological, developmental, cultural and social interest equitably', it immediately switches to Brundtland-style sustainable development discourse, with a call for 'socially, environmentally and economically sustainable' development (RSA 1998a: s.3.2, 2.3). The idea of sustainability entails 'the integration of social, economic and environmental factors into planning, implementation and decision-making so as to ensure that development serves present and future generations' (RSA 1998a: s.1.29), which in turn follows from the constitution's approach to 'justifiable economic and social development' (RSA 1996: s.24.b).

Thus NEMA (RSA 1998a: s.2.4.a) stipulates avoidance (or where that is impossible minimisation and remedy) of 'the disturbance of ecosystems and loss of biological diversity . . . ; pollution and degradation of the environment . . . ; disturbance of landscapes and sites that constitute the nation's cultural heritage . . . ; [and] waste . . .' It continues by insisting

> that the use and exploitation of non-renewable natural resources is responsible and equitable, and takes into account the consequences of the depletion of the resource; that the development, use and exploitation of renewable resources and the ecosystems of which they are part do not exceed the level beyond which their integrity is jeopardised; that a risk-adverse and cautious approach is applied, which takes into account the limits of current knowledge about the consequences of decisions and actions; and that the negative impacts on the environment and people's environmental rights be anticipated and prevented, and where they cannot altogether be prevented, are minimised and remedied.

Hence prevention is better than cure, but qualifications are made consistently so that sources of environmental harm and damage located deep within the economic system are ultimately not challenged.

But here too an environmental justice thread is woven into the legal rhetoric. NEMA's founding principles recognised that 'environmental justice must be pursued so that adverse environmental impacts shall not be distributed in such a manner as to unfairly discriminate against any person, particularly vulnerable and disadvantaged persons'

(RSA 1998a: s.2.4.c). However, 'adverse environmental impact' is not defined and, although capable of wide interpretation, there is a threat that a narrow reading of NEMA's definition of 'environment' will nullify the broader social intent of the principle. For, that foundational definition (RSA 1998a: s.1.11):

> the surroundings within which humans exist and that are made up of—the land, water and atmosphere of the earth; micro-organisms, plant and animal life; . . . the interrelationships among and between them; and the physical, chemical, aesthetic and cultural properties and conditions of the foregoing that influence human health and wellbeing

is, after all, an ecocentric approach which explicitly avoids clarifying in plain language *social, living and working environments* (Lukey 1995: 40). In a context where a relatively untransformed judicial bench retains strong class, race, gender and other relations to the privileged of society, clear legislative language is vital, and NEMA's implicit distinction between human health and wellbeing, and environmental health and wellbeing, leaves the law more amenable to an eco-tourist's conception of environmental sustainability than to meeting the needs of someone from poor or working-class roots.

To illustrate, while NEMA safeguards the refusal to do environmentally hazardous work (RSA 1998a: s.29), this section is curiously silent on potential, threatened or actual health threats associated with particular work practices. The balance of convenience is clearly in the hands of employers, for workers are required to comply with technical and complex administrative requirements. There is, thus, access to environmental information in NEMA—including, under certain circumstances, privately held information—and added protection for whistle-blowers (RSA 1998a: s.30). Yet the extent of employer disclosure will ultimately depend both on Open Democracy legislation not yet passed by parliament (where considerable pressure will be exerted by corporate interests) and regulations promulgated by the Minister of Environmental Affairs and Tourism. Such ministerial regulations must be 'reasonable' (RSA 1998a: s.30.2), i.e. objectively justifiable in the circumstances, which leaves significant room for manoeuvre, particularly in an age of commercially protected information.

In sum, NEMA's principles are internally qualified or simply do not go far enough to address distributional issues, the root causes of environmental damage and harm, and practical power relationships on the legal battlefield. Likewise, NEMA's compliance and enforcement provisions contain relatively far-reaching provisions which, at first blush, resonate with social and environmental justice values. But these provisions contain substantial terminological loopholes following compromises with key corporate-industrial interests. The 'polluter pays' principle is fundamental, requiring that

> every person, who causes, has caused or may cause significant pollution or degradation of the environment must take reasonable measures to prevent such pollution or degradation from occurring, continuing or recurring, or, insofar as such harm to the environment is authorised by law or cannot reasonably be avoided or stopped, to minimise and rectify such pollution or degradation (RSA 1998a: s.28.1).

But again the qualifier 'reasonable' can be invoked when there is any alleged economic hardship or job loss associated with pollution-control measures.

Moreover, those who are obliged to take 'reasonable measures' include the

> owner of land and or premises, a person in control of land or premises or a person who has the right to use the land or premises on which or in which any activity is or was performed or undertaken; or any other situation exists, which causes, has caused or is likely to cause significant pollution or degradation of the environment (RSA 1998a: s.28.2).

South Africa's legacy of brutal land dispossession and land tenancy should have suggested the need for sensitivity as to the relative priority given to *which* polluter must pay, and, to compound matters, there is very little prospect for prosecution of predecessors-in-title. For, while NEMA boldly declares an intention to consider any person who 'is or was responsible for, or directly or indirectly contributed to, the pollution or degradation or the potential pollution or degradation', there is no specification of whether, for example, lenders, technical specialists or predecessors-in-title can be brought into the liability net. As for costs that may be recovered, again these must be 'reasonable', and no mention is made of indirect social costs.

The provisions of the constitution dealing with the enforcement of rights (RSA 1996: s.38) are replicated and given effect in NEMA (RSA 1998a: s.32), including the re-introduction of class action into the South African court process and cost protection for group-plaintiffs. Nonetheless, these are premised on access to justice being available to all; given fiscal constraints and residual class privilege, this simply does not exist in South Africa. In short, possibilities for integrating compliance and enforcement provisions given the existing system of civil and criminal justice do not appear to be in the least bit realistic.

The constitution (RSA 1996: s.44.2) sanctions national government to set minimum uniform norms and standards regarding provincial and municipal legislation, with space given for specific and technical issues pertinent to regional and local settings. But again, in the interstices of practical legislative implementation in a context of a severely compromised transition process, semi-federalism has been repeatedly entrenched, and is evident in the supreme law of the land. Activists' concerns about uneven legislation and regulatory control in respect of the environment were ignored in the constitution. Environment and pollution control are 'concurrent' national and provincial government legislative responsibilities and, even more worrying, exclusive legislative competence has been granted to the provinces and municipalities in regard to monitoring and regulating waste disposal (whether this includes hazardous waste disposal is left unclear). As a result, NEMA's chapter on integrated environmental management amplifies asymmetry in an already terribly uneven regulatory and administrative environment (RSA 1996: ch. 5). It also surrenders socio-ecological regulatory power to other (non-environmental) national and provincial departments, with the result that the most significant polluters—the mines—will continue to enjoy protection from, for instance, the rigours of far-reaching impact assessments prior to commencement of prospecting or mining operations. Many of the same legislative weaknesses are evident in the 1998 National Water Act (NWA).

The NWA and the question of basic needs

The NWA came into operation in October 1998, replacing the 1956 Water Act. Its core objectives are (RSA 1998b: s.2):

1. Meeting the basic human needs of present and future generations
2. Promoting equitable access to water
3. Redressing the results of past racial and gender discrimination
4. Promoting the efficient, sustainable and beneficial use of water in the public interest
5. Facilitating social and economic development
6. Providing for growing demand for water use
7. Protecting aquatic and associated ecosystems and their biological diversity
8. Reducing and preventing pollution and degradation of water resources
9. Meeting international obligations
10. Promoting dam safety
11. Managing floods and droughts

As with NEMA, ecological modernism discourse underpins the NWA, particularly the calls for sufficiency and sustainability (undefined) in the public interest and the facilitation of social and economic development. In the Brundtland mode, intergenerational equity and the meeting of basic human needs are fundamental provisions. Yet the extent to which the NWA legislates the protection, use, development, conservation, management and control of water resources, in relation to the country's vast unmet human needs, is nevertheless questionable.

Here the NWA's concept of an abstract 'reserve' of water resources to meet both basic needs and the integrity of aquatic ecosystems is a key international legal innovation. But the basic needs provision is itself reliant on interpretations of the 1997 Water Services Act, the constitutionally enshrined rights of access to sufficient water (RSA 1996: s.27) and environmental rights as discussed above. Those interpretations are, unfortunately, subject to the vagaries of administrative decision-making and regulatory prescription by the Minister of Water Affairs and Forestry.

The lack of clarity on meeting basic needs is carried through to the pricing strategy provided for in the NWA (RSA 1998b: s.56), which obliges the Water Minister to 'consider measures necessary to support the establishment of tariffs by water service authorities', and in particular to 'make allowance' for lifeline and progressive block tariffs. Yet neither the NWA nor the Water Services Act provide clues as to what is meant by a lifeline tariff, which gives rise to somewhat arbitrary determinations of the 'minimum' amount of water per day required to sustain human life and hygiene. For the ANC's first term in office, and indeed for the foreseeable future, the RDP *short-term* objective of 25 l per person per day is used, and has become not a minimum in actual water projects, but the effective *maximum* for which small pipes are installed. Nor is this amount guaranteed as a free entitlement; as noted above, official policy is that marginal cost should be met by consumers. Thus, although laudable for including the recognition of sufficient water for basic human needs, the NWA suddenly stops short, in the modernist mode, of granting the full ambit of this notion. (As noted earlier, the threat and reality of water cut-offs actually intensified over the ANC's first term, as a result of a burgeoning municipal fiscal crisis and an extremely tough 'credit control' mandate given to municipalities by DCD.) Interpretation of these issues will again be left to the courts, which remain a highly inadequate forum for the environmental and social justice values mandated by the Constitution.

The NWA proceeds to introduce a wide definition of 'water use' (RSA 1998b: s.21), including abstraction of water from a water resource, storing water, impeding or diverting the flow of water as well as the discharging or disposing of water found underground if this is necessary for the efficient continuation of an activity or for the safety of people (i.e. in underground mining operations). The NWA constitutes a legislative shift from a system that facilitated acquisition of private use rights in water to a public system where allocation of water-use rights is administratively determined on a licensing basis, which in turn will be influenced by an abstract water market as set out in the pricing policy. Riparianism, the doctrine developed in South African Common Law, English law and apartheid law, is also abolished in the NWA.

Yet here, too, where the opportunity arises for a great leap forward for social and environmental justice, the NWA gives protection to 'existing lawful water uses' (RSA 1998b: s.32), i.e. 'during a period of two years immediately before the date of commencement of this Act; or which has been declared an existing lawful water use . . .'. It is only through the compulsory licensing process (RSA 1998b: s.43-48) that existing lawful water uses are ultimately challenged, but this is constrained by the spirit of the orthodox economic approach, namely residual (and sacrosanct) property relations under the riparian system. The point was to avoid challenge to the NWA on the grounds of the constitution's protection of private property. However, as a result, payment of compensation can be claimed where 'severe prejudice to the economic viability of an undertaking' has resulted in 'financial loss suffered in consequence' of a lesser water use being authorised or a substantial reduction in water use imposed through the compulsory licensing process (RSA 1998b: s.22.6). The budget for the Department of Water Affairs and Forestry does not, however, contain provision for major compensation, and indeed the water services budget came under fierce attack—at one point suffering mid-year cuts of 67%—from the Department of State Expenditure during the mid-1998 period of foreign financial turmoil, which in turn catalysed intensified fiscal discipline.

Though written in apparently more plain and accessible language than the NEMA, ultimately the fulfilment of the rights guaranteed in the NWA are dependent on the say-so of a water tribunal (established under the NWA) and the courts. Again, given South Africa's untransformed civil and criminal justice system, serious concern arises as to the extent to which the NWA will deliver meaningful social and environmental justice. Given South Africa's extraordinary maldistribution of water resources, the NWA's light treatment of redistribution and its somewhat fickle provisions for implementation together raise serious concerns over whether any progress towards 'equity', repeated so often in the NWA, will occur in reality.

Conclusion

The world has witnessed, since the early 1970s, three broad discourses emerging around environmental management. The area between these tends to be grey, and partisans often move fitfully—often largely rhetorically—between the camps. But challenges in South African environmental and water management provide a sense of how these discourses play themselves out, in a country characterised both by a dramatic political power shift and by residual economic domination by corporate interests. It is evident from this review that, notwithstanding stated sentiments consistent with sustainable development and even environmental justice discourses, the hegemonic perspective favours the privileges and prejudices of élites and of those companies that still wish society to take the overall burden of externalised environmental costs. It is in this sense that both the generation of socio-ecological inequality and the failure of South Africa to achieve even a modicum of ecological modernisation, can be traced not just to existing power relations but deeper, to economic interests.

This is all widely understood, and does not go unchallenged. One expression of the implications of uneven political power relations for moral discourses about environmental management was provided by Albie Sachs (1990: 139), who in 1995 was named a Constitutional Court Judge:

> People who have washing machines have no right to condemn others who dirty streams with their laundry. Those who summon up energy with the click of a switch should hesitate before denouncing persons who denude forests in search of firewood. It is undeniably distasteful to spend huge sums on saving the white rhino when millions of black children are starving.

Notwithstanding South Africa's rights-based rhetoric and various attempts to tinker with environmental management problems through technical, market-oriented solutions, the imperatives of ecological exploitation and the impossibility of more fundamental reversals of environmental degradation are obvious. In contrast, what is required in environmental management is to start with the very ingredient missing from virtually all post-apartheid government initiatives: popular mobilisation. In this sense, virtually all issues associated with the survival of society's oppressed communities are environmental management problems which can only be understood and tackled through an increasing convergence of green, brown, feminist, racial/ethnic justice, and class politics ('militant particularisms', as David Harvey describes them). That kind of serious environmentalism, Harvey (1996: 400-401) insists, must

> deal in the material and institutional issues of how to organise production and distribution in general, how to confront the realities of global power politics and how to displace the hegemonic powers of capitalism not simply with dispersed, autonomous, localised, and essentially communitarian solutions (apologists for which can be found at both the right and the left ends of the

> political spectrum), but with a rather more complex politics that recognises how environmental and social justice must be sought by a rational ordering of activities at different scales. The reinsertion of 'rational ordering' indicates that such a movement will have no option, as it broadens out from its militant particularist base, but to reclaim for itself a non-co-opted and non-perverted version of the theses of ecological modernisation. On the one hand that means subsuming the highly geographically differentiated desire for cultural autonomy and dispersion, for the proliferation of tradition and difference within a more global politics, but on the other hand making the quest for environmental and social justice central rather than peripheral concerns.
>
> For that to happen, the environmental justice movement has to radicalise the ecological modernisation discourse.

As economic orthodoxy continues to prevail in so many areas of South African environmental management, and as ecological modernisation discourses, policies and legislation fall far short of resolving environmental crises, it is to more radical confrontations with powerful forces that South Africa's environmental justice movements will be inexorably drawn.

Bibliography

Abubakar, S., and P. Sutton (1988) 'Indonesia: Time to Talk in Terms of Millions', *Pulp and Paper International* 30.1 (January 1988): 40-44.
Advance Agro (1994) *Fact Sheet* (Bangkok: Advance Agro, April 1994).
Al-Akhbar (1997) '*Al-Akhbar* investigates burying wastes in the western Alexandrian Desert', *Al-Akhbar*, 28 March 1997: 1.
Al-Baradei, L. (1998) 'Management of Foreign Aid Directed to the Field of Environment in Egypt, 1985–1995' (PhD dissertation, Faculty of Economics and Political Science, Cairo University).
Alcoa (1994) 'Adopting a New Approach to Water Management', *Alcoa and the Environment* (Corporate Newsletter; Pittsburgh, PA: Aluminum Company of America).
Alcoa (1995a) *Alcoa Environmental Management Systems Resource Document* (Pittsburgh, PA: Aluminum Company of America).
Alcoa (1995b) *Alcoa International Environmental Audit Protocol: Air* (Pittsburgh, PA: Aluminum Company of America).
Alcoa (1995c) *Position on Key Environmental Issues* (Pittsburgh, PA: Aluminum Company of America).
Alcoa (1996) *First Things First: 1995 Alcoa Environment, Health and Safety Annual Report* (Pittsburgh, PA: Aluminum Company of America).
Alcoa (1997a) *Alcoa Update 1996 Annual Report* (Pittsburgh, PA: Aluminum Company of America).
Alcoa (1997b) *1996 Alcoa Environment, Health and Safety Annual Report* (Pittsburgh, PA: Aluminum Company of America).
Alcoa-Köfém (1996a) *Company Procedures and Practices of Environmental Protection* (Székesfehérvár, Hungary: Alcoa-Köfém).
Alcoa-Köfém (1996b) *Storm Water System* (Székesfehérvár, Hungary: Alcoa-Köfém).
Alexander, W. (1994) 'Exceptional Kerala: Efficiency of Use of Resources and Life Quality in a Non-Affluent State', *Gaia* 3.4: 211-26.
AMCHAM (1998) *Doing Business in Costa Rica* (San José, Costa Rica: The Costa Rican–American Chamber of Commerce; *http://www.businesscostarica.com/*).
American Chamber of Commerce in Egypt (1997) *Privatization in Egypt: An Update* (Cairo: American Chamber of Commerce in Egypt).
Amin, S. (1993) 'Can environmental problems be subject to economic calculations?', *Monthly Review* 43 (December 1993): 16-32.
ANC (African National Congress) (1994) *The Reconstruction and Development Programme, Johannesburg* (Johannesburg: ANC).
Andorno, L., (1997) *La Protección del Medio Ambiente en el Ambito del Mercosur* (Buenos Aires: Derecho Ambiental).
Angulo, L., and J. Chelela (1994) *Balancing Societal Goals and Oil Development: The Caño Limon, Colombia Experience* (Proceedings of the 14th World Petroleum Congress; New York: John Wiley).
API (American Paper Institute) (1986) *How Paper Came to America* (New York: American Paper Institute).
API (American Paper Institute) (1987) *Paper and Paper Manufacture* (New York: American Paper Institute).
APKI (Indonesian Pulp and Paper Association) (1993) *Indonesian Paper Trade Directory 1993 (With ASEAN Supplement)* (Jakarta: APKI).
Aquino, P. (1998) 'Privatización Impulsa la Inversión Ambiental', *Informativo Mensual de la Sociedad Nacional de Minería, Petróleo y Energía* 7.7: 30.
Arthur D. Little (1996) *Environmental Regulation of the Petroleum Industry in South America* (Cambridge, MA: Arthur D. Little Inc.).

Ashton, C. (1996) 'Values drive leadership: Environmental Leadership and Accountability', *Environmental Excellence*, June 1996: 3-6.
Ausubel, J. (1994) 'Directions for Environmental Technologies', *Technology in Society* 16.2: 139-54.
Bandyopadhyay, D. (1997) 'People's Participation in Planning: Kerala Experiment', *Economic and Political Weekly* 32.39: 2450-54.
BAPPENAS (Badan Perencanaan Pembangunan Nasional) (1992) 'Water Resources for Sustainable Use in Indonesia', *International Seminar Proceedings*, Bogor, Indonesia, 29 October–1 November 1992.
Barkin, D. (1994) 'Las organizaciones no gubernamentales ambientalistas en México', in A. Glender and V. Lichtinger (eds.), *La diplomacia ambiental: México y la Conferencia de las Naciones Unidas sobre Medio Ambiente y Desarrollo* (Mexico: Fondo de Cultura Económica): 342-62.
Barkin, D. (1998) *Wealth, Poverty, and Sustainable Development* (Mexico: Editorial Jus and Centro de Ecología y Desarrollo).
Barkin, D., and C. Pailles (1998) 'Water as an Instrument for Sustainable Regional Development', *Arid Lands Newsletter* 44 (*http://ag.arizona.edu/OALS/OALN/ALN/aln44/barkinfinal.html*)
Barkin, D., and M.A. Garcia (1999) 'The Social Construction of Deforestation in Mexico: A Case Study of the 1998 Fires in the Chimalapas Rainforest', *http://www.wrm.org.uy/english/u_causes/regional/l_america/Chimalapas.html*.
Baxter International (1997) *1996 Environment, Health, and Safety Report* (Deerfield, IL: Baxter International).
Beck, N. (1998) *The Next Century: Why Canada Wins* (Toronto: HarperCollins).
Berdyaev, N. (1916) *The Meaning of Creativity* (Moscow); English translation: *The Meaning of Creative Art* (London/New York: Victor Gollancz, 1955).
Berry, M.A., and D.A. Rondinelli (1998) 'Proactive Environment Management: A New Industrial Revolution', *Academy of Management Executive* 12.2: 38-50.
Berry, W. (1986) *The Unsettling of America* (San Francisco: Sierra Club Publications).
Bezlepkin, A. (1998) 'A logger can be put in jail' ('Lesoruba mozhno zasudit'), *Noviye Izvestiya*, 7 March 1998.
Bond, G.G. (1996) 'Global Product Stewardship: A Challenge for the Multinational Corporation', *Environmental Management Today* 7: 26-27.
Bond, P. (1999) *Cities of Gold, Townships of Coal: Essays on South Africa's New Urban Crisis* (Trenton, NJ: Africa World Press).
Bond, P., G. Dor and G. Ruiters (1999) 'Transformation in Infrastructure Policy, from Apartheid to Democracy: Mandates for Change, Continuities in Ideology, Frictions in Delivery', in M. Khosa and Y. Muthien (eds.), *Infrastructure for Reconstruction in South Africa* (Pretoria: Human Sciences Research Council; London: Asgate Press).
Bragd, A., G. Bridge, F. Hond and P. Jose (1998) 'Beyond Greening: New Dialogue and New Approaches for Developing Sustainability', *Business Strategy and the Environment* 7: 179-92.
Broad, R. (1994) 'The Poor and the Environment: Friends or Foes?', *World Development* 22.6: 811-22.
Brown, L., M. Romer and C. Flavin (1998) *Vital Signs: The Environmental Trends that are Shaping our Future* (New York: Worldwatch Institute).
Bush, M.B. (1997) *Ecology of a Changing Planet* (Upper Saddle River, NJ: Prentice–Hall).
Cairncross, F. (1992) *Costing the Earth: The Challenge for Governments, the Opportunities for Business* (Boston, MA: Harvard Business School Press).
Cameron, J. (1993) 'The Precautionary Principle: Core Meaning, Constitutional Framework and Procedures for Implementation', in *Conference on The Precautionary Principle: A New Approach to Environmental Management 20–21 September, Sydney* (Sydney: Institute of Environmental Studies, University of New South Wales).
Cappelle, D. (1996) 'Statement by the RMI Secretary of Health and the Environment to the Second United Nations Conference on Human Settlement', *http://www.un.org/Conferences/habitat/eng~stat/14/mli14.txt*, 14 June 1996.
Carrere, R., and L. Lohmann (1996) *Pulping the South* (London: Zed Books).
Carson, R. (1962) *Silent Spring* (Boston, MA: Houghton Mifflin).
Cavanagh, J., and S. Anderson (1997) *International Financial Flows: The New Trends of the 1990s and Projections for the Future* (Washington, DC: Institute for Policy Studies).
CECODES (1995) *Cambiando el Rumbo* (Bogotá: CECODES).
CECODES (1997) *Cambiando el Rumbo* (Bogotá: CECODES).
Centre for Earth Science Studies (1992) *Project on Panchayat Level Resource Mapping for Decentralised Planning with People's Participation* (First Annual Report; Thiruvananthapuram, India: Centre for Earth Science Studies).

Centre for Science and Environment (1985) *The State of India's Environment 1984–85: The Second Citizens' Report* (New Delhi: Centre for Science and Environment).

CERI (Canadian Energy Research Institute) (1998) *Work Plan, Canada–Colombia, A CERI–CIDA Colombia Project* (Calgary: CERI).

Chance, N.A., and E.N. Andreeva (1995) 'Sustainability Equity and Natural Resource Development in Northwest Siberia and Arctic Alaska', *Human Ecology* 23.2: 217-40.

Cheru, F. (1992) 'Structural Adjustment, Primary Resource Trade and Sustainable Development in Sub-Saharan Africa', *World Development* 20.4: 497-512.

China Accreditation Committee (1998) 'China and ISO 14001', *China ISO 14000 Certification Magazine* 1: 11.

Choucri, N. (1993) 'Multinational Corporations and the Global Environment', in N. Choucri (ed.), *Global Accord: Environmental Challenges and International Responses* (Cambridge, MA: MIT Press).

Chudnovsky, D., G. Lugones and M. Chidiak (1995) *Comerciao Internacional y Medio Ambiente: El Caso Argentino* (Estudio preparado a solicitud de UNCTAD; Buenos Aires: CENIT).

Clarkson, M.B.E. (1995) 'A Stakeholder Framework for Analyzing and Evaluating Corporate Social Performance', *Academy of Management Review* 20.1: 92-117.

Claus, G., and K. Bolander (1982) 'Environmental Carcinogenesis. The Threshold Principle: A Law of Nature', in G.J. Halasi-kun (ed.), *Pollution and Water Resources* (Columbia University Seminar Series, vol. 15, part 1; New York: Pergamon Press).

Cohen, A.J. (1983) 'The Economic Determination of Technological Change: A Theoretical Framework and a Case Study of the US Pulp and Paper Industry' (PhD thesis; Palo Alto, CA: Stanford University, Dept of Economics).

Cohen, M.A., S.A. Fenn and J.S. Naimon (1995) *Environmental and Financial Performance: Are they Related?* (Washington, DC: Investor Responsibility Research Center).

Cole, M.A., A.J. Rayner and J.M. Bates (1997a) 'The Environmental Kuznets Curve: An Empirical Analysis', *Environment and Development Economics* 2.4: 401-16.

Cole, M.A., A.J. Rayner and J.M. Bates (1997b) 'The Environmental Impact of the Uruguay Round' (Research Paper No. 97/20; Nottingham, UK: Centre for Research in Economic Development and International Trade [CREDIT], University of Nottingham).

Cole, M.A., A.J. Rayner and J.M. Bates (1998) 'Trade Liberalisation and the Environment: The Case of the Uruguay Round', *The World Economy* 21.3: 337-47.

Collier, G. (1994) *Basta! Land and the Zapatista Rebellion in Chiapas* (Oakland, CA: Food First).

Connell, J., and M. Maata (1992) *Environmental Planning, Climate Change and Potential Sea Level Rise: Report on a Mission to the Republic of the Marshall Islands* (Apia, Western Samoa: South Pacific Regional Environmental Programme).

Cooper, G. (1997) 'No glamour for Disney's sweatshop toilers', *The Independent*, 10 October 1997: 3.

Costanza, R. (1992) 'Toward an Operational Definition of Ecosystem Health', in R. Costanza, B.D. Haskell and B.G. Norton (eds.), *Ecosystem Health: New Goals for Environmental Management* (Washington, DC: Island Press): 239-56.

Costanza, R., and B. Patten (1995) 'Defining and Predicting Sustainability', *Ecological Economics* 15: 193-96.

Costanza, R., and H.E. Daly (1992) 'Natural Capital and Sustainable Development', *Conservation Biology* 6: 37-46.

Costanza, R., and L. Cornwell (1992) 'The 4P Approach to Dealing with Scientific Uncertainty', *Environment* 34.9 (November 1992): 12-42.

Costanza, R., *et al.* (1995) 'Sustainable Trade: A New Paradigm for World Welfare. Environment', *Environment* 37.5: 17-20.

Daly, H., and J. Cobb (1994) *For the Common Good: Redirecting the Economy toward Community the Environment and Sustainable Development* (Boston, MA: Beacon Press).

Daly, H.E. (1977) *Steady-State Economics: The Economics of Biophysical Equilibrium and Moral Growth* (San Francisco: Freeman).

Daly, H.E. (1990) 'Sustainable Growth: An Impossibility Theorem', *Development* 3.4: 45-47.

Daly, H.E. (1991) *Steady-State Economics: Second Edition with New Essays* (Washington, DC: Island Press).

Daly, H.E. (1992) 'Allocation, Distribution and Scale: Towards an Economics that is Efficient, Just and Sustainable', *Ecological Economics* 6.3: 185-93.

Daly, H.E. (1993) 'The Perils of Free Trade', *Scientific American* 269.5: 24-29.

Davy, A. (1997) 'Environmental Management Systems: ISO 14000 Issues for Developing Countries', in C. Sheldon (ed.), *ISO 14000 and Beyond: Environmental Management Systems in the Real World* (Sheffield, UK: Greenleaf Publishing).

DCD (Department of Constitutional Development) (1997) *Municipal Infrastructure Investment Framework* (Pretoria: Department of Constitutional Development).
de Mello Lemos, M.C. (1998) 'The Politics of Pollution Control in Brazil: State Actors and Social Movements Cleaning up Cubatao', *World Development* 26.1: 75-87.
de Soto, H. (1989) *The Other Path: The Invisible Revolution in the Third World* (London: I.B. Travis).
Dow Chemical Corporation (1997) *1996 Environment, Health and Safety Report* (Midland, MI: Dow Chemical).
Drummond, I., and T.K. Marsden (1995) 'Regulating Sustainable Development', *Global Environmental Change* 5.1: 51-63.
ECAFE (Economic Commission on Asian and the Far East) and FAO (Food and Agriculture Organisation) (1962) *Pulp and Paper Development in Asia and the Far East* (ECAFE and FAO conference proceedings, Tokyo, 17–31 October 1960; Bangkok: United Nations).
ECLAC (Economic Commission for Latin America and the Caribbean) (1997) 'Barreras Estadounidenses al Comercio con América Latina y El Caribe', *http://www.eclac.cl/espanol/noticias/comunicados/barreras.htm*, 28 October 1998.
Economist (1992) *The Economist*, 8 February 1992.
EEAA and EU Delegation (1998) *A Strategic Plan for St Katherine Protectorate* (unpublished document; Cairo).
Ehrenfeld, J.R., and J. Howard (1996) 'Setting Environmental Goals: The View from Industry', in National Research Council, *Linking Science and Technology to Society's Environmental Goals* (Washington, DC: National Academy of Sciences Press): 281-325.
Ekins, P. (1993) 'Making Development Sustainable', in W. Sachs (ed.), *Global Ecology: A New Arena of Political Conflict* (London: Zed Books).
EM (1999) 'Europe's recycling laws costing packagers $10 billion a year', *EM: Air & Waste Management Association's Magazine for Environmental Managers*, January 1999: 18.
Environmental News Network (1998) 'El Niño spurs rise in global average sea level', *http://www.un.org/Conferences/habitat/eng~stat/14/mli14.txt*, 9 December 1998.
EPA (US Environmental Protection Agency) (1990) *Environmental Investments: The Cost of a Clean Environment* (Report of the Administrator of the Environmental Protection Agency to the Congress of the United States; Washington, DC: EPA, November 1990).
EPA (US Environmental Protection Agency) (1995) *EPA Office of Compliance Sector Notebook Project: Profile of the Nonferrous Metals Industry* (Washington, DC: EPA).
EPE Infoservice (1997) *EPE Newsletter*, 1997.
Epstein, M. (1995) *Management Accounting Guideline 37, Implementing Corporate Environmental Strategies* (Hamilton, ON, Canada: The Society of Management Accountants of Canada).
EPW Research Foundation (1994) 'Social Indicators of Development. II. Inter-State Disparities', *Economic and Political Weekly* 29 (21 May 1994): 1300-308.
ESCAP (Economic and Social Commission for Asia and the Pacific) and United Nations Center on Transnational Corporations (1988) *Transnational Corporations and Environmental Management in Selected Asian and Pacific Countries* (New York: United Nations).
Eskeland, G., and E. Jimenez (1991) 'Policy Instruments for Pollution Control in Developing Countries', in *SPES: Seminar on Economy and Ecology in Sustainable Development*, Society for Economic and Political Studies, Jakarta, 6–7 May 1991.
Evans, P. (ed.) (1997) *State–Society Synergy: Government and Social Capital in Development* (Berkeley, CA: University of California Press).
Ezquerra, E.R. (1994) *Empresas lideres en desarrollo, aplicación y difusión de tecnologias ambientalmente racionales en América Latina: El caso de Maestranza Iquique SA-Hetland Process y empresas pesqueras asociadas a Corpesca, Chile* (Documento CEPAL, LC/R.1152/Rev.3, 18 de marzo de 1994).
Fairbanks, M., and S. Lindsay (1997) *Plowing the Sea: Nurturing the Hidden Sources of Growth in the Developing World* (Boston, MA: Harvard Business School Press).
Fankhauser, S. (1995) *Valuing Climate Change: The Economics of the Greenhouse* (London: Earthscan).
Farrell, A. and Hart, M. (1998) 'What does sustainability really mean? The Search for Useful Indicators', *Environment* 40.9: 5-9, 26-31.
Fedyanin (1998) 'Russia : Champion of Corruption', *Novaya Gazeta* 40.512 (13 October 1998).
FESCOL (1997a) *La Gestión Ambiental Empresarial en Manizales: Un Diagnóstico Preliminar* (Manizales, Colombia: FESCOL).
FESCOL (1997b) *La Gestión Ambiental Empresarial en Pereira: Un Diagnóstico Preliminar* (Manizales, Colombia: FESCOL).
Feshbach, M., and A. Friendly (1992) *Ecocide in the USSR: Health and Nature under Siege* (New York: Basic Books).

Fiana & Partners (1998) *Kompass Egypt Financial Directory* (Cairo: Al Ahram Commercial Press).

Fiana & Partners (1999) *Kompass Auto: Official Guide to the Egyptian Automotive Sector, 1998–99* (Cairo: Al Ahram Commercial Press).

Fikry, Z. (1997a) 'Unknown waste materials cause panic in Burg al-Arab', *Al-Wafd*, 25 March 1997: 1.

Fikry, Z. (1997b) 'German experts and public sector company behind the disaster of burying wastes in Alexandria', *al-Wafd*, 26 March 1997: 1.

Financial Times (1995) 'Privatising European Energy: Executive Summary', *Joint Implementation: Opportunities for Business Under the UN Framework Convention for Climate Change* (Executive Summary of Deborah Adams; Management Report May 1995; *http://www.ftenergy.com/general/genrsl1.htm*).

Financial Times (1996) 'World Bank chief accuses staff of blocking reforms', *Financial Times*, 29 March 1996.

Fine, B. and Z. Rustomjee (1996) *The Political Economy of South Africa: From Minerals-Energy Complex to Industrialisation* (London: Hirst; Johannesburg: Wits University Press).

Flury, H. (1998) 'Impulsar Proyectos Mineros', *Peru Minero* 6.15: 14-17.

FoEE (Friends of the Earth, Europe) (1996) *Sustainable Europe* (Brussels: FoEE).

Forest News (1998) *Electronic Bulletin of Russian Socio-Ecological Union* 13 (August 1998).

François, J.F., B. McDonald and H. Nordstrom (1995) 'Assessing the Uruguay Round', in W. Martin and L.A. Winters (eds.), *The Uruguay Round and the Developing Economies* (World Bank Discussion Paper No. 307; Washington, DC: World Bank).

Franke, R.W. (1993) *Life is a Little Better: Redistribution as a Development Strategy in Nadur Village, Kerala* (Boulder, CO: Westview Press).

Franke, R.W., and B.H. Chasin (1994) *Kerala: Radical Reform as Development in an Indian State* (Oakland, CA: Institute for Food and Development Policy): 13.

Franke, R.W., and B.H. Chasin (1995) 'Kerala State: A Social Justice Model', *Multinational Monitor* 16.7-8: 25-28.

Franke, R.W., and B.H. Chasin (1997) 'Power to the Malayalee People', *Economic and Political Weekly* 32.48: 3061-69.

Freeman, R.E. (1984) *Strategic Management: A Stakeholder Approach* (Boston, MA: Pitman).

French, H.F. (1997) 'When foreign investors pay for development', *Worldwatch Magazine* 10.3 (May/June 1997): 8-17.

Fuggle, R.F. and M.A. Rabie (eds.) (1992) *Environmental Management in South Africa* (Cape Town: Juta).

Galbraith, J.K. (1992) *The Culture of Contentment* (Harmondsworth, UK: Penguin).

Gallup International Institute (1993) *Health of the Planet* (Princeton, NJ: Gallup).

Garcia, D. (1994), *Reconciliation of Trade and Environmental Policies: The Case of Colombia* (UNCTAD Case Studies; Geneva: UNCTAD).

Garcia, P. (1998) 'Environmental Management in Multinational Oil and Gas Exploration and Production Corporations in Latin America' (Masters Degree Project; Calgary, AB, Canada: Faculty of Environmental Science, University of Calgary).

Ghilarov, A. (1996) 'What does "Biodiversity" mean: Scientific Problem or Convenient Myth?', *TREE* 11.7: 304-306.

Gladwin, T.N., J.J. Kennelly and T.-S. Krause (1995) 'Shifting Paradigms for Sustainable Development: Implications for Management Theory and Research', *Academy of Management Journal* 20.4: 874-907.

Glazyrina, I.P., and V. Glazyrin (1997) 'Pathways to Sustainability in a Transitional Economy: Approach to the Nature Use Regulation in Eastern Siberia', in T. Sellis and D. Georgulis (eds.), 'Urban, Regional, Environmental Planning and Informatics to Planning in an Era of Transition', *Proceedings of Athens International Conference*, National Technical University of Athens, Greece, 22–24 October 1997: 1-6.

Gleckman, H., and R. Krut (1996) 'Neither International nor Standard: The Limits of ISO 14001 as an Instrument of Global Corporate Environmental Management', in C. Sheldon (ed.), *ISO 14001 and Beyond: Environmental Management Systems in the Real World* (Sheffield, UK: Greenleaf Publishing): 45-59.

Glinkina, S. (1998) 'The Ominous Landscape of Russian Corruption', *Transitions*, March 1998.

Goble, P. (1999) 'Where reforms trump resources', RFE/RL *Newsline*, 7 January 1999 (*http://206.241.72.7/newsline/1999/01/070199.html*).

Godard, O. (1998) 'On Markets and the Conditions of a Profitable Use of Economic Instruments for Environmental Policy in Countries in Transition to Market', in J. Becvar and M. Kokine (eds.), *Role of Economic Instruments in Integrating Environmental Policy with Sectoral Policies* (Proceedings of the Workshop, Prunovice, Czech Republic, 8–10 October 1997; New York/Geneva: Economic Commission for Europe/United Nations): 11-21.

Gofman, K.G., and E.V. Ryumina (1994) 'Credit Relationship between Society and Nature', *Economics and Mathematical Methods* 30: 17-30.

Goodland, R. (1997) 'Biophysical and Objective Environmental Sustainability', in A.K. Dragun and K.M. Jakobsson (eds.), *Sustainability and Global Environmental Policy* (Cheltenham, UK: Edward Elgar): 63-96.

Government of Costa Rica (1998) *Uniform Reporting Format: National Programme on Activities Implemented Jointly u nder the Pilot Phase* (San José, Costa Rica: Costa Rican Office on Joint Implementation [OCIC]; *http://www.unfccc.de/fccc/ccinfo/aijprog/aij_pcri.htm*).

Government of Kerala (1997) *Economic Survey* (Thiruvananthapuram, India: Kerala State Planning Board).

Government of Norway (1997) *Uniform Reporting Format: National Programme on Activities Implemented Jointly under the Pilot Phase* (Oslo: Ministry of Foreign Affairs, Department of Natural Resources and Environmental Affairs; *http://www.unfccc.de/fccc/ccinfo/aijprog/aij_pnor.htm*).

Government of Poland (1997) *Uniform Reporting Format: National Programme on Activities Implemented Jointly under the Pilot Phase* (Warsaw: National Fund for Environmental Protection and Water Management, JI-Secretariat, International Department [NFOSiGW]; *http://www.unfccc.de/fccc/ccinfo/aijprog/aij_ppol.htm*).

Government of Sweden (1998) *Uniform Reporting Format: National Programme on Activities Implemented Jointly Under the Pilot Phase* (Stockholm: The Swedish National Board for Industrial and Technical Development on Activities Implemented Jointly, Environmentally Adapted Energy System in the Baltic Region and Eastern Europe [NUTEK]; *http://www.unfccc.de/fccc/ccinfo/aijprog/aij_pswe.htm*).

Government of the United States (1997) *Uniform Reporting Format: National Programme on Activities Implemented Jointly Under the Pilot Phase* (Washington, DC: US Initiative on Joint Implementation; *http://www.unfccc.de/fccc/ccinfo/aijprog/aij_pusa.htm*).

Greenpeace Mediterranean Quarterly (1997) *Greenpeace Mediterranean Quarterly Newsletter* 2 (Malta: Greenpeace Mediterranean Office).

Grumbine, E. (1990) 'Protecting Biological Diversity through the Greater Ecosystem Concept', *Natural Areas* 10: 114-20.

Gumbleton, K., and A. Bhargava (1995) *The North American Development Bank and the Border Environmental Cooperation Commission: Current Progress and Future Prospects* (Claremont, VT: The Tomas Rivera Center).

Gumilev, L.N. (1990) *Ethnogenesis and the Biosphere* (Moscow: Progress Publishers).

Gweida, N. (1997) 'Report of the Environmental Affairs Authority confirmed safety of the burying procedures and lack of danger to public health', *al-Ahram*, 4 April 1997.

Haapaniemi, P. (1996) 'Alcoa builds a superhighway', *Journal of Business Strategy* 17.1: 24-25.

Hadlock, C.R. (1994) 'Multinational Corporations and the Transfer of Environmental Technology to Developing Countries', *Journal of International Environmental Affairs* 6.2: 149-74.

Hagg, C. (1984) 'The OECD Guidelines for Multinational Enterprises: A Critical Analysis', *Journal of Business Ethics* 3: 71-76.

Hall, S., and C. Williams (1993) *Block 16: Conoco's 'Green' Oil Strategy (A)* (Boston, MA: Harvard Business School).

Hallowes, D. (1997) *Briefings on Six Environmental Sectors* (Pietermaritzburg, South Africa: Environmental Justice Networking Forum).

Hanafi, Pratomo (1994) 'Impact of New Government Regulations on Future Existence of Pulp Mill', *Proceedings of 48th Appita Annual General Conference, Melbourne, Australia, 1–6 May 1994* (Carlton, Victoria: Australia–New Zealand Pulp and Paper Industry Technical Association).

Hansen-Kuhn, K. (1993) 'Sapping the Economy: Structural Adjustment in Costa Rica', *The Ecologist* 23.5 (September/October 1993): 179-84.

Harding, E. (1992) *Review of Environmental Law: Republic of the Marshall Islands (RETA 5403)* ('Strengthening Environment Management Capabilities in Pacific Island Developing Countries' series; Sydney: South Pacific Regional Environment Programme).

Harrison, A. (1994) 'The Role of Multinationals in Economic Development: The Benefits of FDI', *The Colombia Journal of World Business* 26 (Winter 1994): 6-11.

Hart, K. (1998) *Sung for Anidreb: A Brief History of the Marshall Islands* (Majuro, RMI: Marshall Islands Publishing).

Hart, S.L., and G. Ahuja (1996) 'Does it pay to be green? An Empirical Examination of the Relationship between Emission Reduction and Firm Performance', *Business Strategy and the Environment* 5: 30-37.

Harvey, D. (1996) *Justice, Nature and the Geography of Difference* (Oxford: Basil Blackwell).
Heller, P. (1995) 'From Class Struggle to Class Compromise: Redistribution and Growth in a South Indian State', *Journal of Development Studies* 31.5: 645-72.
Heller, P. (1996) 'Social Capital as a Product of Class Mobilization and State Intervention: Industrial Workers in Kerala, India', *World Development* 24.6: 1055-71.
Heller, T.C. (1997) 'Additionality, Transactional Barriers and the Political Economy of Climate Change', a working paper based on a paper presented at the *Conference on International Environmental Agreements and Climate Change, Venice, 6–7 May 1997* (organised by the Fondazione Eni Enrico Mattei and the Stanford Energy Modeling Forum).
Hellman, J.S. (1998) 'Winners Take All: The Politics of Partial Reform in PostCommunist Transitions', *World Politics* 50.2 (January 1998): 203-34.
Hemenway, C.G. (1996) 'Ford catches ISO 14000 fever', *Environmental Management Today* 7: 1, 12, 14.
Henderson, H. (1990) 'From Economism to Systems Theory and New Indicators of Development', *Technological Forecasting and Social Change* 37: 213-33.
Hettige, H., P. Martin, M. Singh and D. Wheeler (1994) *The Industrial Pollution Projection System* (Washington, DC: World Bank).
Hill, J., D. Fedrigo and L. Marshall (1997) *Banking on the Future* (London: Green Alliance).
Holdgate, M. (1996) *From Care to Action: Making a Sustainable World* (Washington, DC: Taylor & Francis).
Holling, C.S. (1986) 'The Resilience of Terrestrial Ecosystems: Local Surprise and Global Change', in C.C. William and R.E. Munn (eds.), *Sustainable Development of the Biosphere* (New York: Cambridge University Press for the International Institute for Applied Systems Analysis): 292-320.
Holling, C.S. (1992) 'Cross-Scale Morphology, Geometry and Dynamics of Ecosystems', *Ecological Monographs* 62.4: 447-502.
Hopkins, N.S., S.R. Mehanna and S. el-Haggar (1998) *Social Response to Environmental Change and Pollution in Egypt Cairo* (Cairo: Social Research Center, American University in Cairo).
Hurst, P. (1990) *Rainforest Politics: Ecological Destruction in South-East Asia* (London: Zed Books).
IBTCI (International Business and Technical Consultants, Inc.) (1998) *Quarterly Review for 1 July to 30 September 1998 for the USAID Privatization Project* (Cairo: IBTCI).
ICC (International Chamber of Commerce) (1994) *The Business Charter for Sustainable Development* (Paris: ICC).
ICEL (Indonesian Centre for Environmental Law) (1994) *Report on Analysis of Policies, Regulations, Programs, and Institutions that Affect Industrial Pollution Control* (Jakarta: ASEAN Environmental Improvement Project).
IIED (International Institute for Environmental Development) (1996) *Towards a Sustainable Paper Cycle* (London: IIED).
IIF (Institute of International Finance) (1997) *Capital Flows to Emerging Market Economies* (Washington, DC: IIF, January 1997).
Instituto de Desarrollo Ademando (1994) *Medio Ambiente y Competitividad: Case Sector Expeortador Clinleno* (UNCTAD Case Studies; Geneva: UNCTAD).
Instituto de Ingenieros de Minas del Peru (1998) 'Antamina: Un Megaproyecto en su Totalidad', *Mineria* 46.253: 18-21.
Inter-American Development Bank, Organisation of American States, United Nations Economic Commission for Latin America and the Caribbean (1999) 'Free Trade Area of the Americas, Official Web Page', *http://www.ftaa-alca.org/EnglishVersion/alca_e.htm*, 16 February 1999.
Isaac, T.M.T., R.W. Franke and M.P. Parameswaran (1997) 'From Anti-Feudalism to Sustainable Development: The People's Science Movement', *Bulletin of Concerned Asian Scholars* 29.3: 34-44.
Jackson, S.L. (1997) *The ISO 14001 Implementation Guide: Creating an Integrated Management System* (New York: John Wiley).
Jackson, T. (1997) 'Facing up to a Challenging Opposition', *Financial Times*, 31 October 1997: 16.
Jakarta Post (1996a) 'RI's bureaucracy the worst in ASEAN: Survey', *Jakarta Post*, 12 September 1996.
Jakarta Post (1996b) 'World Bank vows to pull out of tainted projects', *Jakarta Post*, 5 October 1996.
Jakarta Post (1996c) 'Peat land project facing irrigation problems', *Jakarta Post*, 5 October 1996.
Jakarta Post (1996d) 'Sudjana denies allegations of bank transfer fraud', *Jakarta Post*, 12 December 1996.
Jeffrey, R. (1992) *Politics, Women and Well-Being: How Kerala Became a Model* (London: Macmillan).
Joint Implementation Network (1995) 'Netherlands' Policy Statement on JI', *JiQ* 2.3 (September 1995; *http://northsea.nl/jiq/nether.htm*).
Joint Implementation Network (1996) 'USIJI Second Round Approval', *JiQ* 2.1 (April 1996; *http://northsea.nl/jiq/USA.htm*).

Joint Implementation Network (1997) 'Netherlands' JI Registration and Certification Procedure Approved', *JiQ* 3.2 (July 1997; *http://northsea.nl/jiq/nether.htm*).
Jones, D.R. (1996) 'A Gold Medal Salute to the Aluminum Company of America', *Environmental Management Today*, May/June 1996: 5.
Kaimowitz, D., G. Thiele and P. Pacheco (1999) 'The Effect of Structural Adjustment on Deforestation and Forest Degradation in Lowland Bolivia', *World Development* 27.3 (March 1999): 505-20.
Kannan, K.P. (1995) 'Public Intervention and Poverty Alleviation: A Study of the Declining Incidence of Rural Poverty in Kerala, India', *Development and Change* 26.4: 701-27.
Kannan, K.P., K.R. Thankappan, V.R. Kutty and K.P. Aravindan (1991) *Health and Development of Rural Kerala* (Trivandrum, India: Kerala Sastra Sahitya Parishhad).
Kerala State Planning Board (1996) *People's Campaign for the Ninth Plan: An Approach Paper* (Thiruvananthapuram, India: Kerala State Planning Board, People's Campaign Cell).
Kerr, M.G. (1995) 'Looking at Environmental Management through the Lens of Quality' (Press Release; Mississauga, Canada: Nortel).
Kienle, E. (1998) 'More than a Response to Islamism: The Political Deliberalization of Egypt in the 1990s', *Middle East Journal* 42.2: 219-35.
Kimerling, J. (1996) 'Oil, Lawless and Indigenous Struggles in Ecuador's Oriente', in H. Collison (ed.), *Green Guerrillas: Environmental Conflicts and Initiatives in Latin America and the Caribbean* (Nottingham, UK: Russell Press).
Kirkland, L., and D. Thompson (1997) 'Forces Driving Environmental Management in Oil and Gas Companies', *Environmental Geosciences* 4.4: 171-76.
Kirkland, L., and D. Thompson (1999) 'Challenges in Designing, Implementing and Operating an Environmental Management System', *Business Strategy and the Environment* 8: 128-43.
Kolk, A. (1996) *Forests in International Environmental Politics. International Organisations, NGOs and the Brazilian Amazon* (Utrecht, Netherlands: International Books).
Kolk, A. (1998) 'From Conflict to Cooperation: International Policies to Protect the Brazilian Amazon', *World Development* 26.8: 1481-93.
Kolk, A. (2000) *The Economics of Environmental Management* (Harlow, UK: Financial Times/Prentice–Hall).
Kolk, A., and E. van der Weij (1998) 'Financing Environmental Policy in East Central Europe', *Environmental Politics* 7.1: 53-68.
Konnikov, E.G., M.I. Kuzmin, V.A. Lbov, G.L. Mitrofanov and K.Sh. Shagzhiev (1996) 'Mineral Resources of the Lake Baikal Region and Sustainable Development', in V.A. Koptyug and M. Uppenbrink (eds.), *Sustainable Development of the Lake Baikal Region* (NATO ASI Series, Partnership Sub-Series 2, Environment, vol. 6; Heidelberg: Springer Verlag): 33-58.
Korten, D.C. (1995) *When Corporations Rule the World* (London: Earthscan).
Koslowski, J., and G. Hill (1993) *Towards Planning for Sustainable Development: A Guide for the Ultimate Environmental Threshold (UET) Method* (Brookfield, VT: Ashgate Publishing).
Kothandapani, D. (1994) 'Phoenix aims to rise after a year of crises', *Bangkok Post*, 18 April 1994.
Kroesa, R. (1991) *Sustainable Paper Production: Specific Actions for Environmental Compatibility* (Vancouver: Greenpeace International, May 1991).
Kumar, R. (1995) *Industrial Policies and Industrial Competitiveness: Are they compatible?* (Vienna: UNIDO Global Forum).
Laabs, J.J. (1996) 'Alcoa unit president forced to resign after failing to report safety violations', *Personnel Journal* 75.9: 12.
Lackey, R. (1998) 'The Seven Pillars of Ecosystem Management', *Landscape and Urban Planning* 40: 21-30.
Le Prestre, P. (1989) *The World Bank and the Environmental Challenge* (London/Toronto: Associated University Press).
Lemaire, D. (1996) *Lessons from Canadian Corporations Operating in Emerging Markets* (Ottawa: The Conference Board of Canada).
Leonard, H.J. (1982) 'Environmental Regulations, Multinational Corporations and Industrial Development in the 1980s', *Habitat International* 6.3: 323-41.
Leonard, H. J. (1984) *Are environmental regulations driving United States industry overseas? An Issue Report* (Washington, DC: The Conservation Foundation).
Leonard, H.J., and C.J. Duerksen (1980) 'Environmental Regulations and the Location of Industry: An International Perspective', *Columbia Journal of World Business* 15.2: 52-68.
Leopold, A. (1987) *Sand County Almanac* (New York: Oxford University Press).
Letsie, D., and P. Bond (1999) 'The Impact of Large-Scale Infrastructure Projects on Basic Needs: The Case of the Lesotho Highlands Water Project', in M. Khosa and Y. Muthien (eds.), *Infrastructure for Reconstruction in South Africa* (Pretoria: Human Sciences Research Council; London: Asgate Press).

Levin, M.I., and M.L. Tsirik (1998) 'Corruption as an Object of Mathematical Modelling', *Economics and Mathematical Models, 'Nauka'* 34.3: 40-62.

Levy, N.M. (1996) *Micronesia Handbook* (Chico, CA: Moon Publications, 4th edn).

Luken, R.A., and A.C. Freij (1996) 'Cleaner Industrial Production in Developing Countries and Potential Cost Savings for Developing Countries', in Organisation for Economic Co-operation and Development (OECD), *The Environment Industry: The Washington Meeting* (Paris: OECD).

Lukey, P. (1995) *Health before Profits* (Johannesburg: Environmental Justice Networking Forum and Friedrich Ebert Stiftung).

Lutter, S. (1991) *Precautionary Principle versus Assimilative Capacity Approach: A Review from the Interface between Marine Science and Policy Making* (ICES/CM/1991/E:11; Copenhagen: Marine Environmental Quality Committee, International Council for the Exploration of the Sea).

MacNeill, J., P. Winsemius and T. Yakushiji (1991) *Beyond Interdependence. The Meshing of the World's Economy and the Earth's Ecology* (New York/Oxford, UK: Oxford University Press for the Trilateral Commission).

Mail and Guardian (1996) *Mail and Guardian*, 20 November 1996.

Manas, B. (1995) 'A Bit of ISO Irony in Sprawling Saõ Paulo (Alcoa Aluminio, SA)', *American Metal Market* 103: 20A.

Marchak, M. Patricia (1995) *Logging the Globe* (Montreal: McGill–Queens University Press).

Marland, G., R.J. Andres and T.A. Boden (1994) 'Global, Regional and National CO_2 Emissions', in T.A. Boden, D.P. Kaiser, R.J. Sepanski and F.W. Stoss (eds.), *Trends '93: A Compendium of Data on Global Change* (ORNL/CDIAC-65; Oak Ridge, TN: Carbon Dioxide Information Analysis Centre, Oak Ridge National Laboratory): 505-84.

Maximov, V. (1998) 'No railroad, but the money is gone' ('Dorogi net, a denezhki tyu-tyu'), *Novaya Gazeta* 50.522 (21 December 1998).

May, P., and O. Segura Bonilla (1997) 'The Environmental Effects of Agricultural Trade Liberalisation in Latin America: An Interpretation', *Ecological Economics* 22.1 (July 1997): 5-18.

Mayer, J. H. (1996) 'Trees vs Trees: Indigenous Agroforestry and Industrial Timber Plantations in West Kalimantan' (PhD thesis; Berkeley, CA: University of California, Department of City and Regional Planning).

Mayhew, N. (1997) 'Fading to Grey: The Use and Abuse of Corporate Executives' Representational Power', in R. Welford (ed.), *Hijacking Environmentalism: The Corporate Response to Sustainable Development* (London: Earthscan).

McKibben, B. (1995) *Hope, Human and Wild* (Boston, MA: Little Brown).

McLuhan, M. (1964) *Understanding Media: The Extensions of Man* (New York: Mentor Books).

McLuhan, M., and Q. Fiore (1967) *The Medium is the Message* (New York: Bantam Books).

Mechede, T. (1997) 'Mercury Decontamination of a Chloralkali Plant in Alexandria, Egypt' (unpublished paper; Cairo).

Merriam-Webster, Inc. (1998) *Merriam-Webster's Collegiate Dictionary* (Springfield, MA: Merriam-Webster, 10th edn)

Miller Freeman, Inc. (1991) *International Pulp and Paper Directory, 1992–93* (San Francisco: Miller Freeman, Inc.).

Minerales de Colombia SA (1998) *Mining in Colombia: Gold, Emerald and Other Business* (Santafé de Bogotá, Colombia: Ministerio de Minas y Energía).

Miniska, I. (1997) 'Occupational Health at Alcoa-Köfém', *Alcoa-Köfém Newsletter* 25.5: 5-6.

Ministry of Reconstruction and Development (1995) *Urban Development Strategy* (Pretoria: Ministry of Reconstruction and Development).

Mnatsakanian, R. (1992) *Environmental Legacy of the Former Soviet Republics* (Edinburgh: University of Edinburgh).

Montgomery, D.R., G.E. Grant and K. Sullivan (1995) 'Watershed Analysis as a Framework for Implementing Ecosystem Management', *Water Resources Bulletin* 31.3: 369-86.

Morrison, R.C. (1987) *A Technological History of Papermaking and Related Materials: Notes for Paper Conservators* (Canberra: Canberra College).

Morse, B., and T. Berger (1992) *Sardar Sarovar: Report of the Independent Review* (Ottawa: Resource Futures International).

Myers, J. (1999) 'The Big Squeeze', *Canadian Economic Outlook*, 12 February 1999 (Canadian Business: Special Issue).

Naim, M. (1994) 'The World Bank: Its Role, Governance and Organizational Culture', in Bretton Woods Commission, *Bretton Woods: Looking into the Future* (Background papers; Washington, DC: Bretton Woods Commission): 273-88.

Nation (1994) 'Top rice exporter will build paper plant in Thailand', *The Nation*, 14 April 1994.
National Heritage Institute (1997) *Environmental Degradation and Migration: A US/Mexico Case Study* (San Francisco, CA: National Heritage Institute).
Natural Resources and Environment Programme (1995) *The Monitoring and Control of Industrial Hazardous Waste Management in Thailand* (Bangkok: Thailand Development Research Institute).
Newsline (1998) RFE/RL Newsline 'Lebed, key industrialist tangle' (10 December 1998; *http://206.241.72.7/newsline/1998/12/101298.html*); 'Lebed comes under pressure to cede powers' (*http://206.241.72.7/newsline/1998/12/221298.html*, 22 December 1998).
Norton, B.G. (1992) 'A New Paradigm of Environmental Management', in R. Costanza, B.G. Norton and B.D. Haskell (eds.), *Ecosystem Health* (Washington, DC: Island Press): 23-41.
O'Connor, D. (1994) *Managing the Environment with Rapid Industrialisation: Lessons from the East Asian Experience* (Paris: OECD).
O'Neill, P. (1996) 'To Alcoa Shareholders', in *Alcoa Update 1996 Annual Report* (Pittsburgh, PA: Aluminum Company of America).
O'Neill, P. (1998) 'To Alcoa Shareholders', in *Alcoa 1997 Annual Report* (Pittsburgh, PA: Aluminum Company of America).
O'Riordan, T., and J. Cameron (eds.) (1994) *Interpreting the Precautionary Principle* (London: Earthscan).
OECD (Organisation for Economic Co-operation and Development) (1986) *Expenditures, Costs and Benefits* (Paris: OECD).
OECD (Organisation for Economic Co-operation and Development) (1993) *Environmental Data Compendium 1993* (Paris: OECD).
OECD (Organisation for Economic Co-operation and Development) (1995) *Environmental Data Compendium 1995* (Paris: OECD).
OECD (Organisation for Economic Co-operation and Development) (1998) 'Environmental Financing in Russian Federation', in A. Zamparutti (ed.), *OECD Proceedings, Nizhniy Novgorod Workshop, November 1996* (Paris: OECD).
Office of Environmental Policy and Planning (1997a) *Thailand: Policy and Prospective Plan for Enhancement and Conservation of National Environmental Quality: 1997–2016* (Bangkok: Ministry of Science, Technology and Environment).
Office of Environmental Policy and Planning (1997b) *Thailand State of Environment 1995–1996, Executive Summary* (Bangkok: Ministry of Science, Technology and Environment).
Oka Watershed Council (1992) *Agreement on Joint Use and Protection of Water Resources in the Oka Basin (Soglasheniye o sovmestnom ispolzovanii I okhrane vodnikh resursov basseina r.Oki)* (Draft; Moscow: Oka Watershed Council).
Otero, M., G. Estafanell and E. Trigo (1992) *Conservación de los recursos naturales, medio ambiente y comercio internacional: Una visión desde América Latina y el Caribe* (San José, Costa Rica: IICA).
Panayotou, T. (1993) *Green Markets: The Economics of Sustainable Development* (San Francisco: Institute for Contemporary Studies Press): 129-32.
Pappens, R. (1993) 'Sabah's Solutions to a Slow Start', *Pulp and Paper International* 35.6 (June 1993): 32-36.
Parameswaran, M.P. (2000) 'What does the Kerala "model" signify? Towards A Possible "Fourth World"?', in G. Parayil (ed.), *Kerala's Development Experience: Reflections on Sustainability and Replicability* (London/New York: Zed Books).
Parasnis, M., and C. Bunyagidj (1998) *Contribution to the Formulation of National Cleaner Production Policies in Thailand* (Bangkok: Thailand Environment Institute).
Parayil, G., and F. Tong (1998) 'Pasture-Led to Logging-Led Deforestation in the Brazilian Amazon: The Dynamics of Socio-Environmental Change', *Global Environmental Change* 8.1: 63-79.
Parfenov, V. (1996) 'On the Draft of the Strategy of Sustainable Development in Russia: "Towards a Sustainable Russia" ', *Bulletin of the Center of Russian Environmental Policy* 2.6: 4-6.
Pearce, D. (1993) *Blueprint 3: Measuring Sustainable Development* (London: Earthscan).
Perciasepe, R. (1994) 'EPA's Watershed Approach to Ecosystem Management', *Fisheries* 19.4: 4.
Percy, S. (1997) 'Whither Joint Implementation? Climate progress is possible through Joint Implementation', *Resources for the Future Weathervane*, *http://www.weathervane.rff.org/pointcpoint/pcp2/percy.html*.
Piasecki, B.W. (1995) *Corporate Environmental Strategy: The Avalanche of Change Since Bhopal* (New York: John Wiley).
Pimenta, F.C.P. (1987) 'Multinational Corporations and Industrial Pollution Control in São Paulo, Brazil', in C.S. Pearson (ed.), *Multinational Corporations, Environment and the Third World* (Durham, NC: Duke University Press): 198-220.

PIRC (Pensions Investment Resources Consultancy Ltd) (1997) *The Committee on Corporate Governance: A Response from PIRC Ltd* (London: PIRC).
Pizzorusso, A. (1998) 'Reflections from Philips Electronics, NA: Lessons from Winning the WEC Gold Medal', *Corporate Environmental Strategy* 5.4: 60-64.
Plas, J.M. (1996) *Person-Centered Leadership: An American Approach to Participatory Management* (Thousand Oaks, CA: Sage Publications).
PMTF (Portfolio Management Task Force) (1992) *Effective Implementation: Key to Development Impact* (Washington, DC: World Bank).
Pollitzer, S. (1968) 'Thailand: Progress at Siam Kraft Mill', *Pulp and Paper International* 10.9 (August 1968): 172.
Polterovich, V.M. (1998) 'Factors of Corruption', *Economics and Mathematical Models, 'Nauka'* 34.3: 30-39.
Popper, K. (1992) *The Logic of Scientific Discovery* (London: Routledge).
Porter, M.A. (1990) *The Competitive Advantage of Nations* (New York: Free Press).
PPI (*Pulp and Paper International*) (1970a) 'Canada gives aid in study of Sabah Forest potential', *Pulp and Paper International* 12.9 (August 1970): 22.
PPI (*Pulp and Paper International*) (1970b) 'Integrated mill raises Thailand's output by 400%', *Pulp and Paper International* 12.5 (May 1970): 41-43ff.
PPI (*Pulp and Paper International*) (1980) 'Malaysia: Sabah government revives plans for large complex', *Pulp and Paper International* 22.11 (October 1980): 32.
PPI (*Pulp and Paper International*) (1981) 'Indonesia: Country's first newsprint mill will use bagasse and rice straw', *Pulp and Paper International* 23.13 (December 1981): 38.
PPI (*Pulp and Paper International*) (1986) 'Indonesia: New dissolving pulp mill set to start late 1988', *Pulp and Paper International* 28.5 (May 1986): 29.
PPI (*Pulp and Paper International*) (1991) 'Indonesia: Inti Indorayon joins pulp flood', *Pulp and Paper International* 33.9 (September 1991): 7-8.
PPI (*Pulp and Paper International*) (1992) 'Indonesia: Government promotes pulp and paper', *Pulp and Paper International* 34.7 (July 1992): 81.
Prakash, B.A. (1994) 'Demographic Trends in Kerala', in B.A. Prakash (ed.), *Kerala's Economy: Performance, Problems, Prospects* (New Delhi: Sage Publications): 43-60.
Prism (1994) 'Transnational Corporations and Global Environmental Policy', *Prism*, 1st quarter 1994.
Pryde, P.R. (1991) *Environmental Management in the Soviet Union* (Cambridge: Cambridge University Press).
Przeworski, A. (1986) 'Some Problems in the Study of the Transition to Democracy', in G. O'Donnell, P. Schmitter and L. Whitehead (eds.), *Transitions from Authoritarian Rule* (Baltimore, MD: Johns Hopkins University Press).
Public Citizen and RMALC (1996) *Broken Promises: The Border Betrayed* (Washington, DC: Public Citizen).
Ramachandran, V.K. (1995) 'A Note on Kerala's Development Achievements', *Monthly Review* 47.1: 19-24.
Ratcliffe, J. (1978) 'Social Justice and the Demographic Transition: Lessons from India's Kerala', *International Journal of Health Services* 8: 123-44.
Redclift, M. (1987) *Sustainable Development: Exploring the Contradictions* (London: Methuen).
Redclift, M. (1994) *Sustainable Development: Exploring the Contradictions* (London: Routledge).
Reed, D. (ed.) (1992) *Structural Adjustment and the Environment* (Boulder, CO: Westview Press).
Reeve, D. (1996) 'Indonesia', in A. Miller and M. Quilty (eds.), *Australia in Asia: Communities of Thought* (Melbourne: Oxford University Press).
Republica de Colombia, Ministerio del Medio Ambiente (1995) *Plan Nacional de Desarrollo Ambiental. El Salto Social: Hacia el Desarrollo Humano Sostenible* (Bogotá: Ministerio del Medio Ambiente).
Republica de Colombia, Ministerio del Medio Ambiente (1998) *Programa Hacia 'Una Producción Más Limpia': Avances y Perspectivas 1995–1998* (Bogotá: Ministerio del Medio Ambiente).
Republika (1993) 'What is the Harvard team for?', *Republika*, 20 February 1993.
Responsabilidad Integral (1997) *Un Camino Hacia el Desarrollo Sostenible* (Bogotá: Responsabilidad Integral).
ReThink Paper (1998) 'State-by-State Guide to Ecological Paper Retailers, Printers, And Manufacturers', 17 June 1998 (San Francisco: Earth Island Institute; *http://www.earthisland.org/ei/paper/stateguide.html*).
Reuters News Service (1994) 'Thailand: Phoenix chief responds to Globex ad campaign', 10 June 1994.
Revista do Alumíno (1992) 'Modern Techniques help in the preservation of the Amazon', *Revista do Alumíno* 3 (June 1992): 8-12.

Reznik, B., and V. Golovnin (1997) 'Mafia and the Sea', *Izvestia* 200-202 (21–23 October 1997).
Riad, W. (1997) 'They lied by saying it was nuclear wastes', *al-Ahram*, 6 April 1997: 26.
RMI Online (1998) 'Internet Guide to the Republic of the Marshall Islands', *http://www.rmiembassyus.org*, 1998.
Robins, N., and S. Roberts (1997) *Unlocking Trade Opportunities* (Report by the International Institute for Environment and Development for the UN Department of Policy Co-ordination and Sustainable Development; London: IIED).
Rondinelli, D.A., and G. Vastag (1998) 'Private Investment and Environmental Protection in Central and Eastern Europe: Alcoa-Köfém in Hungary', *The European Management Journal* 16.4: 422-30.
Rondinelli, D.A., and M.A. Berry (1997) 'Industry's Role in Air Quality Improvement: Environmental Management Opportunities for the 21st Century', *Environmental Quality Management* 7: 31-44.
Roome, J. (1995) 'Water Pricing and Management: World Bank Presentation to the SA Water Conservation Conference' (unpublished paper; South Africa, 2 October 1995).
Rosenberg, G.S., G.P. Krasnoshekov, Yu.M. Krilov, V.A. Pavlovskiy, A.S. Pisarev and S.A. Chernikova (1998) *Stable Development: Myths and the Reality* (Tolyatti, Russian Federation: IEVB).
Roylance, F.D. (1997) 'Struggle: US nuclear tests and westernisation have crippled the Marshall Islands, which has contracted the University of Maryland at Baltimore to recommend reforms', *The Baltimore Sun*, 26 October 1997.
RSA (Republic of South Africa) (1996) *The Constitution of the Republic of South Africa* (Cape Town: RSA).
RSA (Republic of South Africa) (1998a) *National Environmental Management Act* (Cape Town: RSA).
RSA (Republic of South Africa) (1998b) *National Water Act* (Cape Town: RSA).
Sachs, A. (1990) *Protecting Human Rights in a New South Africa* (Cape Town: Oxford University Press).
Sadowski, Y. (1991) *Political Vegetables? Businessman and Bureaucrat in the Development of Egyptian Agriculture* (Washington, DC: Brookings Institution).
Said, M. (1997) 'Dangerous Surprise: Matruh governor refused the German company's request and Hamam City Council agreed to bury the nuclear wastes', *al-Masa'*, 30 March 1997: 1.
Sanchez Triana, E., and E. Uribe Botero (1994) *Contaminación Industrial en Colombia* (Bogotá: Departamento Nacional de Planeación y PNUD).
Sanyal, R.N., and J.S. Neves (1991) 'The Valdez Principles: Implications for Corporate Social Responsibility', *Journal of Business Ethics* 10: 883-90.
Schmidheiny, S., and F. Zorraquin (1996) *Financing Change: The Financial Community, Eco-efficiency, and Sustainable Development* (Cambridge, MA: MIT Press).
Schmidheiny, S., and the Business Council for Sustainable Development (1992) *Changing Course: A Global Business Perspective on Development and the Environment* (Cambridge, MA: MIT Press).
Schot, J., and K. Fischer (1993) 'Introduction: The Greening of the Industrial Firm', in K. Fischer and J. Schot (eds.), *Environmental Strategies for Industry: International Perspectives on Research Needs and Policy Implications* (Washington, DC: Island Press): 1-33.
Schroyer, T. (ed.) (1997) *A World that Works: Building Blocks for a Just and Sustainable Society* (New York: Bootstrap Press).
Sen, A.K. (1992) *Inequality Reexamined* (Cambridge, MA: Harvard University Press).
Sen, A.K. (1993) 'The Economics of Life and Death', *Scientific American*, May 1993: 40-47.
Sen, A.K. (1994) 'Freedoms and Needs: An Argument for the Primacy of Political Rights', *The New Republic*, 10 January 1994: 31-38.
Server, O.B. (1996) 'Corruption: A Major Problem for Urban Management. Some Evidence from Indonesia', *Habitat International* 20.1: 23-41.
Shao, H. (1998) 'The Relationship between ISO 14000 and China's Foreign Trade', *China ISO 14000 Certification Magazine* 1: 12.
Shaw, R.P. (1989) 'Rapid Population Growth and Environmental Degradation: Ultimate versus Proximate Factors', *Environmental Conservation* 16.3: 199-208.
Simpson, R.D., and R.L. Bradford (1996) 'Taxing Variable Cost: Environmental Regulation as Industrial Policy', *Journal of Environmental Economics and Management* 30: 282-300.
Simpson, R.D., R.A. Sedjo and J.W. Reid (1996) 'Valuing Biodiversity for Use in Pharmaceutical Research', *Journal of Political Economy* 104.1: 163-85.
Singh. J.B., and V.C. Lakham (1989) 'Business Ethics and the International Trade in Hazardous Waste', *Journal of Business Ethics* 8.11: 889-99.
Singh, N. (1976) *Economics and the Crisis of Ecology* (New Delhi: Oxford University Press).
Slocombe, S. (1993) 'Implementing Ecosystem-Based Management', *BioScience* 43.9: 612-22.
Smith, A. (1997) 'Bananas: Straightening up a Bent World', *Ethical Consumer* 49 (October/November 1997).

Smith, C., and A. Voinov (1996) 'Resource Management: Can it sustain Pacific Northwest fishery and forest systems?', *Ecosystem Health* 2: 145-58.
Smith, M. (1997) *The US Paper Industry and Sustainable Production: An Argument for Restructuring* (Cambridge, MA: MIT Press).
Socolow, R., C. Andrews, F. Berkhout and V. Thomas (eds.) (1994) *Industrial Ecology and Global Change* (Cambridge, UK: Cambridge University Press).
Soderbaum, P. (1998) 'Ecological Economics' (unpublished manuscript; Vasteras, Sweden: Malardalen Hogscola).
Solow, R.M. (1991) *Sustainability: An Economist's Perspective* (WHOI; Woods Hole, MA: Marine Policy Center).
Sonnenfeld, D.A. (1996a) 'Greening the Tiger? Social Movements' Influence on the Adoption of Environmental Technologies in the Pulp and Paper Industries of Australia, Indonesia, and Thailand' (Sociology PhD thesis; Santa Cruz, CA: University of California).
Sonnenfeld, D.A. (1996b) 'The Ghost of Wesley Vale: Environmentalists' Influence on Innovation in Australia's Pulp and Paper Industry', *Competition and Change* 1.4 (Fall 1996): 379-401.
Sonnenfeld, D.A. (1998a) 'From Brown to Green? Late Industrialization, Social Conflict, and Adoption of Environmental Technologies in Thailand's Pulp and Paper Industry', *Organization and Environment* 11.1 (March 1998): 59-87.
Sonnenfeld, D.A. (1998b) 'Tragedy and Innovation: Social Movements, Environment, and Technology in Indonesia's Pulp and Paper Industry', *Asia Pacific Viewpoint* 39.1 (April 1998): 95-110.
Sonnenfeld, D.A. (1999) 'Vikings and Tigers: Finland, Sweden and Adoption of Environmental Technologies in Southeast Asia's Pulp and Paper Industries', *Journal of World-Systems Research* 5.1 (Spring 1999): 26-47 (*http://csf.colorado.edu/ wsystems/jwsr.html*).
Spennemann, D.H.R. (1992) 'Concept of population control goes a long way back', *The Marshall Islands Journal* 23.2 (10 January 1992): 15.
SPES (1992) *Pembangunan Berkelanjutan: Mencari Format Politik* (Jakarta: PT Gramedia).
Stein, R., and C. Tucker (1997) 'Environmental Rights in the Bill of Rights: An Opportunity to Develop the South African Environmental Jurisprudence', *The Human Rights and Constitutional Law Journal of Southern Africa* 1: 5.
Subhadhira, S., and M. Samart (1984) 'A Thai Village History: Ban Ngio' (Khon Kaen University, Thailand).
Summers, R., and A. Heston (1991) 'The Penn. World Table (Mark 5): An Expanded Set of International Comparisons', *The Quarterly Journal of Economics* 106.2: 327-68.
Susangkarakarn, V. (1971) 'Thailand: $16-million project launched to produce kenaf pulp', *Pulp and Paper International* 13.8 (July 1971): 147.
Symonds, J. (1996) 'The Mobil Survey: More than 127,000 ISO Certificates', *ISO 9000 News* (November/December 1996): 1-5.
Tanner, D., R. Bellamy and C. Mason (1997) *Environmental Management Asia 1997: A Guide to ISO 14000* (London: Asia Environmental Trading Co. Ltd; Singapore: The Regional Institute of Environmental Technology).
Tahija, J. (1993) 'Swapping Business Skills for Oil', *Harvard Business Review*, September/October 1993: 64-77.
Teilhard de Chardin, P. (1927) *Hymne de l'univers* (Paris); English translation: *Hymn of the Universe* (New York: Harper & Row, 1969).
Thailand Environment Institute (1997a) *Development of Economic Tools in Industrial Environmental Management* (Bangkok: Thailand Environment Institute).
Thailand Environment Institute (1997b) *Cleaner Technology in Thailand* (Bangkok: Thailand Environment Institute).
Thompson, D. (1997) 'Environmental Management', in T. Fleming (ed.), *Environmental Management and Canadian Society* (Toronto: ITP Nelson): 219-50.
Tibor, T., and I. Feldman (1996) *ISO 14000: A Guide to the New Environmental Management Standards* (Chicago: Irwin).
Turovskiy, A. (1998) 'Agro-Ecological Society', *Eco News No. 41* 4.146 (20 December 1998, *http://solar.rtd.utk.edu/~valery/econews/econews.html*).
TWS (The Wilderness Society) (1992) 'Protecting, Preserving and Promoting Wilderness: Annual Report 1991–92', *Wilderness News* 130 (Sydney: TWS, December 1992): 13-16.
Tyler Miller, G., Jr (1994) *Living in the Environment: Principles, Connections, and Solutions* (Belmont, CA: Wadsworth).
Ukhtomskiy (1998) 'Did you get a call from Yeltsin?' ('Ot Yeltsina ne zvonili?'), *Novaya Gazeta* 48.520 (8 December 1998).

UNCSD (United Nations Council for Sustainable Development) (1997) *Overall Progress Achieved since the United Nations Conference on Environment and Development: Report of the Secretary General. Addendum: Changing Consumption and Production Patterns Chapter 4, Agenda 21* (New York: UNCSD).

UNCTAD (United Nations Conference on Trade and Development) (1991) *Environment and International Trade* (United Nations Document A/Conf.151/PC/48; Geneva: United Nations).

UNCTAD (United Nations Conference on Trade and Development) (1993) *Environmental Management in Transnational Corporations: Report on the Benchmark Corporate Environmental Survey* (New York: United Nations).

UNCTAD (United Nations Conference on Trade and Development) (1995a) *Effects of environmental policies, standards and regulations on market access and competitiveness, with special reference to developing countries, including with least developed among them, and in light of UNCTAD empirical studies* (Report by the UNCTAD Secretariat, Trade and Development Board, Ad Hoc Working Group on Trade, Environment and Development; Geneva: UNCTAD).

UNCTAD (United Nations Conference on Trade and Development) (1995b) *Recent Trends in International Investment and Transnational Corporations* (Geneva: United Nations).

UNCTAD (United Nations Conference on Trade and Development) (1997) *World Investment Report: Transnational Corporations, Market Structure and Competitive Policy* (New York: United Nations).

UNDP (United Nations Development Programme) (1994) *Human Development Report 1994* (New York: Oxford University Press).

UNDP (United Nations Development Programme) (1998) *Trade and Environment: Capacity Building for Sustainable Development* (New York: UNDP).

UNDP (United Nations Development Programme) (1999) *Human Development Report 1999* (New York: UNDP).

UNEP (United Nations Environment Programme) (1993) *Environmental Data Report 1993–94* (Oxford, UK: Blackwell).

UNICEF (1995) *The State of the World's Children, 1995* (Oxford, UK: Oxford University Press).

UNIDO (United Nations Industrial Development Organisation) (1992) *Proceedings of the Conference on Ecologically Sustainable Industrial Development, Copenhagen, 1991* (Vienna: UNIDO).

UNIDO (United Nations Industrial Development Organisation) (1996) *Global Economic Database* (Vienna: UNIDO).

United Nations (1992a) *World Investment Directory: Developed Countries* (New York: United Nations).

United Nations (1992b) *World Investment Report 1992* (New York: United Nations).

United Nations (1993) *Agenda 21: Programme of Action for Sustainable Development* (New York: United Nations).

United Nations (1995) 'Decision 5/CP.1. Framework Convention on Climate Change, Conference of the Parties', in *Report of the Conference of the Parties on its First Session, Held at Berlin from 28 March to 7 April 1995* (Addendum FCCC[CP/1995/7/Add.1]; *http://www.unfccc.de/fccc/ccinfo/dec5cp.htm*).

United Nations (1997) 'Kyoto Protocol to the United Nations Framework Convention on Climate Change', *Framework Convention on Climate Change, Conference of the Parties. Third Session, Kyoto, 1–10 December 1997* (Addendum FCCC[CP/1997/L.7/Add.1] 10 December 1997).

United Nations (1998) 'Review of the Implementation of Commitments and of Other Provisions of the Convention. Activities Implemented Jointly: Review of the Progress Under the Pilot Phase (Decision 5/CP.1)', *Second Synthesis Report on Activities Implemented Jointly* (Note by the Secretariat; UNFCCC Secretariat, FCCC/CP/1998/2, 2 October 1998).

US Initiative on Joint Implementation (1995) 'Conference Notebook', *Program Conference to Support the Second Round Proposal Process, Crystal Gateway Marriott, Arlington, VA, 31 May–1 June 1995* (Washington, DC: US Initiative on Joint Implementation).

USGAO (1995) *North American Free Trade Agreement: Structure and Status of Implementing Organizations* (GAO/GGE-95-10BR; Washington, DC: USGAO).

Varillas, A. (1998) 'Los Límites de la Protección Conferida por los Estudios de Impacto Ambiental y los Programas de Adecuación y Manejo Ambiental', *Informativo Mensual de la Sociedad Nacional de Minería, Petróleo y Energía* 7.7: 14-18.

Vastag, G., S. Kerekes and D.A. Rondinelli (1996) 'Evaluation of Corporate Environmental Management Approaches: A Framework and Application', *International Journal of Production Economics* 13: 193-211.

Vernadsky, V.I. (1945) 'The Biosphere and the Noosphere', *American Scientist* 33.1: 1-12; repr. Moscow: Nauka, 1989.

Veron, R. (1998) 'The "New" Kerala Model: Lessons for Sustainable Development', *Department of Geography Seminar*, School of Oriental and African Studies, London, 17 March 1998 (London: Mimro).

Vitalis, R. (1995) *When Capitalists Collide* (Berkeley, CA: University of California Press).

Voinov, A.A, and R. Costanza (1999) 'Watershed Management and the Web', *Journal of Ecosystem Management* 56: 231-45.

Voinov, A.A. (1998) 'Paradoxes of Sustainability', *Journal of General Biology* 59: 209-18.

von Weizsäcker, E., A. Lovins and L.H. Lovins (1997) *Factor Four: Doubling Wealth, Halving Resource Use. The New Report to the Club of Rome* (London: Earthscan).

Wade, R. (1997) 'Greening the Bank: The Struggle over the Environment, 1970–1995', in D. Kapur, J.P. Lewis and R. Webb (eds.), *The World Bank: Its First Half Century. Perspectives* (Washington, DC: Brookings Institution Press): 611-734.

WALHI (Wahana Lingkungan Hidup Indonesia) and YLBH (Yayasan Lembaga Bantuan Hukum Indonesia) (1992) *Mistaking Plantations for Indonesia's Tropical Forest* (Jakarta: WALHI/YLBH).

Wallich, P. (1995) 'A Mystery Inside a Riddle Inside an Enigma', *Scientific American*, March 1995.

Wapenhans, W.A. (1994) 'Efficiency and Effectiveness: Is the World Bank Group well prepared for the task ahead?', in Bretton Woods Commission, *Bretton Woods: Looking into the Future* (Background papers; Washington, DC: Bretton Woods Commission): 289-304.

Waterbury, J. (1993) *Exposed to Innumerable Delusions* (Cambridge: Cambridge University Press).

WCED (World Commission on Environment and Development) (1987) *Our Common Future* (Oxford, UK: Oxford University Press).

Wescott, W.F. (1992) 'Environmental Technology Co-operation: A Quid-Pro-Quo for Transnational Corporations and Developing Countries', *The Colombia Journal of World Business,* Fall/Winter 1992: 145-53.

WHO (World Health Organisation)/UNEP (United Nations Environment Programme) (1992) *Urban Air Pollution in Megacities of the World* (Oxford, UK: Blackwell).

Wiemann, J., T. Bunning, G. Danne, C. Hagenmaier, F. Kolling, R. Siller and A. Wender (1994) *Ecological Product Standards and Requirements as a New Challenge for Developing Countries' Industries and Exports: The Case of India's Leather, Textile and Refrigeration Industries* (Berlin: German Development Institute).

Williams, M., and P. Petesch (1993) *Sustaining The Earth: Role of Multilateral Development Institutions* (Washington, DC: Overseas Development Council).

Wilson, A. (1994) *GATT, Trade Liberalization, and the Environment: An Economic Analysis* (Washington, DC: Report for Congress, Report No. 94-291 E; Congressional Research Service).

WIM (Wahana Informasi Masyarakat) (n.d.) *PT. IIU Funding Report: A Working History Finance Negotiations for PT. Inti Indorayon Utama* (Medan, North Sumatra, Indonesia: Wahana Informasi Masyarakat).

Wimberly, R.C. (1993) 'Policy Perspectives on Social, Agricultural and Rural Sustainability', *Rural Sociology* 58: 1-29.

World Bank (1992a) *World Development Report 1992: Development and the Environment* (Oxford, UK: Oxford University Press).

World Bank (1992b) *Annual Report* (Washington, DC: World Bank).

World Bank (1994–95) *Urban Infrastructure Investment Framework* (Washington, DC: Southern Africa Department, World Bank).

World Bank (1994a) *Economywide Policies and the Environment: Emerging Lessons from Experience* (Washington, DC: World Bank).

World Bank (1994b) *Global Economic Prospects and the Developing Countries* (Washington, DC: World Bank).

World Bank (1994c) *Indonesia Environment and Development: Challenges for the Future* (Washington, DC: World Bank).

World Bank (1994d) *World Development Report 1994: Infrastructure for Development* (New York: Oxford University Press).

World Bank (1996a) *A Mining Strategy for Latin America and the Caribbean* (Technical Paper No. 345; Washington, DC: World Bank).

World Bank (1996b) *Transition* (Washington, DC: World Bank, September/October 1996).

World Bank (1997a) *The Strategic Compact: Renewing the Bank's Effectiveness to Fight Poverty* (Washington, DC: World Bank Planning and Budgeting Department, 13 February 1997).

World Bank (1997b) *Implementing the Compact (Final Text)* (Washington, DC: World Bank Planning and Budgeting Department, 9 May 1997).

World Bank (1997c) *World Development Report 1997: The State in a Changing World* (New York: Oxford University Press).

World Bank (1998) *Annual Report* (Washington, DC: World Bank).

World Bank Group (1995) *Mainstreaming the Environment* (Washington, DC: The World Bank).
World Bank Group (1997) *Joint Implementation: Theoretical Considerations with Perspectives from the Industrial and Land Use Sectors. Part 1: Policy Context and Aims of the Report* (Washington, DC: The World Bank Group; *http://www-esd.worldbank.org/aij/econji.htm*).
World Resources Institute (1997) *World Resources 1996–97* (New York: Oxford University Press).
Worldwatch Institute (1998) 'Implementing the Kyoto Protocol: Fourth Conference of the Parties, Buenos Aires, 2–14 November 1998' (*http://www.islandpress.org/global/climate/buenosaires.html*, 20 November 1998).
Yeltsin, B. (1997) President's address to the Federal Assembly (Poslanie Prezidenta RF Federal'nomy Sobraniyu) (Moscow).
Zotin, A.I., and R.S. Zotina (1993) *Phenomenological Theory of Development, Growth and Ageing* (Russian language; Moscow: Nauka).

Biographies

David Barkin is Professor of Economics at the Xochimilco Campus of the Universidad Autonoma Metropolitana in Mexico City. He is a member of the Mexican Academy of Sciences and of the National Research Council. He teaches courses in international economics as well as on rural development and sustainability. He has published extensively on these problems; his latest books include: *Wealth, Poverty and Sustainable Development* and *Distorted Development: Mexico in the World Economy*.

Patrick Bond is Associate Professor at the University of the Witwatersrand Graduate School of Public and Development Management in Johannesburg; he received his PhD from the Johns Hopkins University Department of Geography and Environmental Engineering. He is the author of five books on Southern Africa, and served the first African National Congress government as drafter of several seminal development white papers and other policy documents. He works closely with social movements in South Africa and Zimbabwe, and is a voluntary research associate with the Alternative Information and Development Centre (*http:\\www.aidc.org.za*).

Matthew Cole is a lecturer in Environmental Economics in the Department of Economics, University of Birmingham, UK. His research interests include trade and the environment and the relationship between economic development, industrial composition and the environment.

Mike Di (Chang Xing) is the Chief Representative of ERM Certification and Verification Service Company in China, and also the resident researcher in the Center for Economic and Social Studies on the Environment of ULB University in Belgium. He was awarded an honorary Master's degree in International Politics by the ULB University (Belgium) in 1992 and a European Master's degree in Environmental Management Studies by the European Association for Environmental Management Education in 1995. He is an environmental management specialist focusing on the ISO 14001 EMS international standard, since early 1996 devoting himself to the promotion of ISO 14001 implementation and certification in China. He is a registered environmental auditor and has conducted many ISO 14001 audits for both MNCs operating in China and Chinese local companies.

Percy Garcia has a BEng (Petroleum) and a MEDes (Environmental Science). He worked for five years in the oil and gas industry for a multinational corporation in the areas of operation, production and reservoir engineering. Currently, his PhD research at the University of Calgary, Canada, focuses on 'Means of Achieving Sustainable Development Goals within Natural Resource-Based Corporations in Latin America'.

Irina Glazyrina obtained her PhD in Mathematics at Novosibirsk State University. Her principal scientific interests are mathematical models and methods in natural resource management. Concurrently, for the last five years she has worked in comprehensive multidisciplinary environmental programmes. Currently she is a regional manager in the GEF Project 'Conservation of Biodiversity in Russia', which is an application of an ecosystem approach to the Khilok River watershed management programme.

Julia Gonzalez has an Honours Bachelors Degree in Science and is a Graduate Student in Environmental Science at the Faculty of Environmental Design, University of Calgary, Canada. Her research concerns Environmental Management and the Mining Sector of Latin America. She is employed as a Environmental Scientist at AGRA Earth & Environmental Ltd.

Neil Harrison is an Assistant Professor in the Department of Political Science at the University of Wyoming, USA. Born and raised in England, and educated there and in the United States, he is experienced in management in three countries. Professor Harrison has published articles on climate change, sustainable development, the influence of science on international environmental policy, and technological innovation. His book, *Constructing Sustainable Development*, is forthcoming from SUNY Press.

Gilbert S. Hedstrom is a Vice-President of Arthur D. Little, Inc., and a Managing Director of the company's Environmental, Health and Safety Consulting business. His major consulting activities focus on helping companies around the world increase the effectiveness of their environmental, health and safety management programmes.

Murray Glyn Jones joined Shell Prospecting & Development as Health, Safety and Environment Manager in August 1996, having worked in environmental and safety management for Shell Canada since 1981. He is responsible for the consultation programme with international and local stakeholders and the delivery of health, social and environmental benefits to the people of the Camisea region. With a Masters degree in Environmental Engineering, Murray worked on legislation with the Provincial Government of Ontario, Canada, from 1973 to 1979 and for the following two years he was with the Dutch Environment Ministry.

Peter Koffel's background lies in Indonesia's politics and culture, though he has been researching Indonesia's 'state of the environment' for the last decade with the Institute for Science and Technology Policy at Murdoch University, Perth, Western Australia. He has been involved in bilateral environmental exchange programmes, working on river water quality in Indonesia and has initiated an annual clean-up day for the Brantas River, East Java. He has worked as an environmental consultant for foreign aid projects in Java and has been involved in environmental studies curriculum development for universities in Java.

Ans Kolk is senior researcher at the Institute for Environmental Management, Faculty of Economics, University of Amsterdam, the Netherlands. Her areas of research and publication are environmental management and corporate social responsibility, particularly in relation to multinational corporations' strategies, and international environmental policy. Articles in English have been published in a range of international journals, including *World Development*, *Business Strategy and the Environment*, *Transnational Corporations*, *International Environmental Affairs*, *International Journal of Environment and Pollution*, *Environmental Politics* and *Corporate Environmental Strategy*. Her latest book, *The Economics of Environmental Management* (Financial Times/Prentice–Hall, 2000), presents a theoretical and practical update of environmental management.

Emilio Latorre studied Electrical Engineering at the Universidad de los Andes in Bogotá, Colombia, and has a PhD in Urban and Regional Planning from the University of Toulouse, France. He was the Director of the Ecological Action Committee at the Universidad del Valle in Cali, Colombia, for nine years. He is a member of the Board of Directors of the Regional Environmental Authority for the Cauca Valley Department in Colombia (CVC). He has written several books, including *General Systems Theory: An Approach to Problem Solving*, *Municipality and Environmental Planning in Colombia*, and, more recently *Enterprise and Environment in Colombia*. He is a full-time Professor in the Department of Production and Operations Research and the Director of the Environmental Study Unit of the Engineering Faculty of the Universidad del Valle.

Ralph Luken worked as a senior staff economist for the US Environmental Protection Agency, Washington, DC, between 1979 and 1990, and as Chief of Economic Studies between 1982 and 1990, supervising economic analyses of regulatory activities and the EPA's economic research programme. He joined the United Nations Industrial Development Organisation (UNIDO) in 1990 as Senior Environmental Advisor, responsible for in-house environmental training programmes, for formulating and reviewing environment-related projects and for technical support for the UNIDO Conference on Ecologically Sustainable Industrial Development. Ralph initiated the joint UNIDO–UNEP National

Cleaner Production Centers Programme. Since 1995, his duties have included support for a global network on the industrial dimension of national sustainable development strategies, the promotion of environmental management systems and eco-labels (ISO 14000) and in-house environmental training and advice. He is currently in charge of the overall management of the Cleaner Production Programme.

Ronald A.N. McLean is a Vice-President of Arthur D. Little, Inc., and a Managing Director of the firm's Environmental, Health and Safety Consulting business. Based in Brussels, he helps transnational companies improve their global EHS capabilities.

Bernhard H. Metzger is a Vice-President of Arthur D. Little International and leads the company's Environmental Impact and Risk Assessment Practice. He has managed major environmental baseline assessments, impact assessments and other projects for oil and gas and other industries worldwide.

Damian Miller is a MacArthur Research Scholar and PhD candidate at the Judge Institute of Management Studies, Cambridge University, UK. His research concerns enterprise development and the diffusion of solar photovoltaic technology in rural India and Indonesia.

Titus Moser is a PhD candidate at the Judge Institute of Management Studies, Cambridge University, UK, with funding from the ESRC and Environmental Resources Management. His research concerns the Colombian and Peruvian petroleum industries and the responsiveness of oil companies to their environmental and social impacts.

Yacob Mulugetta is a Lecturer at the Centre for Environmental Strategy at the University of Surrey, UK. His academic interest covers broad areas of development and environment, and his particular research expertise lies in sustainable energy issues. He is currently involved in a series of projects looking into the problems associated with energy stress and environmental degradation in developing countries, and the extent to which renewable energy resources can contribute to the alleviation of these problems.

Mandar Parasnis, of the Thailand Environment Institute (TEI), a leading non-profit NGO in Thailand, established and is responsible for the Cleaner Technology Information Centre at TEI and is also working on a number of national and international environmental management-related projects focusing on policy studies, training, environmental information management and regional networking. He co-ordinates *Asia Pacific Cleaner Production Network*, an e-mail discussion forum on the Internet.

Govindan Parayil is on the faculty of the Division of Social Science at the Hong Kong University of Science and Technology.

Bruno Pavoni obtained his Doctorate in Chemistry from the University of Padua, Italy, in 1974. At present he is Associate Professor of Environmental Chemistry at the University of Venice. Since 1979, he has been involved in a number of research projects, aiming at studying environmental aspects of the lagoon of Venice, the inland territory and the northern Adriatic sea. He is leading an INTAS-funded project for Russia and CIS on Ecological Analysis of Point and Non-point Pollution in Watersheds.

Barbara A. Ribbens, a visiting Assistant Professor of Management, obtained her PhD from the University of Connecticut, USA. She studies career threats and organisational learning relationships to strategy formulation and the natural environment.

Eric Ribbens, an Assistant Professor of Biology, obtained his PhD from the University of Connecticut. USA. A plant ecologist, he studies dispersal pattern implications for population strategies, emphasising the survival of rare species.

Sarah Roberts is a Research Associate for the Sustainable Consumption and Trade Initiative at the International Institute for Environment and Development (IIED). She has advised, researched and managed a wide range of projects on sustainable consumption, trade, business and the environment for organisations including the OECD, UN DESA, World Business Council for Sustainable Development and the Norwegian Ministry of Environment.

Nick Robins is Programme Co-ordinator of the Sustainable Consumption and Trade Initiative at the International Institute for Environment and Development (IIED). He has advised, researched and managed a wide range of projects on sustainable consumption, trade, business and the environment for organisations including the OECD, UN DESA, World Business Council for Sustainable Development and the Norwegian Ministry of Environment. Nick Robins also manages an IIED programme on European aid and foreign policy.

Dennis A. Rondinelli is the Glaxo Distinguished International Professor of Management at the Kenan-Flagler Business School and director of the Center for Global Business Research at the Frank Hawkins Kenan Institute of Private Enterprise, University of North Carolina at Chapel Hill, USA. Dr Rondinelli has authored and edited 16 books and published more than 200 articles on environmental management, international business and economic development. He has served as an advisor and consultant to the World Bank, the US Agency for International Development and various United Nations agencies. He received his PhD from Cornell University.

David A. Sonnenfeld is Assistant Professor of Sociology, Washington State University, USA. He received his PhD in Sociology from the University of California, Santa Cruz, in 1996. Currently, he is conducting research on environmental reform in Thailand's electronics industry. During the 1998–2000 academic years, he is Ciriacy-Wantrup Visiting Scholar Fellow in Natural Resource Economics at the University of California, Berkeley.

Jeannie Sowers is a PhD candidate in Comparative Politics at Princeton University, NJ, USA, where she is writing a dissertation on the political economy of environmental issues in Egypt. She obtained her BA from Harvard University in 1989, and an MA from Princeton University in 1996. She worked on housing and environmental issues in Washington, DC, and Los Angeles before graduate school, and has lived and studied in Egypt, Israel and India.

Robyn Stein has a BA and LLB from Wits University in Johannesburg and an LLM from the London School of Economics. She is an attorney specialising in environmental and water law, and served as Special Adviser to South Africa's Minister of Water Affairs and Forestry from 1996 to 1998, when she participated in drafting the Water Services Act, the National Water Act and the National Environmental Management Act. She is a member of the National Water Advisory Council and the Interim Dam Safety Committee.

Dixon Thompson is a professor of environmental science and has extensive experience in environmental management research, teaching and consulting. He played a key role in designing and implementing the Environmental Science Program, University of Ancash, Peru and an interdisciplinary University of Calgary Master's Degree in Energy and the Environment, which is taught in Quito, Ecuador.

Gyula Vastag is assistant professor in the Department of Marketing and Supply Chain Management at the Eli Broad Graduate School of Management, Michigan State University, East Lansing, Michigan, USA. He served as Citibank International Fellow from 1991 to 1993 and as Senior Research Associate from 1993 to 1996 at the Kenan Institute of Private Enterprise, University of North Carolina at Chapel Hill. He is a founding member and associate director of the Global Manufacturing Research Group. Dr Vastag received his PhD from the Budapest University of Economic Sciences.

Alexey Voinov received his PhD in Ecological Modeling in 1982 from Moscow State University. Since then, his research has been concerned with systems analysis and simulation modeling in ecology. In the 1980s he succeeded in establishing one of the first Russian private environmental consulting companies: ECOLEX Laboratory. His major research interests are modelling of ecosystems, systems analysis in ecology and economics, decision-support systems and educational software. He is currently working at University of Maryland Institute for Ecological Economics, USA, on watershed landscape modelling and management.

Frank Vorhies is the head of the Economics Unit of IUCN: The World Conservation Union and is based at its headquarters in Gland, Switzerland. He is a specialist in the economics of biodiversity with particular interests in biodiversity incentives and biodiversity finance. Before joining IUCN in 1995 as their first economist, he worked from the African Wildlife Foundation in Nairobi, Kenya. He also spent several years in South Africa working on the economics and business of nature conservation. Frank has a PhD in Economics from the University of Colorado at Boulder, USA.

Walter Wehrmeyer is the BG Surrey Scholar at the Centre for Environmental Strategy of the University of Surrey, working on contaminated land and the regeneration of brownfield sites. His research interests lie within corporate environmental policy, environmental management systems and strategy formation, risk communication and participative approaches towards urban regeneration as well as environmental and sustainability performance indicators. He is Adjunct Professor at the Graduate School of Business of Curtin University of Technology, Perth, Western Australia, and full member of the Institute of Environmental Management.

Nadezhda Zharova received her PhD in Physics and Mathematics in 1991. Her scientific interests lie in the field of ecosystem management and simulation modelling in ecology. Since late 1992 she has been working at the University of Venice. The main concern of her current study is analysis of the ecological situation in the Veneto region, in particular the study of possible impacts of different internal factors and man-made perturbations on aquatic and watershed environments.

Index